Trauma

Trauma

Contemporary Directions in
Theory, Practice, and Research

EDITORS

Shoshana Ringel
University of Maryland, Baltimore

Jerrold R. Brandell
Wayne State University

Los Angeles | London | New Delhi
Singapore | Washington DC

Los Angeles | London | New Delhi
Singapore | Washington DC

FOR INFORMATION:

SAGE Publications, Inc.
2455 Teller Road
Thousand Oaks, California 91320
E-mail: order@sagepub.com

SAGE Publications Ltd.
1 Oliver's Yard
55 City Road
London EC1Y 1SP
United Kingdom

SAGE Publications India Pvt. Ltd.
B 1/I 1 Mohan Cooperative Industrial Area
Mathura Road, New Delhi 110 044
India

SAGE Publications Asia-Pacific Pte. Ltd.
33 Pekin Street #02-01
Far East Square
Singapore 048763

Acquisitions Editor: Kassie Graves
Editorial Assistant: Courtney Munz
Production Editor: Kelle Schillaci
Copy Editor: Barbara Corrigan
Typesetter: C&M Digitals (P) Ltd.
Proofreader: Victoria Reed-Castro
Indexer: Will Ragsdale
Cover Designer: Gail Buschman
Marketing Manager: Stephanie Adams
Permissions Editor: Adele Hutchinson

Copyright © 2012 by SAGE Publications, Inc.

Printed in the United States of America

Library of Congress Cataloging-in-Publication Data

Trauma : contemporary directions in theory, practice, and research / [edited by] Shoshana Ringel, University of Maryland, Baltimore, Jerrold R. Brandell, Wayne State University.

p.; cm.
Includes bibliographical references and index.

ISBN 978-1-4129-7982-5 (paper : alk. paper)

1. Post-traumatic stress disorder. I. Ringel, Shoshana, editor. II. Brandell, Jerrold R., 1952- editor. [DNLM: 1. Stress Disorders, Post-Traumatic. 2. Models, Psychological. 3. Stress Disorders, Post-Traumatic--therapy. WM 172]

RC552.P67T7476 2011 616.85′21—dc22 2010050861

This book is printed on acid-free paper.

11 12 13 14 15 10 9 8 7 6 5 4 3 2 1

Contents

Introduction _____

Although there has been much scholarship devoted to the study of trauma, the field has expanded rapidly during the past decade as a result of several significant developments. From an earlier focus on the interpersonal aspects of trauma, including child abuse and domestic violence, traumatic experiences have taken on a political and social dimension, for example, the events of 9/11, the war on terror, and combat trauma associated with recent wars in Afghanistan and Iraq. Finally, the rash of school shootings in American public schools, increasingly linked to the problem of bullying, has also entered the domain of public awareness. These social and political phenomena have added to the magnitude of traumatic experiences in everyday life and created a more complex task for mental health professionals dealing with the effects of trauma.

This book will present new developments in the conceptualization of trauma and trauma-related interventions from diverse clinical perspectives, including cognitive-behavioral therapy, psychodynamic therapy, and attachment theory. Clinical chapters will focus on various populations and themes associated with trauma: the use of art therapy with children who suffer loss and bereavement and who lost a parent during the 9/11 terror attacks, the impact of bullying on school children, developmental trauma in the lives of gay men, cultural and historical trauma among Native Americans, and finally, the impact of combat trauma on Israeli soldiers and the link between traumatic experiences encountered in combat and the grief associated with the loss of comrades and commanders.

Because of its broad scope as well as its emphasis on the application of diverse theoretical viewpoints to a variety of posttraumatic situations, we believe this anthology represents a new and different, transtheoretical approach to clinical scholarship on trauma. Indeed, no social work text of which we are aware, and few written by authors with other professional backgrounds, has focused specifically on theoretical and clinical issues associated with trauma.

This book is designed to provide a clear and accessible description of contemporary theoretical perspectives on trauma as well as clinical applications for treatment with a variety of populations, including both research outcomes on the utility of the approach and clinical vignettes to illustrate its usefulness.

The following is the outline of the book:

Chapter 1. Overview

This chapter explores the history of trauma treatment for "shell-shocked" soldiers during World Wars I and II and after the Vietnam War. It considers the inclusion of PTSD in the American Psychiatric Association's *Diagnostic and Statistical Manual* in the 1980s and the influence of the women's movement on examining sexual abuse and violence against women. Finally, recent controversies regarding debriefing procedures in the aftermath of 9/11 and current trends regarding diagnosis and treatment of complex PTSD and developmental trauma are discussed.

Part I. Theoretical Frameworks

Chapter 2. Cognitive-Behavioral Theory

In this chapter, the authors begin with a summary of cognitive-behavioral therapy and its application to clinical practice with traumatized individuals, including learning theory, cognitive models that address an overactive schemata regarding danger, failure to discriminate between safe and unsafe, cognitive dissonance, and disengagement from the trauma memory. Cognitive and behavioral approaches to treatment are also described, including cognitive restructuring (Beck), systematic desensitization (Wolpe), imaginal exposure and prolonged exposure therapy (Foa), virtual reality exposure, eye movement desensitization and reprocessing (Shapiro), and self-instructional therapy (Meichenbaum). The chapter concludes with a review of empirical evidence regarding cognitive-behavioral therapy and behavioral treatment approaches.

Chapter 3. Psychoanalytic Theory (Part I)

This chapter examines the development of psychodynamic thinking in relation to trauma, including Freud's earliest conception of loss and bereavement, Ferenczi's work with survivors of sexual abuse, Rank's theory of birth trauma, and the British (independent) object relations group including Fairbairn, Winnicott, and Balint. The chapter concludes with an examination of self psychological perspectives on trauma, illustrated in part through a case example.

Chapter 4. Psychoanalytic Theory (Part II)

Contemporary relational and intersubjective writers, including Benjamin, Ghent, Bromberg, and Bach, and their ideas regarding dissociation, mastery and submission, and "the third" are described in this chapter. The chapter also examines Davies and Frawley as well as Shane, Shane, and Gale and their contributions to the understanding of patient-therapist traumatic enactments; Stolorow's intersubjective traumatology theory; and Lichtenberg, Lachmann, and Fosshage's contemporary self psychological approach to trauma. Brief clinical vignettes are used to highlight these differing conceptions of trauma.

Chapter 5. Attachment Theory, Infant Research, and Neurobiology

In this chapter, attachment theory as applied to the study of trauma and disorganization is examined in detail. Bowlby's work on children's separation and loss is also summarized. Another focus is that of attachment disorganization and its sequelae in children and adults, highlighting the contributions of Mary Main, Lyons-Ruth, Liotti, Solomon, George, and others. The work of infant researchers including Beebe and Tronick is also presented in regard to infant/parent disorganization. The Adult Attachment Interview and the four attachment criteria are then discussed as they relate to traumatic experiences. Finally, neurobiological findings in regard to attachment disorganization are presented, including the work of Schore and others.

Part II. Clinical Applications With Selected Populations

Chapter 6. Art Therapy With Traumatically Bereaved Children

Art therapy has been used effectively in the treatment of traumatized client populations for many years. As a nonverbal, sensory-based, enactive modality with narrative and symbolic potential, art making within a therapeutic relationship can access aspects of trauma experience that evade verbal processing. Brain research supports art therapy as a treatment that promotes hemispheric integration, linking the verbal with the nonverbal while containing affect. Specific techniques have been developed by art therapists, such as the instinctual trauma response to work with PTSD. Parental loss for children is considered traumatic, even when anticipated, due to the developmental stage of the child. When the death is sudden and violent, as in accident, suicide, or murder, actual trauma intensifies and complicates the grieving process. Art therapy application to bereavement work with children is the focus of this chapter. Case examples illustrate its effectiveness with specific traumatizing aspects of loss. Highlighted is work with children who lost parents in the 9/11 terror attacks.

Chapter 7. Military Bereavement and Combat Trauma

The stresses and traumas of combat and intervention paradigms have been studied intensively in the United States and Israel. In contrast, combat bereavement has not received due attention. The authors review post-traumatic stress in the military and current directions in intervention work. In particular, they distinguish between two main themes: PTSD due to life threat in combat and the experiences of interpersonal loss associated with the loss of valued "buddies" and commanding officers. The chapter concludes with research and clinical findings, with particular attention to work with combat bereavement and trauma in Israel.

Chapter 8. The Trauma of Bullying Experiences

This chapter offers an overview of bullying among children and adolescents. The various forms and their effects are reviewed, including direct (e.g., physical and verbal bullying), indirect (e.g., rumors and exclusion), and cyber forms (e.g., use of electronic technology to threaten, harass, and damage reputations). Research demonstrating the devastating effects of the various forms of bullying is also presented. As defined in this chapter, bullying is conceived as a relationship problem that requires relational solutions at the various levels of a child's or youth's social world, including individual, peers, school, family, community, and society. The chapter discusses the ways in which bullying of children and adolescents can be experienced as traumatic. A case example is also offered to highlight the importance of validation and attunement by adults to prevent or diminish the likelihood that a child or youth will experience bullying as traumatic.

Chapter 9. Traumas of Development in the Gay Male

This chapter examines the theme of trauma as it relates to the experience of being gay in contemporary American society. Themes include the specific issues associated with being gay and human immunodeficiency virus, gay identity formation, coming out, and the social oppression of gay men.

Chapter 10. Cultural and Historical Trauma Among Native Americans

This chapter provides clinicians with information to enable them to recognize cultural and historical trauma and to be sensitive to its effects when developing and implementing intervention plans with Native Americans. The concepts of cultural and historical trauma are defined, and a discussion of pertinent theories (e.g., Alexander, Brave Heart, Salzman, and others) is provided. The nature of Native American cultural and historical trauma is also described, and its psychological and social effects across generations of Native Americans are addressed. The interactive effects of cultural and historical trauma and current personal traumas are examined. Finally, clinical issues such as assessment, cultural sensitivity, and appropriate intervention strategies are explained.

Chapter 11. The Effects of Trauma Treatment on the Therapist

In exploring the impact that trauma treatment has on the clinician, this chapter examines concepts of vicarious trauma, secondary trauma, and associated constructs that seek to understand the deleterious effects of providing clinical services to traumatized individuals. The chapter explores the role of empathic immersion in this process and situates this occupational hazard in psychodynamic and relational frames. Empirical evidence that demonstrates the impact of trauma work on the clinician is reviewed, and recommendations are given for minimizing and moderating its negative dimensions. Finally, this chapter discusses the impact that vicarious trauma may have on the clinical process.

1 Overview

History of Trauma Theory

The relationship between trauma and mental illness was first investigated by the neurologist Jean Martin Charcot, a French physician who was working with traumatized women in the Salpetriere hospital. During the late 19th century, a major focus of Charcot's study was hysteria, a disorder commonly diagnosed in women. Hysterical symptoms were characterized by sudden paralysis, amnesia, sensory loss, and convulsions. Women comprised the vast majority of patients with hysteria, and at the time, such symptoms were thought to originate in the uterus. Until Charcot, the common treatment for hysteria was hysterectomy. Charcot was the first to understand that the origin of hysterical symptoms was not physiological but rather psychological in nature, although he was not interested in the inner lives of his female patients. He noted that traumatic events could induce a hypnotic state in his patients and was the first to "describe both the problems of suggestibility in these patients, and the fact that hysterical attacks are dissociative problems—the results of having endured unbearable experiences" (van der Kolk, Weisaeth, & van der Hart, 1996, p. 50). In Salpetriere, young women who suffered violence, rape, and sexual abuse found safety and shelter, and Charcot presented his theory to large audiences through live demonstrations in which patients were hypnotized and then helped to remember their trauma, a process that culminated in the abrogation of their symptoms (Herman, 1992).

Pierre Janet, a student of Charcot, continued to study dissociative phenomena and traumatic memories. Janet investigated the influence of patients' traumatic experiences on personality development and behavior. He recognized that patients' intense affects were reactive to their perceptions of the traumatic events that happened to them, and he found that through hypnosis and abreaction, or reexposure to the traumatic memories, patients' symptoms could be alleviated (van der Kolk, Weisaeth, et al., 1996). In his early studies of hysteria (1893–1895), Freud, too, was initially influenced by Charcot and adopted some of his ideas. In *Studies on Hysteria* (1893), coauthored with Josef Breuer, Freud suggested that

> we must point out that we consider it essential for the explanation of hysterical phenomena to assume the presence of a dissociation, a splitting of the content of consciousness. [T]he regular and essential content of a hysterical attack is the recurrence of a physical state which the patient has experience earlier. (cited in van der Kolk, Weisaeth, et al., 1996, p. 30)

Freud and Breuer termed traumatic dissociation "hypnoid hysteria" and highlighted its relationship to a traumatic antecedent. In 1896, Freud suggested that "a precocious experience of sexual relations . . . resulting from sexual abuse committed by another person . . . is the *specific cause* [italics added] of hysteria . . . not merely an agent provocateur" (1896/1962, p. 195, cited in van der Kolk, Weisaeth, et al., 1996, p. 54). In the 1880s, Freud and Breuer as well as Janet independently concluded that hysteria was caused by psychological trauma. They agreed that unbearable reactions to traumatic experiences produced an altered state of consciousness that Janet called "dissociation." According to Janet, dissociation manifested in hysterical symptoms (Herman, 1992). Putting the emotions into words and reconstructing the past helped alleviate the patients' symptoms.

However, Freud eventually moved from what has been termed "seduction theory" to conflict theory (see Chapter 3 for a more detailed discussion of this development), suggesting that it was not memories of external trauma that caused hysterical symptoms but rather the unacceptable nature of sexual and aggressive wishes. What his followers neglected to notice, however, was that whereas Freud privileged intrapsychic theory and fantasy over external trauma, he did suggest that it was possible for external trauma to influence the patient's state of mind (Diamond, 2004). Ferenczi (1933/1955) was the only one among Freud's followers who regarded his patients' stories of childhood sexual abuse as veridical recollections, but he remained somewhat of an outsider in the psychoanalytic movement during his lifetime, his theories gaining favor only in the decades following his untimely death in 1933.

Crisis intervention methods to address traumatic events developed gradually, with the establishment of the first suicide hotline in 1902 in San Francisco. Psychological "first aid" was then further developed in the context of military combat. During World War I, psychiatrists observed that soldiers returned with "shell shock" syndrome. Psychological first aid was first developed to help World War I soldiers overcome their symptoms of uncontrollable weeping and screaming, memory loss, physical paralysis, and lack of responsiveness (Herman, 1992). The goal of psychological first aid was to provide a short intervention that would help the soldiers recover and return to the front as soon as possible. It was observed that by providing intervention close to the front and soon after deployment, traumatized soldiers were able to overcome their shell shock symptoms and return to active combat duty. In 1923, following World War I, Abram Kardiner started to treat traumatized U.S. war veterans (Kardiner, 1941). Like Janet and Freud, he observed the nature of reenactment, a central construct in modern trauma theory, and noted that "the subject acts as if the original traumatic situation were still in existence and engages in protective devices which failed on the original occasion" (p. 82; also cited in van der Kolk, Weisaeth, et al., 1996, p. 58). Kardiner also foresaw an important controversy that continues to haunt trauma therapists, that is, whether to bring the traumatic memories into the patient's consciousness or to focus on stabilization (van der Kolk, van der Hart, & Marmar, 1996). Although earlier trauma theorists blamed the soldiers' symptoms on their poor moral character, Kardiner understood that any man could be affected by the atrocities of war and that the traumatic symptoms were a normal response to an unbearable situation.

Kardiner and his colleague Herbert Spiegel argued that the most powerful intervention against overwhelming terror was "the degree of relatedness between the soldier, his immediate fighting unit, and their leader" (Herman, 1992, p. 25). Consequently, treatment for traumatized soldiers during the Second World War focused on minimizing separation between these soldiers and their comrades and providing brief intervention methods such as hypnosis. Kardiner and Spiegel warned, however, that cathartic experiences and hypnosis by themselves, without consistent follow-up, were not sufficiently helpful and that unless the traumatic memories were integrated in consciousness the improvement would not last (Kardiner & Spiegel, 1947, cited in Herman, 1992). During World War II, psychiatrists reintroduced hypnosis as a treatment for trauma, and the U.S. Army instituted the use of "group stress debriefing" (Shalev & Ursano, 1990, cited in van der Kolk, Weisaeth, et al., 1996, p. 59).

After World War II, studies on the impact of prolonged stress and trauma on concentration cam survivors coincided with observations of combat stress. Henry Krystal (1968, 1978, 1988) was a psychoanalyst who studied outcomes of prolonged traumatization on concentration camp survivors, observing that "traumatized patients come to experience emotional reactions merely as somatic states, without being able to interpret the meaning of what they are feeling" (van der Kolk, Weisaeth, et al., 1996, p. 60). Krystal elaborated on the diagnosis of alexithymia, a typical syndrome in chronically traumatized people. He described the effect of trauma on the capacity to experience, identify, and verbalize feelings as well as physiological needs and these patients' tendency to somatize affective experiences, express themselves in an overly concrete manner, and their lack of capacity to symbolize and dream. McDougall, who also worked with traumatized patients, suggested that it was not the absence of affect that was the issue. Instead, she stated, her patients "were not suffering from an inability to experience or express emotions, but from an inability to contain and reflect over an excess of affective experiences" (McDougall, 1989, p. 94).

Contemporary trauma theory in civilian contexts developed following the 1942 Cocoanut Grove fire in Boston. During that fire, 493 people perished in a nightclub, many of them trampled to death. Following the tragedy, Dr. Lindemann, who treated a number of the survivors, observed that they displayed common responses. He began to theorize about normal grief reactions, including preoccupation with lost loved ones, identification with the deceased, expressions of guilt and hostility, disorganization, and somatic complaints (Lindemann, 1944). Caplan, who also worked with the survivors of the Cocoanut Grove fire, was the first to systematically describe the components of crisis. He spoke of people's being

> in a state of crisis when they face an obstacle to important life goals, . . . an obstacle that is, for a time, insurmountable by the use of customary methods of problem solving. A period of disorganization ensues, a period of upset, during which many abortive attempts at solution are made. (Caplan, 1961, p. 18)

During the same time Parad was interested in examining the impact of particular types of crises and identified five components that affected victims' abilities to cope with overwhelming life events:

- The stressful event poses a problem which is by definition insoluble in the immediate future.
- The problem overtaxes the psychological resources of the family, since it is beyond their traditional problem solving methods.
- The situation is perceived as a threat or danger to the life goals of the family members.
- The crisis period is characterized by tension which mounts to a peak, then falls.
- Perhaps of the greatest importance, the crisis situation awakens unresolved key problems from both the near and distant past. (Parad & Caplan, 1960, pp. 11–12)

During the Vietnam War, soldiers and veterans returned with incapacitating symptoms that often developed into chronic problems affecting their capacity to cope with, and function in, civilian life. Many of them started to abuse drugs and alcohol, behaved violently toward their partners, or became homeless and unemployable. Lifton and Shatan, who worked with Vietnam veterans, conducted "rap groups" for the veterans, during which they could share their experiences with their comrades and receive validation and support. Based on their work, Lifton and Shatan identified 27 common symptoms of "traumatic neurosis" (Lifton, 1973). These symptoms were catalogued based on the authors' observations of veterans as well as on their readings of Kardiner and the literature on Holocaust survivors and victims of accidents, which they compared with clinical records of Vietnam veterans. Many of these symptoms were later included in the *Diagnostic and Statistical Manual of Mental Disorders* (third edition; *DSM-III*) diagnosis of posttraumatic stress disorder (PTSD) and utilized in panel discussions leading to the inclusion of this diagnosis (van der Kolk, Weisaeth, et al., 1996). Figley (1978) also contributed to the growing treatment literature on Vietnam veterans, and Shay (1994) made theoretical contributions to the understanding of the long-term impact of combat trauma on Vietnam veterans by applying Greek mythological imagery. He used, for example, the story of Achilles to anchor his discussion of Vietnam veterans' experiences and psychological wounds.

Along with combat trauma and the trauma of Holocaust survivors, trauma in the lives of women moved from the private domain of the home to the public arena as a consequence of the women's movement in the 1970s. Women's consciousness-raising groups shared common characteristics with the Vietnam veterans' rap groups in that they were based on open sharing, validation, and support and "helped overcome barriers of denial, secrecy and shame" (Herman, 1992, p. 29). The purpose was not only to provide psychological healing but to bring about social change in policies and institutions. An epidemiological survey by Diana Russell in the 1980s of more than 900 women chosen at random showed that 1 woman in 4 had been raped and 1 woman in 3 had been sexually abused in childhood, statistics that were quite shocking insofar as such problems had been well hidden and denied until that era (Russell, 1984). The first rape crisis center opened in 1971, and a more comprehensive understanding and treatment of domestic violence followed (Herman, 1992). Additional contributions to the understanding of types of trauma and their impact were made by Lenore Terr (1979) through her work with children involved in a school bus kidnapping in Chowchilla, California.

PTSD and the *DSM-III*

Psychological trauma and PTSD were not included in the *DSM* until 1980, when returning Vietnam War veterans presented with severe symptoms and clearly needed prolonged psychological services. Advocates for combat veterans and mental health professionals collaborated in bringing these events and their aftermath to public view (Herman, 1981, 1992; van der Kolk, Weisaeth, et al., 1996). Together with advocates of battered women, rape victims, and abused children, these clinicians brought their influence to bear on the *DSM-III* committees, and all of these groups were included under the diagnosis of PTSD in 1980. Veterans' advocates, mental health professionals, and others working with victims of domestic violence and adult survivors of childhood incest/sexual abuse reported similar symptoms in their traumatized clients. Many had been further victimized owing to social stigmata and a lack of understanding of their behavioral, emotional, and cognitive symptoms. In addition to advocating for the acceptance of PTSD diagnosis, women's advocates opposed the inclusion of certain personality disorders that they regarded as being sexist and/or culturally biased, such as masochistic and histrionic personality disorders.

The *DSM* diagnosis of PTSD addressed immediate symptoms following combat experiences, rape, domestic violence, and child abuse; symptoms were then categorized along four clusters: intrusive reexperiencing, avoidance, hyperarousal, and hypervigilance, with general symptoms of anxiety and dysphoria in addition (Ford & Courtois, 2009). Although the PTSD diagnosis addresses the symptoms of posttraumatic stress, it does not focus on causes in a patient's early developmental history, which may include childhood abuse and neglect; nor does it offer a more complex and comprehensive view of psychosocial stressors and daily functioning that exert influence over all areas of adult life.

Complex Traumatic Stress Disorder

As stated above, although the diagnosis of PTSD included the comprehensive symptoms of trauma, it did not address early antecedents in childhood, the impact on long-term social and professional functioning, and the role of trauma in personality disorders. Herman (1992) was the first to suggest that "Complex PTSD" be included as a new diagnosis that would address the multiple origins of trauma and their impact on all aspects of a person's life. She noted that frequently, women with borderline personality disorder were marginalized by mental health professionals who failed to understand the connection between their early experience of sexual abuse and their present personality structure. More recently, Courtois developed the comprehensive diagnosis of complex trauma (Courtois, 2004, 2009), which she explains as the "inability to self regulate, self organize, or draw upon relationships to regain self integrity" (Ford & Courtois, 2009, p. 17). Complex trauma is "associated with histories of multiple traumatic stressors and exposure experiences, along with severe disturbances in primary care giving relationships" (Ford & Courtois, 2009, p. 18). It can lead to substance abuse, unemployment, and homelessness and affects all psychosocial aspects of living. A diagnosis of complex traumatic stress disorder calls for a treatment model that addresses the immediate posttraumatic symptoms as well as psychosocial counseling, substance abuse treatment, domestic violence interventions, and assistance in improving professional and interpersonal skills as well as in obtaining housing.

Developmental Trauma Disorder

Along with the recognition of complex traumatic stress disorder and its impact on all aspects of the person's life, van der Kolk (2005) recommended the inclusion of a new diagnosis, which he called developmental trauma disorder, for children with complex developmental trauma histories. This diagnosis is distinct from other childhood diagnoses such as ADHD, oppositional defiant, and conduct disorder in that it specifically addresses the consequences of early trauma in relation to abuse and neglect. Van der Kolk noted that a study by Kaiser Permanente of 17,337 members revealed that 11% reported having been emotionally abused as children, 30.1% reported early physical abuse, and 19.9% reported sexual abuse (van der Kolk, 2005). This survey shows that childhood abuse is much more common than previously known and that those children deprived of intervention or treatment of early abuse symptoms will likely suffer from behavioral, emotional, and cognitive disturbances for the rest of their lives. In addition, early trauma affects the neurological development of young children, who may not be able to develop the neuronal structures necessary to process information, regulate emotions, and categorize experiences. This can lead to poor impulse control, aggression, difficulty in interpersonal relationships, and poor academic performance because of their inability to concentrate. In later development, such children may develop self-harming and substance abuse disorders in an effort to regulate their emotional arousal, owing to their difficulty in self-soothing and affect regulation. Van der Kolk suggested that multiple exposures to childhood traumas, including "abandonment, betrayal, physical or sexual assaults, or witnessing domestic violence" (2005, p. 406) can have negative sequelae that continue to reverberate throughout childhood, adolescence, and adulthood.

Trauma in Contemporary Life

Traumatic stress has become more prevalent and complex in contemporary American life as a result of the mass trauma of 9/11, the ongoing war against terrorism, and ongoing wars in Iraq and Afghanistan, which have led to an increased incidence of PTSD in returning military personnel. In the immediate aftermath of 9/11, mental health professionals treated survivors based on the principles of critical incident stress debriefing procedures (Everly & Mitchell, 1999; Mitchell, 1983). This treatment approach is based on the assumption that encouraging expression of one's thoughts and feelings about the traumatic event soon after it happens will bring about relief and resolution of symptoms (Seery, Silver, Holman, Ence, & Chu, 2008). However, to date there are few data to show that expressing one's thoughts and feelings immediately after trauma is a good way of coping. Although some studies indicate that trauma expression results in better mental health, research has shown that the mean amount of time between the target event and the participant's disclosure is 15 months, well beyond the limits of early intervention (Frattaroli, 2006). A meta-analysis by van Emmerik, Kamphuis, Hulsbosch, and Emmelkamp (2002) shows that critical incident stress debriefing does not significantly improve PTSD and other trauma-related symptoms such as general anxiety and depression. In addition, Sherman, Zanotti, and Jones (2005) found that survivors of 9/11 who chose not to discuss the trauma they experienced showed better mental health outcomes for 2 years after 9/11 than people who chose to express their feelings and discuss their experiences. As a result of these studies, trauma intervention methods have become less intrusive and are now based on stabilization and psychosocial approaches (Basham & Miehls, 2006; Briere & Scott, 2006; Ford & Courtois, 2009).

More recently, as a result of the wars in Iraq and Afghanistan, which have entailed multiple, long deployments for military personnel, the violent death of peers, and the high incidence of physiological and psychological trauma, the rates of complex PTSD have been increasing. Complex PTSD affects both these soldiers and their families and requires new intervention approaches. Prolonged exposure techniques (Foa, 2006; Foa et al., 2005) immediately following the event, although helpful to some patients, have been found to be far too intense for others. Moreover, the treatment dropout rate is quite high (K. Basham, personal communication, 2009). A phase-based approach that would include stabilization techniques, education, and social skills training may be more effective in helping these soldiers integrate their experiences, adapt to civilian life and to their role in their families, and return to productive lives (Ford & Courtois, 2009).

Contemporary Approaches to Trauma

In this volume, we have tried to include traumatized groups that are less familiar to professional audiences to contribute to the dissemination of new knowledge. The emphasis in this book is on clinical interventions with a number of specific communities. Although limitations of space have made it impossible to cover all contemporary treatments in this volume, we would like to mention the important role of body-based therapies, including somatic therapy (Levine) and sensorimotor psychotherapy (Fisher & Ogden, 2009). These therapies are particularly significant in trauma work, where experiences are frequently stored in nonverbal parts of the brain such as the amygdala and in sensory organs. Body-based therapies help clients access traumatic experiences that are not yet available for verbal narration and cognitive reflection. Many clients require processes other than talk therapy to make the material available to conscious awareness.

Sensorimotor therapy is influenced by several bodies of literature, including mindfulness practice, attachment theory, and neurobiology, particularly Schore's (2003) work on affect regulation, and also by Peter Levine's somatic therapy model (Levine, 1997). Although no formal research has been done on this model, there is clinical evidence of its usefulness with traumatized clients. The model focuses on both body and mind, but rather than focusing on verbal and analytical skills, the interaction of thought, feeling, bodily sensation, and movement is emphasized through mindfulness observations of the "here and now." Sensorimotor therapists help clients

> regulate arousal by carefully tracking physical sensations for signs of dysregulation, by asking questions that direct attention to relationships between bodily response and narrative content, by teaching clients to recognize the physical signs that indicate dysregulated or hyperarousal, and by encouraging them to experiment with specific somatic interventions that promote regulation. (Fisher & Ogden, 2009, p. 317)

The therapist encourages the client to express experience through action and arm and bodily movements, which may be either protective or aggressive in nature. The therapeutic process includes phases of stabilization, memory and emotion work, and finally integration.

Another group of treatments showing promise with traumatized clients is mindfulness meditation–based therapies. Although these have not been specifically developed to address trauma, they have been effective in the management of stress, pain, and chronic and terminal illness. There has been much research on mindfulness-based therapy that has entered the health care field and is rapidly becoming part of a treatment protocol in hospitals and health care settings. Mindfulness therapies are inspired by Eastern meditation practices, and all share common elements. In addition to dialectical behavioral therapy, other mindfulness-based therapies have been developed and show promise in the treatment of borderline personality disorder, anxiety, depression, and pain management. To date, these models include dialectical behavioral therapy (Linehan, 1993a, 1993b), developed for borderline personality disorders; acceptance and commitment therapy (Hayes & Strosahl, 2004); mindfulness-based cognitive therapy (Segal, Williams, & Teasdale, 2002); and mindfulness-based stress reduction (Kabat Zinn, 1990, 2003, 2005).

The principles common to all of these models include the following:

- accepting internal experiences as they are, even when difficult, and observing them with curiosity, openness, and compassion;
- integrating mindfulness skills with change-based strategies, which suggests that although there is an attitude of patience and acceptance, there is also an emphasis on teaching skills for change (e.g., affect regulation and social skills); and
- decentering or defusion: observing experiences as transitory mental states, such that the client learns to recognize that thoughts and feelings pass and change and there is no need to immediately react or identify oneself with what one is thinking and feeling.

The goals of such treatment are increasing awareness of the present-moment experience, including sensations, thoughts, feelings, and environmental stimuli; cultivating an accepting nonjudgmental stance; reducing symptoms; developing self-exploration and insight; developing wisdom and compassion; and finally, living in accordance with values such as love, compassion, integrity, and honesty (Baer & Huss, 2008). Unlike cognitive-behavioral therapy, mindfulness-based models advocate staying with states of mind, feelings, and physical sensations rather than using distraction strategies or restructuring thoughts and beliefs (cognitive restructuring). States of mind might include traumatic memories, physical pain and discomfort, negative thoughts, and intense feeling states. The client learns to allow, accept, and welcome mental states and bodily sensations without trying to fix them or change them.

Outline of the Book

In this book, we will address contemporary developments in the principal theoretical models that deal with trauma, including cognitive-behavioral, psychodynamic, and attachment theories. Although this volume is not intended to comprehensively address all populations and communities affected by various kinds of traumas, we have tried to select groups that the literature has not yet fully addressed. This book will include discussions of interventions with children who experienced 9/11 through the death of family members, adolescents who have been subjected to bullying, combat trauma, practice with traumatized gay men, and intergenerational trauma among Native Americans. Finally, the impact on the clinician and the implications for teaching and supervision will be discussed.

Although there has been much scholarship devoted to the study of trauma, the field has expanded rapidly during the past decade as a result of several significant developments. From an earlier focus on the interpersonal aspects of trauma, including child abuse and domestic violence, traumatic experiences have taken on political and social dimensions, for example, the events of 9/11, the war on terror, and combat trauma associated with recent wars in Afghanistan and Iraq. Finally, the rash of school shootings in American public schools, increasingly linked to the problem of bullying, has also recently entered the public consciousness. These complex social and political phenomena have added to the magnitude of traumatic experiences in everyday life and created a more challenging task for mental health professionals dealing with trauma and its aftermath. Accordingly, this volume will present new developments in the conceptualization of trauma and trauma-related interventions from diverse theoretical and clinical perspectives, with special attention to emerging clinical groups and populations.

References

American Psychiatric Association. (1980). *Diagnostic and statistical manual of mental disorders* (3rd ed.). Washington, DC: Author.

Baer, R., & Huss, D. (2008). Mindfulness and acceptance-based therapy. In J. Lebow (Ed.), *Twenty-first century psychotherapies* (pp. 123–166). Hoboken, NJ. John Wiley.

Basham, K., & Miehls, D. (2006). *Transforming the legacy: Couple therapy with survivors of childhood trauma.* New York: Columbia University Press.

Briere, J., & Scott, C. (2006). *Principles of trauma therapy: A guide to symptoms, evaluation and treatment.* Thousand Oaks, CA: Sage.

Caplan, G. (1961). *An approach to community mental health.* New York: Grune & Stratton.

Courtois, C. (2004). Complex trauma, complex reactions: Assessment and treatment. *Psychotherapy: Theory, Research, Practice, Training, 41*(4), 412–425.

Diamond, D. (2004). Attachment disorganization: The reunion of attachment theory and psychoanalysis. *Psychoanalytic Psychology, 21*(2), 276–299.

Everly, G., & Mitchell, J. (1999). *Critical incident stress management (CISM): A new era and standard of care in crisis intervention.* Ellicott City, MD: Chevron.

Ferenczi, S. (1955). The confusion of tongues between the adult and the child: The language of tenderness and the language of passion. In M. Balint (Ed.), *Final contributions to the problems and methods of psychoanalysis* (pp. 156–167). New York: Brunner/Mazel. (Original work published 1933)

Figley, C. (1978). *Stress disorders among Vietnam veterans: Theory, research and treatment implications.* New York: Brunner/Mazel.

Fisher, J., & Ogden, P. (2009). Sensorimotor psychotherapy. In C. Courtois & J. Ford (Eds.), *Treating complex traumatic stress disorders: An evidence based guide* (pp. 312–328). New York: Guilford.

Foa, E. (2006). Psychosocial therapy for posttraumatic stress disorder. *Journal of Clinical Psychiatry, 67,* 40–45.

Foa, E., Hembree, E., Cahill, S., Rauch, S., Riggs, D., Feeny, N., et al. (2005). Randomized trial of prolonged exposure for posttraumatic stress disorder with and without cognitive restructuring: Outcome at academic and community clinics. *Journal of Consulting and Clinical Psychology, 73*(5), 953–964.

Ford, J., & Courtois, C. (2009). Defining and understanding complex trauma and complex traumatic stress disorders. In C. Courtois & J. Ford (Eds.), *Treating complex traumatic stress disorders* (pp. 13–30). New York: Guilford.

Frattaroli, J. (2006). Experimental disclosure and its moderators: A meta analysis. *Psychological Bulletin, 132,* 823–865.

Freud, S. (1962). The aetiology of hysteria. In J. Strachey (Ed.), *The standard edition of the complete psychological works of Sigmund Freud* (Vol. 3, pp. 189–221). London: Hogarth. (Original work published 1896)

Hayes, S., & Strosahl, K. (2004). *A practical guide to acceptance and commitment therapy.* New York: Springer.

Herman, J. (1981). *Father-daughter incest.* Cambridge, MA: Harvard University Press.

Herman, J. (1992). *Trauma and recovery.* New York: Basic Books.

Kabat Zinn, J. (1990). *Full catastrophe living: Using the wisdom of your body and mind to face stress, pain and illness.* New York: Delacorte.

Kabat Zinn, J. (2003). Mindfulness based intervention in context: Past, present, and future. *Clinical Psychology: Science and Practice, 10,* 144–156.

Kabat Zinn, J. (2005). *Coming to our senses.* New York: Hyperion.

Kardiner, A. (1941). *The traumatic neuroses of war.* New York: Hoeber.

Kardiner, A., & Spiegel, H. (1947). *War, stress and neurotic illness: The traumatic neuroses of war.* New York: Hoeber.

Krystal, H. (Ed.). (1968). *Massive psychic trauma.* New York: International Universities.

Krystal, H. (1978). Trauma and affects. *Psychoanalytic Study of the Child, 33,* 81–116.

Krystal, H. (1988). *Integration and self healing: Affect, trauma and alexithymia.* Hillsdale, NJ: Analytic Press.

Levine, P. (1997). *Waking the tiger: Healing trauma.* Berkeley, CA: North Atlantic Books.

Lifton, R. (1973). *Home from the war: Vietnam veterans: Neither victims nor executioners.* New York: Simon & Schuster.

Lindemann, E. (1944). Symptomatology and management of acute grief. *American Journal of Psychiatry, 101,* 141–148.

Linehan, M. (1993a). *Cognitive behavioral treatment of borderline personality disorder.* New York: Guilford.

Linehan, M. (1993b). *Skills training manual for treating borderline personality disorder.* New York: Guilford.

McDougall, J. (1989). *Theaters of the body.* New York: Norton.

Mitchell, J. (1983). When disaster strikes: The critical incident stress debriefing process. *Journal of Emergency Medical Services, 8,* 36–39.

Parad, H., & Caplan, G. (1960). A framework for studying families in crisis. *Social Work, 5*(3), 3–15.

Russell, D. (1984). *Sexual exploitation: Rape, child sexual abuse, and sexual harassment.* Beverly Hills, CA: Sage.

Schore, A. (2003). Early relational trauma, disorganized attachment and the development of predisposition to violence. In M. Solomon & D. Siegel (Eds.), *Healing trauma: Attachment, mind, body, and brain* (pp. 107–167). New York: Norton.

Seery, M., Silver, R., Holman, A., Ence, W., & Chu, T. (2008). Expressing thoughts and feelings following a collective trauma: Immediate responses to 9/11 predict negative outcomes in a national sample. *Journal of Counseling and Clinical Psychiatry, 76*(4), 657–667.

Segal, Z., Williams, J., & Teasdale, J. (2002). *Mindfulness based cognitive therapy for depression: A new approach to preventing relapse.* New York: Guilford.

Shalev, A., & Ursano, R. (1990). Group debriefing following exposure to traumatic stress. In J. E. Lundeberg, U. Ott, & B. Rybeck (Eds.), *War medical services* (pp. 192–207). Stockholm, Sweden: Forsvarets Forskningsanstalt.

Shay, J. (1994). *Achilles in Vietnam: Combat trauma and the undoing of character.* New York: Atheneum.

Sherman, M., Zanotti, D., & Jones, D. (2005). Key elements in couples therapy with veterans with combat-related posttraumatic stress disorder. *Professional Psychology: Research and Practice, 36*(6), 626–633.

Terr, L. (1979). Children of Chowchilla: A study of psychic trauma. *Psychoanalytic Study of the Child, 34,* 552–623.

van der Kolk, B. A. (2005). Developmental trauma disorder: Toward a rational diagnosis for children with complex trauma histories. *Psychiatric Annals, 35*(5), 401–408.

van der Kolk, B. A., van der Hart, O., & Marmar, G. (1996). Dissociation and information processing in posttraumatic stress disorder. In B. A. van der Kolk, A. C. McFarlane, & L. Weisaeth (Eds.), *Traumatic stress: The effects of overwhelming experience in mind, body and society* (pp. 303–327). New York: Guilford.

van der Kolk, B. A., Weisaeth, L., & van der Hart, O. (1996). History of trauma in psychiatry. In B. A. van der Kolk, A. McFarlane, & L. Weisaeth (Eds.), *Traumatic stress: The effects of overwhelming experience on mind, body and society* (pp. 47–76). New York: Guilford.

van Emmerik, A., Kamphuis, J., Hulsbosch, A., & Emmelkamp, P. (2002). Single session debriefing after psychological trauma: A meta analysis. *Lancet, 360,* 766–771.

PART I

Theoretical Frameworks

2

Cognitive-Behavioral Theory

A. Antonio González-Prendes and Stella M. Resko

Cognitive-behavioral therapy (CBT) approaches are rooted in the fundamental principle that an individual's cognitions play a significant and primary role in the development and maintenance of emotional and behavioral responses to life situations. In CBT models, cognitive processes, in the form of meanings, judgments, appraisals, and assumptions associated with specific life events, are the primary determinants of one's feelings and actions in response to life events and thus either facilitate or hinder the process of adaptation. CBT includes a range of approaches that have been shown to be efficacious in treating posttraumatic stress disorder (PTSD). In this chapter, we present an overview of leading cognitive-behavioral approaches used in the treatment of PTSD. The treatment approaches discussed here include cognitive therapy/reframing, exposure therapies (prolonged exposure [PE] and virtual reality exposure [VRE]), stress inoculation training (SIT), eye movement desensitization and reprocessing (EMDR), and Briere's self-trauma model (1992, 1996, 2002). In our discussion of each of these approaches, we include a description of the key assumptions that frame the particular approach and the main strategies associated with the treatment. In the final section of this chapter, we review the growing body of research that has evaluated the effectiveness of cognitive-behavioral treatments for PTSD.

CBT

Three fundamental assumptions underscore cognitive-behavioral models of treatment (D. Dobson & Dobson, 2009; K. Dobson & Dozois, 2001). The first assumption is that cognitive processes and content are accessible and can be known. Although in many instances specific thoughts or beliefs may not be in one's immediate awareness, with proper training and practice individuals can become aware of them. The second key assumption is that our thinking mediates the way that we respond to environmental cues. From this perspective, people do not just react emotionally or behaviorally to life events. Instead, CBT holds that the way we think about our reality is central to how we react to that reality. The third fundamental assumption of CBT is that such cognitions can be intentionally targeted, modified, and changed. Consequently, when such cognitions are changed in the direction of more rational, realistic, and balanced thinking, the individual's symptoms will be relieved, and the person will have increased adaptability and functionality. This change can occur as a result of the individual's working alone, perhaps with the use of self-help material, or through engagement with a trained practitioner in one of the various CBT approaches.

CBT and PTSD

Traditionally, CBT approaches to treatment of PTSD have been driven by two broad theoretical orientations that aim to explain the way fear is developed and processed. These orientations are learning theory (Mowrer, 1960; Wolpe, 1990) and emotional-processing theory (Clark & Ehlers, 2004; Ehlers & Clark, 2000; Foa & Kozak, 1986; Foa, Steketee, & Rothbaum, 1989; Hembree & Foa, 2004; Rachman, 1980).

Learning Theories

Learning theories are most often associated with behavioral approaches that focus on modifying behavior by manipulating environmental cues (i.e., antecedents or reinforcers). Learning theories have focused on explaining how the mechanisms of fear and avoidance of the traumatic memory associated with PTSD are conditioned, activated, and reinforced. From this perspective, unhealthy fears may develop from a single traumatic episode or from exposure to a series of unpleasant events (Wolpe, 1990). Fears can be acquired on the basis of association through classical conditioning, or they can be learned vicariously through the process of observation (Bandura, 1977, 1986). That is, a person may learn to react with fear by observing others' fearful reactions to specific objects or events.

Mowrer's (1956) two-factor theory represents one of the first attempts to provide a behavioral explanation for the acquisition and maintenance of fear associated with PTSD (Cahill, Rothbaum, Resick, & Follette, 2009; Hembree & Foa, 2004). Mowrer suggested that emotions are learned through a two-part process that includes both classical and operant conditioning. Anticipatory fear is acquired through the process of classical conditioning, and relief from this fear takes place when the danger signal is terminated through active avoidance of the feared object or situation, thus creating a secondary rein-forcement of the avoidance behavior (i.e., operant conditioning) (Feather, 1963). In the classical conditioning model, unhealthy fear may develop when an otherwise neutral condition (e.g., being in an elevator) is associated with an unpleasant or dangerous outcome (e.g., an assault). In this case the person may find himself or herself reacting to the neutral condition with the same level of fear associated with the dangerous event. Furthermore, it is possible that through the process of generalization the fear and avoidance may then expand to other places or situations that remind the individual of the trauma. These reminders or thoughts may trigger the same anticipatory fear response and engender the same avoidance behaviors associated with the original stimulus. Moreover, the avoidant behavior becomes operantly conditioned as it provides the person with relief from the unpleasant experience of fear and anxiety.

Although traditional learning theories explain the acquisition of fear and the process of avoidance seen in PTSD, these theories are criticized for falling short of explaining the full spectrum of PTSD symptoms (see Foa et al., 1989; Hembree & Foa, 2004). Of particular note is the inability to account for generalization of fear across dissimilar situations and the failure to include thoughts, appraisals, and meaning concepts (i.e., dangerousness) associated with the traumatic memory.

Emotional-Processing Theory

Emotional-processing theory (Foa & Kozak, 1986; Foa & Riggs, 1993; Rachman, 1980) provides an integrated framework to analyze and explain the onset and maintenance of PTSD. This theoretical approach combines insight from learning, cognitive, and behavioral theories of PTSD and builds on the idea that it is not unusual for emotional experiences to continue to affect one's behaviors long after the event originally associated with the emotion has passed. This emotional reexperiencing can engender a pattern of avoidance of the trauma memory and sustain the presence of PTSD (Foa et al., 1989; Foa & Jaycox, 1999). Foa and Kozak suggest that emotions are represented by information structures in memory. In the case of fear, the associated memory includes information specific to the feared stimulus, overt responses (i.e., verbal, physiological, and behavioral) to the stimulus, and the meaning that the individual has attached to that stimulus. The overall func-tion of this information structure is to help the individual escape or avoid the perceived threat or danger (Foa & Kozak, 1986). Therefore, it is the meaning attached to the memory, usually in the form of a feeling of dangerousness or some catastrophic outcome (e.g., "I will die"; "I will lose control"; "I will faint") that prevents the individual from confronting the traumatic memory and effectively processing the information, emotionally and cognitively, underlying the memory. Thus, the individual reacts to the memory with the same cognitive, affective, and behavioral responses associated with the original trauma. In effect, the individual fear structure is virtually stuck in a moment in time that has now passed but that has not been processed or digested in an effective and healthy manner.

Foa and Kozak (1986) defined emotional processing as the activation and modification of the memory structure that underlies the fear. This process includes, first, creating access to the complete memory of the event to reactivate the fear structure through the process of exposure (i.e., imaginal, in vivo, virtual reality) and, second, helping the individual access new information incompatible with the existing maladaptive information to modify the fear structure to engender a healthier response to the memory.

Cognitive Conceptualization of PTSD

Evidence suggests that the way individuals emotionally and cognitively process a traumatic experience contributes to the development and maintenance of PTSD (Clark & Ehlers, 2004; Ehlers & Clark, 2000; Foa & Kozak, 1986; Smucker, 1997). Persistent PTSD occurs when an individual processes a traumatic event in a manner that leads the person to recall the event with the same sense of seriousness and danger felt at the time of the original trauma (Clark & Ehlers, 2004; Ehlers & Clark, 2000). It is the individual's interpretation and appraisal of the trauma and the ensuing memory that contribute to persistent PTSD. Therefore, cognitive therapy for PTSD focuses on teaching clients how to identify, evaluate, and reframe the dysfunctional cognitions related to the specific trauma and its sequelae that contribute to the intense negative emotions and behavioral reactions (Ehlers & Clark, 2000; Hembree & Foa, 2004). Yet not all individuals who experience trauma develop PTSD (Foa, Ehlers, Clark, Tolin, & Orsillo, 1999). Why is that?

Foa and Riggs (1993) and Foa and Rothbaum (1998) suggested that persons with PTSD are characterized by two flawed central beliefs that relate to how these individuals evaluate themselves and the world. The first belief is that the self is incompetent. The second belief, reflecting the individual's worldview, is that the world is a threatening and dangerous place. For these individuals, the traumatic event often serves as confirmation of their beliefs antedating the trauma. This interpretation is supported by Dunmore, Clark, and Ehlers (1999), who studied cognitive factors that contributed to the onset and maintenance of PTSD in 92 assault victims and compared those who developed PTSD with those who did not. They reported that cognitive factors associated with the onset and persistence of PTSD included beliefs relative to devaluation of the personality (e.g., "I am a loser"; "I am disgusting"), one's safety (e.g., "There is no safe place"; "People have bad intentions"), and the world (e.g., "The world is dark"; "There is no justice in this world"). Individuals who possess these beliefs would then tend to feel a more persistent and intense sense of apprehension and uncertainty and would be more likely to interpret traumatic events as being characteristic of a dangerous world. Such interpretation may result in fear and avoidance of what is perceived as a dangerous place. Second, the view of the self as incompetent diminishes the person's ability to cope with adversity. An individual who sees the self in this way is less likely to feel capable of coping with the pain of the actual trauma or the unpleasantness of the memory and would instead feel overwhelmed and crushed by the weight of the trauma memory.

A central theme contributing to the onset and persistence of PTSD is a perception of ongoing threat, even when the trauma occurred in the distant past (Dunmore et al., 1999). Furthermore, the expectation of a threat activates and maintains the disabling anxiety associated with PTSD. Other individuals are able to frame a traumatic event as a unique and isolated occurrence that does not alter their broader views of the world or self (Clark & Ehlers, 2004). These individuals are more likely to process the trauma emotionally and cognitively in a way that leads to healing and successful recovery.

The cognitive conceptualization of PTSD acknowledges the presence of overly active danger schemas (A. T. Beck, Emery, & Greenberger, 1985; Ehlers & Clark, 2000; Hembree & Foa, 2004). A person with PTSD is likely to have recurrent false alarms brought on by an exaggerated sense of danger. As we have already noted, this can happen even if the trauma happened long ago. Researchers have advanced several explanations of why some individuals experience this persistent, exaggerated sense of threat. One explanation is the process of avoidance and "seeking safety" (Dunmore et al., 1999; Najavits, Weiss, Shaw, & Muentz, 1998). Retreating to a safe place represents a less threatening alternative than facing the situations, places, or experiences that activate fears, vulnerabilities, and negative beliefs about oneself and one's environment. As Foa et al. (1989) have argued, this process may work for some anxieties (e.g., phobias). However, the varying and unstable nature of situations that engender fear in the person with PTSD makes the attainment of a safe place, which lessens the anxiety through the avoidance of feared situations, more difficult. Nonetheless, avoidance of situations that the person associates with the original trauma does not allow the person with PTSD opportunities to evaluate the validity of erroneous beliefs or to gain corrective emotional experiences.

Cognitive Therapy for PTSD

The goal of cognitive therapy for PTSD is to teach clients cognitive-reframing strategies. Such techniques help clients to identify and restructure trauma-related, irrational beliefs that engender unhealthy negative emotions and lead to dysfunctional behaviors, typically in response to memories of, or situations associated with, the trauma (Hembree & Foa, 2004). Cognitive therapy for

PTSD may also include some form of exposure to the trauma memory in the form of either repeated exposure to related images (Foa, Rothbaum, Riggs, & Murdock, 1991) or a written narrative of the trauma (Resick & Schnicke, 1992). The process described by Hembree and Foa and rooted in Beck's cognitive therapy model (A. T. Beck, 1976; A. T. Beck et al., 1985) includes identifying the irrational and dysfunctional cognitions that fuel the negative emotional and behavioral responses, systematically evaluating the validity and functionality of such cognitions by assessing evidence that both supports and contradicts their validity and functionality, and summarizing and synthesizing the uncovered evidence and using it to reframe the irrational thoughts into more realistic, balanced, rational, and functional perceptions of self, the world, and the future. In cognitive therapy there are two mechanisms that are central to the therapeutic process: collaborative empiricism and the Socratic method (A. T. Beck et al., 1985; J. S. Beck, 1995). Collaborative empiricism, or collaborative hypothesis testing (Scott & Freeman, 2010), refers to the formation of a therapeutic alliance in which the client and therapist work together, using Socratic questioning to uncover and evaluate supporting or contradictory evidence of the targeted belief. The Socratic method, also called Socratic questioning, employs the posing of open-ended questions to help the client recover information/knowledge that he or she already possesses and that is relevant to the targeted problem. The objective is a reevaluation of a previously held erroneous conclusion and the construction of a new perspective (Scott & Freeman, 2010). Cognitive therapy models to treat PTSD are similar in that they are trauma focused and include education as well as cognitive and exposure strategies (Clark & Ehlers, 2004; Ehlers & Clark, 2000; Resick & Schnicke, 1992).

Ehlers and Clark Model

In their CBT model for the treatment of PTSD, Clark and Ehlers (2004) and Ehlers and Clark (2000) specified three therapy goals for the treatment of PTSD: (a) reduce intrusions and reexperiencing of the traumatic memory, (b) modify excessive negative appraisals, and (c) eliminate dysfunctional cognitive and behavioral strategies. Ehlers and Clark proposed a treatment model that incorporates the following elements:

• *Detailed assessment interview.* The objectives of this process are to identify possible problematic cognitive themes that need to be addressed in treatment, specify the worst aspects and most painful moment associated with the trauma, underscore predominant emotions associated with the event, illuminate problematic appraisals of the trauma sequelae, identify specifics of the problematic and dysfunctional cognitive and behavioral attempts to cope (i.e., how has the client tried to put the trauma behind him or her, how does the client deal with intrusions, and what does the client fear will happen if he or she allows him- or herself to dwell on the trauma?), and identify the characteristics of the trauma memory and intrusions.

• *Rationale for treatment.* A key aspect of cognitive therapy is to ensure that the client understands the rationale behind the therapeutic strategies employed. This rationale should include an explanation of the nature of PTSD and its symptoms; of how the client's attempts to cope with the trauma, most likely through avoidance, may produce temporary relief from anxiety but can indeed contribute to maintaining the symptoms of the disorder; and that to counteract this process of avoidance and fully process the trauma, it will be necessary to confront the unpleasant memory.

• *Thought-suppression experiment.* This strategy allows the client to understand how attempts to suppress intrusive memories by pushing them away from the consciousness paradoxically reinforces and increases the impact of such memories. Instead, a client is encouraged to use an alternative approach and not to try to push the memory from consciousness but rather to accept it, observe it, and allow it to come and go, as if the client were watching a twig floating, bobbing up and down, and passing along in a stream of water.

• *Education.* Ehlers and Clark (2000) suggested educating and providing the client with access to information that may help rectify mistaken assumptions about possible physical damage associated with the trauma.

• *Reclaiming one's life.* This strategy aims to help the client reclaim aspects (e.g., activities and other pursuits) of his or her life that were given up as a result of the trauma. As Ehlers and Clark (2000) suggested, this process helps the client become "unstuck" from that moment in the past when he or she experienced the trauma. Instead, the client attempts to reclaim the former self by reconnecting with lost interests and social contacts.

• *Reliving with cognitive restructuring.* Cognitive behavioral approaches to the treatment of PTSD generally include some form of reliving or revisiting the trauma. A key aspect of this step is to make sure that the client fully understands the rationale behind this strategy. The client is then asked to revisit the trauma, recounting the original event with as much detail and as vividly as possible. This helps the client construct a detailed account of the trauma, while at the same time connecting with the feelings and cognitions associated with it. This process is discussed in more detail in the Exposure Therapies section.

• *In-vivo exposure.* The process of in-vivo exposure revolves around revisiting reminders of the original trauma that have been systematically avoided in the past. This may include exposure to the site, smells, sounds, activities, and other powerful reminders of the trauma. This process helps the client to discriminate between the harmless reminders of the trauma and the danger of the actual trauma, to challenge patterns of overgeneralization that have led the client to avoid elements unrelated to the original trauma, and to challenge the various irrational appraisals attached to the sequelae of the trauma.

• *Identifying triggers of intrusive memories or emotions.* This procedure aims to enhance the process of discriminating between past stimuli at the time of the trauma and present stimuli. The client is encouraged to monitor carefully the context within which the intrusions occur and the triggers (e.g., sensations, feelings, situations, cognitions) associated with these intrusions. This is followed by a detailed discussion of similarities and differences of the past and present context of the triggers, facilitating a higher level of stimulus discrimination.

• *Imagery techniques.* Ehlers and Clark (2000) suggested the use of imagery to help the client elaborate and change the meaning of the trauma memory. In a way, imagery may help the client tie loose ends (e.g., saying good-bye to a friend or relative) and help bring closure to aspects of the trauma.

Cognitive Processing Therapy (CPT)

CPT was developed to help rape victims address the symptoms of PTSD (Resick & Schnicke, 1992). At the core of CPT's conceptual framework of PTSD is the conflict that may exist between old information stored by the individual in various schemata and new information derived from the trauma. In cases in which a person acquires new information that does not conform to existing schemata, either the new information is assimilated into the existing schemata or the existing schemata are altered to accommodate the new information. Resick and Schnicke (1992) proposed that the symptoms of PTSD are indeed the result of conflict between new information (e.g., "I have just been raped") and existing schemata (e.g., "Nice women do not experience rape"). The authors went on to point out that these conflicts may be concerned not only with themes of danger and safety (e.g., "The world is dangerous"; "My home is not a safe place") but also with other themes reflecting self-esteem, competence, and/or intimacy. Thus, the focus of CPT is on helping clients resolve "stuck points" that represent conflicts between prior schemata and new information derived from the traumatic experience.

As described by Resick and Schnicke (1992), the process of CPT flows through several components. Treatment typically takes place during 12 sessions of group therapy consisting of 1½ hours per session. Initially clients are educated in information processing, specifically related to their rape. A written assignment helps clients explore the personal meaning they ascribe to the traumatic event. Clients are also taught to differentiate feelings from thoughts, as well as to recognize the connection between cognitions (i.e., self-statements) and feelings. The exposure component of CPT asks clients to revisit their traumatic event by writing a detailed account of their rape, which is then read back in therapy and at home. Emphasis is placed on helping clients have a full experience of their emotions both during the writing process and during the later reading of the account. In this manner CPT encourages clients to experience their emotions more fully. According to Resick and Schnicke the rationale behind this exercise is to counteract the tendency of rape victims to suppress or avoid the overwhelming emotions experienced in association with the assault and to identify stuck points that may represent areas of incomplete processing. The cognitive therapy component of CPT involves teaching clients how to identify, challenge, and reframe maladaptive beliefs and recognize faulty thinking patterns. During this portion of treatment, there is a sequential presentation of five domains of beliefs affected by the trauma: safety, trust, power, esteem, and intimacy. These beliefs form the core of a model about psychological responses to trauma and the relationship between traumatic experiences and cognitive schemas, described by McCann, Sakheim, and Abrahamsom (1988). Homework assignments and group discussion are part of treatment, along with suggestions for adaptive self-statements that help clients resolve conflict and get past stuck points.

In the next-to-last session of CPT, the participants are again asked to write an account of the meaning of the event, without referring to the earlier writing. The last session focuses on a final analysis of their beliefs about intimacy, a discussion of the writing assignment, and a review of goals and plans for the future. Resick and Schnicke (1992) added that throughout the length of treatment, participants should be reminded that the central goal of therapy is to equip them with necessary skills for managing their own individual idiosyncratic thinking patterns and maladaptive beliefs.

Exposure Therapies (PE and VRE)

In light of the fact that avoidance is held to be a central mechanism in the maintenance of anxiety disorders including PTSD, it follows that some form of exposure to the feared objects, situations, images, and memories is an essential and central component for overcoming such fear. This applies to the successful treatment of anxiety disorders in general and PTSD in particular. Exposure therapies focus on the activation of affective and cognitive processes associated with the trauma to facilitate the healthy processing of the trauma. Exposure approaches vary in the degree of contact and the level of intensity of the exposure to the feared object. Some approaches use graduated exposure, a series of hierarchical steps from least to most anxiety provoking that the individual confronts in the course of treatment. Other techniques use a flooding approach in which there is a more abrupt confrontation with the object of avoidance. Exposure therapy can also take the form of imaginal exposure, with the person imaginally revisiting the feared situation, or in-vivo exposure, in which the person confronts the feared object face-to-face. The length of the exposure exercise may be brief or prolonged. Some exposure approaches such as systematic desensitization (Wolpe, 1990) combine graduated exposure with relaxation strategies, whereas others, such as PE (Foa & Kozak, 1986), do not pair the exposure with relaxation.

PE

PE, also referred to as imaginal exposure, consists of repeated imaginal reliving of the traumatic memory along with in-vivo exposure exercises to confront trauma-related situations, that is, objects or other environmental cues that trigger pathological anxiety and fear (Hembree & Foa, 2004). In 1986, Foa and Kozak argued that some form of exposure leading to confrontation with a feared object is an effective form of treatment for anxiety and an essential aspect for the corrective emotional processing of pathological fear. The authors further argued that to reduce pathological fear, the fear structure must be activated through some form of exposure, and then information incompatible with the fear structure must be introduced. The goal of the exposure is twofold: to provide an opportunity for the emotional processing of the trauma and to facilitate new learning, in the form of cognitive restructuring of maladaptive beliefs associated with the trauma.

Cahill et al. (2009) and Hembree and Foa (2004) discussed several mechanisms by which exposure to the trauma memory (and associated cues) leads to improvement in PTSD. First, habituation is facilitated by repeated exposure, imaginal and in vivo, to the trauma memory and associated cues. As clients revisit the memory and retell the story, they begin to feel less anxious and learn that they do not have to use avoidance to decrease anxiety. However, the experience of exposure goes beyond habituation as it also provides a corrective cognitive experience (i.e., new learning), underscoring the fact that avoidance is not necessary to reduce the level of anxiety. Second, actively confronting the memory, in essence, blocks the process of avoidance. Third, the process of exposure, facilitated by supportive and empathic therapists, helps clients debunk the notion that thinking about the trauma is dangerous. This process helps to undermine the unhealthy idea often held by individuals with PTSD that thinking about the trauma is as dangerous as the trauma itself. Fourth, through repeated exposures to the trauma memory, clients begin to differentiate aspects associated with the past original trauma from present situations to which they have generalized the fear and anxiety. As a result, the trauma is framed as a unique event rather than culminating in an overgeneralization that the world is dangerous or that one is incompetent. By decreasing generalization, the anxiety and fear projected onto nontrauma-related situations begin to dissipate. Fifth, repeated imaginal exposures allow clients to reevaluate and reframe the negative meanings that they attach to themselves. Sixth, as individuals gradually and repeatedly successfully engage in the confrontation of the trauma memory and its associated cues, they begin to feel more in control of their lives, with an increasing sense of competence and mastery. Effective exposure therapy not only has the effect of habituation but also helps clients to challenge and reframe their original view of self as incompetent and weak (Cahill et al., 2009; Hembree & Foa, 2004).

The process of exposure therapy generally ranges from 9 to 12 individual sessions, of approximately 90 minutes in length, offered weekly or biweekly (Foa et al., 1991; Foa et al., 2005; Hembree & Foa, 2004). According to Hembree and Foa (2004), there are four integral components to PE treatment: education, breathing retraining, imaginal exposure to the trauma memory, and in-vivo exposure between sessions to factors or cues associated with the trauma. The first two sessions are normally devoted to gathering background information, explaining the treatment rationale, educating the client about PTSD and its sequelae, breathing retraining, and planning treatment. In Session 3, the process of imaginal exposure begins. The client is asked to sit comfortably, close his or her eyes, and imagine as vividly as possible the actual trauma. Then the client is asked to recount aloud the details of the trauma, using the present tense as if it were happening now, and to use the pronoun *I* as he or she retells the story. As the client recounts the trauma, he or she is encouraged to verbalize the emotions, cognitions, and sensations experienced. This process goes on for approximately 60 minutes, during which time the client is asked to recount that trauma several times. The therapist remains nonintrusive, except for brief interjections to ask for more detail, elicit emotional reactions, or assess the level of the client's anxiety. With each retelling of the trauma, the client is encouraged to provide more vivid details about the event, while at the same time engaging in a deeper level of emotional connection to the trauma. Exposure sessions are tape-recorded and serve as homework assignments, to which the client is instructed to listen daily. Additional homework assignments include in-vivo exposure to environmental cues, along with feared and avoided situations that have been deemed by the client and therapist to be safe (Foa et al., 1991). The following sessions (Sessions 4 to 9 or 12) continue in a similar fashion, with repeated imaginal exposure, tape recording of the session, and homework assignments. In the final session, the client is asked to summarize what was learned in treatment and discuss his or her progress.

VRE

VRE is a relatively new form of graduated exposure therapy for the treatment of PTSD. VRE integrates real-time computer-generated simulation, body-tracking devices that respond to the user's head and body motions, other sensory input (e.g., odors and sounds), and visual displays to create a virtual reality environment that allows the client to immerse him- or herself in the feared and avoided situation (Parsons & Rizzo, 2008; Rothbaum, Ruef, Litz, Han, & Hodges, 2003). VRE for PTSD was initially developed for the treatment of veterans of the Vietnam War (Rothbaum et al., 1999;

Rothbaum, Hodges, Ready, Graap, & Alarcon, 2001). A participant in VRE wears a head-mounted display and headphones into which images and sounds are conveyed. The clinician administering the treatment can follow the virtual environment on a computer screen and simultaneously trigger stimulus delivery to tailor the experience to the participant (Rizzo et al., 2006). One benefit of the VRE approach is that it can overcome certain disadvantages that some clients may experience with traditional imaginal exposure: difficulty visualizing or evoking the trauma memory, reluctance to repeatedly narrate the trauma, and failure to engage emotionally or sense the trauma (Cukor, Spitalnick, Difede, Rizzo, & Rothbaum, 2009; Rizzo et al., 2006). Emotional processing and engagement are key aspects of imaginal exposure, and without those elements, the chances for therapeutic success are diminished (Cahill et al., 2009; Jaycox, Foa, & Morral, 1998). Because VRE has the ability to deliver multiple sensory cues and engage the client's attention with eyes open, it is hypothesized that the obstacles can be more effectively overcome through its administration. This is because the client is able to become more deeply immersed in the traumatic experience (Cukor et al., 2009). Similarly, Alsina-Jurnet, Carvallo-Beciu, and Gutierrez-Maldonado (2007) suggested that VRE offers advantages over in-vivo exposure, for which the logistics of the exposure can be complex and limiting.

In addition to Vietnam War scenarios, virtual environments depict situations of rural and urban combat associated with the Iraq War (e.g., Virtual Iraq) (Rizzo et al., 2006) and the World Trade Center attack of 9/11/01 (Difede & Hoffman, 2002). Most recently, Baños et al. (2009) have reported the development of a versatile virtual reality system, EMMA's World, which can recreate a large spectrum of situations. EMMA's World provides an alternative to current virtual reality systems that target very specific populations with very specific traumas (e.g., Vietnam, Iraq, World Trade Center) by allowing for individualized environments that can be applied to different problems with different populations, such as veterans as well as victims of sexual assault, childhood abuse, disasters, and automobile accidents, among others (Baños et al., 2009).

Although there is some variability in the application of VRE, a review of various studies reveals that a typical pattern entails weekly or biweekly individual therapy sessions. These sessions typically last 90 minutes and include preexposure preparation, exposure to the computer-generated audio and visual stimuli, and debriefing (Alsina-Jurnet et al., 2007; Difede & Hoffman, 2002; Gerardi, Rothbaum, Ressler, Heekin, & Rizzo, 2008; North, North, & Coble, 1998; Reger & Gahm, 2008; Rothbaum et al., 2003). The length of treatment ranges from 4 to 12 weeks. Pretreatment preparation involves an assessment through a clinical interview and the use of self-report, identification of most traumatic memories and a subjective rating of the intensity of the distress associated with each memory using Subjective Units of Distress, and baseline data for psychometric measures and physiological responses (i.e., heart rate and skin conductance). Rothbaum et al. (2003) suggested that including psychophysiological measures provides a more accurate and objective evaluation than self-reporting as to whether negative emotional arousal is alleviated within a session.

Session 1 of VRE generally entails familiarization of the client with treatment procedures and the equipment to be used, an explanation of treatment rationale, psychoeducation about trauma and its sequelae, breathing retraining, and a review of traumatic memories to elicit specific details. Exposure begins during the second session, and the participant generally progresses at his or her own pace. The therapist has access to the virtual environment using a computer screen and is able to gradually introduce sensory stimuli to meet the specific needs of the client while encouraging the client to concentrate on the traumatic memory and associated negative emotions. During the exposure sessions, the therapist asks for a Subjective Units of Distress rating of the client's anxiety every 5 minutes (Rothbaum et al., 2003), and the participant may be exposed to one or more of the virtual environments. Following the exposure scenarios, the participant undergoes a 15-minute debriefing session and breathing retraining. The debriefing sessions focus on the client's reactions to the virtual environment and emotional processing of the experience.

The additional exposure sessions follow a similar pattern, with some variations. In the Difede and Hoffman (2002) study, the authors indicated that each scenario in the virtual reality menu was repeated until there was at least a 50% decrease in Subjective Units of Distress associated with each exposure. In the Rothbaum et al. (2003) study, psychophysiological reactions were measured, to evaluate change within and between sessions.

EMDR

EMDR was initially developed by Francine Shapiro (1989a, 1989b) to reduce the distress of traumatic memories. After initial reports of high success rates in treating PTSD within a short period of time, EMDR quickly became the focus of much debate and research (Devilly & Spence, 1999). The process involves a three-pronged approach that addresses the etiology of a traumatic event (the past), the triggers of the PTSD symptoms (the present), and the development of templates to cope with upsetting events (the future) (Shapiro, 2007). With EMDR, the therapist uses directive questioning to desensitize the client through a brief imagined exposure to the traumatic memory (Shapiro, 2001). The client is asked to provide a negative or dysfunctional cognition of the trauma and identify places in the body where the physical sensations are felt. After focusing on the traumatic memory and negative cognition, emotion, and physical sensations, the client receives bilateral stimulation. The alternating stimulation is a unique though controversial aspect of EMDR. Most commonly, it involves therapist-directed saccadic eye movements, with the therapist moving his or her fingers back and forth in front of the client's face after instructing the client to follow the movement with his or her eyes (Shapiro, 2001). Other dual-attention tasks, such as finger tapping on alternating sides and presenting sounds or light on alternating sides, have also been used (Davidson & Parker, 2001). This sequence is repeated until the accompanying level of disturbance has subsided and the dysfunctional cognitions about the trauma have been ameliorated (Shapiro, 2007).

Although EMDR has been widely adopted (e.g., Veterans Health Administration and Department of Defense, 2004) and thousands of clinicians have been trained in EMDR (Cahill, Carrigan, & Frueh, 1999), it has been the subject of intense controversy. The effectiveness of the eye movement component of EMDR has been questioned because several studies have found that EMDR outcomes are not enhanced by eye movements (e.g., Cahill et al., 1999; Devilly & Spence, 1999; Pitman et al., 1991; Renfrey & Spates, 1994). Rather notably, EMDR has also been critiqued for the absence of an empirically validated model explaining its effectiveness (Gunter & Bodner, 2008; Perkins & Rouanzoin, 2002; Rodenburg, Benjamin, de Roos, Meijer, & Stams, 2009). Several hypotheses have been proposed to explain the treatment mechanism underlying EMDR. Stickgold (2007), for example, has suggested that EMDR may activate a neurobiological state similar to REM sleep. Others have suggested a working-memory account of EMDR that posits that unpleasant memories become less vivid and less emotional when eye movements use up the brain's resources for processing visuospatial information (Gunter & Bodner, 2008; Kavanagh, Freese, Andrade, & May, 2001). Because an understanding of EMDR's treatment mechanism is lacking, additional research is needed.

SIT

SIT is designed to help bolster clients' coping skills as well as their confidence in using their skills effectively in anxiety-provoking situations (Meichenbaum, 1993, 1996). It has been used as a treatment model to assist individuals facing the aftermath of trauma and, on a preventive basis, as a means of self-inoculation against future stressors (Meichenbaum, 1996). SIT utilizes a three-phase, overlapping approach: conceptualization, development of strategies rehearsal, and application/follow-through. The approach to implementing these phases will vary depending on the nature of the trauma (i.e., acute time-limited stressors vs. prolonged ongoing repetitive stressors) and the resources and coping abilities of the client (Meichenbaum, 2007).

During the initial conceptualization phase the goal is to establish a collaborative relationship with the client while enhancing the client's understanding and awareness of the nature of PTSD and the response to the trauma. After the client has developed an understanding of PTSD and the dynamics behind the symptoms, treatment moves to the skills acquisition and rehearsal phase. The goal of this phase is to provide the client with cognitive and behavioral skills to manage and reduce the anxiety associated with the trauma. These skills include cognitive restructuring, relaxation and breathing techniques, thought stopping, covert modeling, problem solving, interpersonal communication skills, attention diversion, and self-instructional training. These are tailored to the specific stressors faced by the client and are rehearsed in session, employing role-play, during which the therapist teaches and models the specific skills. During the application and follow-through phase, the client is expected to apply the learned skills to memories related to the trauma and to increasing levels of stressful cues outside the therapy session. Techniques such as modeling, role-playing, and graduated in-vivo exposure continue to be used through this phase. During this phase of treatment the therapist focuses on reinforcing the client's successful application of the skills learned in therapy to events in his or her life outside therapy as well as troubleshooting any problems or setbacks that may arise in that process.

Relapse prevention strategies and attributional procedures are used throughout SIT to ensure that the client can identify triggers and high-risk situations and also give him- or herself proper credit for gains made and the successful application of coping skills (Meichenbaum, 1996). In most cases SIT will consist of 8 to 15 one-hour sessions, weekly or biweekly, with follow-up booster sessions scheduled 3 to 12 months after therapy (Meichenbaum, 2007).

The Self-Trauma Model

The self-trauma model developed by Briere (1996, 1997, 2002) integrates aspects of humanistic, psychodynamic, and cognitive-behavioral theories. The model was initially developed to assist adults who were victims of child abuse and views PTSD as a self-healing mechanism in which painful events are blocked or avoided (Briere, 2002). These blockers, such as substance abuse and dissociative disorders, can impede emotional processing and recovery. In the self-trauma model, cognitive and behavioral avoidance are ameliorated by enhancing affect-regulation skills before proceeding to exposure therapy. These skills frequently include relaxation, breath training, identification and discernment of emotions, and anticipation and countering of intrusive thoughts (Briere & Scott, 2006). Consistent with other exposure methods, the aim of the self-trauma model is to alter a client's conditioned emotional response to a traumatic memory through exposure and activation of feelings the client had at the time of the trauma (Briere, 2002). If this process is carried out in a safe and therapeutic environment, tailored to the client's individual characteristics and concerns, traumatic responses will be eliminated. Drawing on psychodynamic models, and given that abuse affects relationships and development, the therapeutic relationship is a critical aspect of the process that can countercondition relational trauma and facilitate the client's ability to develop positive relationships (Briere, 2002).

Empirical Evaluations of CBT Treatments for PTSD

When evaluated from a broad perspective, there is substantial evidence supporting the efficacy of several CBTs for the treatment of PTSD, including exposure therapy, EMDR, and SIT (Benish, Imel, & Wampold, 2008; Bisson & Andrew, 2007; Bisson et al., 2007; Bradley, Greene, Russ, Dutra, & Westen, 2005; Foa, Dancu, et al., 1999; Foa, Davidson, & Frances, 1999; Foa et al., 1991; Ponniah & Hollon, 2009; Seidler & Wagner, 2006). At the same time, however, consensus does not exist with regard to the relative efficacy of these treatments (Benish et al., 2008), and no specific treatment has yet proven to be the gold standard in the treatment of PTSD (Lee, Taylor, & Drummond, 2006; McFarlane & Yehuda, 2000).

In a meta-analysis of randomized studies published in the English language ($N = 38$), Bisson et al. (2007) concluded that trauma-focused CBT (TFCBT) and EMDR are effective in treating PTSD on an individual basis. There was also limited support for the use of stress management and group CBT to alleviate symptoms of PTSD. The results of the analysis also indicated that nontrauma-focused therapies did not have clinically significant effects on PTSD. The authors explain that this is a possible result of the limited number of studies available and not necessarily as a sign of ineffectiveness. Another study conducted by Bisson and Andrew (2007) further supports the notion that TFCBT is more effective than wait-list controls or treatment as usual to reduce symptoms of PTSD and associated levels of depression and anxiety. TFCBT ($d = 1.36$) and stress management ($d = 1.14$) were also found to be more effective than other therapies.

Bradley et al. (2005) conducted a multidimensional, meta-analytic review of studies published between 1989 and 2003 on psychotherapies for PTSD ($N = 26$) that included 44 treatment conditions. The treatment conditions studied included 13 exposure treatments, 5 cognitive therapy, 9 cognitive therapy plus exposure, 10 EMDR, and 7 *other*. The authors concluded that the results support the use of treatments that include exposure, cognitive therapy, and EMDR to treat PTSD. Effect sizes were largest in pre-post comparisons ($d = 1.43$), in contrast to wait-list controls ($d = 1.11$) or supportive controls ($d = 0.83$). Consistent with previous studies, treatments for combat-related PTSD had the lowest effect size (Bradley et al., 2005). A large effect size ($d = 1.52$) was found between measures taken right after completion of treatment and follow-up measures taken at least 6 months after treatment (two studies provided follow-up measures at the 12-month posttreatment point). The authors concluded that based on the results of their meta-analysis, treatments including exposure, cognitive therapy, and EMDR are effective for the treatment of PTSD.

In another meta-analytic study, Ponniah and Hollon (2009) reviewed randomized studies ($N = 57$) published up until the end of 2008, irrespective of trauma, and concluded that TFCBT is efficacious in the treatment of PTSD. Exposure, with or without cognitive restructuring, was found to produce greater reductions in PTSD symptoms when compared with no treatment or minimal interventions, relaxation training, and supportive counseling. That study also found that cognitive restructuring alone, without exposure, was more efficacious than treatment as usual and relaxation training. The authors also concluded that EMDR is efficacious to treat PTSD, although they tempered their support of EMDR, citing that fewer studies have been conducted with this condition and many of the studies included a mixed trauma sample. SIT was found to be "possibly efficacious" for the treatment of PTSD.

A meta-analytic study ($N = 7$) directly comparing EMDR treatment adhering to Shapiro's (1995) protocol against TFCBT with exposure as the main form of intervention concluded that both conditions are equally efficacious (Seidler & Wagner, 2006). Prior meta-analyses (Bradley et al., 2005) had supported the efficacy of both treatments. Nonetheless, the results from this analysis do not support the notion that one treatment is superior to the other (Seidler & Wagner, 2006). The authors underscore two limitations of this review: the relatively small number of studies that compare EMDR to TFCBT and the fact that results are based on clients who completed treatment. Both study groups had substantial numbers of dropouts (EMDR—21%, TFCBT—23%).

Several meta-analytic reviews of outcome studies suggest that EMDR is an efficacious treatment for PTSD (Bisson & Andrew, 2007; Bisson et al., 2007; Bradley et al., 2005; Davidson & Parker, 2001; van Etten & Taylor, 1998), possibly as effective as exposure therapies (e.g., Ironson, Freund, Strauss, & Williams, 2002; Lee, Gavriel, Drummond, Richards, & Greenwald, 2002; Rothbaum, Astin, & Marsteller, 2005). In five studies using clinician-based assessments of PTSD symptoms, EMDR resulted in significantly better outcomes than wait-list controls or treatment as usual (Standardized Mean Difference = –1.51; 95% confidence interval, –1.87 to –1.15) (Bisson & Andrew, 2007). Other researchers, however, have critiqued the evidence base for EMDR (e.g., Herbert et al., 2000; McNally, 1999), noting several controlled studies with contradictory results that did not support the efficacy of EMDR (e.g., Devilly & Spence, 1999; Jensen, 1994). These scholars are concerned by the aggressive marketing and dissemination strategies by EMDR's developers and have argued that EMDR may simply be a variant of exposure therapy (Herbert et al., 2000). There also has been considerably less evidence for incremental efficacy that would indicate EMDR is a significant improvement over other established PTSD treatments (Rodenburg et al., 2009).

SIT, PE, and the combination of the two have been found to effectively reduce PTSD symptoms, as well as anxiety and depression in female victims of assault (Foa, Dancu, et al., 1999; Foa et al., 1991). The 1991 study involved 45 female victims of rape or attempted rape randomly assigned to one of four conditions: PE, SIT, supportive counseling, and wait list. The results indicated that SIT was most effective in reducing symptoms immediately following treatment. PE was also effective in reducing symptoms at posttreatment, and it showed greater results at the follow-up measures. Both treatments showed significant reductions of symptoms when compared to supportive counseling and wait list. According to Foa et al. (1991), SIT appears to provide more immediate relief of symptoms because its focus is on anxiety management. On the other hand, PE may produce some immediate increases in anxiety as the result of the exposure to the traumatic memory. However, the emotional processing of the trauma with cognitive reframing of its theme of dangerousness may result in longer lasting effects. The efficaciousness of SIT and PE was supported by Foa, Dancu, et al. (1999) in a comparison of PE, SIT, and a combination of the two to treat PTSD in female assault victims. That comparison revealed that all three active treatment conditions were superior to wait list in reducing symptoms of PTSD and depression, but there were not significant differences among those three (Foa, Dancu, et al., 1999). Ninety-six women started treatment, of whom 63% were Caucasian and 36% African American. The assaults included rape, attempted rape, and nonsexual incidents such as aggravated assault. Assessments were conducted at pre- and posttreatment as well as the 3-, 6-, and 12-month follow-up periods. Treatment gains were maintained at follow-up measures. Although there were no significant differences among the three treatment conditions, PE produced lower anxiety levels than the combination of exposure and SIT. The PE treatment also produced larger effect sizes than both SIT and PE-SIT on measures of PTSD symptoms, depression, and anxiety (Foa, Dancu, et al., 1999).

Empirical Status of VRE for PTSD

Although the use of VRE is a relatively new approach to treating PTSD and the research behind it is limited, the results of the few available outcome studies show significant promise for the use of VRE as a viable option for treating PTSD. There are a number of studies that assert the effectiveness of VRE for treatment of anxiety disorders other than PTSD (North et al., 1998; Parsons & Rizzo, 2008; Power & Emmelkamp, 2008). However, here we have chosen to discuss a sample of studies that have focused on PTSD exclusively. Difede et al. (2007) evaluated a sample of 21 mostly middle-aged males following the attacks on the World Trade Center. The participants were randomly assigned to VRE (n = 13) or wait list (n = 9). The results revealed significant decreases across all domains of PTSD symptoms, as measured by the clinician-administered PTSD Scale (Blake et al., 1995) and a large effect size of 1.54 for between-groups posttreatment comparisons. The findings suggest that VRE is an effective tool for enhancing exposure therapy to treat rescue workers involved in civilian disasters. In a single case study conducted by Difede and Hoffman (2002) with a 26-year-old, single, African American woman with PTSD symptoms after the World Trade Center attacks, the results suggest that VRE is effective in the treatment of PTSD in that case. Posttreatment measures indicated that the individual showed significant decreases over time in subjective units of distress, related to each of the exposure activities. That is, as treatment went on, the woman reported feeling less distressed when confronting the traumatic scenarios. The client also showed significant reductions in standardized measures of depression and PTSD, including all three main symptom clusters of PTSD: reexperiencing, avoidance, and arousal. In this case, by the end of six exposure sessions, the client no longer met criteria for PTSD, as rated by independent CBT evaluators. Other single case studies conducted with Vietnam and Iraq War veterans have also shown participants to have benefited from receiving VRE for PTSD (Hodges et al., 1999; Reger & Gahm, 2008; Rothbaum et al., 2003).

In an open clinical trial (Rothbaum et al., 2001), 16 Vietnam veterans with PTSD participated in VRE. Ten participants completed treatment, and 9 completed all posttreatment assessments. Most of the participants were taking psychotropic medications at the time of the trial. Although the sample was small and the authors discuss limitations to generalizability, pre- to post-treatment comparison showed statistically significant changes from baseline to a 6-month follow-up in clinician-rated PTSD symptoms. The authors report that at the 6-month follow-up mark, all of those completing treatment reported a reduction in PTSD symptoms from 15% to 67%, including significant reductions in the three major symptom clusters of PTSD. Baños et al. (2009) evaluated 19 individuals (6 men and 13 women) with traumatic stress–related problems who had been diagnosed with PTSD, adjustment disorder, or pathological grief. The results indicate that participants experienced significant reductions in measures of depression and negative affect and significant increases in positive affect measures. Moreover, participants also indicated significant increases in treatment expectations and satisfaction.

The available research suggests that VRE may be a viable form of treatment for PTSD and could be used as a stand-alone form of treatment or as part of a comprehensive therapy approach for persons suffering from stress related to either combat or civilian trauma (Rizzo et al., 2006). Although additional research is needed to solidify the benefits and effectiveness of VRE with different types of trauma and different populations, VRE offers the advantage of creating scenarios to allow victims to re-create the traumatic event under controlled conditions that facilitate habituation and cognitive restructuring (Rothbaum et al., 2001).

Comments on Current Research

One of the criticisms of the research on the use of CBT to treat PTSD was raised in a meta-analysis (N = 15) conducted by Benish et al. (2008). The criticism states that in the reviewed studies, comparisons were often made with wait-list groups or conditions usually labeled as "supportive therapy" that are not meant to be therapeutic (Benish et al., 2008). The authors indicate that the results of their meta-analysis, focusing on comparisons with "bona fide psychotherapies," suggest that TFCBT is no more efficacious than other nontrauma-focused "bona fide psychotherapies." These conclusions were challenged by Ehlers et al. (2010) on the basis that Benish et al. failed to take into account the supposition that research into the relative effectiveness of treatments for PTSD needs to show that those treatments are indeed more effective than natural recovery and, perhaps most important, that the continued increases in effect sizes during the past two decades coming out of research on TFCBT underscore that content of treatment (i.e., trauma focused vs. nontrauma focused) does indeed matter.

Other limitations that have been cited regarding the evaluation of cognitive-behavioral approaches to treatment of PTSD include the consistently high number of dropouts (Bisson & Andrew, 2007; Seidler & Wagner, 2006) and the lack of sufficient evidence to assert that positive changes attained during treatment are sustained over time (Bisson & Andrew, 2007; Bradley et al., 2005). Regarding follow-up measures, Bradley et al. (2005) suggested that follow-up should continue at least to the 2-year posttreatment mark to provide stronger evidence of the long-term impact of treatment. Bradley et al. also criticized current research because of the exclusion criteria used to select participants for the studies as well as because of the lack of information provided regarding co-occurring conditions associated with PTSD. Both issues limit the generalizability of findings to community-based treatment populations (Bradley et al., 2005).

According to Bradley et al. (2005), commonly used exclusion criteria often include substance abuse or dependence, suicide risk, or other co-occurring conditions. However, these criteria would effectively exclude clients who are commonly part of community-based treatment for PTSD. At the same time, Bradley et al. argue that few studies provide adequate information about comorbid Axis I (e.g., anxiety, depression, substance abuse disorders) or Axis II (e.g., personality disorders) conditions, a common occurrence with PTSD. According to Yen et al. (cited in Bradley et al., 2005), about 35% of individuals with personality disorders also meet criteria for PTSD. Similarly, none of the studies reviewed by Bradley et al. reported PTSD with comorbid psychotic symptoms despite studies that suggest a common co-occurrence (Bradley et al., 2005). To address these issues, the authors offer the following recommendations to make research findings more relevant to community-based clinicians: Researchers should provide detailed justification for their exclusion criteria, exclusion criteria in future studies should apply only when it is medically necessary, and due to the exclusion of participants with comorbid conditions, researchers should clearly specify the particular client populations for whom they suggest their findings can be generalized.

Another limitation of the research literature is that none of the evaluated therapies have been tested across a broad range of trauma groups. Therefore, it is difficult to draw conclusions about which trauma patients might benefit from which methods (Ponniah & Hollon, 2009; Seidler & Wagner, 2006). One cannot assume that because a certain treatment works with a specific trauma (e.g., rape), it will work with other types of trauma (e.g., combat, accidents). This concern notwithstanding, Ponniah and Hollon (2009) indicated that there is evidence to suggest that TFCBT is effective for assault-related and automobile accident traumas. Therefore, future research should move beyond evaluating the general efficacy of treatment to establish which type of trauma is more likely to benefit from which treatment and to establish evidence-based treatments with diverse client populations. Specifically regarding the use of EMDR, Seidler and Wagner (2006) suggested that more research is needed to define the specific contribution of the eye movement component to treatment outcomes.

Summary and Conclusions

As we have discussed in this chapter, the available evidence supports the notion that trauma-focused cognitive behavioral treatments (i.e., those that incorporate either imaginal, virtual reality, or written narrative exposure) and EMDR are efficacious therapies for PTSD. Exposure strategies designed to revisit the trauma memory are intended to produce activation of the fear structure. This process allows for corrective emotional engagement with the trauma memory while at the same time providing opportunities to modify and reframe dysfunctional and irrational cognitions (Hembree & Foa, 2004). However, although the available research supports the use of cognitive-behavioral approaches to treat PTSD, it also underscores three general areas of attention for future studies, namely, the following: (a) Future research should be able to identify with greater specificity those clients who are most likely to benefit from the various cognitive-behavioral approaches for PTSD. Current attrition rates highlight that not all study participants respond well to treatment and those who do not respond well are more likely to drop out (Cahill et al., 2009). This may entail discriminating more particularly the type of treatment that would benefit specific types of trauma (e.g., combat, rape, accidents) as well as specific groups of individuals, that is, effectively matching treatment to a particular client problem or characteristic (Vonk, Bordnick, & Graap, 2006). For example, researchers could ask, Who is more likely to benefit from prolonged imaginal exposure as opposed to VRE? or, Who is more likely to benefit from CPT? or From EMDR? Is treatment equally effective across diverse racial or ethnic groups? (b) As Bradley et al. (2005) suggested, future researchers should also seek to increase the length of follow-up measures to at least a 2-year mark to provide stronger evidence for the long-term effects of treatment. (c) We also agree with Bradley et al.'s recommendation that researchers provide more detailed information about comorbid conditions of the sample participants as well as justification for exclusion criteria indicating the intended populations to whom the treatment effects are generalized. This information would be beneficial for clinicians in the field seeking to implement evidence-based practices with their client populations.

References

Alsina-Jurnet, I., Carvallo-Beciu, C., & Gutierrez-Maldonado, J. (2007). Validity of virtual reality as a method of exposure in the treatment of test anxiety. *Behavior Research Methods, 39*, 844–851.

Bandura, A. (1977). Self efficacy: Toward a unifying theory of behavioral change. *Psychological Review, 84*, 191–215.

Bandura, A. (1986). *Social foundation of thought and action: A social cognitive theory*. Englewood Cliffs, NJ: Prentice Hall.

Baños, R. M., Botella, C., Guillen, V., García-Palacios, A., Quero, S., Breton-Lopez, J., et al. (2009). An adaptive display to treat stress related disorders: EMMA's World. *British Journal of Guidance & Counselling, 37*, 347–356.

Beck, A. T. (1976). *Cognitive therapy of the emotional disorders*. New York: Penguin.

Beck, A. T., Emery, G., & Greenberger, R. L. (1985). *Anxiety disorders and phobias: A cognitive perspective*. New York: Basic Books.

Beck, J. S. (1995). *Cognitive therapy: Basics and beyond*. New York: Guilford.

Benish, S. G., Imel, Z. E., & Wampold, B. E. (2008). The relative efficacy of bona fide psychotherapies for treating post-traumatic stress disorder: A meta-analysis of direct comparisons. *Clinical Psychology, 28*, 746–758.

Bisson, J., & Andrew, M. (2007). Psychological treatment of post-traumatic stress disorder (PTSD). *Cochrane Database of Systematic Reviews, 2007*(3), Article No. CD003388.

Bisson, J. I., Ehlers, A., Matthews, R., Pilling, S., Richards, D., & Turners, S. (2007). Psychological treatments for chronic post traumatic stress disorders: Systematic review and meta-analysis. *British Journal of Psychiatry, 190*, 97–104.

Blake, D. D., Weathers, F. W., Nagy, L. M., Kaloupek, D. G., Gusman, F. D., Charney, D. S., et al. (1995). The development of a clinician-administered PTSD scale. *Journal of Traumatic Stress, 8*, 75–90.

Bradley, R., Greene, J., Russ, E., Dutra, L., & Westen, D. (2005). A multidimensional meta-analysis of psychotherapy for PTSD. *American Journal of Psychiatry, 162*, 214–227.

Briere, J. (1992). *Child abuse trauma: Theory and treatment of the lasting effects*. Newbury Park, CA: Sage.

Briere, J. (1996). *Therapy for adults molested as children: Beyond survival, revised and expanded edition* (2nd ed.). New York: Springer.

Briere, J. (1997). Treating adults severely abused as children: The Self-Trauma Model. In D. A. Wolfe, B. McMahon, & R. D. Peters (Eds.), *Child abuse: New directions in treatment and prevention across the lifespan* (pp. 177–204). Thousand Oaks, CA: Sage.

Briere, J. (2002). Treating adult survivors of severe childhood abuse and neglect: Further development of an integrative model. In J. E. B. Myers, L. Berliner,

J. Briere, T. Reid, & C. Jenny (Eds.), *The APSAC handbook on child maltreatment* (2nd ed., pp. 1–26). Thousand Oaks, CA: Sage.

Briere, J., & Scott, C. (2006). *Principles of trauma therapy: A guide to symptoms, evaluation and treatment.* Thousand Oaks, CA: Sage.

Cahill, S. P., Carrigan, M. H., & Frueh, B. C. (1999). Does EMDR work? And if so, why? A critical review of controlled outcome and dismantling research. *Journal of Anxiety Disorders, 13*(1/2), 5–33.

Cahill, S. P., Rothbaum, B. O., Resick, P. A., & Follette, V. M. (2009). Cognitive-behavioral therapy for adults. In E. B. Foa, T. M. Keane, M. J. Friedman, & J. A. Cohen (Eds.), *The effective treatment for PTSD: Practice guidelines from the International Society for Traumatic Stress Studies* (pp. 139–222). New York: Guilford.

Clark, D. M., & Ehlers, A. (2004). Posttraumatic stress disorders from cognitive theory to therapy. In R. L. Leahy (Ed.), *Contemporary cognitive therapy: Theory, research, and practice* (pp. 141–160). New York: Guilford.

Cukor, J., Spitalnick, J., Difede, J., Rizzo, A., & Rothbaum, B. O. (2009). Emerging treatments for PTSD. *Clinical Psychology Review, 29,* 715–726.

Davidson, P. R., & Parker, K. C. H. (2001). Eye movement desensitization and reprocessing (EMDR): A meta-analysis. *Journal of Consulting & Clinical Psychology, 69*(2), 305–316.

Devilly, G. J., & Spence, S. H. (1999). The relative efficacy and treatment distress of EMDR and a cognitive-behavior trauma treatment protocol in the amelioration of posttraumatic stress disorder. *Journal of Anxiety Disorders, 13*(1/2), 131–157.

Difede, J., Cukor, J., Jayasinghe, N., Patt, I., Jedel, S., Spielman, L., et al. (2007). Virtual reality exposure therapy for the treatment of posttraumatic stress disorder following September 11, 2001. *Journal of Clinical Psychiatry, 68,* 1639–1647.

Difede, J., & Hoffman, H. G. (2002). Virtual reality exposure therapy for World Trade Center post-traumatic stress disorder: A case report. *Cyber Psychology & Behavior, 5,* 529–535.

Dobson, D., & Dobson, K. S. (2009). *Evidenced-based practice of cognitive-behavioral therapy.* New York: Guilford.

Dobson, K., & Dozois, D. (2001). Historical and philosophical basis of cognitive-behavioral therapy. In K. Dobson (Ed.), *Handbook of cognitive-behavioral therapies* (pp. 3–39). New York: Guilford.

Dunmore, E., Clark, D. M., & Ehlers, A. (1999). A prospective investigation of the role of cognitive factors in persistent posttraumatic stress disorder (PTSD) after physical or sexual assault. *Behaviour Research and Therapy, 39,* 1063–1084.

Ehlers, A., Bisson, J., Clark, D. M., Creamer, M., Pilling, S., Richards, D., et al. (2010). Do all psychological treatments really work the same in posttraumatic stress disorder? *Clinical Psychology Review, 30,* 269–276.

Ehlers, A., & Clark, D. M. (2000). A cognitive model of posttraumatic stress disorder. *Behaviour Research and Therapy, 38,* 319–345.

Feather, N. T. (1963). Mowrer's revised two-factor theory and the motive-expectancy-value model. *Psychological Review, 70,* 500–515.

Foa, E. B., Dancu, C. V., Hembree, E. A., Jaycox, L. H., Meadows, E. A., & Street, G. P. (1999). A comparison of exposure therapy, stress inoculation training, and their combination for reducing posttraumatic stress disorder in female assault victims. *Journal of Consulting and Clinical Psychology, 67,* 194–200.

Foa, E. B., Davidson, J. R. T., & Frances, A. (1999). The expert consensus guidelines series: Treatment of posttraumatic stress disorder. *Journal of Clinical Psychiatry, 60*(16), 4–76.

Foa, E. B., Ehlers, A., Clark, D. M., Tolin, D. F., & Orsillo, S. M. (1999). The Posttraumatic Cognitions Inventory (PTCI): Development and validation. *Psychological Assessment, 11*, 303–314.

Foa, E. B., Hembree, E. A., Cahill, S. P., Rauch, S. A. M., Riggs, D. S., Feeny, N. C., et al. (2005). Randomized trial of prolonged exposure for posttraumatic stress disorder with and without cognitive restructuring: Outcome at academic and community clinics. *Journal of Consulting and Clinical Psychology, 73*, 953–964.

Foa, E. B., & Jaycox, L. H. (1999). Cognitive-behavioral theory and treatment of posttraumatic stress disorder. In D. Spiegel (Ed.), Efficacy and cost-effectiveness of psychotherapy (pp. 23–61). Washington, DC: American Psychiatric Press.

Foa, E. B., & Kozak, M. J. (1986). Emotional processing of fear: Exposure to corrective information. *Psychological Bulletin, 99*, 20–35.

Foa, E. B., & Riggs, D. S. (1993). Posttraumatic stress disorder in rape victims. In J. Oldham, M. B. Riba, & A. Tasman (Eds.), *Annual review of psychiatry* (Vol. 12, pp. 273–303). Washington, DC: American Psychiatric Association.

Foa, E. B., & Rothbaum, B. O. (1998). *Treating the trauma of rape: A cognitive behavioral therapy for PTSD.* New York: Guilford.

Foa, E. B., Rothbaum, B. O., Riggs, D. S., & Murdock, T. B. (1991). Treatment of posttraumatic stress disorder in rape victims: A comparison between cognitive-behavioral procedures and counseling. *Journal of Counseling and Consulting Psychology, 59*, 715–723.

Foa, E. B., Steketee, G., & Rothbaum, B. O. (1989). Behavioral/cognitive conceptualizations of post-traumatic stress disorder. *Behavior Therapy, 20*, 155–176.

Gerardi, M., Rothbaum, B. O., Ressler, K., Heekin, M., & Rizzo, A. (2008). Virtual reality exposure therapy using Virtual Iraq: A case report. *Journal of Traumatic Disorders, 21*, 209–213.

Gunter, R. W., & Bodner, G. E. (2008). How eye movements affect unpleasant memories: Support for a working-memory account. *Behaviour Research and Therapy, 46*(8), 913–931.

Hembree, E. A., & Foa, E. B. (2004). Promoting cognitive change in posttraumatic stress disorder. In M. A. Reinecke & D. A. Clark (Eds.), *Cognitive therapy across the lifespan: Evidence and practice* (pp. 231–257). New York: Cambridge University Press.

Herbert, J. D., Lilienfeld, S. O., Lohr, J. M., Montgomery, R. W., O'Donohue, W. T., Rosen, G. M., et al. (2000). Science and pseudoscience in the development of eye movement desensitization and reprocessing: Implications for clinical psychology. *Clinical Psychology Review, 20*(8), 945–971.

Hodges, L. F., Rothbaum, B. O., Alarcon, R., Ready, D., Shahar, F., Graap, K., et al. (1999). A virtual environment for the treatment of chronic combat-related post-traumatic stress disorder. *CyberPsychology & Behavior, 2*, 7–14.

Ironson, G., Freund, B., Strauss, J., & Williams, J. (2002). Comparison of two treatments for traumatic stress: A community-based study of EMDR and prolonged exposure. *Journal of Clinical Psychology, 58*(1), 113–128.

Jaycox, L. H., Foa, E. B., & Morral, A. R. (1998). Influence of emotional engagement and habituation on exposure therapy for PTSD. *Journal of Consulting & Clinical Psychology, 66*, 185–192.

Jensen, J. A. (1994). An investigation of eye movement desensitization and reprocessing (EMDR) as a treatment for posttraumatic stress disorder (PTSD) symptoms of Vietnam combat veterans. *Behavior Therapy, 25*(2), 311–325.

Kavanagh, D. J., Freese, S., Andrade, J., & May, J. (2001). Effects of visuospatial tasks on desensitization to emotive memories. *British Journal of Clinical Psychology, 40*(3), 267–280.

Lee, C. W., Gavriel, H., Drummond, P., Richards, J., & Greenwald, R. (2002). Treatment of PTSD: Stress inoculation training with prolonged exposure compared to EMDR. *Journal of Clinical Psychology, 58,* 1071–1089.

Lee, C. W., Taylor, G., & Drummond, P. (2006). The active ingredient in EMDR: Is it traditional exposure or dual focus of attention? *Clinical Psychology & Psychotherapy, 13,* 97–107.

McCann, I. L., Sakheim, D. K., & Abrahamsom, D. J. (1988). Trauma and victimization: A model of psychological adaptation. *Counseling Psychologist, 16,* 531–594.

McFarlane, A. C., & Yehuda, R. (2000). Clinical treatment of posttraumatic stress disorder: Conceptual challenges raised by recent research. *Australian and New Zealand Journal of Psychiatry, 34,* 940–953.

McNally, R. J. (1999). EMDR and mesmerism: A comparative historical analysis. *Journal of Anxiety Disorders, 13*(1/2), 225–236.

Meichenbaum, D. (2007). Stress inoculation training: A preventative and treatment approach. In P. M. Lehrer, R. L. Woolfolk, & W. S. Sime (Eds.), *Principles and practice of stress management* (3rd ed., pp. 497–518). New York: Guilford.

Meichenbaum, D. H. (1993). Stress inoculation training: A 20-year update. In P. M. Lehrer & R. L. Woolfolk (Eds.), *Principles and practice of stress management* (2nd ed., pp. 373–406). New York: Guilford.

Meichenbaum, D. H. (1996). Stress-inoculation training for coping with stressors. *Clinical Psychologist, 49,* 4–7.

Mowrer, O. H. (1956). Two-factor learning theory reconsidered, with special reference to secondary reinforcement and the concept of habit. *Psychological Review, 63,* 114–128.

Mowrer, O. H. (1960). *Learning theory and behavior.* New York: John Wiley.

Najavits, L. M., Weiss, R. D., Shaw, S. R., & Muentz, L. R. (1998). "Seeking safety": Outcome of a new cognitive-behavioral psychotherapy for women with posttraumatic stress disorder and substance dependence. *Journal of Traumatic Stress, 11,* 437–456.

North, M. M., North, S. M., & Coble, J. R. (1998). Virtual reality therapy: An effective treatment for the fear of public speaking. *International Journal of Virtual Reality, 3,* 1–6.

Parsons, T. D., & Rizzo, A. A. (2008). Affective outcomes of virtual reality exposure therapy for anxiety and specific phobias: A meta-analysis. *Journal of Behavior Therapy and Experimental Psychiatry, 39,* 250–261.

Perkins, B. R., & Rouanzoin, C. C. (2002). A critical evaluation of current views regarding eye movement desensitization and reprocessing (EMDR): Clarifying points of confusion. *Journal of Clinical Psychology, 58*(1), 77–97.

Pitman, R. K., Altman, B., Greenwald, E., Longpre, R. E., Macklin, M. L., Poire, R. E., et al. (1991). Psychiatric complications during flooding therapy for posttraumatic stress disorder. *Journal of Clinical Psychiatry, 52*(1), 17–20.

Ponniah, K., & Hollon, S. D. (2009). Empirically supported psychological treatments for adult acute stress disorder and posttraumatic stress disorder: A review. *Depression and Anxiety, 26,* 1086–1109.

Powers, M. B., & Emmelkamp, P. M. G. (2008). Virtual reality exposure therapy for anxiety disorders: A meta-analysis. *Journal of Anxiety Disorders, 22,* 561–569.

Rachman, S. (1980). Emotional processing. *Behavior Research & Therapy, 18,* 51–60.

Reger, G. M., & Gahm, G. A. (2008). Virtual reality exposure therapy for active duty soldiers. *Journal of Clinical Psychology: In Session, 64,* 940–946.

Renfrey, G., & Spates, C. R. (1994). Eye movement desensitization: A partial dismantling study. *Journal of Behavior Therapy and Experimental Psychiatry, 25*(3), 231–239.

Resick, P. A., & Schnicke, M. K. (1992). Cognitive processing therapy for sexual assault victims. *Journal of Consulting and Clinical Psychology, 60,* 748–756.

Rizzo, A., Pair, J., Graap, K., Manson, B., McNerney, P. J., Wiederhold, B., et al. (2006). A virtual reality exposure therapy application for Iraq War military personnel with post-traumatic stress disorder: From training to toy to treatment. In M. Roy (Ed.), *NATO advanced research workshop on novel approaches to the diagnosis and treatment of posttraumatic stress disorder* (pp. 235–250). Washington, DC: IOS Press.

Rodenburg, R., Benjamin, A., de Roos, C., Meijer, A. M., & Stams, G. J. (2009). Efficacy of EMDR in children: A meta-analysis. *Clinical Psychology Review, 29*(70), 599–606.

Rothbaum, B. O., Astin, M. C., & Marsteller, E. (2005). Prolonged exposure versus eye movement desensitization and reprocessing (EMDR) for PTSD rape victims. *Journal of Traumatic Stress, 18,* 607–616.

Rothbaum, B. O., Hodges, L., Alarcon, R., Ready, D., Shahar, F., Graap, K., et al. (1999). Virtual reality exposure therapy for PTSD Vietnam veterans: A case study. *Journal of Traumatic Stress, 12*(2), 263–271.

Rothbaum, B. O., Hodges, L. F., Ready, D., Graap, K., & Alarcon, R. D. (2001). Virtual reality exposure therapy for Vietnam veterans with posttraumatic stress disorder. *Journal of Clinical Psychiatry, 62,* 617–622.

Rothbaum, B. O., Ruef, A. M., Litz, B. T., Han, H., & Hodges, L. (2003). Virtual reality exposure therapy of combat-related PTSD: A case study using psychophysiological indicators of outcome. *Journal of Cognitive Psychotherapy: An International Quarterly, 17,* 163–178.

Scott, J., & Freeman, A. (2010). Beck's cognitive therapy. In N. Kazantzis, M. A. Reinecke, & A. Freeman (Eds.), *Cognitive and behavioral theories in clinical practice* (pp. 28–75). New York: Guilford.

Seidler, G. H., & Wagner, F. E. (2006). Comparing the efficacy of EMDR and trauma-focused cognitive-behavioral therapy in the treatment of PTSD: A meta-analytic study. *Psychological Medicine, 36,* 1515–1522.

Shapiro, F. (1989a). Efficacy of the eye movement desensitization procedure in the treatment of traumatic memories. *Journal of Traumatic Stress, 2*(2), 199–223.

Shapiro, F. (1989b). Eye movement desensitization: A new treatment for posttraumatic stress disorder. *Journal of Behavior Therapy and Experimental Psychiatry, 20,* 211–217.

Shapiro, F. (1995). *Eye movement desensitization and reprocessing, basic principles, protocols and procedures.* New York: Guilford.

Shapiro, F. (2001). *Eye movement desensitization and reprocessing: Basic principles, protocols, and procedures* (2nd ed.). New York: Guilford.

Shapiro, F. (2007). EMDR and case conceptualization from an adaptive information processing perspective. In F. Shapiro, F. Kaslow, & L. Maxfield (Eds.), *Handbook of EMDR and family therapy processes* (pp. 3–36). New York: John Wiley.

Smucker, M. R. (1997). Post-traumatic stress disorder. In R. Leahy (Ed.), *Practicing cognitive therapy: A guide to interventions* (pp. 193–220). Northvale, NJ: Jason Aronson.

Stickgold, R. (2007). Of sleep, memories and trauma. *Nature Neuroscience, 10*(5), 540–542.

van Etten, M. L., & Taylor, S. (1998). Comparative efficacy of treatments for post-traumatic stress disorder: A meta-analysis. *Clinical Psychology and Psychotherapy, 5*(3), 126–144.

Veterans Health Administration and Department of Defense. (2004). *VA/DoD clinical practice guideline for the management of post-traumatic stress.* Washington, DC: Veterans Health Administration.

Vonk, E., Bordnick, P., & Graap, K. (2006). Cognitive-behavioral therapy for post-traumatic stress disorder: An evidence-based approach. In A. R. Roberts & K. R. Yeager (Eds.), *Foundations of evidence-based social work practice* (pp. 323–335). New York: Oxford University Press.

Wolpe, J. (1990). *The practice of behavior therapy* (4th ed.). New York: Pergamon.

3

Psychoanalytic Theory (Part I)

Jerrold R. Brandell

Beginning with the classical formulations of Sigmund Freud, the concept of trauma has gradually attained a superordinate status in the psychoanalytic literature. Indeed, the idea of trauma runs as a common thread across generational and ideological lines in psychoanalysis and has been addressed by every major psychoanalytic school, from Freud and Breuer's earliest forays into the treatment of hysteria to the relational theories of contemporary psychoanalysis. In this chapter, we will begin by exploring Freud's conceptions of trauma, paying close attention to his views on hysteria, the concept of danger situations, and the ego's signal anxiety and defensive functions. This will be followed by a discussion of the trauma in relation to object loss. In succeeding sections of the chapter, the centrality of trauma as a theme in the work of Otto Rank and Sandor Ferenczi, two of Freud's earliest disciples, will be explored in depth. We shall then turn to the literature associated with British object relations theories, examining the contributions of such writers as W. R. D. Fairbairn, D. W. Winnicott, and Michael Balint. Finally, views of trauma associated with psychoanalytic self psychology and the seminal writings of Heinz Kohut and his followers will be discussed and illustrated through the use of a brief clinical vignette.[1]

Trauma Defined

Before discussing various psychoanalytic contributions to our understanding of trauma, it may be helpful to begin by defining the term. In everyday discourse, the word *trauma* is often used more or less interchangeably with *stress,* which has led to a gradual erosion of meaning and clarity. Difficult

---

[1]A separate chapter will detail the contributions of the newest psychoanalytic psychology, relational psychoanalysis, to our understanding of trauma.

writing assignments, excessive workload, anxiety-generating conversations—virtually anything that causes some measure of stress may now be popularly characterized as traumatic. Such generic usage has led to a trivialization of the concept, but it has also led to a blurring of the distinction between traumatic events and traumatic response (Allen, 2001). A somewhat more clinically useful definition of *trauma*, appearing in *Webster's New College Dictionary*, defines trauma as "an emotional shock that creates substantial and lasting damage to the psychological development of the individual, generally leading to neurosis; something that severely jars the mind or emotions" (Webster, 1995, p. 1173). Such a definition is more in keeping with psychoanalytic conceptions of trauma; it establishes that trauma is not an event but a response to an event and, further, that it represents an enduring adverse response to an event (Allen, 2001, p. 6).

In their glossary of psychoanalytic terminology and concepts, Moore and Fine offer the following definition. Although their definition is arguably more compatible with classical and object relational ideas, they consider trauma to represent

> the disruption or breakdown that occurs when the psychic apparatus is suddenly presented with stimuli, either from within or without, that are too powerful to be dealt with or assimilated in the usual way. A postulated stimulus barrier or protective shield is breached, and the ego is overwhelmed and loses its mediating capacity. A state of helplessness results, ranging from total apathy and withdrawal to an emotional storm accompanied by disorganized behavior bordering on panic. Signs of autonomic dysfunction are frequently present. (Moore & Fine, 1990, p. 199)

Other psychoanalytic writers have made useful distinctions between "relatively impersonal trauma" (e.g., natural disasters, technological disasters, automobile accidents) and "interpersonal trauma" (e.g., criminal assault, rape, sexual harassment, war, and political violence), arguing that traumas associated with the latter group are, generally speaking, far more problematic and likely to culminate in serious mental disorders than those in the former group (Allen, 2001). In other chapters of this volume, some of these topics will be considered in substantially greater depth. However, this chapter's focus is limited to psychoanalytic conceptions of trauma, to which we now turn.

Freudian Conceptions of Trauma

As suggested in an earlier chapter, foundational psychoanalytic conceptions of trauma are traceable to Sigmund Freud's ideas regarding the treatment of hysteria, which are rooted in the seminal *Studies on Hysteria,* a work he coauthored with Josef Breuer more than a century ago (1893–1895). In the introductory chapter of this work, Freud and Breuer quickly established the importance of "external events" in giving rise to and shaping hysterical symptoms. At times, the connection between a particular precipitating event and the outbreak of hysterical illness was relatively uncomplicated to discern, as the following example illustrates: "We may take as a very commonplace instance a painful emotion arising during a meal but suppressed at the time, and then producing nausea and vomiting which persists for months in the form of hysterical vomiting" (1893–1895/1961, p. 4).

At other times, Freud and Breuer asserted, the connection between the external event and the appearance of symptoms was more symbolic in nature, and therefore somewhat more challenging to deconstruct. It is significant, however, that Freud and Breuer made a clear connection between hysteria and the traumatic or "war" neuroses, suggesting that the common element in both is the affect of fright. In fact, they argued that "any experience which calls up distressing affects—such as fright, anxiety, shame, or physical pain—may operate as a trauma" (S. Freud & Breuer, 1893–1895/1961, p. 6).

Freud and Breuer also focused on the importance of "abreaction" or catharsis as a means of discharging such pent-up affects. Relief from hysterical symptoms, they wrote, could be achieved via the "cathartic method," a procedure originally developed by Josef Breuer, the aim of which was to facilitate release of suppressed emotions. Many psychoanalytic historians have observed that the early conceptions of trauma and its treatment via the cathartic method rely heavily on principles of psychological functioning rooted in the physicalistic science of Freud's era, most notably the writings of Gustav Fechner. Accumulating psychic energy or tensions are presumed to require "discharge" in the interest of maintaining the organism's *constancy,* a corollary of which is that humans seek to avoid unpleasure or eliminate it via the most expedient route. In the case of hysterical illness, Freud and Breuer hypothesized, abreaction of the psychic tensions had for various reasons simply not occurred, leading to a "damming up" of psychic energy. In Freud's early view, such "dammed up energy," or *libido,* a term he later adopted, needed to be released for the patient's symptoms to be ameliorated.

Freud's Experimentation With Hypnosis

Although Freud was at first highly enthusiastic about the beneficial effects of hypnotic treatment with his hysterical patients, he soon discovered that the initial symptom relief his hysterical patients reported could not be sustained over time. This, however, is but one of several reasons advanced in an effort to explain his gradual disillusionment with the technique. It has been suggested that Freud's lack of skill in using hypnotic techniques may have been a factor (Erika Fromm, personal communication, 1997). Ernest Jones has underscored Freud's retrospective claim, made some time after his decision to discontinue hypnotic treatment of his hysterical patients, that hypnosis obscured the patient's resistance. The basic problem with hypnosis was not that it did away with the resistance but rather that resistance was circum-navigated; thus, such treatment could yield only imperfect data and temporary success (Jones, 1955).

Fromm and Nash offer a somewhat different explanation. Modeling his work after that of his mentors, Charcot and Bernheim, Freud relied on what have been termed *authoritarian* techniques for inducing the hypnotic trance state in his patients. He frequently would place his hand on the patient's forehead, exerting slight pressure, or even hold the patient's head between his palms and give the command to sleep. In his work with Emmy von N, considered a paradigmatic illustration of the dynamic treatment of hysteria, Freud "sternly positioned his index finger in front of the patient's face and called out 'Sleep!'" (S. Freud & Breuer, 1893–1895/1961, cited in Fromm & Nash, 1997, p. 16). Fromm and Nash observe that although such techniques for trance induction seem very peculiar by contemporary standards for hypnotherapeutic practice, they would have been regarded as quite conventional practice among physicians in Freud's day (S. Freud & Breuer, 1893–1895/1961, cited in Fromm & Nash, 1997, p. 16). They maintain that Freud turned away from hypnosis because the technique as he had used it "had more to do with coercion than understanding" (Fromm & Nash, 1997, p. 16). The notion of treating a patient coercively to obtain data was at variance with Freud's scientific ideal, that of detached neutrality.

At about the same time that Freud gave up hypnotic treatment in favor of a new clinical approach that emphasized such critical elements as free association, interpretation, and transference, he also reluctantly relinquished what is now commonly referred to as the "seduction hypothesis." According to Freud's original seduction theory, a veritable occurrence of sexual molestation perpetrated on the child by an adult is presumed to have taken place, although Freud finally replaced this theory with a more purely psychological one. He concluded that such reports, in many if not most instances, were a function of unconscious, intrapsychically based desires and conflicts rather than veridical, historically based, experienced events. Nevertheless, even years later, Freud continued to believe that "seduction has retained a certain significance for etiology," observing that in the cases of Katharina and Fraulein Rosalia H, the patients had been sexually assaulted by their fathers (Gay, 1988).

Trauma, Danger Situations, and the Function of the Defenses

Freud's ideas about the nature and mechanism of psychic trauma evolved gradually. Although as I have already suggested, Freud's early understanding of trauma depended to a considerable degree on actual, experienced events, he ultimately came to understand and define trauma quite differently. When he wrote about the topic in 1917, Freud observed,

> We apply it to an experience which within a short period of time presents the mind with an increase of stimulus too powerful to be dealt with or worked off in the normal way . . . [thus resulting] . . . in permanent disturbances of the manner in which the energy operates. (1917/1961e, p. 275)

However, less than 10 years later, in his seminal *Inhibitions, Symptoms, and Anxiety* (S. Freud, 1926/1961c), Freud's emphasis had changed. First, he further clarified the difference "between anxiety as a direct and automatic reaction to a trauma and anxiety as a *signal* [italics added] of the danger of the approach of such a trauma" (p. 80). With his new emphasis on the "signal anxiety" function of the ego, Freud was able to offer a more satisfying explanation for how traumatic states might be averted or prevented, namely, through the organism's avoidance of the helplessness and incapacitating anxiety associated with traumatic states. This in turn depended on the organism's capacity to give itself a small degree of anxiety to take expedient action (i.e., signal anxiety). Second, Freud seemed less focused on trauma as representing a redistribution of psychic energy and more interested in the ego's role in preventing or mitigating such trauma, a development tied to the expanded and more fully articulated conception of the ego and its functions presented just 3 years earlier, in *The Ego and the Id* (S. Freud, 1923/1961b). Finally, Freud elaborated on the traumatic potential of various normative, developmental experiences, which have also been termed "danger situations."

Freud's discovery that childhood wishes were regularly associated with anxiety (i.e., fear) led him to conclude that such fears fall into one of four basic categories, each representing a specific danger situation. The earliest and most basic anxiety involved the loss of the object (mother or primary caretaker); the next, developmentally speaking, arose from the child's fear of losing the object's love; the third involved the fear of punishment, particularly by genital mutilation/castration; and the last, the internalized fear of one's own moral precepts or conscience, which depended on the establishment of a functioning superego. According to Freud's classical theory, when a wish comes to be associated with any of these dangers, the impulse toward enactment leads to a dramatic increase in anxiety. Such anxiety may increase to traumatic levels without the supervention of reassuring caregivers or without other, independent measures. In Freud's view, the child gradually learns ways to diminish these anxieties, which are termed *defense operations* or simply *defenses*. Perhaps the most important of these is repression, which is sometimes referred to as the "paradigmatic defense." Repression involves a shifting of attention away from tempting but dangerous wishes, so that they effectively are barred from consciousness. Freud, his disciples, and several succeeding generations of psychoanalysts eventually identified at least 22 major and 26 minor defenses (Laughlin, 1979). It is of some importance, however, that in Freud's estimation, no defense is fully effective in warding off anxiety, and this is arguably most true in the instance of anxiety that stems from a traumatic experience. Finally, although any specific defense or constellation of defenses may be employed in the service of protecting an individual from the incapacitating anxiety associated with a traumatic experience, the more "primitive" dissociative defenses (i.e., depersonalization, derealization) are the most frequently encountered in clinical work with traumatized patients.

In *Studies on Hysteria,* Freud wrote of a "splitting of the mind," following a psychic trauma, a term that was eventually replaced by the more familiar *dissociation.* Dissociation is defined as an altered state of consciousness, designed to protect a subject from experiences of an overwhelmingly traumatic nature. When the experience involves distortions of the subject's bodily self-experience only, the term *depersonalization* is sometimes used; when the distortions involve apprehension of external stimuli, the term *derealization* may be employed. *Fugue states* and *hysterical conversion reactions* are also dissociative in nature. Early childhood trauma, Freud and Breuer concluded as early as 1893, led to a repeated overuse of dissociation to the point at which it became the "individual's primary psychological defense, manifesting itself in dramatic alterations in the experience of self and world" (Fromm & Nash, 1997, p. 221).

Object Loss, Grief, and Mourning

As I suggested in the preceding section, the loss of an object constitutes the most significant form of early anxiety and, under certain circumstances, may be considered traumatic. At the same time, it is recognized that mourning, the process through which psychic equilibrium is reestablished after an object loss, is incompatible with the experience of trauma; indeed, successful mourning carries with it the great likelihood that a loss will not be experienced as an enduring trauma. Before discussing traumatic loss, however, it may be useful to clarify the difference between traumatic loss and the mourning process associated with normal bereavement.

Mourning is most often initiated by the loss through death of a (real) object but may also occur in connection with other forms of loss, for example, the loss of a limb or other body part, physical abilities, one's belief in an ideal, or one's freedom (Moore & Fine, 1990). Aggrieved individuals report a predominant mood of pain and exhibit a loss of interest in the outside world. They are preoccupied with memories of the lost object and are largely incapable of making new emotional investments (Moore & Fine, 1990). The capacity of an individual to complete the process of mourning is affected by a range of factors, such as the level of object maturity the individual has achieved, the capacity to tolerate painful affects, how successful the individual is in regulating self-esteem, how dependent he or she has been on the object, and the exact circumstances of the loss (Moore & Fine, 1990). Moreover, mourning is believed to occur in stages and, when successful, leads to a healing of the ego and the restoration of psychological well-being. Psychoanalytic authors have suggested that the work of mourning includes three phases, which unfold in an epigenetic fashion:

- understanding, accepting, and coping with the loss and its circumstances;
- the mourning proper, which involves withdrawal of attachments to and identifications with the lost object (decathexis); and
- resumption of an emotional life in harmony with one's level of maturity, which frequently involves establishing new relationships (recathexis) (Moore & Fine, 1990, p. 122).

But what of traumatic loss? When is a loss traumatic, and which features are likely to culminate in such an experience of loss? Although traumatic loss is certainly possible in adulthood, developmental immaturity and reliance on objects increases the potential for loss of a meaningful object to trigger a traumatic reaction in childhood. Put somewhat differently, children and adolescents who have suffered the loss of a parent or other important caregiver are on that account alone more likely to experience the loss as traumatic, other factors being equal. The circumstances of the loss (e.g., prolonged illness vs. sudden death from natural causes or parental suicide) can also have great significance. Nevertheless, there is a certain danger in applying this probability to all losses occurring in childhood or adolescence. Anna Freud observes,

> Whenever I am tempted to call an event in a child's or adult's life "traumatic," I shall ask myself some further questions. Do I mean the event was upsetting, that it was significant for altering the course of further development; that it was pathogenic? Or do I really mean traumatic in the strict sense of the word, i.e., shattering, devastating, causing internal disruption, by putting ego functioning and ego mediation out of action? (1967, p. 242)

The general utility of Anna Freud's admonition notwithstanding, there is now general consensus in the field of child psychoanalysis that death of one's parent in childhood or adolescence is an event of such magnitude that it taxes even the most emotionally resilient child's capacities (Altschul & Pollock, 1988). Such a loss may indeed be "shattering" and "devastating," to use Anna Freud's litmus test, despite the fact that the capacity of children to mourn a loss is now generally acknowledged as possible. However, various factors tend to complicate and derail the mourning process in children and adolescents.

As mentioned above, the child is naturally dependent on the parent for continuous support and assistance in negotiating the course of development. However, in many instances, the surviving partner, owing to that person's own preoccupation with the loss, may be less available for the child to lean on. Families may also deal quite differently with the death of a family member. In some families, grieving children may be admonished to be strong for the surviving parent, or there may be an expectation that sad affects should be expressed during the period of acute mourning, but not later, as though the mourning process were well defined and finite. Less-than-ideal alternate child care arrangements may be forced on the child, and so forth. Although none of these variables alone may be responsible for a pathological mourning process, the child's greater vulnerability to disruptions in cognitive, affective, and social development certainly increases the probability that such a process may unfold. In one psychoanalytic author's opinion, parental "death is almost always traumatic in the disruption it brings to the ongoing life of the family and the flooding of the child's experiencing and integrative capacities" (Samuels, 1990, p. 22).

Otto Rank and Birth Trauma

Otto Rank (1884–1939) was one of Freud's earliest adherents and is remembered by psychoanalytic historians for several important contributions, including his writings on the human will as a creative force (Rank, 1945) and the process of termination as well as an early, joint undertaking with Sandor Ferenczi widely regarded as a precursor to later efforts to shorten the duration of psychoanalytic treatment (Ferenczi & Rank, 1925). But the work with which Rank's name came almost to be reflexively identified is his 1924 book, *The Trauma of Birth*.

In this work, Rank hypothesized that the experience of birth involved a physical trauma and called forth a very basic form of anxiety in the human infant. Birth is traumatic, in Rank's view, both because it brings about an abrupt end to the nirvana-like intrauterine state and also because the neonate is flooded by stimuli that cannot be mastered. As such, the trauma of birth is understood to represent primal anxiety. There are two basic outcomes in the effort to master such massive anxiety, according to Rank. The first, a fixation of the infant's desire to return to the safety of the womb, results in neurosis, whereas the second, which is adaptive and progressive, culminates in creative productivity (Menaker, 1982).

Freud initially received Rank's work with interest and seemed willing to acknowledge that birth represented the earliest anxiety state. Freud's 1923 footnote to the Little Hans case also reveals a certain acceptance of Rank's thesis. In it, he states, "Rank's view of the effects of the trauma of birth seems to throw special light on the predisposition to anxiety/hysteria which is so strong in childhood" (S. Freud, 1909/1961a, p. 116, Note 2).

However, the Rankian birth trauma also represented a fundamental challenge to Freud's ideas regarding the primacy of the drives. Rank was not unaware of this problem and made some effort to reconcile his view and Freud's by suggesting that castration anxiety was in effect a later phase of the anxiety at birth. But Freud and other psychoanalysts of the time may well have interpreted this differently because Rank's theory seemed to privilege and elevate the mother's contribution to psychological development at the expense of the father (Gay, 1988). Detailed consideration of Rank's ultimate rejection of classical psychoanalytic formulations and, more particularly, of his relationship with Freud is beyond the scope of this chapter, although a brief summary of Freud's views on Rank's thesis may nevertheless be useful as we consider the fate of Rank's ideas regarding trauma.

As suggested above, Freud seemed willing to consider the experience of birth to represent a prototype for later experiences of anxiety—the first situation of danger, as it were. He observes that psychoanalysis had already traced the developmental line connecting

> the first danger-situation and determinant of anxiety with all the later ones, and . . . that they all retain a common quality in so far as they signify in a certain sense a separation from the mother—at first only in a biological sense, next as a direct loss of the object and later as a loss of the object incurred indirectly. (S. Freud, 1926/1961c, p. 151)

Moreover, in the years prior to the publication of Rank's book, Freud had himself observed that "the act of birth is the first experience of anxiety and therefore source and model of the affect of anxiety" (S. Freud, 1900/1961d, pp. 400–401, note 3). However, he was highly critical of Rank's contention that people become neurotic as a direct consequence of their inability to abreact the strength of the trauma experienced in the act of being born and, further, of Rank's view that all subsequent affects of anxiety constitute an effort to abreact the trauma more and more fully. Freud by this time had largely discarded the idea of abreaction as a means of overcoming traumas, based on his earlier failures in treating hysterics hypnotically and via the cathartic method. Although he accepted the idea that powerful affects present at birth serve as a bridge to subsequent danger situations, he rejected the notion that all neuroses are traceable to one original source of trauma.

Although few today accept Rank's thesis as it was originally conceived and formulated, the translation of his ideas regarding the literal, physical trauma of birth to more metaphorical language regarding the universal experience of separation may offer the theory new meaning. Some writers have asserted that Rank's birth trauma theory, to be understood correctly, must be approached from the vantage point of Rank's other, later contributions. Rank, Menaker believes, was really writing about the process of separation and individuation; in effect, his work portrayed the "wish for the oneness of the womb, with its lack of differentiation, and the driving growth toward separateness, uniqueness, and individuation of the ego" (Menaker, 1982, p. 64). In fact, in certain important respects, Rank's ideas adumbrate important theoretical developments in object relations theory that occurred many years after the publication of his book about the birth trauma.

Although Freud and other psychoanalysts of his time rejected Rank's notion of the birth trauma, his ideas have acquired new life in such non-dynamic therapies as Janov's primal therapy, as well as other body-centered psychotherapies. Janov's primal therapy enjoyed some popularity in the 1970s and 1980s. It is based on the idea that childhood trauma creates such unbearable pain that individuals seek escape through neurosis. Through a treatment process that bears an unmistakable similarity to the cathartic method of Breuer and Freud, patients are encouraged to undergo "primals." Although Janov has minimized his ideological debt to Rank, the idea of traumatic birth does seem to be at the center of Janov's theory, as is the necessity for therapeutic rebirth via an abreactive process.

Sandor Ferenczi and "The Confusion of Tongues"

The Hungarian psychoanalyst Sandor Ferenczi (1873–1933) is rightly regarded as one of Freud's most gifted protégés, and his contributions to the psychoanalytic movement, particularly in its early years, are arguably second in importance only to those of Freud himself (Aron & Harris, 1993). However, by the early 1930s, Ferenczi had fallen into disfavor with Freud and the mainstream psychoanalytic movement for several reasons, among them his experimentation with brief psychoanalytic treatment, the perception that he promoted dangerous transference regressions in his patients and tried to cure them through love, his idea of mutual analysis, and undoubtedly, Ferenczi's highly ambivalent and tempestuous relationship with Freud and other members of the Freudian inner circle. Another significant area of contention between Ferenczi and Freud arose in the 1920s and early 1930s, when Ferenczi rehabilitated Freud's earlier notions about the relationship of trauma to childhood sexual seduction, a theoretical position from which Freud and others in the psychoanalytic movement had taken great pains to distance themselves years earlier.

By the mid-1920s, with the publication of such works as *The Ego and the Id* (S. Freud, 1923/1961b) and Abraham's paper about libidinal development (Abraham, 1924/1948), psychoanalysis had not only privileged the primacy of the instincts as a determinant of human psychological life but also charted the course of the libido, viewing such development as a phylogenetically determined process, leading inexorably from an early oral stage to mature, adult, genital sexuality. It has been suggested that Freud gave greater acknowledgment to the role of the environment in *The Ego and the Id* than in earlier publications. Nevertheless, even in that work, forces external to the developing infant still pale in comparison to the overriding importance accorded to purely intrapsychic processes. During the same period, Ferenczi began to oppose these ideas as well as others regarding the pathogenesis of neurotic illness, and he actually restored Freud's ideas about sexual seduction and trauma to a central place in his own theory of neurosis (Van Haute & Geyskens, 2004).

Ferenczi's own theory of trauma had evolved over a period of years, as he paid closer attention to the "child" in his adult patients, or put somewhat differently, to the role of repetition, regression, and acting out in the treatment situation, as well as how such phenomena could be used to clinical advantage (Dupont, 1993). Ultimately, Ferenczi returned to the idea that actual experiences of trauma played a significant role in the creation of neurotic disturbances (Ferenczi, 1930/1999, 1932). Ferenczi emphasized that two phases were involved in the production of a trauma: First, there must be a traumatic event, which may or may not be inherently pathogenic, and second, the event would be subject to denial by significant people in the child's life, most notably the child's mother. The denial of the traumatic event, in Ferenczi's estimation, represented the most important pathogenic component (Dupont, 1993).

These ideas were further elaborated on in Ferenczi's final published paper, "The Confusion of Tongues Between Adults and the Child" (Ferenczi, 1933/1955). It is this paper, perhaps to a greater degree than any other single contribution of Ferenczi, that is responsible for the renewal of interest in his ideas by the current generation of relational psychoanalysts. It is here that Ferenczi asserts that the pathogenicity of trauma, particularly when it is of a sexual nature, cannot be overestimated (Ferenczi, 1933/1955). It may be useful to comment more specifically on Ferenczi's use of the phrase, "confusion of tongues." According to Van Haute and Geyskens (2004),

> Before the trauma, there exists a tie of love between the child and the adult. According to Ferenczi, this intimate relationship is accompanied by all kinds of sexual and oedipal behavior. In play, the child acts out the role of the adult, imitating the adult. . . . In this manner, the relationship between child and adult may assume an erotic form. But Ferenczi emphasizes that for the child, this intimacy remains on the level of *tenderness, imagination and play* [emphasis in the original]. This cannot be said of the adult partner, who interprets as sexual that which the child expresses in the language of tenderness. In that case, the adult considers child's play as sexual desires. . . . In this manner, a confusion of tongues between the child's language of tenderness and the (adult's) language of passion is produced. (p. 90)

The adult then responds with sexual passion to the child's desire for tenderness. Insofar as the child has no real capacity to understand or respond to the sexuality of the adult, he or she experiences powerlessness; the child is unable to protest against this misguided interpretation of her or his aim-inhibited, loving feelings. Once confronted with the adult's mature, frankly sexual behavior, and the adult's "overpowering force and authority," which are experienced as a violent subjugation of the child's will, children demonstrate physical and moral helplessness. The encounter causes massive anxiety, which at a certain juncture "compels them to subordinate themselves like automata to the will of the aggressor, to divine each one of his desires and to gratify these" (Ferenczi, 1933/1955, p. 162). The child's identification with the aggressor, including the introjection of the adult's guilt feelings, then occurs, according to Ferenczi.

The trauma is then typically compounded by denial that follows the act. The act is denied not only by the perpetrator but also by others in the child's environment. Adults react with a combination of denial, disavowal, and incomprehension and punish the child for what are believed to be fabrications or distortions of the perpetrator's benevolence. Or even more insidiously, there is no reaction at all, and the child's efforts to describe the trauma are met with silence. Through the process of introjection, the child takes in all of these various reactions by the adults around him or her. The child identifies not only with the perpetrator's desire, aggression, and projected guilt but also with the denial and silence of the other adults. Significantly, it is through such identificatory processes that the child strives to maintain a connection to those adults on whom he or she depends (Ferenczi, 1933/1955; Van Haute & Geyskens, 2004).

Ferenczi concludes his paper with thoughts about the outcome of such experiences in the child, the clinical consequences of frank sexual abuse. He first speaks of the development of a "precocious maturity," which today might be termed premature sexuality. Ferenczi also explains clinical observations that sexually traumatized patients may have little if any memory of the event as being due in large measure to the disbelief, minimization, and denial exhibited by adults in the child's environment whenever efforts were made to introduce the topic of seduction. In tandem with the child's desire to maintain some sort of loving connection with the parents, such reactions are further reason for the child to disbelieve his or her own veridical recollections and to conclude that the seduction was imagined—simply a fantasy production. However, the memory of the veritable experience of seduction and the attendant trauma do remain, in one sense, alive, although in a fragmented form. Anticipating by several decades the clinical experience of those who work with victims of sexual and other traumas, Ferenczi writes eloquently of a fragmenting of the personality, such that each "split" in the personality behaves as though "it does not know of the existence of the others" (Ferenczi, 1933/1955, p. 165). What is especially remarkable about this portrayal is how well it resonates with contemporary psychoanalytic understanding of the process and phenomena of dissociation, now universally recognized as a hallmark of the posttraumatic adaptation.

Trauma Within the British Object Relations Tradition: The Work of Fairbairn, Winnicott, and Balint

There was considerable divisiveness within the British psychoanalytic community by the early 1940s, primarily the result of theoretical differences between Anna Freud and Melanie Klein, which had given rise to an increasingly contentious and acrimonious professional environment. The failure to reconcile the views of those pledging allegiance to Melanie Klein's object relations school with those who remained loyal to the more traditional formulations of Anna Freud led to growing disharmony and fracture within the psychoanalytic community.[2] Ultimately, a third group emerged, usually referred to as the middle or independent tradition.

The independent group consisted of a number of seminal thinkers, among them W. R. D. Fairbairn, D. W. Winnicott, Michael Balint, and John Bowlby. Because we will be discussing Bowlby's ideas regarding trauma in Chapter 4, the focus here will be on Fairbairn, Winnicott, and Balint. All of these theorists developed object relations theories based on Klein's basic postulate of an infant who is object seeking from the moment of birth. At the same time, "they also all broke with Klein's premise of constitutional aggression . . . proposing instead an infant wired for harmonious interaction and nontraumatic development but thwarted by inadequate parenting" (Mitchell & Black, 1995, pp. 114–115). All have also contributed in significant ways to a vision of trauma sufficiently distinctive from the formulations of Freud and other theorists we have discussed to warrant a separate discussion here.

Fairbairn and the Nature of Libido

Fairbairn believed that libido, the elemental force whose distribution Freud and Abraham had charted in the 1920s, was not pleasure seeking, as they had claimed, but object seeking. In effect, the most fundamental motive in human experience was not for gratification and the discharge of tensions through relationships with others, where the others served simply as the means toward that goal. Rather, seeking connections with others as an end unto itself was the true aim of libido, in Fairbairn's view (Mitchell & Black, 1995). When such connections are thwarted in childhood, whether through the frustration of the child's dependency strivings or because the child's efforts to establish healthy and affirming interactions are not met in

---

[2]For a more detailed description of this epoch in the history of psychoanalysis, the reader is referred to Kohon (1986), Mishne (1993), and Borden (2009).

a reciprocal fashion, the child turns away from external reality. In place of those connections, the child creates a fantasy world of internal objects that contains features of the real-world objects with whom the child cannot establish and maintain a meaningful relationship.

Particularly in his work with schizoid individuals, Fairbairn theorized the existence of traumatic experiences in infancy that had caused such individuals to feel unloved as persons in their own right and also to believe that whatever love they felt for their parents was essentially bad or worthless (Moore & Fine, 1990).

Because Fairbairn believed failures in parenting to be essentially universal, differing only in degree or kind, he theorized that all children defend against such traumagenic experiences through a process of ego splitting.

> The child, in Fairbairn's system, becomes *like* the unresponsive features of the parents: depressed, isolated, masochistic, bullying, and so on. It is through the absorption of these pathological character traits that he feels connected to the parent, who is unavailable in other ways. This internalization of the parents also necessarily creates a split in the ego: part of the self remains directed toward the real parents in the external world, seeking actual responses from them; part of the self is redirected toward the illusory parents as internal objects to which it is bound. (Mitchell & Black, 1995, p. 120)

Fairbairn's theoretical system is, however, a complicated one, for following this early splitting of the ego, a further split occurs, one "between the alluring, promising features of the parents (the *exciting* object) and the frustrating, disappointing features (the *rejecting* object)" (Mitchell & Black, 1995, p. 120). Additional splitting then culminates into what Fairbairn has termed the "libidinal ego," a part of the self tied to the exciting object in which the subject's sense of longing and hope resides, and the "anti-libidinal ego," another part of the self that is identified with the rejecting object and in which "angry and hateful, despising vulnerability and need" are retained (Mitchell & Black, 1995, p. 120).

It is of considerable interest that Fairbairn appears to have been greatly influenced by his early clinical experiences with abused children. He was particularly impressed by the intensity of the attachment and sense of loyalty they demonstrated toward their abusive parents. Indeed, the absence of pleasure or gratification that such children experienced with their abusive parents did not seem to have much discernible effect on the bond between them. Because primarily painful sequelae followed the object-seeking behavior of these children, Fairbairn eventually understood the painful connections such children then experience with others as representing a preferred mode of contact, which led to an endless repetition of the same traumatic pattern in all subsequent relationships.

D. W. Winnicott

Winnicott was an important middle tradition developmental theorist who originally trained as a pediatrician and spent more than 40 years working with infants and mothers. He is known for a number of contributions that have shaped our contemporary understanding of infancy and of the relations between infants and their caregivers. Many important object relations concepts, such as primary maternal occupation, good-enough mothering, the holding environment, and true and false selves, are attributable to Winnicott. At least one of his ideas, that of the transitional object, or security blanket, has gradually attained a degree of popularity and general usage equaled only by such Freudian concepts as the unconscious, the ego, or the idea of wish fulfillment.

Perhaps Winnicott's central idea relative to the experience of trauma is his notion of the true and false self. Winnicott wrote that individuals begin life with a true self, an "inherited potential" representing the infant's core self or essence. In a facilitative environment, the true self, which has been equated with the spontaneous expression of the id, continues to develop and becomes firmly established. The false self, on the other hand, is a facade that the child erects so as to ensure compliance with the mother's inadequate adaptations, whether such maternal failures are in the form of deprivations or impingements on the child's growth (Goldstein, 1995). Infants exposed to such repeated deprivations or impingements are able to survive, but in Winnicott's estimation they are able to do so only at the cost of "living falsely" (Winnicott, 1960; see also Mishne, 1993). Although Winnicott emphasized that the partition or distribution of self-experience into true and false is always present in varying degrees (even in normal infants), the false self has an almost palpable presence in various forms of child and adult psychopathology. Winnicott treated a number of patients with basic pathology of the self, individuals who might have been diagnosed with schizoid or borderline disorders. What impressed him most about such patients was their profound inner alienation. In such patients, "subjectivity itself, the quality of personhood, is somehow disordered" (Mitchell & Black, 1995, p. 124). Winnicott gradually came to understand that these adult patients suffered from "false self disorders," and the bridge he "constructed between the quality and the nuances of adult subjectivity and the subtleties of mother-infant interactions provided a powerful new perspective for viewing both the development of the self" and the process of treatment (Mitchell & Black, 1995, p. 125; see also Brandell, 2004).

Thus, although Winnicott's explicit focus was not on the nature of trauma, the idea of developmental trauma remained very central to most of his theoretical and clinical writings.

Michael Balint

Michael Balint, like his fellow middle traditionalists, imputed great power to the early relations between infants and mothers, and much like his analyst and mentor, Sandor Ferenczi, he believed the root of later pathology was frequently established in the faulty or pathological responses of mothers and other caregivers to children's expression of their needs. With the idea of developmental trauma in mind, we may regard Balint's most important contributions to the object relations literature to reside in his ideas of primary object love and the basic fault.

Based on his clinical work with very disturbed psychoanalytic patients, Balint came to believe that certain individuals "attempt to remedy their own early deprivations by involving or coercing the analyst into granting them unconditional love which they had been deprived of in childhood" (Greenberg & Mitchell, 1983, p. 182). He termed this the search for "primary object love" and expressed the view that it formed the basis for all subsequent psychological phenomena.

However, the search for primary object love is closely if not inextricably tied to traumatic breaches in the earliest relationship between infants and caregivers. Such breaches, in Balint's view, give rise to a "basic fault" (Balint, 1968), a structural rending of the psyche. According to Fonagy and Target (2003), the basic fault may be legitimately considered to constitute the developmental basis for personality disorders. Phenomenologically speaking, individuals exhibiting basic faults have the "underlying feeling that something is not quite right about" them (p. 138), for which they seek out various environmental remedies. Ultimately, many such patients enter psychoanalysis or other forms of treatment, Balint believed, principally seeking to heal these basic disjunctions in the structure of the self. In his work with such patients, Balint experimented with various clinical approaches that were intended to "recapture missed developmental opportunities" as well as to reclaim dissociated parts of the self (Mitchell & Black, 1995, p. 136).

A Self Psychological Vision of Trauma: The Work of Kohut and His Followers

A relative newcomer among the psychoanalytic theories that constitute contemporary psychoanalysis (classical psychoanalysis, ego psychology, object relations theories, and relational psychoanalysis, inter alia), self psychology was introduced by American psychoanalyst Heinz Kohut in a series of essays and books published between 1959 and 1984. Although Kohut originally presented the theoretical and technical innovations of his new psychology within the framework of classical drive theory (Greenberg & Mitchell, 1983; Kohut, 1966, 1971), he later expanded and revised his theory (Kohut, 1977, 1984) into a distinctive and fundamentally new psychoanalytic psychology (Brandell, 2004).

Kohut introduced an entirely new terminology to psychoanalysis, writing of such phenomena as selfobjects, transmuting internalization, self-cohesiveness, and varieties of selfobject experience (e.g., idealizing, mirroring, and partnering).

Although space does not permit a more detailed examination of Kohut's theoretical system, suffice it to say that self psychology encompasses not only a framework for clinical interventions but also a model for understanding certain aspects of normative human development and developmental deviations, as well as a theory of psychopathology.[3]

Kohut's vision of trauma is a distinctive one. Like those of the object relations theorists I discussed in the preceding section, his conception of trauma is fundamentally developmental and intimately tied to the relationship between the child and caregiver. Kohut believed that disturbances in self-functioning, which might take any of a variety of forms (e.g., borderline conditions, pathological narcissism, and other personality disorders as well as depression, anxiety disorders, and sexual perversions), are the result of chronically occurring, traumatic breaches in parental empathy. Such breaches might be the result of parental pathology, environmental uncertainties or deficits, or perhaps a combination of the two, but the end result is that the child's need for healthy affirmation, or for soothing and calming, cannot be met. Somewhat paradoxically, Kohut assumed that lapses in parental empathy are inevitable, even necessary for the healthy development of the child's self. However, these breaches are by definition optimally gratifying and optimally frustrating. As such, they serve as a catalyst for the development of healthy self-structures, furnishing the child with just the right amount of frustration to build a cohesive, fully functioning self-system.

Clinical Case Illustration—"Joe"[4]

Joe, an overweight, 47-year-old, upper-middle-class, Italian American Catholic man, originally came for treatment complaining of difficulty in establishing meaningful autonomy from his parents, a "joyless" marriage, and not being able to derive pleasure from his work. Joe managed the family business, a small smelting and refining company founded by his father and uncle some 50 years earlier, that was located in the industrial corridor of a large northeastern city. Joe's father had been an aggressive and highly successful businessman, although in his personal life, he was weak, ineffectual, and unable to lend Joe any modicum of real emotional support. Joe had never felt that he could count on his father when the chips were down or when in a crisis. At such times, Joe's father was alternately distant or critical and, in general, seemed largely incapable of any meaningful emotional connection with Joe. He was, moreover, unpredictable; he could "blow" at any

---

[3]For a more comprehensive overview of psychoanalytic self psychology, the reader is referred to Kohut (1977, 1984) and Perlman and Brandell (2011).

[4]This illustration is an adaptation of a psychoanalytic case originally described in Brandell (2004, pp. 97–103).

moment. Worse yet, Joe believed that his father was contemptuous of him and had been since childhood.

Relations with his mother were also a source of disappointment and conflict for Joe. From the time he was very young, he found her to be both unreliable and unattuned. She would become very impatient with him when he clung to her at the babysitter's, often leaving him sobbing, and throughout his early and middle childhood, she seemed incapable of furnishing him with the emotional safety he required. In fact, he often found himself in the position of placating her or of calming her down and generally placing her needs before his in what amounted to a reversal if not a parody of the mother-child relationship. Another significant theme in this relationship was Joe's strong sense that his mother was unable to take delight in his appearance. In fact, she shunned him at times, which caused him to feel small, ashamed, and physically repulsive. His struggle to maintain a normal weight, beginning in early childhood, was in some measure due to hereditary factors but was certainly compounded by the fact that food proved a reliable means of alleviating painful affect states and inner emptiness associated with thwarted selfobject needs in both of these relationships.

Although he had never thought of himself as depressed prior to starting treatment, Joe now recognized many of his reactions—both at work and at home—as being depressive in nature. Even when he was successful in cementing a lucrative business deal, for example, it wasn't enough to make him happy. He also acknowledged that raising his kids, which he believed should be a source of genuine gratification, was instead burdensome and draining. After 6 months of analysis, Joe revealed a recurring fantasy that for him was particularly disturbing and humiliating. In the fantasy, he is traveling alone on a deserted stretch of highway, and he stops at an isolated rest area. He walks into the men's room and is rather surprised to find another man standing near the rear by the toilet stalls. This man cannot be seen clearly because he is in the shadows. Without hesitating, Joe kneels down in front of the other man, unzips his fly, and begins to perform fellatio. At first, he feels excitement as the man's penis becomes erect, and then, at the moment of orgasm, he feels a sense of both power and primal satisfaction. This is as far as the fantasy goes. Even though Joe had had this fantasy for years, he had spoken of it only once before, during a session with his former therapist. At that time, he had expressed concern that it may mean he is gay. Although the therapist tried to reassure him that this seemed very unlikely to her, she "also moved off the topic pretty quickly."

Discussion

Joe suffered from what has been most aptly characterized in self psychology as a depletion depression. In self psychological terms, Joe failed to attain self-cohesiveness owing to the unremitting series of traumatic disappointments that he had suffered in his relationships with both his parents. Indeed, Joe's history was replete with such selfobject failures. Joe's mother, who was chronically overburdened, evinced a marked insensitivity and lack of attunement with her son's emotional needs, further compounded by her own pathological reliance on him as a soothing and calming selfobject. Joe's father, despite his many successes in the business world, had little wisdom to impart to his son and was rarely if ever able to serve as a fount of strength or steadfastness for Joe. Lacking in self-confidence and inner vitality, Joe had gradually come to feel an emptiness that could not be assuaged in his marriage; it was not alleviated in interaction with his children or even at work in his business relationships. He felt devitalized and impotent, was subject to mercurial fluctuations of mood, and was also markedly sensitive to narcissistic slights. Joe's capacity for the regulation of his self-esteem was minimal, inasmuch as he was highly reliant on the positive valuation of others.

Conclusion

As I stated at the beginning of this chapter, conceptions of trauma have been a central focus of the theoretical and clinical literature in psychoanalysis for more than 100 years. Ever since Freud's earliest experiments with hypnosis and the cathartic method in his work with hysterical patients, psychoanalysis has sought to understand the nature and manifestations of trauma and how it may be successfully addressed using psychodynamic treatment approaches. In this century-long odyssey, various ideas have at different times been privileged, only later to be cast aside or supplanted by newer understandings.

Trauma has sometimes been used in a narrower or more limited sense, such that it is carefully differentiated from anxiety and neurotic states (e.g., in the work of Anna Freud and Erna Furman). Other conceptions of trauma, however, place it at the very center of all pathology (e.g., Rank's conception of birth trauma) or emphasize the veridical basis of trauma (e.g., Ferenczi) rather than viewing most posttraumatic illness as arising from inner fantasies and the conflicts to which they give rise (e.g., Freud). Some theorists, most notably those whose work is associated with the British or independent tradition in object relations theory, have tried to understand the relationship of developmental traumas to the ordering of an individual's inner object or representational world. Finally, other psychoanalytic renderings of trauma emphasize the ubiquitous nature of trauma within a parent-child relational milieu in which chronic psychological disappointments occur (e.g., Kohut).

References

Abraham, K. (1948). A short study of the development of the libido. In *Selected papers on psycho-analysis* (pp. 418–450). London: Hogarth. (Original work published 1924)

Allen, J. (2001). *Traumatic relationships and serious mental disorders*. New York: John Wiley.

Altschul, S., & Pollock, G. (1988). *Childhood bereavement and its aftermath*. Madison, CT: International Universities Press.

Aron, L., & Harris, H. (1993). Sandor Ferenczi: Discovery and rediscovery. In L. Aron & H. Harris (Eds.), *The legacy of Sandor Ferenczi* (pp. 1–35). Hillsdale, NJ: Analytic Press.

Balint, M. (1968). *The basic fault: Therapeutic aspects of regression*. London: Tavistock.

Borden, W. (2009). *Contemporary psychodynamic theory and practice*. Chicago: Lyceum.

Brandell, J. (2004). *Psychodynamic social work*. New York: Columbia University Press.

Dupont, J. (1993). Michael Balint: Analysand, pupil, friend, and successor to Sandor Ferenczi. In L. Aron & H. Harris (Eds.), *The legacy of Sandor Ferenczi* (pp. 145–157). Hillsdale, NJ: Analytic Press.

Ferenczi, S. (1932). *The clinical diary of Sandor Ferenczi* (J. Dupont, Ed., M. Balint & N. Jackson, Trans.). Cambridge, MA: Harvard University Press.

Ferenczi, S. (1955). Confusion of tongues between adults and the child. In *The selected papers of Sandor Ferenczi: Vol. 3. Final contributions to the problems and methods of psychoanalysis* (pp. 156–167). New York: Basic Books. (Original work published 1933)

Ferenczi, S. (1999). The principle of relaxation and neo-catharsis. In *Selected writings* (pp. 275–292). London: Penguin. (Original work published 1930)

Ferenczi, S., & Rank, O. (1925). *The development of psychoanalysis*. New York: Nervous and Mental Diseases.

Fonagy, P., & Target, M. (2003). *Psychoanalytic theories: Perspectives from developmental psychopathology*. New York: Brunner-Routledge.

Freud, A. (1967). Comments on trauma. In S. Furst (Ed.), *Psychic trauma* (pp. 233–245). New York: Basic Books.

Freud, S. (1961a). Analysis of a phobia in a five-year-old boy. In J. Strachey (Ed. & Trans.), *The standard edition of the complete psychological works of Sigmund Freud* (Vol. 10, pp. 1–149). London: Hogarth Press. (Original work published 1909)

Freud, S. (1961b). The ego and the id. In J. Strachey (Ed. & Trans.), *The standard edition of the complete psychological works of Sigmund Freud* (Vol. 19, pp. 1–66). London: Hogarth Press. (Original work published 1923)

Freud, S. (1961c). Inhibitions, symptoms, and anxiety. In J. Strachey (Ed. & Trans.), *The standard edition of the complete psychological works of Sigmund Freud* (Vol. 20, pp. 75–175). London: Hogarth Press. (Original work published 1926)

Freud, S. (1961d). The interpretation of dreams. In J. Strachey (Ed. & Trans.), *The standard edition of the complete psychological works of Sigmund Freud* (Vols. 4–5, pp. 1–751). London: Hogarth Press. (Original work published 1900)

Freud, S. (1961e). Introductory lectures on psychoanalysis. In J. Strachey (Ed. & Trans.), *The standard edition of the complete psychological works of Sigmund Freud* (Vol. 17, Part 3, pp. 243–496). London: Hogarth Press. (Original work published 1917)

Freud, S., & Breuer, J. (1961). Studies on hysteria. In J. Strachey (Ed. & Trans.), *The standard edition of the complete psychological works of Sigmund Freud* (Vol. 2, pp. 1–321). London: Hogarth Press. (Original work published 1893–1895)

Fromm, E., & Nash, M. (1997). *Psychoanalysis and hypnosis.* Madison, CT: International Universities Press.

Gay, P. (1988). *Freud: A life for our time.* New York: Norton.

Goldstein, E. (1995). *Ego psychology and social work practice.* New York: Free Press.

Greenberg, J., & Mitchell, S. (1983). *Object relations in psychoanalytic theory.* Cambridge, MA: Harvard University Press.

Jones, E. (1955). *The life and work of Sigmund Freud: Vol. 2. 1901–1919, years of maturity.* New York: Basic Books.

Kohon, G. (Ed.). (1986). *The British school of psychoanalysis: The independent tradition.* London: Free Association Books.

Kohut, H. (1966). Forms and transformations of narcissism. *Journal of the American Psychoanalytic Association, 14,* 243–272.

Kohut, H. (1971). *The analysis of the self.* New York: International Universities Press.

Kohut, H. (1977). *The restoration of the self.* New York: International Universities Press.

Kohut, H. (1984). *How does analysis cure?* Chicago: University of Chicago Press.

Laughlin, H. (1979). *The ego and its defenses.* Northvale, NJ: Jason Aronson.

Menaker, E. (1982). *Otto Rank: A rediscovered legacy.* New York: Columbia University Press.

Mishne, J. (1993). *The evolution and application of clinical theory.* New York: Free Press.

Mitchell, S., & Black, M. (1995). *Freud and beyond: A history of modern psychoanalytic thought.* New York: Basic Books.

Moore, B., & Fine, B. (1990). *Psychoanalytic terms and concepts.* New Haven, CT: Yale University Press.

Perlman, F., & Brandell, J. (2011). Psychoanalytic theory. In *Theory and practice in clinical social work* (2nd ed.). Los Angeles: Sage.

Rank, O. (1945). *Will therapy and truth and reality.* New York: Knopf.

Rank, O. (1973). *The trauma of birth.* New York: Harper & Row. (Original work published 1924)

Samuels, A. (1990). Parental death in childhood. In S. Altschul & G. Pollock (Eds.), *Childhood bereavement and its aftermath* (pp. 19–36). Madison, CT: International Universities Press.

Van Haute, P., & Geyskens, T. (2004). *Confusion of tongues: The primacy of sexuality in Freud, Ferenczi, & Laplanche.* New York: Other Press.

Webster. (1995). *Webster's new college dictionary II.* Boston: Houghton Mifflin.

Winnicott, D. (1960). The theory of the parent-child relationship. *International Journal of Psychoanalysis, 41,* 585–595.

4

Psychoanalytic Theory (Part II)

Shoshana Ringel

Relational and Intersubjective Perspectives _____

With the emergence of relational and intersubjective perspectives in psychoanalytic treatment, the view of developmental trauma and its implications for psychodynamic treatment have significantly evolved and changed. As stated in the previous chapter, Ferenczi's (1933/1999) work, which was an important precursor to current psychodynamic trauma theory, departed from Freud's conceptualization of trauma as primarily an intrapsychic phenomenon. Ferenczi viewed his adult patients' symptoms as directly related to external traumas in their childhoods, typically sexual abuse by parents and significant others, and believed their accounts of seduction by parents and other family members. He focused on the interpersonal nature of the traumas rather than viewing the symptoms as signifying internal conflicts related to the patients' unacceptable fantasies, wishes, and desires, which Freud attributed to oedipal longings. Ferenczi's emphasis on external trauma, rather than internal conflict, provided the basis for later understanding of child sexual abuse and its impact on the survivors' internal experience and their patterns of bonding with others.

This chapter will examine the meanings of trauma and its aftermath from the perspective of contemporary relational and intersubjective theories, which are influenced by Ferenczi's work, attachment research, and infant studies. Important contributions from a range of psychoanalytic authors, representing various relational, intersubjective, and contemporary self psychological perspectives, will be highlighted, including Stern and Bromberg's view of dissociation and multiplicity; Davies and Frawley's idea of role enactments between adult survivors of sexual abuse and their therapists; Bach, Benjamin, Ghent, and Pizer's formulation of binary positions, paradox, and mastery, submission, and surrender; and intersubjective and contemporary self psychological contributions to the trauma literature by Shane, Shane, and Gale as well as by Stolorow, Lichtenberg, Lachmann, and Fosshage. These writers have been strongly influenced by attachment and infant research with its contributions to the understanding of early attachment trauma and attachment disorganization (see Chapter 5).

Ferenczi's Mutual Analysis and the Relational View of Trauma

In the 1920s, believing that the hierarchical relationship between analyst and patient represented an obstacle to the curative potential of psychoanalysis, Ferenczi briefly experimented with a technique he termed "mutual analysis," which required that the analyst and patient take turns analyzing each other's free associations. However, mutual analysis was misguided in the sense that the therapist-patient relationship is not a symmetrical relationship between two equals but an inherently asymmetrical relationship, with the focus on the patient rather than the therapist. Professional boundaries and the therapist's expertise play an important role in the treatment, particularly in cases in which patients' boundaries have been severely damaged and their trust violated by those closest to them. Ferenczi, however, was ahead of his time in his efforts to achieve greater flexibility and mutuality between patient and therapist, and his work is regarded as an important influence in contemporary relational conceptions of mutuality and the therapist's self-disclosure (Aron & Harris, 1993). Ferenczi contributed to greater interest in the mutual impact that patient and therapist have on one another as well as emphasized the therapist's openness and authenticity. This trend can be discerned in the evolution of the concept of transference and countertransference, from Racker's (1968) construct of complementary and concordant countertransference, to Sandler's (1976) formulation of role responsiveness, to Davies and Frawley's (1994) contemporary idea of patient-therapist role enactments. Davies and Frawley believe that the therapeutic dyad enacts complementary roles based on a patient's history of sexual abuse. These include the victim-perpetrator, the dismissive parent–rejected child, and the victim-rescuer, scenarios in which the therapist may unconsciously assume, for example, the alternating roles of rescuer, perpetrator, and victim. It is easy for a clinician to get pulled into such compelling scenarios and to experience difficulty extricating him- or herself from them, especially if the therapist has a history of trauma. From the relational view, the therapist is increasingly implicated in the enactment and can no longer play the role of the objective outsider who is neutral and anonymous, as formulated in earlier classical conceptions of treatment. Later relational writers (Aron, 1996) suggest that enactments are unavoidable phenomena that help patients and therapists process and work through previously unconscious and dissociated relational patterns and affects.

Adult Survivors of Sexual Abuse:
The Work of Davies and Frawley

In their book about practice with adult survivors of sexual abuse, Davies and Frawley (1994) noted that overwhelming experiences of abuse are associated with a greater degree of personality disorganization in patients. The result is that the ego's capacity for organization, synthesis, and symbolization is overstimulated and flooded, such that the abuse experience becomes one of "unformulated experiential chaos." Davies and Frawley observed that "with no self-reflective observing ego to provide even the rudiments of containment, meaning, and structure to the traumatic events, the child exists in a timeless, objectless, and selfless nightmare of unending pain, isolation, and ultimately, psychic dissolution" (1994, p. 45). In consequence, the usual process of insight work, which privileges introspection and self-reflection, must be substantially modified to reflect these psychic realities.

Dissociated Systems of Self and Object Representation

According to Davies and Frawley, it is not only the memories of specific traumatic experiences that become dissociated from other experiences but also "the organization of mutually exclusive systems of self and object representations" formed in relation to traumatic experiences (1994, p. 45). The therapeutic process, as a result, must achieve integration not only of the memories themselves but also of patients' varying experiences of self in relation to their fragmented worlds of internal objects.

Sudden Regressions and Experiences of Disorganization

Linking their own clinical experiences in treating sexual abuse trauma survivors to both the trauma literature and the concept of insecure attachment, Davies and Frawley assert that the traumatized child's loss of a secure base may constitute the most pernicious and damaging psychological trauma (Davies & Frawley, 1994). Because clients' inner object worlds contain no representations of loving, protective objects, they never develop the capacity for self-calming and self-soothing at times of stress or for containment of the panic-like states, disorganization, and physiologically mediated states of intense hyperarousal. Accordingly, the authors emphasize the importance of the clinician's developing familiarity and relative comfort with the patient's abrupt shifts in mood and disorganizing regressive episodes.

Hyperreactivity and Trauma
Response to Arbitrary Stimuli

The clinician's understanding and success in working with such trauma patients may also be enhanced through recognition of the relationship between seemingly neutral stimuli that co-occur or are temporally associated with the original trauma. Through what is most easily explained as classical conditioning, such neutral stimuli eventually serve as triggers for the traumatic response. Davies and Frawley (1994) also believed such reactions to be consistent with ideas advanced by earlier psychoanalytic authors regarding the foreclosure of symbolic representation (McDougall, 1989) and alexithymia (Krystal, 1993).

Perhaps the most important contribution made by Davies and Frawley (1994), however, inheres in their strong endorsement of the treatment relationship as the vehicle through which "soothing, undoing, and redoing" of the traumatized patient's life must finally occur. They assert that such processes are possible only insofar as the patient is able to form a significant object relationship with the therapist. Although the abreaction of traumatic memories does constitute one aspect of this treatment process, the focus on the abusive relationship in the context of a new, therapeutic relationship is essential. As stated above, Davies and Frawley devote considerable attention to the transference-countertransference matrix and the therapist's "willingness to know" the patient fully (Davies & Frawley, 1994).

The relational view emphasizes the intersubjective dynamics between therapist and patient around enactments stemming from the trauma the patient has experienced. Enactments are seen as unavoidable but also as instrumental in helping patients process and understand the previously unconscious relational patterns that they find themselves in, their impact on others, and their perception and interpretation of others' words and behaviors.

Fluidity and Multiplicity
Rather Than a Cohesive Self

Relational psychoanalysis has shifted from an emphasis on a single cohesive self (see the discussion about Kohut in Chapter 3) to a view of internal experience as constructed from multiple self states that are linked to one another through self-awareness, a sense of continuity, and an overarching coherence (Bromberg, 2003b). The goal of treatment with traumatized patients is to help them become conscious of previously unconscious, dissociated self states rather than achieving a state of self-cohesion (Bromberg, 1998, 2003a, 2003b). Bromberg suggests that traumatized patients create a mental structure of separate, incompatible self states "so that each can continue to play its own role, unimpeded by awareness of the others" (Bromberg, 2003b, p. 560). Dissociation is

> a means of foreclosing a potentially traumatic encounter with the mind of a needed "other" in the here and now, encounters that could threaten to trigger affective hyperarousal, including shame, without hope of regulating the affect through the relationship itself. (Bromberg, 2003b, p. 560)

Bromberg notes that the dilemma of both therapist and patient is that by developing the capacity for self-reflection, the patient concurrently experiences a threat to the inevitable dismantling of the dissociative structures, thereby creating the possibility for further traumatization by others, including the therapist.

Bromberg notes that contemporary psychodynamic theory has shifted from a focus on resolving intrapsychic conflicts and strengthening the ego to acceptance and awareness of multiple and fluid self states. Starting with Sullivan (1953) and his notion of the "not me" states and Donnell Stern's (1997) work on disowned and disavowed self states in traumatized patients, Bromberg believes in helping these patients identify and express their dissociated affective states. He suggests that patients cannot recognize internal conflict unless they first work through the trauma and "own" their dissociated self states. Once this ownership has occurred, patients are able to tolerate conflict without feeling compelled to dissociate, a familiar response to intolerable experiences (Bromberg, 2003a, 2003b). Donnell Stern addresses the dilemma of the not me states, which are disowned and disavowed by patients. The not me states need to become conscious and better integrated into awareness. Bromberg suggests that therapists' own reflections concerning their dissociative processes with patients are one of the primary tools in the treatment. In summary, the relational perspective views the goal of trauma treatment as more fluid communication between the patient's dissociated self states, the therapist's dissociative processes, and the interplay between them, so that more flexible choices and relationships may become available to patients.

Clinical Example 1

> Jane is a woman in her 60s who experienced severe sexual abuse that began at an early age and continued through her adolescence. Whenever she mentioned parental behaviors that did not make sense to her or asked for confirmation of her memories and observations from her parents, they told her that she was crazy and simply imagining things. Jane grew up believing that she had a wonderful family, and that what happened in her room at night was a monstrous dream that had no bearing on her everyday reality. The memories related to the abuse surfaced very gradually when she was an adult, emerging as

fragmented visual scenes and bodily experiences. To protect against the horror of the abuse and the emotional rejection she experienced from both parents, Jane dissociated her abuse memories until her father's death, at which time she was an adult with her own family. In the aftermath of the abuse, Jane reported experiencing dissociation and an inability to remember everyday interactions. We later understood that she experienced these encounters, especially with her husband, who was prone to inattentiveness and distractibility, as potential threats to her integrity, and she was highly sensitive to feeling rejected and ignored. She experienced memory gaps and found herself in cognitive as well as geographical dislocations without knowing how she got there or which precipitating event had caused her dissociative response. We explored Jane's fragmented memories and her self states as a baby, a child, an adolescent, and an adult woman. Jane, who initially believed her family to be as normal as any other, described family dinners in which religious and political subjects were discussed. However, these memories alternated with others, of nights during which the "monster" entered her room and she experienced a nightmarish reality that made no sense. When she had tried to communicate her observations of these bizarre experiences to her family, she was told that she was crazy, and this contributed to her self-doubt and sense of unreality and depersonalization. Jane's ability to compartmentalize her experience and live in separate self states permitted her to ward off painful memories but also caused unexplained depression and difficulty in trusting her own perceptions.

Together, we tried to identify moments when Jane felt ignored and misunderstood or when she felt that I, as her therapist, was taking over her train of thought and shifting the direction in which she was going. She then began to experience an overwhelming need to withdraw and disappear. We also devoted much of the treatment to looking at and finding ways to link her fragmented memories to emotional states and to gain understanding of the splits in her experience of her family and history. As Jane reported her horrific memories with a matter-of-fact tone, completely devoid of feelings, I could experience my own horror, sadness at her terror, isolation as a child, and numbing at some of the unimaginable events she described. By watching my expression and hearing my reactions, Jane too started to experience her disowned feelings of overwhelming fear, sadness, and despair, feelings that she had dissociated and disavowed. She was now able to make links between previously fragmented memories and to identify her desire to dissociate when remembering the horror or experiencing the slightest rejection and lack of attunement. Jane started to articulate her experience so that we could repair the disruption and continue. She now had greater choice and flexibility in her interactions with others. She could make her need for understanding, recognition, and validation heard and could stay present despite her overwhelming fear.

From Sadomasochism, Mastery, and Submission to Surrender and "The Third"

Sexual accommodation through relationships based on mastery and submission represents an adjustment to early developmental trauma. The inquiry into the dynamics of mastery and submission (or sadomasochism in an earlier classical formulation) is actually a time-honored psychoanalytic tradition. Freud viewed sadomasochism as an oedipal accommodation stemming from the original desire for the opposite-sex parent, as well as the guilt triggered in consequence of this unacceptable wish that culminated in the fantasy of being punished, which is both painful and exciting. Freud called this fantasy, which he saw in some of his patients, the "beating fantasy."[1] Freud concluded that the wish to be beaten by the father is "not only the punishment for the forbidden genital relation, but also the regressive substitute for that relation" (Freud, 1919/1955, p. 189). Bach (1994, 2002, 2006) noted that rather than being an oedipal phenomenon, sadomasochism represents the expression of an earlier developmental trauma and is aimed toward "maintaining the dependent tie to the father or mother or analyst" (Bach, 2002, p. 229). From an attachment perspective, a disruption in early attachment bonds due to parental abuse, lack of nurturing, or loss may culminate in a distortion of love and sexual needs. Bach noted that sexual perversions are a way to seek affect regulation that the parent failed to provide or alternatively that they may represent a desire to "compensate for hidden feelings of deviance and defectiveness" (Bach, 2002, p. 230). He noted that there are parents who are unable to take pleasure in the child and are either distant and affectless or labile and unpredictable. With these parents, children are deprived of a sense of their own agency, they feel abandoned and enraged but cannot express their rage toward their parents for fear of losing an essential bond on which they depend, and they typically direct their anger toward themselves. These children will do whatever is necessary to maintain the tie to the parent, and as a consequence, the sadomasochistic dyad is created. Bach observed that "these sadomasochistic dyads are a closely coupled system without autonomy for either caretaker or child," who in effect have "become each other's slaves" (Bach, 2002, p. 231). The child's rage is thereby directed either toward the self or toward others through sexualized relationships. Sadists and masochists are both dependant on one another to feel real and complete. Bach views the sadomasochistic relationship as a disorder in sexual regulation based on lack of regulation in the earlier child-caregiver relationship.

In her book *The Bonds of Love*, Benjamin (1988) reflected on the dynamic of mastery and submission from a feminist perspective as she described the

---

[1] It is possible that his paper on the subject was based on his work with his daughter Anna who was in analysis with him (Bach, 2002).

story of O. to discuss the nature of sadomasochism in male-female relation-ships. According to Benjamin, mastery and submission occur when women subjugate themselves sexually and emotionally to men to help the men feel powerful and in control and to experience a sense of connection, belonging, and being desirable. In these relationships there is no place for autonomy or mutuality, as each member of the dyad provides disowned and disavowed aspects of the other's self, and each needs the other to experience a sense of agency and aliveness. Benjamin suggested that patients with a history of trauma develop a rigid self-structure that permits only inflexible binary roles of mastery and submission as well as victim and perpetrator, which she calls the "doer and done to." Every subsequent interaction is viewed by the patient from this polarized perspective, and enactments between patient and thera-pist originate from both finding themselves playing these polarized roles from the patient's history. Benjamin noted that another possibility outside the doer and done to paradigm is for patient and therapist to create a third position from which there is a possibility for a new understanding to arise, not con-tingent on the old, dysfunctional roles but offering new options and possi-bilities for relational bonding.

Benjamin (2004) developed the idea of "the third" in a more recent paper wherein she delineates the idea of moving from the dynamic of the doer and done to—the two binary poles that maintain a rigid split between victim and perpetrator—to the development of a third position. She characterized the third in the following way:

> The third is that to which we surrender, and thirdness is the intersub-jective mental space that facilitates or results from surrender. . . . The term surrender refers to a certain letting go of the self, and thus also implies the ability to take in the other's point of view or reality. Thus, surrender refers us to recognition, being able to sustain connectedness to the other's mind while accepting his separateness and difference. Surrender implies freedom from any intent to control or coerce. (Benjamin, 2004, p. 6)

In a relationship in which the child experiences the adult's manipula-tion of the child to meet the needs of the adult, the child adapts a view of a world in which polarized roles are the norm, where the roles of the powerful perpetrator who is in control and the victim who is dependent and submissive are the only options. These roles then structure future relationships, and similar dynamics become enacted between patient and therapist.

Several authors have discussed the notion of a third from different perspec-tives, including Ogden (1994) and Aron (2006). From Benjamin's point of view, the third is a position outside of such polarized, patient-therapist complementarities. Representing the new meaning that emerges between therapist and patient, the third is arrived at through an intersubjective rela-tional process, outside of the doer–done to paradigm. The third offers a different option that allows mutual surrender to each other's experience. Domination and subjugations are then transformed into mutual collaboration and the discovery of alternative options. The third, therefore, offers the analytic dyad a way out of old, rigidly held positions based on the patient's familiar traumatic patterns. Possibilities for mutual negotiation and recognition emerge, and greater flexibility and space become available, thus establishing a new perspective that both patient and therapist can share. In her formulation of the third, Benjamin draws on Winnicott's (1971) idea of the transitional space and Ghent's (1990) reflections on masochism, submission, and surrender. Ghent notes that unlike masochism, with its connotation of distortion and corruption, submission carries the meaning of "a quality of liberation and expansion of the self as a corollary to the letting down of defensive barriers" (p. 108). He adds that unlike submission, in surrender there is no domination and control by another person. Surrender emerges as a consequence of free choice; one surrenders not to a person but to something bigger than oneself, and the decision to surrender entails greater freedom and clarity, such as what one experiences, for example, during intense spiritual practice or in the process of meditation. Pizer (1992) addressed the issue of a binary dilemma between patient and therapist, with each holding onto an inflexible position, from the perspective of the negotiation of paradox. He noted that eventually both members of the therapeutic dyad find a place of validation and inclusion. This differs markedly from the patient's earlier experience of coercion, exploitation, and manipulation by caregivers and the inevitable choice such situations demanded: submission and loss of self or the risk of losing essential emotional bonds.

Ringstrom (2007) contributed to this discussion by offering the idea of playfulness and improvisation between patient and therapist as a way to process unconscious enactments and transform otherwise potentially traumatic interactions based on the traumatized patient's old internal structures. The relational view places the therapist-patient interaction at the center of enacting, processing, and resolving traumatic self states through improvisation and attending to dissociated states in both patient and therapist.

Clinical Example 2

Peter is a gay man in his 40s who grew up with a domineering, manipulative father and a passive and depressed mother. In addition to an isolated and lonely childhood, Peter experienced rejection and occasional violence from peers during his childhood and adolescence because of his sexual orientation and androgynous appearance. He became highly sensitive to perceived criticism and derogation, protecting himself through social withdrawal and ending several relationships because of real or perceived hurts. Peter learned to use his considerable intellect to shore up his self-esteem by viewing others as inferior to him. These familiar patterns of interaction were enacted between Peter and me,[2] causing frequent impasses and disruptions between us. Peter often perceived me as rejecting and critical like his peers and colleagues, unable to understand or empathize with him. In response, I experienced myself being greatly constrained in my expression with Peter, restricted to the role of Peter's cheerleader and empathic listener or pulled into the position of the disappointing, critical, and clueless Other who mistreated Peter like everyone else. The only way we seemed able to overcome the impasse was for me to view everything from Peter's point of view and to abandon my own authentic expression and autonomy.

After several years of establishing trust and talking through endless ruptures and disappointments, I learned to admit my shortcomings and mistakes but also helped Peter accept that despite my limitations, I was willing to be honest and open with him, remain committed to our work together, and do my best to understand him. As our therapeutic space started to open up, Peter brought in wordplay riddles, enjoying my initial clumsiness in figuring out their meaning but appreciating my willingness to be playful and laugh at his considerable wit. Eventually, I became more adept, sometimes even discovering new meanings that he hadn't considered and making him laugh with enjoyment. We found a way to transform our either-or experience into greater mutual play and collaboration. Peter also started to bring in his dreams, and we collaborated in figuring out their meaning, inspired by one another's metaphors and adding additional layers of interpretation. For example, Peter recounted a dream in which he is walking in his mother's house and explained to me that the house represented his mind, with its complex structure and multiple levels and rooms. In the dream, he finds himself in a low, dark attic from which he enters a new office he hadn't known existed, and from there he goes out to a lush, green, and well-tended garden. I added that since the house was a metaphor for his inner self, the attic may have represented his current feelings of darkness and hopelessness; the dream suggested that there was a way out to a well-appointed room and to a lovely garden that he hadn't seen before or known about, a new solution to the old, habitual way he had experienced his situation.

Intersubjective and Contemporary Self Psychology View of Trauma

Morton and Estelle Shane and Mary Gales are psychoanalysts whose theoretical model integrates elements of Kohut's self psychology with features of

---

[2]Shoshana Ringel.

Bowlby's attachment model and also draws on such bodies of literature as infant research, developmental systems research, and human neuroscience. However, what makes their work especially relevant for this discussion is the prominence they have accorded trauma as an overarching theme and conceptual organizer in their theoretical model.

As one of their basic theoretical premises, these authors observe that only in the instance of secure attachment is there an appropriate balance between parent and child, in which the child demonstrates a "predominant pattern of attachment behavior in connection with a parent manifesting a predominant pattern of parenting behavior" (Shane, Shane, & Gales, 1997, p. 26). They then state that all three categories of insecure attachment reveal "a *traumatically* [italics added] inverted pattern wherein the child appears to parent the parent, but . . . on more detailed examination, is actually preoccupied with the parent in ways that interfere with the child's self and self-with-other consolidation" (Shane et al., 1997, p. 26). For the Shanes, this represents the essence of trauma, which begins with a traumatic attachment to the parent. In their view, then, trauma is equated with developmental outcomes that spring from constitutional and environmental failure, whether such failures involve actual abuse and destructive behavior on the parents' part or are the result of parental absence, neglect, depression, or abandonment (Shane et al., 1997).

The Shanes observe that higher order consciousness, which carries with it the capacity for an integrated experience of past, present, and future, is intimately bound with the continuity of the self. However, when a self has been exposed to trauma, it lacks such a sense of continuity, and this is most transparent in dissociative disorders (Shane et al., 1997). The authors believe that the

> self-protective (defensive) strategy of dissociation, so necessary at the time of the original trauma, prevents the symbolic coding of the event, interfering with the ordinary functioning of higher-order consciousness, and in effect keeping this event encoded only in primary consciousness. (Shane et al., 1997, p. 78)

The consequence is an unconsolidated and fragmented self, deficient not only in continuity but also in achieving a stable sense of reality.

Other contemporary psychoanalytic theorists who include in their work principles of self psychology along with findings from attachment theory and infant research are Joseph Lichtenberg, Frank Lachmann, and James Fosshage (1996, 2002; Lichtenberg, 2005). In their writings, these theorists continue to utilize Kohut's ideas of empathic resonance as the therapist's primary mode of listening and attunement and a focus on affect as an essential component of internal experience. They suggest that as a result of early sexual abuse, restricted affect or inability to regulate overwhelming affect are common symptoms in patients and that these require therapists to provide affect regulation, empathic listening, and attention to all aspects of safety and security in the therapeutic milieu so as not to create a retraumatizing environment. Lichtenberg, Lachmann and Fosshage developed a theory of motivational systems that expands on Freud's ideas of sexual and aggressive drives as the primary human motivations. They note that when working with patients with a history of sexual abuse, therapists should keep in mind disruptions in the sexual/sensual motivational system and suggest that in the absence of empathic, attuned, and regulating others, children are unable to learn to manage their intense affect states, specifically states of disruption and distress. Dissociation, disorganized attachment patterns, and controlling behaviors through aggression or caretaking of significant others may be the consequence of these early deficits. Contemporary self psychology continues to focus on affect and affect regulation in the treatment of trauma, with the therapist utilizing empathic resonance to access the patient's internal experience and dissociated states. Affect regulation occurs intersubjectively and is based on current infant research (e.g., Beebe, Lachmann, and Tronick, as noted in Chapter 5, "Attachment Theory"). There is greater understanding of the bidirectional nature of infant-caregiver interactions as well as its corollary, the bidirectional nature of interactions between the patient and the therapist.

Stolorow (2007) offered a theory of trauma based on his own personal experience with his wife's traumatic loss, which is contextualized within intersubjectivity theory and self psychology and also draws from the philosophical ideas of Heidegger, Husserl, and Gadamer. Like the previous authors, Stolorow noted the primacy of affect in human experience and the essential role of the caregiver's regulation of the child's affect state through mirroring and idealization. In the absence of mirroring and regulating others, the child's affect remains painful and overwhelming, and the phenomena of dissociation and disavowal of affect and memory prevail. The therapist's attuned, empathic, and regulating functions provide the possibility of a new intersubjective context that can help change what Stolorow called the patient's "organizing principles" and bring about greater affective flexibility as well as open new intersubjective possibilities. Stolorow posited a theory of trauma based on contextuality, absolutisms, temporality, and what he terms the "ontological unconscious." The focus on contextuality in the writings of Stolorow and Atwood (1992) essentially reflects their view that there is no such thing as the Cartesian notion of an "isolated mind." There is continuous bidirectional influence between inner state and outer environmental factors, between the inner reality of the child and the relational bonds with caregivers, and between patient and therapist. Thus trauma is always the result of confluence between internal and external factors.

Based on his personal experience of loss, Stolorow suggested that the absolutisms that people take for granted in their everyday life, such as a sense of trust, optimism, and objective reality, have no meaning for those who have experienced trauma, who cannot trust in the reliability of everyday events and the security and predictability of everyday life. For trauma survivors, everything seems precarious and subject to sudden destruction and chaos.

They feel isolated and alienated from others who have not experienced their loss and trauma. Stolorow noted,

> It is in the essence of emotional trauma that it shatters these absolutisms, a catastrophic loss of innocence that permanently alters one's sense of being in the world. Massive deconstruction of the absolutisms of everyday life exposes the inescapable contingency of existence on a universe that is random and unpredictable and in which no safety or continuity of being can be assured. (Stolorow, 2007, p. 16)

Similarly, time or temporality has no meaning after the experience of a traumatic event, and the sense of one's self in the context of time become meaningless. For many patients who have experienced trauma, the traumatic past seems to exist in the present time, and there is no sense of present or future apart from the traumatic event. Stolorow suggested that

> it is the ecstatical unity of temporality, the sense of stretching along between past and future, that is devastatingly disturbed by the experience of emotional trauma. Experiences of trauma become freeze framed into an internal present in which one remains forever trapped, or to which one is condemned to be perpetually returned through the port keys supplied by life's slings and arrows. (2007, p. 20)

What Stolorow called the "ontological unconscious" is the loss of the sense of being through affectivity and through language. Experiences with early lack of attunement, especially linguistic attunement, foreclose one's ability to develop a sense of self that includes affect and language, leaving individuals with a body-based emotional experience that is not subject to understanding and articulation. Stolorow suggested that it is through intersubjective bonds that the sense of being develops and is sustained and that only through intersubjective experiences can one heal from the impact of developmental and other types of trauma. Although much of what Stolorow suggested is not new, his interweaving of his own personal experience with loss gives his writing a unique sense of poignancy.

Conclusion

In this chapter I have summarized important contributions to contemporary psychodynamic theories of trauma emerging from relational theory, intersubjectivity, and contemporary self psychology and influenced by attachment findings and infant research. These contemporary conceptions include enactments between the patient and therapist in which the roles of doer and done to are cocreated; the third as a mutual position that helps the patient and therapist enter a new and more fluid relational paradigm outside of the constrictions of doer–done to dynamics; dissociation and a view of multiple, rather than a single, self states; and the intersubjective space between the clinician's personal experience of emotional trauma and the patient's experience of absolutisms, temporality, and ontological unconscious. These contemporary trends point to a greater personal engagement of the therapist in the narrative and self states of the patient; the need to draw, as a therapist, on one's personal experiences of relational disruptions, loss, and trauma; and the capacity to engage with the patient more openly and authentically.

References

Aron, L. (1996). *A meeting of minds: Mutuality in psychoanalysis.* Hillsdale, NJ: Analytic Press.

Aron, L. (2006). Analytic impasse and the third: Clinical implications of intersubjectivity theory. *International Journal of Psychoanalysis, 87,* 349–368.

Aron, L., & Harris, A. (1993). Sandor Ferenczi: Discovery and rediscovery. In L. Aron & A. Harris (Eds.), *The legacy of Sandor Ferenczi* (pp. 1–36). Northvale, NJ: Analytic Press.

Bach, S. (1994). *The language of perversion and the language of love.* Northvale, NJ: Jason Aronson.

Bach, S. (2002). Sadomasochism in clinical practice and everyday life. *Journal of Clinical Psychoanalysis, 11,* 225–235.

Bach, S. (2006). *Getting from here to there: Analytic love, analytic process.* Hillsdale, NJ: Analytic Press.

Benjamin, J. (1988). *The bonds of love: Psychoanalysis, feminism and the problem of domination.* New York: Pantheon.

Benjamin, J. (2004). Beyond doer and done to: An intersubjective view of thirdness. *Psychoanalytic Quarterly, 73,* 5–46.

Bromberg, P. (1998). *Standing in the spaces: Essays on clinical process, trauma and dissociation.* Hillsdale, NJ: Analytic Press.

Bromberg, P. (2003a). One need not be a house to be haunted: On enactment, dissociation and the dread of "not me": A case study. *Psychoanalytic Dialogues, 13,* 689–709.

Bromberg, P. (2003b). Something wicked this way comes: Trauma dissociation and conflict: The space where psychoanalysis, cognitive science and neuroscience overlap. *Psychoanalytic Psychology, 20,* 558–574.

Davies, J., & Frawley, M. (1994). *Treating the adult survivor of childhood sexual abuse: A psychoanalytic perspective.* New York: Basic Books.

Ferenczi, S. (1999). The confusion of tongues between adults and the child. In *Selected writings* (pp. 293–303). London: Penguin. (Original work published 1933)

Freud, S. (1955). A child is being beaten: A contribution to the study of the origin of sexual perversions. In J. Strachey (Ed. & Trans.), *The standard edition of the complete psychological works of Sigmund Freud* (Vol. 17, pp. 175–204). London: Hogarth Press. (Original work published 1919)

Ghent, E. (1990). Masochism, submission, surrender: Masochism as a perversion of surrender. *Contemporary Psychoanalysis, 26,* 108–136.

Krystal, H. (1993). *Integration of self and healing: Affect, trauma, alexithymia.* Hillsdale, NJ: Analytic Press.

Lichtenberg, J. (2005). *Craft and spirit: A guide to the exploratory psychotherapies.* Hillsdale, NJ: Analytic Press.

Lichtenberg, J., Lachmann, F., & Fosshage, J. (1996). *The clinical exchange.* Hillsdale, NJ: Analytic Press.

Lichtenberg, J., Lachmann, F., & Fosshage, J. (2002). *The spirit of inquiry.* Hillsdale, NJ: Analytic Press.

McDougall, J. (1989). *Theaters of the body.* New York: Basic Books.

Ogden, T. (1994). *Subjects of analysis.* Northvale, NJ: Analytic Press.

Pizer, S. (1992). The negotiation of paradox in the analytic process. *Psychoanalytic Dialogues, 2,* 215–240.

Racker, H. (1968). *Transference and countertransference.* New York: International University Press.

Ringstrom, P. (2007). Scenes that write themselves: Improvisational moments in relational psychoanalysis. *Psychoanalytic Dialogues, 17*(1), 69–99.

Sandler, J. (1976). Countertransference and role responsiveness. *International Review of Psychoanalysis, 3,* 43–47.

Shane, M., Shane, E., & Gales, M. (1997). *Intimate attachments: Toward a new self psychology.* New York: Guilford.

Stern, D. (1997). *Unformulated experience: From dissociation to imagination in psychoanalysis.* Hillsdale, NJ: Analytic Press.

Stolorow, R. (2007). *Trauma and human existence: Autobiographical, psychoanalytic and philosophical reflections.* New York: Analytic Press.

Stolorow, R., & Atwood, G. (1992). *The context of being.* Northvale, NJ: Analytic Press.

Sullivan, H. S. (1953). *The interpersonal theory of psychiatry.* New York: Norton.

Winnicott, D. W. (1971). *Playing and reality.* New York: Routledge.

5 Attachment Theory, Infant Research, and Neurobiology

Shoshana Ringel

From its inception, attachment research concerned traumatic events in the lives of young children, and attachment theory developed in the context of children's need for attachment and their consequent response to separation and loss. Indeed, John Bowlby conducted his observations in orphanages and hospitals with children who lost their parents or were separated from them for long periods of time. More contemporary infant researchers including Beebe and her collaborators (Beebe, 2005; Beebe et al., 2000), Tronick (1977, 1998, 2002), Lyons-Ruth (Lyons-Ruth, Dutra, Schuder, & Bianchi, 2006; Lyons-Ruth & Jacobvitz, 2009), and others have focused their investigations on children's disorganized attachment in the wake of such traumas as parental misattunement, abuse, or neglect. Children's disorganized attachment is also linked to caregivers' own unresolved loss and trauma, communicated to the child via verbal or nonverbal signals and thereby transmitted from one generation to the next. Neuroscientific findings show that brain development is closely linked to attachment relationships and that attachment disruptions can interfere with normative development of brain structures.

In this chapter, I will elaborate on Bowlby's theory of children's attachment, separation, and loss; Ainsworth's Strange Situation experiment and her identification of early attachment patterns; and Main and Solomon's (1990) criteria of disorganized attachment. We will also examine the Adult Attachment Interview (AAI) and adult attachment categories, infant research with an emphasis on disorganized attachment, neuroscience and trauma, and mentalization and the treatment of borderline personality disorder (BPD). The chapter concludes with several clinical applications of attachment theory and research.

Bowlby and Ainsworth: Separation and Loss, the Strange Situation

Bowlby's attachment theory was influenced by Spitz's observations of abandoned babies in hospitals, babies who failed to thrive despite the provision of basic needs such as food and shelter. Bowlby was also influenced by Darwin's evolutionary theory, from which he learned the principle of adaptation to a changing environment and the necessity of caregivers' proximity and nurturing of their offspring to ensure survival. He also learned of Harlow's experiments with baby monkeys who were separated from their mothers and preferred the warmth and softness of a wiremesh "mother" covered in terrycloth to the metal wiremesh mother who carried milk bottles (Harlow, 1958). From Harlow, Bowlby recognized that babies need not only food and shelter but also love and nurturing to survive and thrive. Bowlby applied these findings to human babies and realized that physiological provisions alone were not sufficient for optimal development and that emotional nurturing and attentiveness were required for children to thrive. Through his work with children in orphanages and in hospitals, Bowlby recognized the impact of separation and loss on children's development, and consequently, traumatic experiences were the context in which attachment theory took hold (Bowlby, 1973). Ahead of the psychoanalytic community of his time, Bowlby recognized that young children had a profound emotional need for their mothers (or caregivers) and that separation and loss sustained a profound impact on their developmental experiences. With his collaborator, James Robertson, who filmed hospitalized children separated from their mothers, Bowlby observed that children responded to separation in three distinct stages: protest, when the young children would cry inconsolably; despair, when the children became listless, depressed, and uninterested in food or play; and detachment, when attachment needs were readjusted, and the children became engaged with the hospital environment, nurses, and other children but ignored their mothers when they came to visit (Bowlby, 1973). Robertson and Bowlby observed that it took these children some time to trust their mothers again and reach out to them. Bowlby's work also encompassed children's grief and mourning process. He observed that children mourned the death of a parent deeply and that, at times, such grief remained unresolved for many years, either as prolonged mourning or as failed mourning when a secure environment in which to grieve the loss was not available to the child (Bowlby, 1960, 1963). Bowlby's observations were revolutionary at a time when child psychology was in its infancy. Indeed, much clinical work with children was based on Freud's drive theory, in which the real relationship with caregivers was seen as having far less importance than the child's intrapsychic conflicts. At the time, children were treated by mental health professionals without much attention to their actual relationship with their mothers.

Building on Bowlby's work, Mary Ainsworth, who was initially Bowlby's collaborator (and later an accomplished researcher in her own right), developed the Strange Situation experiment, which led to the identification of three distinct attachment styles in children (Ainsworth, Blehar, Water, & Wall, 1978). In the Strange Situation, Ainsworth exposed young children ages 1½ to 2 years of age to experiences of separation and reunion with their mothers.

In a laboratory room fitted with toys, the child would spend a few minutes with his or her mother; a stranger would enter the room and the mother would then leave; the mother would come back; and after a while both the stranger and the mother would leave, and the child would remain alone. Finally, the mother would return a second time. Ainsworth observed that children's behavior varied during experiences of separation and reunion but was particularly distinct during their reunion with their mothers. Securely attached children would demonstrate attachment behaviors, looking at the mother and seeking contact, but these children were also quite comfortable engaging in exploratory behaviors, playing with toys, and in general, conveying curiosity about their laboratory room environment. Although the secure children were distressed when their mothers left, they were easily soothed when they returned, reaching out to be held and soon returning to their play. The "avoidantly attached" children showed apparent independence and autonomy, playing with toys and exploring the room, but lacked interest in their mothers' comings and goings and ignored their return. Observations of interactions between mothers and avoidant children revealed that these mothers were rejecting and discouraging of their children's attachment needs, especially when these children expressed distress, or were overly controlling and intrusive. The avoidant style seemed to be a strategy for protecting children against painful feelings of rejection and intrusive behaviors by their caregivers. Avoidant children did show consistent interest in exploratory behaviors, but attachment behaviors were minimal. However, studies examining cortisol production (obtained through children's saliva) revealed an interesting discrepancy. Although these children did not show obvious interest in the mothers' comings and goings, their cortisol levels increased when the mothers left the room or returned, indicating that emotional needs were present but camouflaged. Ainsworth and her collaborators concluded that avoidant children have learned to hide their longing for attachment and bonding because of their frustrating experiences with their mothers (Ainsworth et al., 1978).

Unlike avoidant children, those with an "anxious-ambivalent" style demonstrate a heightened attachment system but little interest in exploratory activities. These children attend to their mothers' every move, becoming very distressed when they leave the room. Such children are also not easily soothed when their mothers return, responding to the reunion with ambivalent behaviors that include both reaching out to their mothers to be held and pushing their mothers away. Ambivalent children do not show interest in exploratory behaviors away from the mother and display clinginess and hypervigilance over their mothers' every move. Observations of these children's interactions with their mothers revealed mothers who were inconsistently attentive to their children; at times, they were emotionally available and attentive, but at other times, absent and distracted. Such children have developed a strategy to gain their mothers' attention in any way possible. They are intently focused on their mothers' moods and behavior, at the cost of their developmental need for exploration and autonomy.

Through the Strange Situation experiment, Ainsworth et al. (1978) demonstrated the singular importance of the infant's efforts to maintain proximity with a primary caregiver. The child uses the caregiver as a secure base for exploration of unfamiliar environments and flees to the attachment figure as a safe haven during stressful times (Main, Goldwyn, & Hesse, 2002).

Attachment Disorganization and Infant Research

Following Ainsworth, Mary Main and Judith Solomon identified an additional attachment style, which they called "disorganized" (Main & Solomon, 1990). This style was characterized by the child's contradictory behavior patterns and included the following: attachment behaviors that alternated with avoidance, freezing or dazed behaviors, and interrupted movements and expressions. Main and Solomon also identified indications of apprehension in the parent, including the parent's turning or running away and hiding, and disorganization or disorientation in the child, such as the child's wandering, seeming confusion, dazed expression, or rapid changes in affect (Hesse, Main, Abrams, & Rifkins, 2003; Lyons-Ruth & Jacobvitz, 2009). It was found that disorganized behavior in an infant was rooted in fear—either fear of the caregiver or the infant's perception that the caregiver is fearful of the child. Main et al. (2002) observed that certain caregivers' behaviors stimulated disorganized behavior in the child. These behaviors include threatening posture, facial expression, and movements; frightened behavior, such as retreat and backing away from the infant; dissociative behaviors, such as freezing; timid or deferential behaviors; and intimate or sexualized touching and disorganized behaviors, which match the disorganized behaviors observed in the child (Lyons-Ruth & Jacobvitz, 2009). It is important to emphasize that these behaviors were frequently unconscious and stemmed at times from unresolved trauma or loss in the parent's own childhood.

Lyons-Ruth and Jacobvitz (2009) further observed that a significant number of disorganized children suffered abuse and neglect or that the mothers of these children had themselves suffered unresolved loss or trauma. As suggested above, fear plays a major role in the child's response. The child's fear of the caregiver might stem from such behavior as bizarre expressions and movements, hovering too close to the child, or frowning. However, the disorganized child might also perceive the caregiver as being frightened of the child (e.g., when the caregiver backs away or seems timid and anxious around the child, when the caregiver fails to provide a safe haven for the child) (Liotti, 2004). Based on their observation of children and mothers' interactions, Main et al. (2002) developed scales to identify frightened or frightening parental behaviors. These scales include threatening, frightened, dissociative, timid or deferential, sexualized/romanticized, and disorganized behaviors (Hesse, 2009).

In their infant studies, Lyons-Ruth et al. (2006) identified two subgroups of disorganized mother-infant dyads. These are the helpless-fearful dyad (mothers who project anxiety and fear) and the hostile-intrusive dyad (mothers who demonstrate overly intrusive and role-reversing behaviors, such as mocking and teasing, that lead to an unregulated increase in attachment behaviors) (Diamond, 2004). Longitudinal studies with disorganized children show that they express more anger and aggression than secure, avoidant, or ambivalent children (Lyons-Ruth & Jacobvitz, 2009). In disorganized children at 6 years of age, two behavioral patterns were observed: controlling/caregiving behaviors and controlling/punitive behaviors (Moss et al., 2004, cited in Lyons-Ruth & Jacobvitz, 2009). "Disorganized controlling" children exhibit punitive, hostile behaviors toward the parents, ordering them around and humiliating them. "Disorganized caregiving" children demonstrate caring behavior to show that they are preoccupied with the parents' well-being (Hesse, 1999). The latter group has been identified as disorganized in infancy (Diamond, 2004). Although mothers of disorganized caregiving children portray a merger-like relationship with their children, mothers of disorganized controlling children describe themselves as helpless. One mother stated, "I feel him in my space . . . and I think he does too. . . . I might just put out my hand and suddenly he's holding my hand . . . without looking" (Solomon & George, 1999, p. 19).

These infant observations show that the mother's unresolved trauma directly affects the child's disorganized response and contributes more generally to a disorganized attachment pattern in such a child. When Main et al. (2002) and Hesse (1999, 2009) correlated adult attachment patterns from the AAI with children's attachment styles in the Strange Situation, they found that the majority of disorganized children (84%) had a parent with an unresolved/disorganized style, suggesting that attachment trauma is transmitted from parents to children.

Attachment-based trauma is linked to several relational disruptions in childhood. Separation is especially traumatic for young children who do not understand the concept of time and temporary separation and experience the separation from their primary caregiver as an abandonment. Threatened abandonment, therefore, can cause deep anxiety in young children who do not understand the concept of temporary separation or literal truth versus threats. When a caregiver dies, this is universally experienced as an abandonment by infants and young children and may lead to the loss of both physical and emotional security. Finally, the experience of abuse and neglect confronts children with an impossible relational dilemma: The caregiver on whom they are physically and emotionally dependent and who is supposed to love and protect them is also the source of pain and threat.

Beebe (2005) and Tronick (1977, 1998, 2002) showed that nonverbal signals from caregivers can easily become overstimulating. Based on her split-screen, moment-to-moment observations, Beebe (2005) demonstrated how caregivers' facial expressions and movements, such as finger pointing, tickling, and intense gazing, can be frightening and distressing to very young infants. In these situations, infants typically respond by avoiding direct eye contact, turning their heads, and finally crying. These nonverbal communication patterns may lead to coping strategies of withdrawal, dissociation, or disingenuous responses designed to please the caregivers. Slade (2009) demonstrated how children learn to present a "false self" in a video she produced. In the clip, a baby attempts to smile when his adolescent mother hovers too close to his crib and makes frightening faces. Although the mother's intent is to make her baby smile, the baby appears quite terrified though fearful of revealing how scared he really is for fear that the mother will retaliate. When the video was later shown to the mother, she was surprised at how frightening her expressions appeared and was then able to verbalize the child's inner experience and recognize her lack of attunement. Through such observational experiments, Slade trained teen mothers to improve their maternal skills and become more attuned to their babies' internal states of mind.

In his observational experiments with the "still face," Tronick (1977) demonstrated how infants become highly upset when their caregivers show a lack of responsiveness to their cues. During the experiment, the caregiver is required to maintain a flat expression regardless of whether the infant smiles or is distressed. Consequently the infant becomes increasingly more upset as attempts to receive an empathic and mirroring response from the parent are frustrated. These observations show that from an early age, the reciprocal attunement between a child and the caregiver is instrumental in the child's development of self-regulation and self-soothing capacities. Attunement and mirroring also enable the child to recognize his or her affective experiences as well as others' states of mind.[1]

Affect Regulation and the Impact of Early Trauma

Studies with infants show that they develop some capacity for self-regulation early on. This capacity is enhanced through mutual interactions with caregivers, who provide affect regulation to children through verbal and nonverbal behaviors such as cooing, smiling, holding, and other soothing behaviors. Caregivers can either enhance and amplify children's affect or contain and help diminish infants' distress. Adults' soothing and regulating functions are eventually adopted and internalized by children, who learn to soothe and regulate their emotional reactions. However, children whose caregivers are themselves misattuned and unregulated will not have appropriate models and, in consequence, will not learn to regulate their affects.

---

[1]Tronick's experiments will be elaborated on later in this chapter.

They may learn to regulate via withdrawal and dissociation or through puni-tive or aggressive behavior toward others. Such behaviors may include hit-ting, biting, head banging, and later self-harming behaviors or interpersonal violence. As stated above, disorganized children were found to be more aggressive than secure, avoidant, or anxious ones.

Based on his research with infants and their mothers, Tronick (1977, 1998, 2002) elaborated on the dyadic nature of mutual regulation within the child-parent dyad. Tronick's understanding of mutual regulation was influenced by Sander's theory of dynamic systems and the self-regulatory developmental model (Nahum, 2000). Dynamic systems theory helps us to organize observa-tions of stages of interactions between infants and their mothers, starting from concrete behavioral responses and evolving to the infants' efforts to exercise greater initiative and agency in their behavior and to move from behavioral interchange to affective regulation and more complex inner experiences. In their own observational research, Beebe and colleagues (2000) found that secure mutual interactions between mothers and infants are characterized by novelty and flexibility in the process of change and development. However, they note that at one end of the developmental spectrum are highly rigid infant-mothers dyads that evince high mutual dependence and attachment whereas at the other are loosely attached dyads in which infants and mothers appear unresponsive to one another (Beebe et al., 2000). These infant-mother dyads also correspond to the ambivalent-preoccupied and the avoidant-dismissive attachment categories in the AAI.

To examine the mutuality in mother-infant interactions, Tronick and his collaborators developed a "still face" experiment (Tronick, 1977) wherein they observed how infants respond to their mothers' lack of facial responsive-ness. Tronick's infant participants are seen to be trying hard to elicit their mothers' responses, then turning away, again looking back, and finally with-drawing. Tronick hypothesizes that infants will try everything in their power to restore a homeostatic affective balance by eliciting their mothers' respon-siveness and that this homeostatic balance represents a dyadic collaboration between infants and mothers. Such interpersonal dyadic regulation is as important as internal regulation, and the two correspond with one another. Tronick (1998) described an interactive sequence in which the infant pulls the mother's hair, the mother then frowns, and the infant responds by releasing her. Eventually, the mother approaches again with a playful smile, and the infant smiles as well. This interaction suggests that the infant is able to intuit the mother's affective response and react to it with an affective response of his or her own rather than just imitating the mother. Further, it demonstrates mother-infant attunement and mutual regulation. In effect, infants seem to adjust their behavior to repair a state of misattunement.

The cycle of disruption and repair has enormous importance in infant development. Parents' abilities to recognize their own misattuned behaviors and to adjust them or acknowledge these dysjunctions to their children are critical in repairing attachment ruptures. Such efforts also serve to enhance children's sense of agency and security. Through incremental disruption-repair cycles, children learn to deal with frustrations and to recognize difference. Ongoing interactions of this kind between mothers and children contribute to the deepening complexity and sophistication of infants' regulatory systems.

In a related research study using video microanalysis, Beebe and her colleagues (Beebe, 2005) describe how infant self-regulation develops in the context of bidirectional regulation with mothers. From birth, infants show a remarkable capacity to self-regulate through alternating cycles of connection and withdrawal. Beebe (2005) noted that gazing is an important nonverbal signal and that infants alternate between face-to-face play with their mothers and looking away to regulate their arousal. They also learn to turn their heads in a chase-and-dodge sequence with their mothers, an action that is also designed to reduce arousal[2] and engage in facial matching and vocalizing with mothers, who, if they are well attuned, can help build up positive affects and decrease infants' distress. Beebe found that interactive regulation occurs on a continuum, with one extreme characterized by excessive mutual monitoring and the other by withdrawal. These two extremes also appear to parallel anxious-ambivalent and avoidant attachment styles. Such interactions between infants and mothers are designed to regulate emotional arousal and overstimulation through autonomous and dyadic interactions.

Although avoidant and anxious adults may not have experienced the level of trauma linked to the disorganized pattern, they have not developed a sense of felt security based on ongoing affective experiences with their caregivers. Instead, their internal working models are based on a lack of security at times of threat, separation, or loss and/or ongoing experiences that reflect misattunement, rejection, and intrusiveness by caregivers. Two main self-regulation strategies were found in insecurely attached people: hyperactivating and deactivating responses. Hyperactivating patterns were found in those people whose caregiving was from preoccupied, inattentive, or anxious parents who failed to respond to normal signals from the child. In consequence, the child coped by adopting an anxious-ambivalent pattern. Deactivating responses were found in those people whose caregivers were characterized by distancing, rejection, or hostile responses. In this case, the child learned to suppress the need for attention and bonding, ultimately developing an avoidant pattern (Mikulincer & Shaver, 2009).

Studies with secure, avoidant, and anxiously attached adults show that avoidant people attempt to regulate themselves by deactivating their attachment system. They learn to minimize and defend against experiences of threat, separation, and loss in order not to appear needy and vulnerable.

---

[2]*Chase and dodge* refers to a mother's efforts to establish eye contact with her infant; the infant, who experiences this as intrusive, either averts her or his gaze or turns his or her head away from the mother.

Their self-esteem depends on their ability to overappraise themselves to mask their insecurity and vulnerability. Anxious people, however, tend to exaggerate experiences related to threat, separation, and loss and to heighten their affective responses in consequence. They also tend to exaggerate their sense of helplessness and vulnerability and to undervalue themselves. Secure people, on the other hand, appraise themselves realistically and see events and experiences in a realistic manner. Their self-esteem is stable and based on the capacity to admit vulnerabilities, and they also reveal a capacity to adapt to and manage difficult situations (Mikulincer & Shaver, 2009).

Mentalization and the
Impact of Early Trauma

Fonagy and his collaborators (Jurist, Slade, & Bergner, 2008) adopted the concept of mentalization from French psychoanalysts, who had observed a lack of ability to symbolize mental states in some of their patients. In their studies of young children, Fonagy et al. (2002) found that mentalization was not an innate capacity but rather a learned skill based on interactions between children and caregivers, findings that have now been validated by neuroscience and infant research (Beebe & Lachmann, 2002; Coan, 2009; A. Schore, 2003). Mentalization, therefore, is based on mutual interactions between children and parents. Mentalization occurs when parents model to their children how to identify and articulate their affects and cognitions so that their children can learn to identify them and communicate them to others. It also includes children's capacity to read others' states of mind and emotional cues and respond to them empathically. Fonagy suggests that the capacity for mentalization is compromised in many people who have experienced early trauma. Problems with mentalization in young children who have suffered maltreatment manifest in their preference for less symbolic and dyadic play, their lack of empathy for others, poor affect regulation, difficulty in referring to internal mental states, and difficulty understanding emotional (facial) expressions (Fonagy & Bateman, 2008, p. 19).

The process of mentalization develops gradually. Fonagy and Bateman (2008) termed the initial stage "psychic equivalence," in which children mistake their internal states of mind and fantasies for objective reality. For example, Fonagy and Bateman wrote that fear of monsters may translate into the child's belief that a real monster is actually lurking beneath the bed. In this state of mind, children, as well as adults who have difficulty mentalizing, do not differentiate between internal and external reality and have difficulty accepting the validity of opposing perspectives and alternate points of view. The second stage is termed "pretend play." In this stage, children exclude external reality, and their play, both solitary and collaborative, becomes their reality. This state of mind entails dissociation and the fragmentation of inner reality from an external context. Although pretend play is important in developing social skills, creativity, and fantasy life, it may also result in pathological dissociation and the avoidance of external reality (Fonagy & Bateman, 2008; Fonagy et al., 2002).

A parent can help a child move from psychic equivalence and pretend play to the mature stage of mentalization by participating in and mirroring the child's play and fantasy while at the same time providing a relationship rooted in external reality. This promotes the child's capacity to differentiate between self and other and to link pretend activities with external reality (Slade, 2008). Based on their own research and that of others (Sroufe, Egeland, & Kreutzer, 1990), Fonagy and his associates (2002) found that a child with a secure attachment also shows good mentalization capacities. Fonagy et al. (2002) noted that "pretending requires a mental stance involving the symbolic transformation of reality in the presence of and with a view to the mind of others" (p. 48). The caregiver represents external reality but also mirrors the child's internal states without burdening him or her with the caregiver's own subjective needs and affects. Fonagy and colleagues (2002) also noted that verbal communication from the parent to the child and the parent's ability to discuss his or her own mental states and verbalize the child's mental states facilitates reflective functioning in the child.

Children who experience abuse or neglect may develop internal representations of being bad, incompetent, and unworthy or beliefs in a threatening world and dangerous others. These children may then develop psychic equivalences of a frightening, unsafe world in which they are constantly threatened, which mirrors their internal reality, or they may withdraw to a dissociated internal world cut off from external reality, the pretend mode, to create a protected space. Such children also have difficulty interpreting social cues and communication signals from others. They have trouble interpreting others' emotional states and the impact of their behavior and communication on others. Their ability to form accurate, empathic responses is therefore compromised, and they typically project and displace their own affect states onto others. This creates a distorted view of others and of the nature of interactions with them. For example, they may perceive others to be threatening or themselves to be unworthy, damaged, and unlovable. Fonagy and Bateman (2008) suggested that secure attachment is a "practice space" for children to develop mentalization skills because they feel safe in the context of a relationship with a trustworthy caregiver. Secure attachment between children and parents is therefore important for the development of mentalization. Children who experience a traumatic attachment relationship do not have the safety to develop more integrated and symbolic mentalization skills or to build neurobiological structures that form the basis for cognitive and emotional development. According to Fonagy and Bateman, the lack of availability of a secure attachment in the very early years may therefore lead to long-term vulnerability from which it may be difficult to recover (Fonagy & Bateman, 2008).

Abused children find themselves in the dilemma of having to depend on the threatening parent or on the parent who cannot validate or protect them. They do not have a mirroring, safely attuned Other to help them experience and identify their thoughts and affects or to help them differentiate between their state of mind and those of others. Instead, they may have to develop dissociative functions to protect themselves, or they may internalize the abusive and/or nonvalidating parent as a part of their own self-representation to create some sense of self in the absence of an empathic, mirroring caregiver (Fonagy & Bateman, 2008).

Fonagy and Bateman (2008) suggested that BPD develops as a result of deficits in the mirroring and validating responses of others. Most individuals with this disorder have experienced early childhood abuse; this, in turn, has led to distortions in their perceptions of their own mental states and those of others, particularly when they are angry and distressed. As their relationships become more intimate and intense, their accuracy in perceiving their own experience and the experiences of their partners diminishes. Based on a number of studies (Levy, 2005), some using the AAI as a measurement scale, BPD has been strongly linked to insecure attachment and is also associated with disorganized attachment (Fonagy & Bateman, 2008). Individuals with BPD have seriously compromised mentalization functions, ultimately leading to "diffused identity, experience of inauthenticity, incoherence and emptiness, an inability to make commitments, disturbances of body image and gender dysphoria" (Fonagy & Bateman, 2008, p. 141). When emotionally aroused, people with BPD tend to misread their own states of mind and the internal states of others. Children who lack sufficient mirroring by early caregivers would tend to see caregivers "as part of [their] self representation" (Fonagy & Bateman, 2008, p. 142). Such individuals present with psychic equivalence, or a concrete thought process and the inability to consider perspectives other than their own.

Marsha Linehan developed a model she termed "dialectical behavioral therapy" to work with individuals suffering from BPDs. This model is based on cognitive-behavioral therapy and a mindfulness-based approach to treatment, includes a team approach with individual and group modalities, and aims to teach patients affect regulation, self-acceptance, and effective social skills (Linehan, 1993a, 1993b). Dialectical behavioral therapy has demonstrated positive outcomes in treating such patients. More recently, Fonagy and Bateman (2008) developed a mentalization-based, psychodynamic approach for BPD. Their treatment model emphasizes the clinician's attunement and mirroring as well as the gradual building up of a secure base with BPD patients to allow for the introduction of alternative points of view. The model deemphasizes interpretation inasmuch as this psychodynamic technique is deemed inappropriate for patients with severe personality disorders, who may perceive such therapeutic communications as critical and controlling. The clinician's job is to help patients transition from a rigidified, brittle internal structure in which self and other are experienced as being all good or all bad and where alternative views do not exist to a more flexible mode of perception of self and others in which limitations and failures are an acceptable part of ongoing relationships. This development allows for a more flexible and adaptive response to interpersonal conflicts and to other stressful events.

The mentalization-based treatment model considers trauma as well as other contextual sources of personality disorder, such as lack of validation, family chaos, loss and separation, multiple caregivers, neglect, and substance abuse. Fonagy and Bateman (2008) emphasized that "it is less the fact of maltreatment than a family environment that discourages coherent discourse concerning mental states that is likely to predispose the child to BPD" (p. 145). They suggested that such individuals, who possess rigid cognitive structures, cannot benefit from traditional insight-oriented therapy, because they have problems with behavioral and affective dysregulation that requires a more structured approach at times (similar to Linehan's [1993a, 1993b] model of dialectical behavioral therapy). They noted that clinicians must strive for a balance between stimulating the attachment system to assist clients in negotiating intimate relationships and not overstimulating clients to the point of disorganization. In addition, clinicians must promote patients' capacity for mentalization. Common features of the treatment include clinicians' providing patients with a clear treatment structure, enhancing patients' compliance, providing a clear focus for the treatment, encouraging attachment between therapist and patient, and finally integrating individual treatment with other treatment modalities and services.

The Impact of Trauma on Adult Attachment

Following Ainsworth et al.'s (1978) development of the Strange Situation, Main et al. (2002) developed the AAI, a questionnaire designed to analyze an adult's state of mind in relation to attachment, separation, loss, and trauma. The AAI includes questions about the responder's early relationships related to these attachment experiences and his or her reflections on and perceptions of these early experiences. Two indicators Main et al. used to analyze a respondent's transcript were (a) the nature of early relationships described by the respondent, and (b) the states of mind related to these early experiences. Qualities seen to represent an autonomous-secure attachment style include coherence, collaboration (with the interviewer), truthfulness, and focus. The AAI is a research instrument rather than a clinical tool, and it relies on the analysis of written transcripts alone rather than behavioral and nonverbal cues, which are commonly assessed in clinical practice. Metacognition, or reflective functioning, is one of the hallmarks of a secure-autonomous attachment style, and it demonstrates the capacity for insight, reflection, and empathy.

Main et al. (2002) suggested that there are three aspects of metacognition: (a) the ability to see beyond surface appearances; (b) the ability to recognize changes in the self over time; and (c) the ability to recognize and accept differences between self and others. Metacognition or reflective functioning is the capacity to think and reflect on one's mental processes in relation to self and others. In addition to metacognitive skills (as revealed through the AAI interviews), the attributes of the secure-autonomous personality are the capacity

- to maintain a coherent view of one's life and history,
- to accept limitations and imperfections in the self, and
- for empathy for and forgiveness of others despite difficult life experiences.

Put differently, these attributes are the capacity to be self-reflective, empathic, flexible, yet integrated. Main and colleagues (2002) observed that a secure attachment style can be "earned" through positive relational experiences later in life, including the therapeutic process. Therefore, insecure attachment patterns, including the dismissive and preoccupied patterns, are not necessarily fixed but can change over time in response to environmental factors (e.g., a loving marital relationship, mentoring, or a good therapeutic experience). Difficult childhood experiences, therefore, are not the sole determinant of personality style.

In addition to the secure-autonomous category, Main et al. (2002) identified two attachment categories, the "dismissive" and the "preoccupied." The dismissive style is characterized by the respondent's superficial narrative and poor or stereotypical description of childhood experiences and caregivers, such as "I had a wonderful childhood" or "My mother was like all mothers." These adults seem uncomfortable in discussing attachment-based and emotional experiences, have poor insight, and seem to be detached from their feelings. They lack early memories and are either dismissive of their caregivers and attachment experiences or show superficial idealization of them. Dismissive people have been found to have rejecting, emotionally constricted, or intrusive caregivers. Consequently, they have learned to mask their unmet needs and avoid potential disappointments through emotional distancing and pseudoautonomy. They are wary of intimate relationships and tend to have concrete ways of perceiving and communicating their experiences.

Preoccupied adults tend to present with discursive and tangential narratives. They show intense emotional engagement with childhood experiences and caregivers, usually by expressing anger or providing vague, confusing memories on the AAI. They seem not to have developed a sense of self sufficiently individuated from their parents and family of origin. The early experiences of preoccupied people are fragmented and unresolved, and typically they present as needy, dependent, and emotionally labile. Whereas the dismissive style correlates with narcissistic and schizoid personality disorders, the preoccupied attachment pattern correlates with BPD (Blatt & Levy, 2003).

Main et al. (2002) found that the unresolved/disorganized category due to a loss or trauma can accompany any of the above three primary attachment patterns. Although individuals can show autonomy and security overall, they may demonstrate disorganization and lack of resolution in relation to a specific experience of loss or trauma. Unresolved attachment is characterized by sudden changes in speech patterns, disbelief in the death or abuse, and identification with the dead person or with the perpetrator (e.g., these respondents may believe that the dead or abusive person is living inside them). Unresolved/ disorganized individuals may also express a sense of responsibility for the loss or trauma, which is clearly irrational, and possess other irrational beliefs associated with the loss or trauma. They may also provide an extraordinary amount of detail in regard to the event, as though it were intercurrent even if the death or abuse occurred many years ago (Hesse et al., 2003; Main et al., 2002). As stated previously, individuals with an unresolved attachment style may be secure in other areas of their lives, and they typically present with another primary attachment category such as dismissive or preoccupied. It is useful to remember that such individuals are unresolved only in regard to a particular experience of loss or trauma. The personality may not be affected more generally. Symptoms of unresolved patients are similar to symptoms of posttraumatic stress disorder (PTSD) patients, except that the unresolved style is in relation to attachment disruption whereas PTSD concerns other kinds of traumatic events or experiences.

The AAI adult attachment patterns correlate with children's attachment styles in the Strange Situation. For example, the autonomous style correlates with the secure attachment style in children, the preoccupied category correlates with the ambivalent-resistant style, and the dismissive pattern correlates with the avoidant attachment style in children. Whereas the Strange Situation attachment styles are based on behavioral observations, the AAI relies on subjective memories and on the participants' reflections/interpretations. As a result, it possesses considerable clinical utility, especially with psychodynamically based treatment focusing on childhood experiences, the acquisition of insight, and internal, subjective, and often unconscious processes.

It is not clear whether the AAI has been utilized with minority populations or with participants from lower socioeconomic strata. To date, it appears that a majority of research respondents are college students and that most come from middle-class households. In some poor and/or minority communities including African American, Latino, and Native American, it may not be the norm to discuss childhood experiences, disclose one's negative perceptions of parents, or discuss experiences of loss and trauma. In such patient communities, it may take a long time to develop trust, especially with outsiders from a different class, race, or ethnicity (such as the AAI researchers). It is also possible, therefore, that the AAI is culturally biased in favor of middle-class, educated respondents, who may be more articulate and familiar with a process of self-reflection and who tend to be more trusting of strangers.

Contributions of Neuroscience to the Understanding of Trauma

Neuroscience has made important contributions to our understanding of the impact early attachment disruptions have on brain development as well as the cognitive, emotional, and behavioral sequelae of such disruptions. Studies show that the impact of trauma on brain structure is quite significant. The brain is composed of three interdependent sections: the brain stem and hypo-thalamus, primarily associated with the regulation of internal homeostasis; the limbic system, which helps maintain the balance between the internal world and external reality; and the neocortex, which is responsible for ana-lyzing and interacting with the external world. The brain's right hemisphere is involved in nonverbal emotional apprehension and expression, such as tone of voice, facial expression, and visual spatial communication, and is linked to the amygdala, which regulates autonomic and hormonal responses to incoming information. The left hemisphere mediates verbal communica-tion and organizes problem-solving tasks. Failure of left-hemisphere func-tions may occur during states of extreme arousal (e.g., during traumatic experiences) and is believed to be responsible for experiences of derealiza-tion and depersonalization, mental states of mind associated with acute posttraumatic stress (van der Kolk, 2003).

Studies with people who suffer chronic PTSD have shown that the struc-ture of the brain changes as a consequence of traumatic experience. For example, the hippocampus decreases in volume, which suggests problems in the absorption and processing of information that has its origin in the traumatic experience (van der Kolk, 2003). This may signify an ongoing dissociation and misinterpretation of information, resulting in aggressive reactions, withdrawal, and perceptions of events as threats—which are com-mon symptoms of PTSD.

A study in which participants were exposed to the narrative of a traumatic experience demonstrated increased activity only in the right hemisphere, especially in the amygdala where emotional arousal takes place, but there was a significant decrease in activity in the left hemisphere, where interpretation and verbal communication of experiences occur (Rauch et al., 1996, cited in van der Kolk, 2003). High levels of activity in the amygdala may mean inter-ference with the hippocampus functions of evaluation and categorization of information. The consequence of such failures is that the traumatic experi-ences do not become unified and integrated.

One of the major functions of the prefrontal cortex is the regulation of emotions. The right hemisphere is responsible for absorption and processing of emotions through the limbic system, particularly the amygdala, and attends to nonverbal aspects of experience. The left hemisphere, on the other hand, processes emotional arousal, categorizes it, and eventually incorporates it into narrative and language (Coan, 2009). The process of affect regulation occurs both through interaction with the caregiver who helps soothe and provide safety and security to the child and through the internalization of what Bowlby (1973) called "internal working models." The child uses such internal representations of the caregiver to help soothe and regulate arousal. These mental representations exist in both procedural (unconscious) and declarative (conscious) memories. Siegel suggests that

the human mind is a process that regulates patterns in the flow of two elements, energy and information. This flow can occur within one brain or two or more brains, so that mind is created in the interaction between neurophysiological processes and interpersonal relationships. (2003, p. 9)

Procedural memory, which includes emotions, intuition, and fantasy, resides in the right hemisphere and develops through nonverbal interactions between infants and their caregivers. Schore and Schore (2008) suggested that "the mutual regulations between infant and caregiver promote the development and maintenance of synaptic connections during the establishment of functional circuits of the right brain" (p. 11). The left hemisphere, in which explicit (or declarative), linear logical, semantic (factual), and autobiographical (episodic) memory resides, develops through verbal interactions between children and caregivers at a later date (J. Schore & Schore, 2008). Schore and Schore noted that the development of the right brain, which occurs earlier than development of the left brain, "contributes to the development of the emotional self embedded in implicit intersubjective affective transactions" between infant and caregiver (p. 12). These interactions are primarily visual.

Siegel (2003) applied complexity theory to brain development, noting that the developing brain moves toward increasingly complex states, and to the regulation of states of activation through both internal and external constraints. The minds of two individuals become linked as a single adaptive and flexible system that is both highly integrated and highly differentiated to create maximal complexity. In a disorganized attachment, the child shows poor differentiation from caregiver interactions, and the parent is unable to perceive distress or provide regulatory functions to the child. Avoidant-dismissive child-parent dyads are characterized by loose linking and a high level of differentiation but little integration. In contrast, flexibility and integration are characteristics of securely attached child-parent dyads. Such dyads can thereby facilitate, absorb, and survive a wide range of stressful situations and traumatic experiences. Brain structure, affect regulation, personality style, and interpersonal skills are all greatly influenced by early traumatic experiences and attachment disorganization.

Summary and Implications for Treatment

Attachment theory has principally been utilized in research protocols until recently. Within the past decade, attachment principles have been applied to interventions with maltreated children (Marvin, Cooper, Hoffman, & Powell, 2002; Slade, 2008) as well as to the improvement of parent-child interactions that may otherwise lead to insecure and disorganized attachment styles. As stated previously, Slade (2009) described her work with young unwed mothers who are not aware that their intrusive behavior may be interpreted as frightening to their children. After showing the mothers videos of their interactions with their babies, the mothers are able to recognize the impact their behavior has on the children and can begin to understand and empathize with the children's inner experience. Other attachment concepts, including affect regulation, the development of a secure base, and the impact of such attachment security/insecurity on later development are the basis for contemporary psychodynamic models. These models include contemporary self psychology, intersubjectivity, and relational theories. Lessons from attachment theory and infant observation also have contributed to the treatment of trauma. It is now recognized that an important aspect of the clinical process with traumatized patients is stabilization and affect regulation. In effect, clinicians must help clients to develop strategies for self-soothing and self-regulation, en route to the development of more stable and securely based interpersonal relationships. The treatment of complex trauma, in particular, requires that patients and clinicians understand the nature of childhood traumas and their impact on patients' cognitive, affective, and behavioral symptoms as well as on their interpersonal relationships. With the return of combat veterans from two intercurrent wars in Iraq and Afghanistan, PTSD has become a national problem in the United States. Its problems are frequently complicated by the soldiers' earlier traumatic experiences. Such preexisting traumas may exacerbate combat-related symptoms and require longer psychosocial treatment as well as short-term exposure techniques, which are not intended to address developmental and contextual factors.

Another attachment-based model is emotion-focused therapy (EFT), a treatment approach that has been used with combat veterans and their spouses as well as with couples struggling with traumatic histories (Johnson, 2002; Johnson & Courtois, 2009). The principles on which EFT is based are that attachment needs constitute the primary motivation for couples and that attachment bonds provide a natural regulatory system essential for human emotional survival. Johnson (2002) postulated that dependency needs should not be viewed as pathologically based (i.e., through the lens of Western cultural norms); rather, dependency needs constitute universal and normative human needs. Another EFT principle is that secure attachment allows the child, and later the adult, to look to the primary attachment figure for help in regulating overwhelming affects and for the provision of love and support during times of distress. Having a secure attachment history helps people to achieve greater success in intimate relationships; individuals with secure attachment histories are also more flexible, open, and likely to seek closeness at times of crisis. In contrast, insecure and disorganized attachment histories may lead to "demanding, controlling and pursuing roles in adult relationships" (Johnson & Courtois, 2009, p. 375), and those with avoidant histories may become dismissive adults who utilize strategies of withdrawal and distancing from their partners.

Critical elements of the EFT model include assessment of potential violence in the relationship, investigation of the impact of PTSD on each partner's behavior (e.g., self-harm, substance abuse, and other individual safety issues), and education regarding the nature of traumatic stress and its impact on the individual and on the couple. The therapeutic bond is of primary significance in the treatment. Interventions include a focus on partners' emotional experiences and their expression (especially marginalized emotions such as sadness and fear rather than anger) and increasing the capacity for openness and vulnerability between partners. The EFT clinician helps partners to reach out to one another for emotional support and encourages them to respond sensitively and empathically to one another's distress and intimacy needs.

These clinical models utilize attachment principles to provide treatment for traumatized individuals and families and provide a link between (a) empirical findings of attachment theory and infant studies and (b) clinical practice. For attachment-based clinicians, it is important to keep in mind that insecure attachment patterns, such as children's avoidant, anxious-resistant, and disorganized and adults' dismissive, preoccupied, and unresolved patterns, intensify when attachment disruptions occur. It is during times of distress that habitual attachment strategies that are designed to protect against separation, abandonment, and rejection become more strongly manifested. Attachment-based practice helps patients by providing a secure base with their therapists and by helping patients process their fear and anger related to past relational disruptions as well as empathic disruptions with their therapists. The hope is that these patients will learn that other, more flexible strategies are now available for them to resolve these disruptions and to maintain and deepen important relational bonds.

References

Ainsworth, M., Blehar, M., Water, E., & Wall, S. (1978). *Patterns of attachment.* Hillsdale, NJ: Lawrence Erlbaum.

Beebe, B. (2005). Mother-infant research informs mother infant treatment. *Psychoanalytic Study of the Child, 60,* 7–46.

Beebe, B., Jaffe, J., Lachmann, F., Feldstein, S., Crown, C., & Jasnow, M. (2000). Systems models in development and psychoanalysis: The case of vocal rhythm coordination and attachment. *Infant Mental Health Journal, 21*(1/2), 99–122.

Beebe, B., & Lachmann, F. (2002). *Infant research and adult treatment: Co-constructing interactions.* Hillsdale, NJ: Analytic Press.

Blatt, S., & Levy, K. N. (2003). Attachment theory, psychoanalysis, personality development and psychopathology. *Psychoanalytic Inquiry, 23*(1), 102–150.

Bowlby, J. (1960). Grief and mourning in infancy and early childhood. *Psychoanalytic Study of the Child, 15,* 3–39.

Bowlby, J. (1963). Pathological mourning and childhood mourning. *Journal of the American Psychoanalytic Association, 11,* 500–541.

Bowlby, J. (1973). *Attachment and loss: Vol. 2. Separation.* New York: Basic Books.

Coan, J. (2009). Towards a neuroscience of attachment. In J. Cassidy & P. Shaver (Eds.), *Handbook of attachment: Theory, research and clinical applications* (pp. 249–268). New York: Guilford.

Diamond, D. (2004). Attachment disorganization: The reunion of attachment theory and psychoanalysis. *Psychoanalytic Psychology, 21*(2), 276–299.

Fonagy, P., & Bateman, A. (2008). Mentalization based treatment of borderline personality disorder. In E. Jurist, A. Slade, & S. Bergner (Eds.), *Mind to mind: Infant research, neuroscience and psychoanalysis* (pp. 139–166). New York: Other Press.

Fonagy, P., Gergely, G., Jurist, E., & Target, M. (2002). *Affect regulation, mentalization and the development of the self.* New York: Other Press.

Harlow, H. (1958). The nature of love. *American Psychologist, 3,* 673–685.

Hesse, E. (1999). The adult attachment interview: Historical and current perspectives. In J. Cassidy & P. Shaver (Eds.), *Handbook of attachment: Theory, research and clinical applications* (pp. 395–433). New York: Guilford.

Hesse, E. (2009). The adult attachment interview: Protocol, method of analysis and empirical studies. In J. Cassidy & P. Shaver (Eds.), *Handbook of attachment: Theory, research and clinical applications* (2nd ed., pp. 552–598). New York: Guilford.

Hesse, E., Main, M., Abrams, K., & Rifkin, A. (2003). Unresolved states regarding loss or abuse can have "second generation" effects: Disorganization, role inversion and frightening ideation in the offspring and traumatized non-maltreating parents. In M. Solomon & D. Siegel (Eds.), *Healing trauma: Attachment, mind, body and brain* (pp. 57–106). New York: Norton.

Johnson, S. (2002). *Emotionally focused couple therapy with trauma survivors: Strengthening attachment bonds.* New York: Guilford.

Johnson, S., & Courtois, C. (2009). Couple therapy. In C. Courtois & J. Ford (Eds.), *Treating complex traumatic stress disorders: An evidence-based guide* (pp. 371–390). New York: Guilford.

Jurist, E., Slade, A., & Bergner, S. (Eds.). (2008). *Mind to mind: Infant research, neuroscience and psychoanalysis.* New York: Other Press.

Levy, K. (2005). The implications of attachment theory and research for understanding borderline personality disorder. *Development and Psychopathology, 17*(4), 959–986.

Linehan, M. (1993a). *Cognitive behavioral treatment of borderline personality disorder.* New York: Guilford.

Linehan, M. (1993b). *Skills training manual for treating borderline personality disorder.* New York: Guilford.

Liotti, G. (2004). Trauma, dissociation and disorganized attachment: Three strands of a single braid. *Psychotherapy: Theory, Research, Practice, Training, 41*(4), 472–486.

Lyons-Ruth, K., Dutra, L., Schuder, M., & Bianchi, I. (2006). From infant attachment disorganization to adult dissociation: Relational adaptations or traumatic experiences? *Psychiatric Clinical North America, 29,* 63–86.

Lyons-Ruth, K., & Jacobvitz, D. (2009). Attachment disorganization: Genetic factors, parenting contexts, and developmental transformation from infancy to adulthood. In J. Cassidy & P. Shaver (Eds.), *Handbook of attachment: Theory, research and clinical applications* (pp. 666–697). New York: Guilford.

Main, M., Goldwyn, R., & Hesse, E. (2002). *Adult attachment scoring and classification systems.* Unpublished manuscript, Regents of the University of California.

Main, M., & Solomon, J. (1990). Procedures for identifying infants as disorganized/disoriented during the Strange Situation. In M. Greenberg, D. Cicchetti, &

E. M. Cummings (Eds.), *Attachment in the preschool years: Theory, research and intervention* (pp. 121–160). Chicago: University of Chicago Press.

Marvin, R., Cooper, G., Hoffman, K., & Powell, B. (2002). The circle of security project: Attachment based intervention with caregiver pre-school child dyads. *Attachment and Human Development, 4*(1), 107–124.

Mikulincer, M., & Shaver, P. (2009). Adult attachment and affect regulation. In J. Cassidy & P. Shaver (Eds.), *Handbook of attachment: Theory, research and clinical applications* (pp. 503–531). New York: Guilford.

Nahum, J. (2000). An overview of Louis Sander's contribution to the field of mental health. *Infant Mental Health Journal, 21*(1/2), 29–41.

Schore, A. (2003). Early relational trauma, disorganized attachment and the development of predisposition to violence. In M. Solomon & D. Siegel (Eds.), *Healing trauma: Attachment, mind, body and brain* (pp. 107–167). New York: Norton.

Schore, J., & Schore, A. (2008). Modern attachment theory: The central role of affect regulation in development and treatment. *Clinical Social Work Journal, 36*(1), 9–20.

Siegel, D. (2003). An interpersonal neurobiology of psychotherapy: The developing mind and the resolution of trauma. In. M. Solomon & D. Siegel (Eds.), *Healing trauma: Attachment, mind, body and brain* (pp. 1–56). New York: Norton.

Slade, A. (2008). Mentalization as a frame for working with parents in child psychotherapy. In E. Jurist, A. Slade, & S. Bergner (Eds.), *Mind to mind: Infant research, neuroscience and psychoanalysis* (pp. 307–334). New York: Other Press.

Slade, A. (2009). The implications of attachment theory and research for adult psychotherapy. In J. Cassidy & P. Shaver (Eds.), *Handbook of attachment: Theory, research and clinical applications* (pp. 762–782). New York: Guilford.

Solomon, J., & George, C. (1999). The place of disorganization in attachment theory: Linking classic observations with contemporary findings. In J. Solomon & C. George (Eds.), *Attachment disorganization* (pp. 3–32). New York: Guilford.

Sroufe, A., Egeland, B., & Kreutzer, T. (1990). The fate of early experience following developmental change: Longitudinal approaches to individual adaptation in childhood. *Child Development, 61*, 1363–1373.

Tronick, E. (1977). The infant's capacity to regulate mutuality in face to face interaction. *Journal of Communication, 27*, 74–80.

Tronick, E. (1998). Dyadically expanded states of consciousness and the process of therapeutic change. *Infant Mental Health Journal, 19*(3), 290–299.

Tronick, E. (2002). A model of infant mood states and Sandarian affective waves. *Psychoanalytic Dialogues, 12*(11), 73–99.

van der Kolk, B. (2003). Posttraumatic stress disorder and the nature of trauma. In M. Solomon & D. Siegel (Eds.), *Healing trauma* (pp. 168–195). New York: Norton.

PART II

Clinical Applications With Selected Populations

6

Art Therapy With Traumatically Bereaved Children

Laura V. Loumeau-May

Art therapy is effective in the treatment of traumatized client populations. As a nonverbal, sensory-based, enactive modality with narrative and symbolic potential, art making within a therapeutic relationship accesses aspects of trauma experiences that have evaded verbal processing. Brain research supports art therapy as a treatment to promote hemispheric integration—linking the verbal with the nonverbal. Specific techniques developed by art therapists include the Instinctual Trauma Response to work with posttraumatic stress disorder (PTSD). Losing a parent is traumatic for children, even when it is anticipated. When death is sudden and violent, as by accident, suicide, or murder, actual trauma is intensified, and this complicates the grieving process. Art therapy in grief work with children is the focus of this chapter. The author provides case examples from her work at Journeys, a youth bereavement program in northern New Jersey; these illustrate art therapy benefits in healing traumatizing aspects of loss. Also included is discussion of her experiences working with children who suffered the loss of parents in the World Trade Center terrorist attacks of 9/11.

The Use of Art Therapy With Populations Affected by Trauma

Art has long functioned as a response to trauma. While she was confined at the Czech concentration camp Terezin during the Second World War, Friedl Dicker-Brandeis taught children drawing and painting, activities that sustained them (Potok & Volavková, 1993). Japanese Americans placed in relocation camps in the 1940s processed their experiences through art (Gesensway & Roseman, 1987). Globally, children's artwork provides testament to the horrors of war (Geist & Geist, 2002). Communities erect ad hoc public shrines subsequent to the deaths of figures such as Princess Diana or tragedies such as 9/11 (Santino, 2006).

Art therapy, a profession with roots in psychiatry, has been effective in treating trauma for more than 30 years (Stember, 1977). Many traumatized populations have been helped by art therapy, including burn and accident survivors (Chapman, Morabito, Ladakakos, Schreier, & Knudson, 2001; Mallay, 2002; Martin, 2008; Russell, 1999; Wald, 1989), victims of natural disasters (Chilcote, 2007; Lacroix et al., 2007; Orr, 2007; Roje, 1995), veterans (Collie, Backos, Malchiodi, & Spiegel, 2006; Lande, Tarpley, Francis, & Boucher, 2010; Morgan & Johnson, 1995), and rape victims (Amir & Lev-Wiesel, 2007; Cross, 1993; Kaufman & Wohl, 1992; Pifalo, 2002, 2006, 2007, 2009; Serrano, 1989; Spring, 1993, 2004).

Following the 1994 Los Angeles earthquake, Roje (1995) noted that art therapy "enabled children to express internal processes which they had no verbal awareness of and facilitated working through the defenses in order to identify underlying conflicts which hindered recovery" (p. 243). After 3 months all the children had healed, except those who had preexisting trauma history. Collie et al. (2006) outlined the advantages of using art therapy with combat veterans experiencing PTSD. Benefits include the following:

- reconsolidation of implicit and declarative memories,
- progressive symbolic exposure to stimuli perceived as threatening,
- externalization and distancing of trauma narrative through visual form,
- reduction of arousal through the relaxing effects of art making,
- reactivation of positive emotion to counteract the numbing of trauma,
- enhancement of emotional self-efficacy, and
- improved self-esteem.

Pifalo conducted studies to evaluate the use of art therapy with sexually abused children (2002, 2006). She used the Brief Trauma Symptom Checklist for Children to measure symptoms before and after a 10-week art therapy group and conducted a follow-up study 4 years later. Both studies demonstrated a reduction in sexual abuse–identified symptoms subsequent to intervention. Spring (2004) conducted a 30-year study of the graphic forms created by sexually abused women. Specific recurrent imagery was linked with documented experience of sexual assault. Other studies supported that using the Chapman Art Therapy Treatment Intervention, which was designed for "incident-specific, medical trauma" reduced acute stress symptoms (Chapman et al., 2001, p. 101).

Factors Unique to Art Therapy That Address Trauma

Areas of the brain that handle speech and cognition shut down during a traumatic event. Recalling events through words is difficult, but sensorial memory is strong and flashbacks often occur. Flashbacks are primarily visual and are triggered by specific sensory cues (see Figure 6.1).

Figure 6.1   Media coverage of the 9/11 attacks was constant. For the families of the victims, the sound or sight of an airplane could trigger flashbacks to the event.

Art making enables a victim to represent his or her experience by externalizing it into a concrete form (see Figure 6.2).

This object then enables the victim to describe the traumatic event through words, transforming the visual and sensorial memories. A young client was haunted by the visual memory of her dead grandmother's gnarled hands when she and her mother discovered the body. She struggled to get this image out of her mind. Molding it in clay helped her overcome fear so that she could begin to process the loss of her grandmother. Tapping into visual recall should be handled cautiously by a trained art therapy professional with expertise in understanding the power of emergent imagery. One person may struggle to remember events clearly so as to heal through acknowledging the experience, whereas another may be emotionally overwhelmed by recall. Timing is essential and varies among clients according to their developmental levels and the strength of their defenses. Caution must be exercised not to encourage this process prematurely; however, in some cases, recall is encouraged. Steele (2002) described a boy who blocked memory of the night his sister was raped and murdered. A year later he was demonstrating negative behavior with poor emotional and academic functioning. Using a series of drawings to re-create the tragic events, his therapist was able to unblock the memory and get the boy on the path to recovery.

Figure 6.2   One way to review the impact of a traumatic memory is to create a visual representation of it. In this "before and after" picture, a young girl shows how the 9/11 attacks took her father from her.

Art making is sensory based. It utilizes visual, tactile, kinesthetic, and often olfactory and auditory sensations. It is a physical process involving motion, pressure, and rhythm to stimulate or to calm. Consider the difference between ripping or cutting and blending and smoothing; these activities can both reflect emotion and evoke it. Art materials can be cold, wet, sharp, soft, sticky, rough, or smooth; they evoke sensations that trigger sensory-related memories that can be pleasant or negatively charged. Steele and Raider (2001) attributed art-making's ability to access sensory memories to the fact that it is a psychomotor activity. With cases involving bodily trauma, such as physical abuse, the kinesthetic-sensorial aspect of working with art materials is particularly potent.

During creative activity, the artist is continually responding not only to internal images and feelings but also to the impact of embodied imagery as it develops in the artwork in progress. It is common for art therapy clients to rethink, change, or redo an image based on responses to its physical manifestation. Art making is a symbolic and metaphorical re-creation of experience; this is especially so with young children who constantly change an image as they tell a story with it. A drawing may begin as a representation of a beautiful day that dissolves into rain but then shines again as the sun reemerges and flowers blossom. Adolescents and adults are also affected by creating an artwork; the product may be so emotionally laden that they destroy, transform, or discard it. I have previously described the experience of Rachel, a 10-year-old girl who intended to make a mask to represent the face of her father, a victim of 9/11 (Loumeau-May, 2008). While she was painting it, some of the red-orange pigment used to re-create her father's hair color accidentally mingled with the coral pink she used for his flesh, evoking associations of fire, scarring, and burning. In response to this startling unplanned visual occurrence, the child discarded her original intention of creating a portrait and used the paint instead to portray burned flesh and mud burying the lower half of her father's face. The horrific image represented one of many possible scenarios of how he may have died. The art-making process in this case was cathartic (see Figure 6.3).

Figure 6.3   Reacting to the evocative sensorial impact of the red, orange, and brown paints running into each other as she created a portrait mask, Rachel, whose father died on 9/11, changed her plan, instead depicting a burned face partly covered with mud.

To retain such images, once created, is something that clients often are not comfortable with. To do so may actually be retraumatizing. The opportunity to create toxic images and then discard them, termed by Schaverien (1992) the "Scapegoat Transference," can be experienced as cleansing.

The Expressive Therapies Continuum, created by Kagin and Lüsebrink (1978) and further developed by Hinz (2009), is a conceptual model for understanding art dynamics and use of media. A familiarization with the Expressive Therapies Continuum broadens the clinician's appreciation of art's therapeutic potential. The model analyzes four therapeutic levels of art making: kinesthetic/sensory, perceptual/affective, cognitive/symbolic, and creative. The kinesthetic level primarily utilizes motor discharge. Sensory exploration of materials grounds kinesthetic discharge and leads to the ability to form images. The perceptual level is externally focused and mediates relationships with the outside world. The affective level represents emotional involvement with expression. This can deepen and enrich the art-making process or can overwhelm, leading to regression. The cognitive level involves structured, intellectually focused, nonspontaneous work, such as visual problem solving. The symbolic level is characterized by intuitive work and metaphor. This may augment therapy by amplifying the client's interpretation of personal experience. If defenses are worked through by repeated symbolic confrontation, transformation of their emotional value can occur (Lüsebrink, 1990). This stage is usually original and expansive, similar to Schaverien's (1992) definition of the embodied image, wherein works created often have an evocative power and may defy verbal exploration.

The imagery basis of art therapy is powerful and evocative. Images have emotional impact and re-create experiences imagined or real. They operate on both symbolic and abstract levels. One image may encompass a multitude of actual, implied, or potential meanings, including conscious and unconscious intent. An image shows what the client planned and can indicate what the client is not yet ready to explore. The art product is a tangible record that can be revisited at various times during therapy to reexamine its meaning and glean whatever insight it may contain. The image is now an external concrete form that distances it from the creator, thereby providing potential for objectivity and detachment. The client can contemplate it. This empowers the healing process; the client is no longer controlled by the image but is in control of it.

Creative engagement is active rather than passive; the client is doing and making something that requires intent, planning, action, and appraisal. The enactive aspect of the creative process empowers the creator (Steele & Raider, 2001). Clients are imaging, learning, and practicing actions that relieve anxiety, improve self-esteem, and enable them to visualize themselves functioning in the context of transformed lives and worldviews. According to Buk (2009), "on both physiological and psychological levels, the bodily and life-affirming activities of the artist making art can remediate the feelings of helplessness, passivity, and annihilation experienced during the trauma" (p. 62). Creating an actual product encodes the image more effectively than using words or mental rumination alone.

Enactment can precede and stimulate remembrance. Embodied simulation, linked with the mirror neuron system, enhances the artist's ability to symbolically re-create experiences and the observer's ability to empathize with images produced and their emotional content (Buk, 2009). Through companioned viewing, acknowledgment, and containment of dissociated memory images and metaphoric response, the art therapist assists in recall, recognition, and reintegration of intolerable affect-laden memories. In addition to the production of recognizable images, production of nonfigurative symbolic art directives such as mandalas, circular designs that have both a calming effect and symbolic potential for psychic integration, is frequently used in art therapy and has resulted in significant reduction in PTSD symptoms (Henderson, Mascaro, & Rosen, 2007).

Finally, the use of art enhances the narrative aspect of trauma recovery. Although the story can be told with words alone, it is enriched and embodied in visual and material form. It can be presented directly in chronological order as it occurred or indirectly through allegory if the victim is not ready for the former. Moreover, various alternative endings can be considered until the client is able to accept the reality of actual events. Art expression and play therapy techniques such as sand tray and puppetry are not merely play; they provide enactment opportunities to master and transform traumatic experience.

For example, 7-year-old Clara was eagerly awaiting the birth of her baby brother. She came with her mother to the last prenatal visit, where she anticipated seeing the baby's sonogram and hearing her brother's heartbeat. Unfortunately this joyous opportunity did not go as planned. The baby's heartbeat was not present, and the sonogram revealed that he had died in utero. Magnifying Clara's own alarm was her mother's sudden and intense grief reaction. In therapy Clara made frequent use of medical play equipment, including an IV pole, an X-ray machine, an electrocardiogram machine, and a code alert. Puppets and baby doll patients were used to re-create that doctor visit over and over again. Sometimes she cast the therapist as her mother, sometimes as the doctor. Consistent with the psychoanalytic concept of repetition compulsion, Clara re-created the traumatic event repeatedly. However, she revised the ending several times, starting with a scenario in which she undid the original outcome and rescued her brother. The therapist's dramatic mirroring helped her work through closer approximations to the actual event until she reached the point where she had played out the emotional impact of the loss and had grown to accept the reality of her brother's death and her mother's grief.

Another child, Alan, age 9, created time machines in drawing, painting, and clay. He imagined going back in time to prevent his father from committing suicide. After many such symbolic creations, he was able to let go of this fantasy, stating that he realized that unless he could be with his father every minute of every hour, he would not be able to prevent the suicide from happening. He understood that the locus of control was with his father and not himself.

How Trauma Affects the Brain

People who have suffered traumatic events are often unable to express in words the details of their experience. Alexithymia, the inability to understand, describe, and process emotions, couples with posttraumatic dissociation, a disruption in conscious thought or psychological functioning. According to Lester, Wong, and Hendren, "it is hypothesized that patients with PTSD have difficulty restructuring recollections of traumatic histories due to the decreased activity of Broca's area, an area responsible for language processing and higher cognitive functioning" (2003, p. 264). There is a suppression of function of the hippocampus during traumatic experience (van der Kolk, 2006). According to Buk (2009), "this leads to context-free, fearful memories and associations of the trauma that are encoded in implicit, sensorimotor form, are difficult to locate in place and time, and are therefore often impossible to verbally articulate" (p. 62).

Neuroimaging research findings by Jakowski, de Araújo, de Lacerda, de Jesus Mari, and Kaufman (2009) indicate that permanent structural changes to the brain, notably in prefrontal/frontal lobe volumes, as well as alteration in neurotransmitter systems have been found in chronically maltreated children. This implies that early repeated trauma may lead to permanent brain changes associated with psychopathology such as depression. Early neglect and deprivation can result in impairment to the limbic system and critical neuronal cell death, linked with future aggressive behavior and affective dysregulation (Schore, 2003). Rapid increase of dopamine under discrete or prolonged stress can cause DNA mutations in brain tissue.

Art Therapy and the Brain

Benefits of treating trauma victims with art therapy are reinforced by recent findings in neuroscience and psychology (Hass-Cohen & Carr, 2008). Techniques in neuroimaging, specifically functional positron emission tomography and magnetic resonance imaging methods, illuminate our understanding of how different tasks and structures of the brain process information (Lüsebrink, 2004). In a 1996 study, Rausch et al. reported that during victims' exposure to scripts of their traumatic experiences, brain scans of victims displayed arousal in the right hemisphere, particularly the amygdala, concurrent with a lack of left-brain activity in Broca's area (Tripp, 2007).

Brain research supports art therapy as a treatment that promotes hemispheric integration, linking the verbal with the nonverbal functions while containing affect (Gantt & Tinnin, 2009). Right-hemisphere activity is fully operant from birth. It affects the way implicit memory is stored by the brain, responding to and organizing incoming sensory experience. Early secure attachment is optimal for emotional development as well as for maximizing left-brain development and cognitive functioning. Even when verbally accessible, all explicit memories are retrieved through sensory and visual imagery associations. Implicit sensorial memories are processed by the amygdala in the right hemisphere before being sent to the hippocampus for storage and retrieval through explicit means.

By using visual and somatosensory processing, art therapy treats trauma symptoms with directives that reach areas of the brain that elude explicit thought. When an art therapist asks a victim to create an image, the visual representation supersedes words to portray events and emotions. Art making activates the nonverbal (right) brain to reveal the pain and provide a foundation for the verbal (left) brain to express and externalize the traumatic experience, thereby reducing dissociation and alexithymia and generating cognitive and symbolic aspects of memory. Images reveal traumatic experiences and can be described, providing insight to how the experiences have affected thoughts and behavior, thus leading to mental, emotional, and physical healing (Lüsebrink, 2004). With this approach, the trauma victim is able to recontextualize to make the events addressable and promote health and well-being.

Six Art Therapy Protocols Developed for Managing Trauma

The following are specific trauma-focused approaches developed by art therapists.

1. B. Cohen and Cox (1995) proposed a model based on drawing content and style for recognizing and understanding the imagery produced by clients with dissociative identity disorder. These clients experienced prolonged, continual, sexual, and physical abuse during childhood, usually by primary caregivers on whom the victims were dependent. Ongoing abuse is distinct from single-incident trauma in that hyperarousal symptoms are amplified as a result of the continual repetition of trauma (Herman, 1992). These victims' adaptation strategies, such as dissociation, persist long after the abuse has ceased and are more difficult to recover from.

The integrative approach developed by B. Cohen and Cox (1995) for analyzing artwork focuses on structural elements of visual communication. The dissociative identity disorder model lists 10 picture types: system, chaos, fragmentation, barrier, threat, induction, trance, abreaction, switching, and alert. Artwork in each category corresponds to clients' psychological or behavioral states. Identifying the category drawings, especially when repeated, deepens clients' understanding of their experiences and can point toward appropriate therapeutic interventions that will help integrate personalities that have become dissociated.

2. Appleton (2001) created the Art Therapy Trauma Intervention and Assessment Paradigm, which identified four progressive stages (impact, retreat, acknowledgment, and reconstruction) that adolescents recovering from burn traumas experience. Her model can be applied to other forms of trauma. These stages support clients as they cope with initial regression, damage to body image, loss of function, and the need to reconstruct world views.

For each stage Appleton (2001) identified psychological issues, therapeutic goals, and art and graphic features that typically emerge. During the impact stage, burn patients experience shock, depersonalization, disbelief, and the pain associated with their burns. Spontaneous art making is encouraged; clients may tell the trauma story indirectly through metaphor. Relaxation techniques help clients cope with pain and anxiety. Art directives related to the trauma that may lead to catharsis are avoided at this stage as they cause retraumatization.

The retreat stage is characterized by resistance and development of defenses as full consciousness of the permanent effects of the trauma emerges. The therapeutic goal is to build alliance through support. By helping patients use art materials, the therapist assists victims to develop coping mechanisms as well as trust. Encouragement of free exploration of imagery is more effective than the use of directives, which may be met with superficiality or resistance. More success is achieved with nondirective work wherein clients have choices and autonomy.

As patients express painful feelings, including anger, the acknowledgment stage has been reached. Their comfort level with the therapist through art making becomes a foundation for treatment. During this stage, active mourning happens, and clients are able to use media for expressing feelings and exploring issues related to the loss. If clients do not explore these spontaneously, relevant directives to facilitate exploration may be employed. Clients are capable of sustaining longer periods of focus on art making and will create more complex pieces.

In the reconstruction stage, clients integrate coping skills and insights and begin to accept life changes. This stage is marked by a search for the meaning of the trauma and the establishment of new directions in life. More complex directives and projects are possible. Patients are able to review life's changes stemming both from the loss and from internal growth that they are now handling. Memorial projects are appropriate, as are directives such as timelines that help clients view life from different perspectives.

3. Rankin and Taucher (2003) provided a task-focused plan for addressing the psychological needs of trauma and recommending appropriate art therapy directives that focus on recovery. These directives deal with goals of safety planning, self-regulation, trauma narrative, grieving trauma-associated losses, self-concept, worldview revision, self-development, and relational development. Structured collage and writing techniques identify physical and psychic dangers while establishing safety plans early on; these offer cognitive control. Soothing art tasks such as the creation of mandalas, bodywork, and visualization are skills that will help clients regulate intense emotions and become grounded during flashbacks. Trauma narrative, essential to recovery, is encouraged when clients feel ready. Integrating imagery into storytelling activates sensations, emotions, and cognitions of the actual trauma, aiding recall. Narration is structured to provide closure through media or ritual, minimizing negative effects. Extensive trauma or loss may be divided

into segments to prevent overwhelming clients. The final stage involves revising clients' worldviews and concepts of self. A sense of continuity of the self following trauma is achieved through projects such as lifelines. Reframing techniques will help clients acknowledge self-growth resulting from processing trauma.

4. Goodman (2004) used an art therapy protocol that integrated cognitive-behavioral and client-centered approaches when working with families victimized by 9/11 at New York University's Child Study Center. The cognitive-behavioral approach used structured interventions to address trauma-related affects in specific ways. Self-regulating techniques such as systematic relaxation supported gradual exposure to traumatic events during personal narrative. These techniques helped children manage their anxiety both in and outside the therapy sessions. The client-centered aspect of treatment incorporated active listening techniques and acceptance, which addressed the individual needs of the client; clients themselves determined the content and direction of therapy. Combining both approaches has strengths in the treatment of traumatic grief: The first focuses on the trauma quickly, providing concrete skill-building techniques, and the second is gentler, respects clients' defenses, and increases self-determination.

5. The instinctual trauma response, a method developed by Gantt and Tinnin (2007), analyzes typical reactions to trauma and provides a task-oriented treatment using imagery to process the trauma narrative. This method helps resolve dissociation as well as victim mythology. Human responses to trauma are similar to the survival strategies animals use when attacked, namely,

- startle,
- thwarted intention,
- freeze,
- altered state of consciousness,
- body sensation,
- state of automatic obedience, and
- self-repair.

Clients draw "graphic narratives" to narrate each of the seven stages, beginning with a "safe place." In this way, they bring implicit memory into conscious awareness. This series of drawings includes before and after pieces that frame the traumatic experience within the context of clients' ongoing lives. Bilateral stimulations such as the butterfly hug, a tapping on both arms while they are folded, are used to enhance the visual and verbal process. It is only when the complete narrative is integrated sequentially with a beginning, middle, and end that closure can be brought to the trauma. The unification of memory fragments into a coherent story is made possible by the sensorial images that enhance the re-creation of subjective experiential states; through their externalization and representation they become accessible to explicit memory. Once the narrative is complete, treatment works to resolve dissociation. An effective technique is to film a video dialogue. The symbolic act of creation inherent in art making or ritualistic play is instrumental in rewriting "victim mythology" into a reempowered view of self in which trust in personal safety is restored. Viewing the videotapes is evidence to clients as they view themselves in a new light.

6. McNamee (2003, 2004), Talwar (2007), and Tripp (2007) have developed bilateral stimulation techniques based on eye movement desensitization and reprocessing that they combine with art making to transform traumatic memory. These processes stimulate memories from both sides of the brain and promote integration. McNamee directs clients to draw alternately with their dominant and nondominant hands in response to the processing of emotions and conflicts that they themselves identify. Talwar intensifies the aesthetic sensory experience by using paint rather than drawing and combines this with the physical stimulation of standing and moving around the room to select colors during the art making. Tripp has clients create scribble drawings of emotions and cognitions related to traumatic memories while wearing headphones that produce bilaterally alternating tones, music, and sounds as well as pulsating devices placed under each knee. The art therapist carefully monitors and processes the resultant images with the clients; recommended subsequent images build on emerging feelings or are based on a cognitive restructuring of events and perceptions.

Developmental Issues in
Processing Parental Loss in Children

By the age of 15, 5% of American children have experienced the death of a parent. Anticipated loss and traumatic loss are both traumatic due to developmental and dependency factors. Parentally bereaved youth are at risk for psychological disturbance, health problems, poor academic performance, increased delinquency, and lower self-esteem. However, with support, most develop coping skills and do not suffer long-term psychological impairment (Dowdney et al., 1999; Sandler et al., 2003; Silverman, Nickman, & Worden, 1995; Thompson, Kaslow, Price, Williams, & Kingree, 1998).

Grief is experienced differently at each stage of growth. Although they do not yet have the ability to encode this information explicitly, infants undergo emotional trauma if there is a change in their primary caregivers. Depending on the severity of the remaining parent's grief and the availability of alternate caregivers, the death of one parent during a child's infancy can cause significant disturbance to the relational bonding critical to early brain development and hemispheric integration. Infants and toddlers may exhibit regression in feeding, regression in toileting habits, sleep disturbances, and clinging behavior. Until about age 5, most children do not understand that death is permanent. Some may expect the deceased parent to be fixed by God and sent back to them. Focus and attention spans are limited; brain structures are not developed sufficiently to self-regulate. Younger children will exhibit extreme distress one moment and cheerfulness the next. This can lead caregivers, who are grieving themselves, to believe that the children are not affected.

From ages 5 through 7, school-aged children have greater social exposure. They identify as part of an intact family and compare themselves to peers as a measure of normality. Their understanding of death is incomplete. For instance, children of this age may grasp the concept of permanency yet retain magical thinking regarding what causes death or whether it is contagious. Despite increasing ability to negotiate the world outside their homes, they are still quite dependent and necessarily egocentric about how the death will affect their lives. They may display regressive tendencies such as fear of sleeping alone. Somatic symptoms may mimic those of the deceased parent.

From 7 to 11 years, children become scientific in their reasoning. They will express interest in the biological, moral, and spiritual aspects of death. However, grief may take the form of forgetfulness and inability to concentrate in school. Because they understand its finality, they are more capable of realizing that death can happen to anyone—and therefore display fear for themselves and their remaining parent. As they approach adolescence, their ambivalence about sharing feelings and receiving comfort versus being mature and independent increases. Children's peers are often very supportive, even curious, immediately after the death, but then they quickly want their friends to be their "normal" selves again. Occasionally bereaved children and adolescents will switch friends, seeking out others who have experienced loss and therefore understand.

Teens who lose parents are in more danger of becoming "parentified," that is, assuming some duties of the deceased parent. This gives them responsibility and provides support for the surviving parent. Yet this premature adulthood belies their emotional vulnerability and incomplete maturity. Teens are more capable of risk-taking behavior and may act out in dangerous and self-destructive ways. Promiscuity may offer a false sense of intimacy, or substance abuse may numb emotional pain. Rebellion against parental authority is a developmental norm. However, to lose a parent during this stage deprives teens of the opportunity to resolve normal defiance and distancing, leaving them with unresolved relational issues and guilt. The handling of intense emotions is challenging, and defense against regressive dependency becomes even stronger.

Secondary losses, such as the financial impact death has on the family and the redistribution of parenting roles, compound grief for all ages. A stay-at-home parent may have to return to work; another may have to hire caregivers. The energy level, stress, and emotional availability of the remaining parent are compromised in the early stages of grief. Family routines such as meals and bedtimes change. Children may go into after-school care for the first time. Rules, expectations, and approaches to discipline will be different. Homes may be sold; children may have to move in with extended family, forcing them to change schools and distancing them from their peer support network.

Anticipated Versus Sudden Grief

Responses to debilitating terminal illness and death contain aspects of trauma. These responses vary according to the developmental stage of the child. Anthony (1973) discussed fear of abandonment in the young child. He suggested that parental relationships have rooted, mirrored, protected, and defined the child. The younger the child, the more his or her existence is based on connection with the parent; emotional and physical needs must be met for survival. When one parent is ill, typically both are absent; one may be in the hospital being treated while the other is visiting or transporting the ill parent. Despite the provision of alternative caregivers, the child feels abandoned. This is exacerbated by the child's sense of the anxiety that the adults are experiencing.

Many aspects of an illness itself are potentially traumatic to children. Most significant are the physical and behavioral changes in the parent resulting from illness or its treatment. These include weight and hair loss, memory loss, vomiting, falls, the results of surgery, and others. Children and teens are often physically repulsed by these changes and feel guilty about not wanting to touch the sick parent. Younger children may believe that touching their parent will cause harm, or they may fear contagion. Children also have fears associated with the treatment their parent is undergoing. One 5-year-old boy had repeated nightmares, envisioning his father being chained to the wall of a cave with a vampire approaching while at the same time a laser beam was pointed at his father's head. This child was afraid to talk about his dream until after he had sketched a picture of it. The therapist then asked him to tell what happens at the doctor visits. Johnny described how his father would have a blood test and then get radiation therapy. The therapist reflected to Johnny that maybe his father's treatment was even scarier than knowing he had cancer, an illness Johnny did not yet fully comprehend. Johnny was able to acknowledge his fear that certain medical procedures were making his father sick.

Older children and teens understand the permanency of death and the implications of a cancer diagnosis more fully. When the diagnosis is revealed to them, it traumatically shatters their assumptions of a secure family life and a continuing relationship with the ill parent. One 12-year-old girl used a photo-collage to depict such a moment. She placed a picture of two girls sitting on a couch (as she and her sister had been when told the news) inside the open mouth of a shark to convey the devastating impact that the news had on her. In addition to trauma experienced or witnessed, children are more apt to vividly imagine unobserved aspects of the trauma. Jennifer, an 8-year-old girl whose mother was scheduled for a mastectomy, drew how she pictured her mother's surgery. The image featured home and hospital side by side, effectively separating mother and daughter, who were each encapsulated within one of the structures. The buildings were similarly sized and mound shaped with point-tipped roofs, colored a brownish-pink, looking like the breasts her mother was about to lose. In the hospital portion of her drawing, the surgeon looked like a magician levitating Jennifer's prone mother while simultaneously raising a blade as if to saw her in half. Younger children may experience magical thinking related to causality and undoing. Some children feel that the noise they made while playing when told not to disturb an ailing grandparent or the fact that they wished they did not have a younger sibling who always got into their toys is what ultimately caused the death. Johnny, cited above, prayed every night that God would give him cancer to take it away from his father. When he developed a benign tumor on his knee, he thought his prayers had been answered.

When a parent's death is sudden, unanticipated, and violent, as in an accident, suicide, or murder, actual trauma intensifies and complicates the grieving process for the child or adolescent. Thompson et al. (1998) noted that studies on grief indicate that the ability to prepare for an anticipated death usually results in improved coping. Additional factors of violence, proximity to danger, and witnessing or discovering death further intensify the trauma, putting children at risk for childhood traumatic grief (J. A. Cohen, Mannarino, & Deblinger, 2006). This is characterized by the coexistence of unresolved grief and PTSD symptoms. It is theorized that the presence of significant PTSD symptoms is more predictive of future psychiatric and behavioral conditions such as substance abuse, major depression, or borderline personality disorder than the parental loss by itself.

When trauma and grief coexist, trauma must be addressed before grieving can begin. It is not unusual for pleasant memories of the deceased to segue into horrific images of the death. This was true in Rachel's case, cited earlier, when her attempt to paint her father's portrait reverted instead into a dreadful image of how he may have died. In traumatic death, external factors such as media coverage, police investigation, and litigation may intrude on the family's life, further traumatizing and delaying the grief process. Survivors of accidents may be hospitalized and have to undergo surgery or other medical procedures. One 10-year-old boy remained in intensive care for 2 weeks after he survived the car accident that killed his mother. Shards of glass remained in his cheeks and chest, painful reminders of both his own survival and his mother's death.

Causality of a violent and sudden death is a complicating factor in traumatic loss. Guilt and blame, typical in the emotional experience of grief, occur even when there is no source for blame. When there is a perpetrator or negligent cause, justification and intensification of blame is multiplied. Accident, homicide, and suicide contain particular complicating aspects that exacerbate the grief process. With accidental death, there is an arbitrariness that defies reason and challenges potential spiritual meaning making for survivors. In the case of homicide, often the perpetrator is known to the victim. This has relational consequences for the grieving family, especially when anger and blame have a valid target such as the other parent on whom the child has also been dependent (Lev-Wiesel & Sampson, 2001). A family environment characterized by anger, violence, and fear may have led up to the murder. The presence of mental illness or family dysfunction further complicates the ability to process grief. Where suicide has been the cause of death, unique factors in the grieving process include self-blame, anger toward the deceased, loss of idealization of the beloved parent, and the experience of stigma and shame (Kuramato, Brent, & Wilcox, 2009). Children whose parents commit suicide may be biologically at a higher risk for mental illness if that was a factor in the parent's suicide. Many are aware of this as they struggle with identity issues following the death. Anxiety related to inheriting bipolar illness from his father was a preoccupation for Alan, cited earlier. Additionally, "these offspring may have undergone considerable emotional distress prior to parental suicide compared to individuals who experienced other types of parental loss" (Kuramato et al., 2009, p. 148).

Death caused by political violence or terrorism entails a wide variety of factors affecting grief. The 9/11 attacks claimed nearly 3,000 lives on a single day. The deaths, which were intentional, extremely violent, and targeted at the entire country, attracted continuous media coverage. All these factors played significant roles in the grief process for surviving family members.

Individual grief was overshadowed by national grief. Every American citizen identified with the attacks and with the victims, and the entire nation mourned the events, which were experienced in a personal way by all Americans. This is one of the reasons for the long-lasting media attention; the country was telling its trauma narrative and searching for meaning in this horrific event. The national focus on the attacks took the sanctuary of privacy away from the families of the victims. They received massive support, sympathy, and resources coupled with multifaceted focus from strangers, curiosity, and even resentment. Additionally, mental health agencies and practitioners were overwhelmed by the sheer number of individuals in need of support. Grieving families, as well as actual survivors who had witnessed friends' and coworkers' deaths, needed counseling. Rescue workers who witnessed the devastation as they searched for bodies needed counseling. Witness survivors in the streets or in neighboring office buildings during the attacks, in schools or offices that had views of the World Trade Center, and those whose televisions were on when the collapses occurred needed counseling. This overwhelming need for support strained existing resources; priority servicing was implemented. First served were the bereaved families of the victims.

The 9/11 attacks and their repercussions introduced unprecedented bereavement challenges, including the use of citizens in planes as weapons, the collapse of the twin World Trade Towers, the witnessing of victims jumping from flaming buildings, the deaths of rescue workers, the lack of bodies of most victims, laborious extended search efforts, and the implied horror of what loved ones may have actually experienced if they had not been killed instantaneously. The parent of one child with whom I worked was able to speak to her husband by phone prior to his death and could hear the agonizing screams of his coworkers before losing connection with him. For those who had no contact, images of violence, suffering, and disfiguration were contemplated verbally and through art making (Loumeau-May, 2008). The public exposure of families' grief was prolonged through media coverage; repeated broadcasts reiterated the traumatic events and the utter hopelessness of the victims' predicament. Children around the country drew images of the attack as a way of working through their trauma (Goodman & Fahnestock, 2002), whereas children of the victims were trying to avoid exposure to those same images.

Using Art Therapy to Tolerate Memories of Actual and Imagined Horror

Traumatically bereaved children are vulnerable to nightmares and flashbacks to aspects of the loss. Teens Andrew and Monique were settling down for the night when their father had a fatal heart attack. Monique had recurring memories of the paleness of her father's face when she ran into his bedroom at the sound of her mother's screams. Visualization techniques coupled with the act of painting this memory helped her to achieve emotional mastery of this image. Her brother Andrew, conversely, was adept at using intellectualization as a defense. He described numbness and depersonalization associated with his loss. Andrew expressed a desire to remember all the details; he did not want to forget what had occurred. After leading him through a relaxation exercise, I used guided imagery to encourage him to remember, instructing him to focus on the sounds, smells, and images he could recall. Andrew then painted a diagram of his home, color coding stick-figure people and objects to re-create the chaotic events of the evening: his sister getting him out of the shower to assist his mother, administering CPR, letting emergency personnel into the home, witnessing their exit with his father's body, and noticing his sister and grandfather huddled together on the couch downstairs. Remembering the details helped him embody the event and reconnect with his emotions.

Another teen, whose mother died of breast cancer, had nightmares of her mother's being trapped in a burning house. The repeated experience of maternal deprivation due to many emergency hospitalizations combined with witnessing her mother's physical deterioration was traumatic for Patrice. Patrice was asked to draw a detailed image of her dream (see Figure 6.4), after which she related aspects of it to observations of her mother's illness and her own emotional reactions.

Figure 6.4 Patrice could not understand why she had nightmares about her mother's being trapped in a burning house after her mother had died. Although anxious, she drew her dream. Aspects of her mother's cancer and her own helplessness were then processed through talking about the picture.

Following this intervention, her nightmares ceased.

Using Art Therapy to Reduce Stress With Relaxation Techniques

Betty, at age 7, had been present when her grandfather died from a heart attack. Both of her parents had demanding job schedules. Her grandparents, who lived nearby, would pick Betty up from school every day and bring her to their apartment, where she would remain until her parents returned from work. On one such day her grandfather lay down on the couch and died in his sleep. Betty's mother monitored her reactions, surmising that she was handling the loss well. Two years later, however, a strong emotional response was precipitated by a Halloween school assignment to write about a scary event in your life. Betty recalled her grandfather's death in detail with a panicked intensity she had not exhibited at the actual death. She no longer wanted to go to her grandmother's home and refused to go on a family vacation with her—in case the same thing were to happen all over again. In therapy, Betty was asked to visualize and draw a situation in which she felt completely safe and happy. She drew a picture of herself and her father holding hands as they walked along the beach. Betty was asked to visualize this scene as she thought about her grandfather's death. She was further instructed to take the drawing home and keep it in her room where she could look at it and think about how safe it made her feel and to practice visualizing it whenever she felt anxious. This technique worked, and Betty was again able to feel safe in the presence of her grandmother.

Johnny's father's brain cancer went into remission for 5 years. However, he had a recurrence and eventually died. In the months prior to the death, Johnny witnessed seizures and falls as the disease progressed. Johnny felt a strong sense of responsibility for his father and was anxious about going anywhere without him. This interfered with his ability to concentrate in school and to take pleasure in peer activities such as overnight scout camp; he was afraid his father would have a seizure and die when he was not there. When he returned to the Journeys youth bereavement program, a primary aspect of his therapy was to help him manage his anxiety in anticipation of his father's death. Two art therapy exercises proved beneficial to him. In one, he was asked to visualize a situation in which he felt safe, relaxed, empowered, and joyful. Johnny created a picture of this visualization—himself playing basketball (see Figure 6.5).

Figure 6.5   Visualization techniques, reinforced by creating actual images, can be helpful in reducing anxiety. In this stamp picture, Johnny uses his favorite sport, basketball, as a metaphor for "dunking" the anxiety related to his father's brain tumor.

His next task was to practice imagining that the basketball represented thoughts about his father's tumor, and whenever he dunked it through the net, those thoughts would disappear. Johnny was advised to try to practice this exercise and to use his internal image whenever he became anxious about his father at school. This was successful in reducing his anxiety. As his father's death grew near, Johnny had sleep difficulties. As another intervention, Johnny helped create a relaxation tape using his own vision: an image of himself floating in his aunt's pool. His mother and therapist recorded his script, enhanced by music, for his use at bedtime.

Using Art Therapy to Build Vocabulary to Connect Sensorial Memories With Words

When traumatic memory is encoded, both memory and affect can be blocked from discursive recall. This is true for many children who witness their loved ones' sudden deaths. Ten-year-old Emma was present when her father collapsed of a heart attack at the top of the stairs. Lynn and her brother Roger witnessed the final seizure that caused their father's death. Douglas was playing with friends in the backyard when his 3-year-old sister fell into the pool and drowned. In each case, creating spontaneous as well as loss-related imagery enabled the child to select words for the visually revealed affect. Douglas avoided discussing or portraying his loss but became obsessed with weather disasters and intrigued by a picture of Stonehenge hanging in the art room. I provided a book titled *Earthworks and Beyond* (Beardsley, 1984), from which he studied and sketched. Using nature elements as a metaphor, he created detailed pictures of earth sculptures, water, and rainstorms. With each, he became increasingly articulate in discussing emotional equivalents to visual metaphors. Finally he was able to draw his most painful memory—his sister as she lay in her coffin.

Emma was restrained in expressing her emotions. The first project she chose in art therapy was to create an inside and outside mask. Most children create the outside first and sometimes avoid painting the inside. Emma started with the inside and carefully layered it with metallic paint, covering the inner features with what resembled a shield (see Figure 6.6).

She then turned her attention to the outer face, reworking initially naturalistic features many times over many sessions, rendering the face increasingly pale, and finally covering it with papier-mâché and repainting it. What was notable in her creative process was the time and effort it took her to seal off the inner and outer surfaces of this face form, as if to prevent emotions or memories from emerging.

Figure 6.6   Emma, who witnessed the sudden death of her father, chose to seal off the interior of her mask before painting the outside, possibly to guard against feeling.

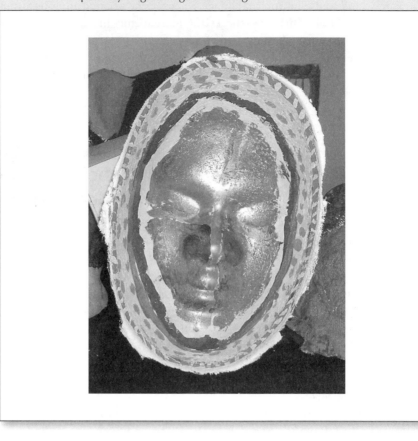

An art therapy exercise I developed that intensifies emotional engagement and potentiates affective expression is the use of tissue paper collage in combination with grief-related music or poetry (Loumeau-May, 2008). Emma, Roger, and Lynn participated in a group in which this technique was used. Emma began her collage in her customary guarded manner but soon became engrossed in ripping, tearing, crushing, and layering tissue paper and adding preprinted lyrics from the songs being played. She initially used bright colors but eventually requested black, adding many splinter-like pieces to her collage. Although it was still difficult for Emma to use her own words, she was able to select lyrics that expressed her pain, including "I won't ever be happy again," which she layered over with black and red tissue paper as if to conceal it (see Figures 6.7 and 6.8).

Through this enactive and multimodal process, Roger also was able to add words to describe his feeling of being forever changed and his loneliness. His sister Lynn never had trouble verbalizing anger. Now she expressed the vulnerability and need to be strong beneath her anger.

Using Art Therapy to Tell the Trauma Narrative

Many art therapy directives help children relate their stories of trauma or loss. Sometimes they will depict the death when they are asked to draw, paint, or sculpt a difficult memory (see Figure 6.9).

Others will avoid or block traumatic memory until they are able to face it. When this occurs metaphoric images can allude to events, or aspects of traumatic imagery may appear in images drawn. Such was the case with many children of 9/11 victims, who, although consciously avoiding the images, unconsciously created plane-like shapes or penetration of buildings.

One boy's father had drowned during Hurricane Floyd when his car broke down and he attempted to walk home in the dark; a dam broke as he was crossing a bridge, and he was swept away by the floodwaters. In the beginning of his bereavement work, David repeatedly drew water images that featured nature as an aggressive, unfriendly force. The images were explored indirectly by discussing the metaphors until he was able to use storyboard format to directly tell the story of his father's death. After he had used this structured format, David was able to talk about the death directly.

Figure 6.8   Emma chose several precut phrases from the songs being played to incorporate in her collage, but she partially concealed some.

Using Art Therapy to Restore Positive Memories of the Lost Object

Children can ascribe damage to the lost parental object when the death has been tragic. This can take several forms: an internalized image of the physical disfigurement experienced by the parent, experiencing the parent as no longer invincible but rather as a victim, or seeing the parent as an unloving monster when the death was self-inflicted. The first and third of the above forms were true in the case of Alan, who felt secure in his father's love and had a normal idealized memory prior to learning that his father had killed

Figure 6.9   Some cannot access words to describe the trauma until they have created images. It was easier for this teen to first sculpt his last memory of his mother grasping her head as she suffered a fatal stroke before he could tell what happened.

himself. Alan struggled with newly ambivalent feelings toward his father before he could grieve. In one drawing he depicted a many-headed grief monster hovering nearby as he prayed at his father's grave. Alan was torn between feeling anger and forgiveness toward his father. Identification with his father was strong. He also identified anxiety about how his loss would ultimately affect the person he would become. A major focus in Alan's therapy, after he had worked through rage, despair, and fear, was reparative work to the memory of his father. His final project was a symbolic still life painting in which he selected objects that had been precious to his father and that represented the memories Alan valued and wanted to retain. This helped him internalize positive aspects of his father's life as well as his love for him.

In contrast, for children who lost parents in 9/11 the damaged memory in the early stages of grief involved the physical embodiment of their parents. The idea that their parents had been burned, crushed, or disintegrated was unfathomable. The use of metallic board in one session suggested mirrors as symbols for viewing the self. This led participants to discuss the fact that they could not remember what their parents looked like just prior to the attacks. They avoided talking about the extreme violence of the death or lack of bodies, both of which compounded the sense of physical destruction. Donald cut out a simple silhouette of a head, neck, and shoulders and without adding features glued it onto a background of white corrugated board (see Figure 6.10).

He said this was a portrait of his father and of himself simultaneously; when he looked into the mirror he could not see either clearly. Such posttraumatic ambiguity demonstrates depersonalization, derealization, identity confusion, and identity alteration—four of the five criteria for dissociation delineated by Steinberg (1997), cited in Amir and Lev-Wiesel (2007). This was exemplified in the image and his understanding of it. Donald would revisit the image of his father several times, coming to terms with his father's death and repairing the internalized damage. He was finally able to create a very different self-portrait in which he combined his and his father's actual images (Loumeau-May, 2008). For many children of 9/11 victims, creating

Figure 6.10   In the absence of bodies, children who lost parents on 9/11 readily imagined violent and disfiguring circumstances of their parents' deaths. Physical connection is part of human bonding. Donald's empty mirror portrait points toward a disconnection that may be a defense against imagining physical damage to his father.

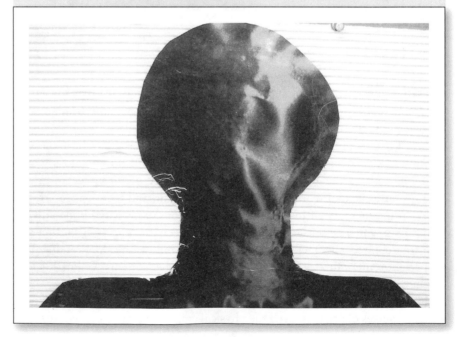

portraits of their deceased parents from photographs was a task that proved helpful in the symbolic restoration of body integrity to memory. Like Alan, Donald also needed to restore his father's image psychologically; he needed to see him again as a hero. This was accomplished through dream exploration, drawing, painting, and bookmaking (Freeman, 2005; Loumeau-May, 2008).

Using Art Therapy to Master Affective Experience Through Action

The creative act is not merely catharsis or release of emotional expression. Its potency lies in mastering and redirecting emotional energy. The act of vicariously and symbolically re-creating authentic affective-laden experience in an art product involves cognition for the planning, construction, and evaluation of the product. Artwork produced within the context of an art therapy session involves communication to the therapist as witness. Internal experience is relived through imaginative recall within a supportive relationship wherein the client's reality is validated. It is transformed and mastered through the ability to portray and share it and the opportunity to distance self from experience afforded by contemplation of the finished product. I have previously compared the art therapy process when used in trauma and bereavement work to Campbell's analysis of the hero's journey (Campbell, 1949; Loumeau-May, 2006). Key features of heroic transformation include a precipitating crisis, deep suffering and questioning, initiative of the hero to search for meaning or reparation, endurance of trials, performance of tasks, companionship, failure (of ego alone) necessitating acceptance of help, and acquisition of treasure (which is usually internal change, insight, or a restructured worldview). This can be considered a model for resiliency. Thus, healing involves a combined ability to endure the pain of reality, accept help, and act by completing grief-related tasks.

Previously cited clinical vignettes in which children depicted traumatic imagery or told the story of the death illustrate this process. In these examples, the creation of the image was instrumental in mastering the affect associated with it. However, facing the pain associated with loss is only part of the heroic journey. Additional grief-related tasks are accomplished through art therapy. Among these are identifying coping skills, evaluating positive family adjustments, symbolically internalizing the strengths of the deceased in revised self-images, and comparing past, present, and future to explore new views of life.

Memorialization projects such as memory boxes, books, or quilts are done toward the end of treatment (see Figure 6.11).

Two and a half years after 9/11, competing architectural plans to rebuild at the World Trade Center site were considered, with the designs aired publically. This provided an opportunity for symbolic closure to children of the

Figure 6.11 A final project that helps children achieve closure is creating a quilt together. In this 9/11 memorial quilt, participants added details with fabric marker and paints to squares they had already designed with cut fabric. One girl is showing how she will grow from a child to an adult. Art therapy intern Tamara Bogdanova led this project.

victims. The children had successfully managed and contained traumatic images, had worked through grief issues, had restored positive memories of deceased parents, and were adjusting to the transformation of their lives. As a final project they discussed the plans and then created their own models. Most preferred to design memorial gardens on the grounds where their parents had died. One young girl indicated that the fact that so many of their loved ones had died there had sanctified the ground. One year earlier these same children had explored the horror of the obliteration of their parents' bodies (Loumeau-May, 2008). Few would have an opportunity to visit the deceased at a cemetery. The place where their parents had spent their last moments of life was where the children could feel close to their spirits. There was a reverence to the focus and care the children took in constructing their designs. They could do something both symbolic and concrete to honor their parents.

Conclusion

Art therapy is uniquely suited to the treatment of trauma. Although more research is indicated, evidence-based practices and current brain research support its use in accessing memories as well as in regulating affect. Trauma-focused techniques developed by art therapists have been successful. Applied to grief, art therapy is particularly effective. Its advantages include the fact that it is an action-based, sensorially evocative modality with narrative and symbolic properties that bypass and complement speech. Bereavement work with children experiencing traumatic loss, as well as those coping with traumatic aspects of anticipated death, was discussed. Specific treatment applications such as visual desensitization, building expressive vocabulary, symbolic reparation of the damaged object, and narration were highlighted.

When one is working with traumatically bereaved children, the initial goal of treatment should be the establishment of safety and comfort. Soothing art activities that offer control and opportunity for metaphor will help the children use defenses effectively while building confidence. This will later yield to expression of feelings and reworking of the experience of the loss. Creative activity stimulates unconscious imagery and affective arousal. The experienced art therapist will recognize when a client is ready for deeper exploration or if the process, material, or imagery has the potential to overwhelm. The therapist can intervene or help the client manage the affect, avoiding retraumatization. It is in this middle stage that more intense trauma and grief work is accomplished. The final stages of traumatic grief work include strengthening coping skills, memorializing the loss, and establishing new goals and a revised worldview. Creating objects that honor the memory of the deceased is empowering and sustains closure.

References

Amir, G., & Lev-Wiesel, R. (2007). Dissociation as depicted in the traumatic event drawings of child sexual abuse survivors: A preliminary study. *The Arts in Psychotherapy, 34*(2), 114–123.

Anthony, E. J. (1973). Mourning and psychic loss of the parent. In E. J. Anthony & C. Koupernik (Eds.), *The child in his family: The impact of disease and death* (Vol. 2, pp. 255–264). New York: John Wiley.

Appleton, V. (2001). Avenues of hope: Art therapy and the resolution of trauma. *Art Therapy Journal of the American Art Therapy Association, 18*(1), 6–13.

Beardsley, J. (1984). *Earthworks and beyond.* New York: Abbeville Press.

Buk, A. (2009). The mirror neuron system and embodied simulation: Clinical implications for art therapists working with trauma survivors. *The Arts in Psychotherapy, 36*(2), 61–74.

Campbell, J. (1949). *The hero with a thousand faces.* New York: Bollingen Foundation.

Chapman, L., Morabito, D., Ladakakos, C., Schreier, H., & Knudson, N. M. (2001). The effectiveness of art therapy interventions in reducing post traumatic stress disorder (PTSD) symptoms in pediatric trauma patients. *Art Therapy Journal of the American Art Therapy Association, 18*(2), 100–104.

Chilcote, R. (2007). Art therapy with child tsunami survivors in Sri Lanka. *Art Therapy Journal of the American Art Therapy Association, 24*(3), 156–162.

Cohen, B., & Cox, C. (1995). *Telling without talking: Art as a window into the world of multiple personality.* New York: Norton.

Cohen, J. A., Mannarino, A. P., & Deblinger, E. (2006). *Treating trauma and traumatic grief in children and adolescents.* New York: Guilford.

Collie, K., Backos, A., Malchiodi, C., & Spiegel, D. (2006). Art therapy for combat-related PTSD: Recommendations for research and practice. *Art Therapy Journal of the American Art Therapy Association, 23*(4), 157–164.

Cross, D. (1993). Family art therapy and sexual abuse. In D. Linesch (Ed.), *Art therapy with families in crisis* (pp. 104–127). New York: Brunner/Mazel.

Dowdney, L., Wilson, R., Maughan, B., Allerton, M., Schofield, P., & Skuse, D. (1999). Psychological disturbance and service provision in parentally bereaved children: Prospective case-control study. *British Medical Journal, 319,* 354–373.

Freeman, V. (2005, October). Between trauma and transformation: The alchemy of art therapy. *Alternative Medicine,* pp. 43–48.

Gantt, L., & Tinnin, L. (2007). The instinctual trauma response. In D. B. Arrington (Ed.), *Art, angst, and trauma* (pp. 168–174). Springfield, IL: Charles C Thomas.

Gantt, L., & Tinnin, L. (2009). Support for a neurobiological view of trauma with implications for art therapy. *The Arts in Psychotherapy, 36*(3), 148–153.

Geist, A. L., & Geist, P. N. C. (2002). *They still draw pictures: Children's art in wartime from the Spanish civil war to Kosovo.* Urbana: University of Illinois Press.

Gesensway, D., & Roseman, M. (1987). *Beyond words: Images from America's concentration camps.* Ithaca, NY: Cornell University Press.

Goodman, R. (2004). Treatment of childhood traumatic grief: Application of cognitive-behavioral and client-centered therapies. In N. Webb (Ed.), *Mass trauma and violence: Helping children and families cope* (pp. 77–99). New York: Guilford.

Goodman, R., & Fahnestock, H. (2002). *The day our world changed: Children's art of 9/11.* New York: Harry N. Abrams.

Hass-Cohen, N., & Carr, R. (Eds.). (2008). *Art therapy and clinical neuroscience.* London: Jessica Kingsley Press.

Henderson, P., Mascaro, N., & Rosen, D. (2007). Empirical study on the healing nature of mandalas. *Psychology of Aesthetics, Creativity, and Art, 1*(3), 148–154.

Herman, J. L. (1992). *Trauma and recovery.* New York: HarperCollins.

Hinz, L. (2009). *Expressive therapies continuum.* New York: Routledge.

Jakowski, A. P., de Araújo, C. M., de Lacerda, A. L. T., de Jesus Mari, J., & Kaufman, J. (2009). Neurostructural imaging findings in children with post-traumatic stress disorder: Brief review. *Psychiatry and Clinical Neurosciences, 63,* 1–8.

Kagin, S., & Lüsebrink, V. B. (1978). The expressive therapies continuum. *Art Psychotherapy, 5*(4), 171–179.

Kaufman, B., & Wohl, A. (1992). *Casualties of childhood: A developmental perspective on sexual abuse using projective drawings.* New York: Brunner/Mazel.

Kuramato, S. J., Brent, D. A., & Wilcox, H. C. (2009). The impact of parental suicide on child and adolescent offspring. *Suicide and Life-Threatening Behavior, 39*(2), 137–151.

Lacroix, L., Rousseau, C., Gauthier, M.-F., Singh, A., Giguère, N., & Lemzoudi, Y. (2007). Immigrant and refugee preschoolers' sandplay representations of the tsunami. *The Arts in Psychotherapy, 34*(2), 99–113.

Lande, R. G., Tarpley, V., Francis, J. L., & Boucher, R. (2010). Combat trauma art therapy scale. *The Arts in Psychotherapy, 37*(1), 42–45.

Lester, P., Wong, S. W., & Hendren, R. L. (2003). The neurobiological effects of trauma. *Adolescent Psychiatry, 27,* 259–282.

Lev-Wiesel, R., & Sampson, T. (2001). Long-term effects of maternal death through parental homicide evidenced from family of origin drawings. *The Arts in Psychotherapy, 28*(4), 239–244.

Loumeau-May, L. (2006, November 16). *Death and the hero quest: Adolescent bereavement and the development of self.* Paper presented at the conference of the American Art Therapy Association, New Orleans, LA.

Loumeau-May, L. (2008). Grieving in the public eye: Art therapy with children who lost parents at the World Trade Center September 11, 2001. In C. Malchiodi (Ed.), *Creative interventions with traumatized children* (pp. 81–111). New York: Guilford.

Lüsebrink, V. (2004). Art therapy and the brain: An attempt to understand the underlying processes of art expression in therapy. *Art Therapy Journal of the American Art Therapy Association, 21*(3), 125–135.

Lüsebrink, V. B. (1990). *Imagery and visual expression in therapy.* New York: Plenum.

Mallay, J. N. (2002). Art therapy, an effective outreach intervention with traumatized children with suspected brain injury. *The Arts in Psychotherapy, 29*(3), 159–172.

Martin, E. S. (2008). Medical art and play therapy with accident survivors. In C. Malchiodi (Ed.), *Creative interventions with traumatized children* (pp. 112–131). New York: Guilford.

McNamee, C. (2003). Bilateral art: Facilitating systematic integration and balance. *The Arts in Psychotherapy, 31*(2004), 229–243.

McNamee, C. (2004). Using both sides of the brain: Experiences that integrate art and talk therapy through scribble drawings. *Art Therapy: Journal of the American Art Therapy Association, 23*(3), 136–142.

Morgan, C. A., III, & Johnson, D. R. (1995). Use of a drawing task in the treatment of nightmares in combat-related PTSD. *Art Therapy Journal of the American Art Therapy Association, 12*(4), 244–247.

Orr, P. (2007). Art therapy with children after a disaster: A content analysis. *The Arts in Psychotherapy, 34*(4), 350–361.

Pifalo, T. (2002). Pulling out the thorns: Art therapy with sexually abused children and adolescents. *Art Therapy Journal of the American Art Therapy Association, 19*(1), 12–22.

Pifalo, T. (2006). Art therapy with sexually abused children and adolescents: Extended research study. *Art Therapy Journal of the American Art Therapy Association, 23*(4), 181–185.

Pifalo, T. (2007). Jogging the clogs: Trauma focused art therapy with sexually abused children. *Art Therapy Journal of the American Art Therapy Association, 24*(4), 170–175.

Pifalo, T. (2009). Mapping the maze: An art therapy intervention following the disclosure of sexual abuse. *Art Therapy Journal of the American Art Therapy Association, 26*(1), 12–18.

Potok, C., & Volavková, H. (1993) . . . *I never saw another butterfly . . . Children's drawings and poems from Terezin concentration camp, 1942–1944.* New York: Schocken Books.

Rankin, A., & Taucher, C. (2003). A task-oriented approach to art therapy in trauma treatment. *Art Therapy Journal of the American Art Therapy Association, 20*(3), 138–147.

Rausch, S., van der Kolk, B. A., Fisler, R., Orr, S., Alpert, N. M., Savage, C. R., et al. (1996). A symptom provocation study of posttraumatic stress disorder using positron emission tomography and script driven imagery. *Archives of General Psychiatry, 53,* 380–387.

Roje, J. (1995). LA '94 earthquake in the eyes of children: Art therapy with elementary school children who were victims of disaster. *Art Therapy Journal of the American Art Therapy Association, 12*(4), 237–243.

Russell, J. (1999). Art therapy on a hospital burn unit: A step toward healing and recovery. In C. Malchiodi (Ed.), *Medical art therapy with children* (pp. 133–152). London: Jessica Kinglsey.

Sandler, I. N., Ayers, T. S., Wolchik, S. A., Tein, J.-Y., Kwok, O.-M., Haine, R. A., et al. (2003). The family bereavement program: Efficacy evaluation of a theory-based prevention program for parentally bereaved children and adolescents. *Journal of Consulting and Clinical Psychology, 71*(3), 587–600.

Santino, J. (2006). *Spontaneous shrines and public memorialization of death.* New York: Palgrave Macmillan.

Schaverien, J. (1992). *The revealing image: Analytical art psychotherapy in theory and practice.* London: Jessica Kingsley.

Schore, A. N. (2003). Early relational trauma, disorganized attachment, and the development of a predisposition to violence. In M. F. Solomon & D. J. Siegel (Eds.), *Healing trauma: Attachment, mind, body, and the brain* (pp. 107–167). New York: Norton.

Serrano, J. S. (1989). The arts in therapy with survivors of incest. In H. Wadeson, P. Durkin, & D. Perach (Eds.), *Advances in art therapy* (pp. 114–125). New York: John Wiley.

Silverman, P. R., Nickman, S., & Worden, J. W. (1995). Detachment revisited: The child's reconstruction of a dead parent. In K. J. Doka (Ed.), *Children mourning, mourning children* (pp. 131–148). Washington, DC: Hospice Foundation of America.

Spring, D. (1993). *Shattered images: Phenomenological language of sexual trauma.* Chicago: Magnolia Street.

Spring, D. (2004). Thirty-year study links neuroscience, specific-trauma PTSD, image conversion, and language translation. *Art Therapy Journal of the American Art Therapy Association, 21*(4), 200–209.

Steele, W. (2002). Using drawing in short-term trauma resolution. In C. Malchiodi (Ed.), *Handbook of art therapy* (pp. 139–151). New York: Guilford.

Steele, W., & Raider, M. (2001). *Structured sensory intervention for traumatized children, adolescents and parents.* Lewiston, NY: Edwin Mellen Press.

Steinberg, M. (1997). Assessing posttraumatic dissociation with the structured clinical interview for *DSM-IV* dissociative disorders. In J. P. Wilson & T. M. Keane (Eds.), *Assessing psychological trauma and PTSD* (pp. 429–448). New York: Guilford.

Stember, C. J. (1977). Printmaking with abused children: A first step in art therapy. *American Journal of Art Therapy, 16*(3), 104–109.

Talwar, S. (2007). Accessing traumatic memory through art making: An art therapy trauma protocol (ATTP). *The Arts in Psychotherapy, 34*(1), 22–35.

Thompson, M., Kaslow, N., Price, A., Williams, K., & Kingree, J. (1998). Role of secondary stressors in the parental death-child distress relation. *Journal of Abnormal Child Psychology.* Retrieved September 7, 2008, from http://findarticles.com/p/articles

Tripp, T. (2007). A short term therapy approach to processing trauma: Art therapy and bilateral stimulation. *Art Therapy Journal of the American Art Therapy Association, 24*(4), 176–183.

van der Kolk, B. A. (2006). Clinical implications of neuroscience research in PTSD. *Annals of the New York Academy of Sciences, 1071,* 277–293.

Wald, J. (1989). Severe head injury and its stages of recovery explored through art therapy. In H. Wadeson, J. Durkin, & D. Perach (Eds.), *Advances in art therapy* (pp. 181–203). New York: John Wiley.

7

Military Bereavement and Combat Trauma

Simon Shimshon Rubin, Ruth Malkinson, Dan Koren, Shahar Mor Yosef, and Eliezer Witztum

The psychological effects of exposure to the stresses and horrors of combat have been studied extensively during the past four decades. This body of literature has significantly furthered our understanding of the nature and course of the experience of trauma both during and after combat (Foa, Keane, Friedman, & Cohen, 2008; Sundin, Fear, Iversen, Rona, & Wessely, 2010). Quite surprisingly, however, this literature tells us relatively little about the bereavement features of combat trauma (Mor Yosef, 2003). The overarching goal of this chapter is to address this lacuna in the literature on the psychological sequelae of bereavement as a result of combat and to heighten clinician awareness of its significance. To accomplish this, first we begin by addressing issues in trauma and more specifically the interface of trauma and bereavement. The Two-Track Model of Bereavement is introduced to assist us in this. Next, we discuss relevant preliminary empirical data of both a quantitative and qualitative nature related to loss of comrades and the experience of trauma. Finally, we consider the implications of the above for understanding and, where necessary, intervening with soldiers who have lost comrades in combat.

Combat Trauma and Military Bereavement

The recognition that many soldiers suffer debilitating psychological responses to the stresses and traumas of combat is today widely acknowledged by both

The authors wish to thank Yoav Laron for his contributions to this chapter.

the general public and the medical establishments. This acknowledgment has led to a tidal wave of studies that have attempted to identify pre-, peri-, and posttraumatic factors that increase or decrease the risk for these debilitating responses. Despite the massive interest in factors contributing to posttraumatic stress and resiliency following combat, the significance of the loss of comrades during combat has received very little attention (Pivar & Prigerson, 2005). Consequently, relatively little is known about the mutual relationship between grief and bereavement reactions over dead comrades and posttraumatic stress reactions following combat. This chapter is motivated by the view that grief and interpersonal military bereavements deserve closer consideration in an effort to understand the factors that affect soldiers and the painful and stressful experiences to which they are subject. Clinical implications follow from this premise. Knowledge of the bereavement literature and intervention strategies from that domain are needed alongside expertise in trauma in the evaluation and treatment of distressed soldiers who have lost comrades.

Currently, the death of comrades in arms is typically refracted through a single trauma lens that assigns to such deaths the status of yet another of the multiple stresses of combat. The psychological import of the experience can be interpreted to mean that the death serves to heighten the soldier's awareness of the threat to his or her own life. A decidedly different approach would emphasize the interpersonal significance of the loss of comrades and commanders for the surviving soldier. In such a view, a unique component of what makes combat a particularly difficult and harrowing experience stems from the threat to self as well as to others who are meaningful to the individual. The affiliative and attachment bonds that form in the relationships among soldiers vary greatly and may serve any number of adaptive functions. What they share, however, is a significance that has much in common with family relationships. Nuclear and extended family groupings involve and link people together so they are connected beyond mere instrumental assistance to each other. In similar fashion, soldiers are involved and invested in the nuclear and extended military units they belong to. These are not abstract concepts but reflect the "we" connections to particular individuals with whom the soldiers have meaningful relationships.

In this chapter, we will utilize theory, clinical observation, and preliminary empirical findings to make the case for a bifocal perspective on traumatic combat experiences in which comrades are killed. Our view is that such events contain two elements: (a) a life-threatening component to self and other (central to most conceptions of a stressful event and constituting Criterion A of posttraumatic stress disorder [PTSD] in the *Diagnostic and Statistical Manual of Mental Disorders* [fourth edition, text revision; *DSM-IV-TR*] [American Psychiatric Association, 2000], which results in a range of stress symptomatologies), and (b) a bereavement component that relates very specifically to the death of the particular soldiers who died and should be assessed and addressed as an independent variable. Although the two dimensions of combat experiences may not be fully separable, their independent conceptualization can provide a clearer view of the traumatic experiences of surviving combatants. In particular, the separation raises more clearly the question of how the loss of a comrade can be, in and of itself, a bereavement experience of traumatic proportions.

Historical and Theoretical Background

The development and emotional sequelae of trauma have been a source of controversy and discussion within the medical and therapeutic community for more than a century and a half. In the ensuing years these controversies have only intensified, a fact that is illustrated by the frequent changes and transformations of psychiatric nosology relative to the diagnosis of trauma.

In the 1860s, the British medical literature reported the first description of individual reactions to injuries caused in railway accidents. Patients complained not only of physical pain but also of emotional distress, which they often described in great detail (Kinzie & Goetz, 1996). The syndrome came to be known as Railway Spine. Other forms of trauma-related clinical terminology as the result of combat have a much longer history in literature. Early descriptions of combat traumas surface in the Homeric stories of the Greek wars. In more recent times, variations of medical terms used in conjunction with such traumas include *Soldier's Heart, War Neurosis, Shell Shock, Battle Fatigue, Battle Shock,* and *Combat Reaction* (Lamprecht & Sack, 2002). These terms attempt to form an associative link between specific psychophysiological responses to military trauma. They were heavily influenced by prevailing cultural conventions concerning trauma and the reaction to it. The first two editions of the *DSM* (American Psychiatric Association, 1958, 1968) defined the sequelae of trauma as reaction to stress ("Gross Stress Reaction"). This diagnosis was classified within the transient situational personality disorders. The implications were straightforward, communicating that if the disorder was not transient and situational, the phenomenology was not primarily a response to external stress, and these diagnoses were not to be used (Witztum & Kotler, 2000).

Today, the accepted term is *posttraumatic stress disorder,* which was introduced in the late 1970s and entered the official nomenclature in the 1980 revision of the *DSM* (American Psychiatric Association, 1980). In PTSD, the symptomatic state can now be "prolonged" or "chronic." This diagnosis reflects the clinical awareness that traumatic events can have severe, extensive, and protracted emotional and mental sequelae.

The formal recognition of PTSD in 1980 represented a paradigm shift in the way that psychiatric trauma was interpreted. Hitherto, it was argued that if a healthy individual suffered psychological effects as a result of a life-threatening event, these would resolve naturally, in a manner akin to a self-healing wound and without long-term effects (Jones & Wessely, 2007). The discovery of a so-called delayed stress syndrome during the Vietnam War appeared to show that healthy soldiers subjected to the trauma of combat could suffer chronic, adverse effects that were not apparent at the time of their exposure (Figley, 1978).

In Israel, the combination of brief repeated wars and protracted military conflict under conditions of existential threat influences Israeli ethos, social conventions, and public discourse in myriad ways. Not surprisingly, these factors influence how combat trauma and PTSD have been managed within Israel (Witztum, Levy, & Solomon, 1996). In addition to medical conventions, the role of social factors in responding to war-related trauma, stress, and their emotional sequelae and classification are part of the society's responses (Witztum, Malkinson, & Rubin, 2001). Inasmuch as the emotional core content of a combat stress reaction is an overwhelming feeling of vulnerability and existential helplessness, it is clear that such a response is an affront to the military mindset. For the state of Israel, these experiences also run counter to the sense of safety, mastery, assertiveness, and self-control that the founders of Israel and its pioneers strove to inculcate in the native-born Israelis or *Sabras*. The archetype of the new Jew liberated from millennia of vulnerability by virtue of the return to the Jewish homeland served important purposes for Israeli society. Society could not readily incorporate a range of psychological combat reactions into its narrative. Emotional distress due to combat was associated with weakness and not with the idealized picture of the Jewish warrior—in the past or the present (Malkinson & Witztum, 2000).

Similar to the Vietnam conflict for the United States, the Yom Kippur War of 1973 was an important and painful lesson for Israeli society and led to many important conceptual changes (Rabinovich, 2004). The Israeli psychiatric establishment became acutely aware of combat stress reaction (Levy, Witztum, & Solomon, 1996). The events demonstrated to the nation both its collective vulnerability and that of the Israeli native-born warrior. This vulnerability was recognized as a reality that had to be dealt with without further repression or denial. Owing to the high psychiatric morbidity of this war, the mental health department of the military and its functions were greatly expanded. This expansion was felt particularly in frontline facilities targeted for acute combat stress reaction casualties. At the same time, the physical casualty rate was high. Per capita, Israel suffered 3 times as many casualties in 3 weeks of fighting in 1973 as the United States did during almost a decade of combat in Vietnam. The final toll was 2,688 soldiers killed. Although the figures from the 1948 War of Independence—some 6,373 killed in action—approached a staggering 1% of the Jewish community, the impact of the 1973 war was arguably more traumatic (Lorch, 2003). This was because the population's great sense of security in 1973 was shattered by the unforeseen outbreak of hostilities.

It is noteworthy that whereas the symptomatic effects of the posttraumatic reactions have received extensive consideration in Israel, the significance of the death of comrades in arms has not been recognized as a contributing factor (Garb, Bleich, & Lerer, 1987). No doubt, the wide variation of traumatogenic combat experiences to which soldiers are exposed contributes to this perspective. Many include threat but not necessarily bereavement. Furthermore, many soldiers exposed to combat and to the loss of comrades do not manifest significant dysfunction or receive a diagnosis of depression or stress disorder. In Israel's military as well as those of other nations, this response is considered a sign of hardiness or resilience. Yet in the domain of interpersonal relationships and bonds, lack of interest or distress following the loss of comrades when danger is past may be considered a sign of potential difficulty rather than a mark of hardiness and resilience (Rubin, Malkinson, & Witztum, 2008). Psychologically speaking, the ability to function efficiently in combat despite comrade loss would be considered adaptive in the short term. To continue to remain unaffected and impervious to the death of comrades years later, however, is no longer considered adaptive and may then reflect deficiencies rather than desired qualities.

The predominant approach to trauma views death from the perspective of the threat to the soldier's well-being and security. Simply put, one's life is in danger. The life threat associated with exposure to combat, however, is also the threat to one's comrades in arms and to the military unit. In this formulation, individuals are viewed as distinct persons making up the soldier's unit and leadership. They are important as specific individuals, close associates, and members of the military family to which a soldier feels that he or she belongs. The unit functions as a whole comprising individuals who live, fight, and train together. When a loss occurs, the unit loses its sense of integrity—almost as though a piece of it has been torn away and is missing. This affects not only the unit as a whole but also the individual soldiers. In such a formulation, the death of these figures necessitates looking beyond the language of threat to the survivor. In addition, one can reconfigure one's perspective to consider the interplay of trauma and bereavement with particular attention to interpersonal relationships and bonds.

Trauma and the Two-Track Model of Bereavement

Orienting to loss and bereavement requires us to consider or address several basic concepts in the bereavement field to better understand the impact of loss on persons connected to the deceased (Malkinson, 2007; Malkinson, Rubin, & Witztum, 2000, 2005). Although the literature is vast, our goal is to clarify several vectors that will allow us to better understand the trauma-bereavement interface for soldiers. We do this by summarizing the Two-Track Model of Bereavement. This model advocates an approach to loss with attention to biopsychosocial functioning on one hand and relationship to the deceased following loss on the other.

The Two-Track Model of Bereavement is conceived as a scaffolding, intended to capture more fully the experience of the response to interpersonal loss (Rubin, 1981, 1992, 1999). It builds on the core understanding that reworking the relationship to the deceased and coming to grips with grief and mourning are critical components of understanding bereavement (Bowlby,

1980; Freud, 1917/1957). In accord with revisions and modifications of the psychodynamic and interpersonal approaches to loss, an important domain within the two-track framework considers the outcome of bereavement through the prism of the nature and change in the preloss tie to the deceased (Rubin, 1984; Stroebe, Gergen, Gergen, & Stroebe, 1992). At the same time, however, the model remains focused on functioning. This domain is associated with the stress and trauma aspects of the loss experience. With the attention to functioning, the outcome of the bereavement experience is conceived as a biological, behavioral, cognitive, and emotional process fundamentally similar to the response of individuals to situations of crisis, trauma, and stress (Crisp & Priest, 1972; Malkinson et al., 2000; Rubin, Malkinson, & Witztum, 2003). Researchers and clinicians associated with this approach have historically been relatively unconcerned with the significance of the bond to the deceased. Instead, the extent of change, symptoms of various types, and behavioral difficulties following loss, as with many other stressor events, have been of primary interest.

The importance of combining these two perspectives resulted in a series of theoretical and research articles advocating for a bifocal approach to the experience of bereavement (Rubin, 1981, 1984, 1992, 1999). In this model, the process of adaptation to interpersonal loss is understood as linked to the disruption of homeostatic functioning but also as relating and reconfiguring aspects of the relationship to the deceased. The Two-Track Model of Bereavement addresses functioning and the quality and nature of the continuing attachment to the deceased when significant others die.

The Two-Track Model of Bereavement has relevance for military bereavement in situations in which comrades in arms are killed. The current criteria for exposure to traumatic stimuli in the *DSM-IV-TR* include direct personal exposure to life threat and harm or such exposure to a family member or close associates. In combat situations in which compatriots or commanding officers are killed, a double experience of loss and life threat to self and "family" occurs. The death is a safety-shattering traumatic event as well as a bereavement event.

As stated in the *DSM-IV,* a person must have direct personal experience with threatened death or injury to self, have witnessed an event that threatened another, or have learned about an event that involves violent death or harm to a family member or other close associate (American Psychiatric Association, 1994, p. 467, Criterion A1). From the language of the criterion, the traumatic exposure element is not limited to a combat situation wherein the survivor was personally present in a life-threatening situation. The loss of life of a comrade or commander is sufficient, in and of itself, to constitute a traumatogenic factor. Keeping in mind the unique bereavement and grief components, however, is important. They require the clinician to consider the significance of the survivor's connection to the individual who was killed and the survivor's experience of mourning and bereavement. Somewhat surprisingly, the bereaved person does not always recognize the significance of the interpersonal loss for its impact on him- or herself. The bereaved, too, relates to what has occurred primarily from the life threat–trauma perspective.

The implications of the Two-Track Model of Bereavement are relevant for theory, research, and intervention. To determine the individual's response to such events involving trauma and bereavement, it is valuable to assess the extent to which the soldier's response proceeds along both tracks of this model of response to loss. The clinical implications of the model derive directly from the focus on both the functional and relational aspects of the response to loss. The extent to which interventions will need to deal with either or both domains of the response to the trauma and loss events follow from the results of the bifocal assessment inherent in the Two-Track Model of Bereavement. A schematic summary of the assessment schema based on the Two-Track Model of Bereavement is presented in Table 7.1 (Rubin, Malkinson, & Witztum, in press).

Table 7.1   The Two-Track Model of Bereavement for Military Bereavement

Track I: Biopsychosocial Functioning	Track II: Relationship to the Deceased
a. Where are the difficulties in biopsychosocial functioning? b. Where are the indications of strength and resilience?	a. What is the death story, and how is it related to the survivor's connection to the deceased? b. What is the narrative of the current and recollected relationship to the deceased?
1. Anxious affect 2. Depressive affects and cognitions 3. Somatic concerns 4. Symptoms and syndromes targeting trauma 5. Familial relationships and/or relationship with identified military core group 6. General interpersonal relationships with noncore persons 7. Self-esteem and self-system 8. Matrix of personal meanings and worldview 9. Ability to respond adequately to demands of work or similar roles 10. Investment in life tasks that are meaningful to bereaved	1. Reconnection and missing the deceased 2. Imagery, memory, and physical experience of deceased and/or death event 3. Emotional involvement, closeness, and distance vis-à-vis the deceased 4. Positive affects and negative affects associated with the deceased and/or death 5. Preoccupation with death event and/or the deceased 6. Positive perceptions of the deceased and the relationship 7. Presence of conflict surrounding the deceased, the relationship, and/or the loss event 8. The loss trajectory: Reconfigure "stages" of loss to represent features of response (e.g., shock, searching, disorganization, and reorganization) 9. Self-system vis-à-vis the deceased 10. Indications of how memorialization may interact and transform relationship with deceased

The application of the model to loss varies. The circumstances of the loss event are often relevant as the way the death occurs is often intertwined with the narrative about the deceased. In all losses, the time elapsed since death is influential, but precisely in cases where bereavement does not recede in importance, time is often frozen in place. In cases of military loss, the degree of personal exposure to life threat and the absence of time for mourning and grief can serve to hamper the bereavement process. Naturally, biopsychosocial functioning is affected negatively by many factors, and bereavement and traumas are among them. At the same time, the accessibility and organization of the relationship to the deceased, however, is very specifically focused on a particular bereavement. As such, examination of the relationship domain allows for an in-depth examination of the status of that bereavement. The consideration of integrating intervention requirements and opportunities follows directly from the focus on the relationship to the deceased (Malkinson, Rubin, & Witztum, 2006).

Trauma and Bereavement Research: Preliminary Empirical Findings

Does the significance of interpersonal loss in combat deserve consideration as a distinct mechanism that interacts with other aspects of the trauma of combat exposure? A number of clinicians and researchers believe that it should be so considered (Neria & Litz, 2004; Pivar & Prigerson, 2005).

Weiss (2001) has differentiated between attachment and affiliative bonds and relationships. Attachment relationships, such as to one's parents, spouse, and first-degree family members, are exclusive and have deep emotional meanings that relate to self and other and security needs. The broader affiliative relationships (e.g., more distant relatives, friends, and colleagues) are focused on achieving mutual ends but typically lack the deeper emotional meanings associated with attachment relationships. "Relationships can be important without having embedded within them the bond of attachment. Endings of relationships that are emotionally important yet not based on attachment bonds give rise to distress but not to grief" (Weiss, 2001, p. 60).

The powerful bonds and relationships of soldiers in military units do not conform to the distinctions suggested by Weiss (2001). The bonds formed by soldiers in a combat unit often blend affiliative and attachment features. The significance of these relationships for militarily bereaved can be seen in studies that report the strongest stress symptoms among soldiers exposed to both combat and the loss of a buddy. In long-term studies examining World War II veterans decades later, the impact of buddy loss remains a factor in the psychological world of the veterans (Elder & Clipp, 1988; Harvey, Stein, & Scott, 1995). Similar results for Vietnam veterans introduce the interpersonal component into consideration of the traumatic elements of wartime but also raise questions about how the interpersonal aspects of such losses play out over time (Widdison & Salisbury, 1990).

The suppression of grief among soldiers responding to the deaths of lost buddies is maintained by several factors. One important component is the absence of societal recognition of the soldier as mourner. Without legitimacy to grieve, soldiers are left with what Doka (1989) called "disenfranchised grief." It is associated with an absence of social support and often results in the bereaved themselves being unable to legitimize their own emotions and distress as part of an important mourning experience. In a small country such as Israel, connections with family members of the deceased are possible, but they are often of limited assistance to the grieving soldier. The natural family is distinct from the military family, and the former often do not understand what the soldiers have gone through. When former soldiers are denied the option of dealing with their grief, a variety of symptoms pertaining to the traumatic nature of their combat service may result. The loss of comrades in arms contributes to the development of symptom pictures understood as stress reactions, but they may also be thought of as bereavement reactions.

Pivar and Field's (2004) study of unresolved grief among Vietnam veterans admitted to the Veterans' Administration inpatient treatment center for treatment of PTSD is noteworthy in this connection. Their participants were in their early 50s, and some 30 years had passed since they had lost comrades in arms. Nonetheless, on the main bereavement measure, they had average grief scores that were in the range of conjugally bereaved persons who had lost spouses within the previous 6 months. In addition, the grief symptoms were shown to be sharply distinguished from symptoms of PTSD as well as symptoms of depression. In additional analyses of the data, attachment to men in the unit, closeness to a buddy, and number of losses were associated with symptoms of grief but not symptoms of trauma or depression.

These findings led Pivar and Field to conclude that

> the results offer compelling support for bereavement researchers and practitioners who advocate the importance of recognizing unresolved grief as a separate diagnostic category from anxiety and depressive disorders. The high levels of grief specific symptoms reported by the participants . . . suggested that unresolved grief played a significant role in the distress suffered by combat veterans. (2004, p. 753)

Such research fits with earlier work examining the impact of bereavement and the value of viewing loss bifocally through both a bereavement lens and a trauma lens. Zisook and colleagues (Zisook, Chentsova-Dutton, & Shuchter, 1998) examined 350 widows and widowers and found that approximately 10% had PTSD-like symptoms 2 months postloss. At 13 months, some 40% of those identified earlier were meeting full criteria for PTSD. This held true both in cases of chronic illness and with relatively unexpected and accidental deaths. The impact of unnatural death such as suicide was more highly associated with the PTSD classification. Their research considered many aspects of the response to loss in their sample, but the combination of bereavement and trauma features was particularly helpful. That is because it also supports the importance of carving out a bereavement component separate from the consideration of trauma.

Further support for bereavement's being a separate dimension of the overall reaction to trauma comes from a study from our own group (Rubin et al., 2009). We subjected the ratings of 354 bereaved individuals on the Two-Track Bereavement Questionnaire to an exploratory factor analysis. The factor analysis identified a unique factor that was related to the perception of trauma by the bereaved person (Rubin et al., 2009). This finding suggests that in interpersonal loss, the perception of trauma is a significant factor affecting many bereaved persons. Nonetheless, to focus on only the trauma component is to ignore other aspects of the interpersonal dislocation of bereavement. It is important to note that this perception-of-trauma factor was elevated in cases of unexpected and violent death as well as in all cases of child death irrespective of external circumstances.

The significance of violence and its ability to interfere with the processing of interpersonal loss has been documented in recent years in cases of individual violence such as homicide and suicide as well as terrorism (Ryncarson, 2006). In an important web-based study assessing the prevalence of complications of grief and bereavement as well as comorbidity for other disorders in 704 persons bereaved in the 9/11 attacks, the prevalence of PTSD for the bereaved population in the study was dramatic (Neria et al., 2007). Complications of grief (a screening diagnosis emphasizing difficulties in functioning and strong yearning for the deceased) ranged from 22.6% for non–family members to 64.8% for parents bereaved of children. High comorbidity was present for other disorders among those who had complications of bereavement. Overall, 43.3% of those who screened positively for complicated bereavement were also seen to suffer from PTSD. This study argues for the importance of considering bereavement independently alongside trauma.

Bereavement and Combat: Lessons From the Israeli Experience

In the next section, we present a combination of quantitative and qualitative data to support our position that the experience of military bereavement is a significant factor that should be considered both independently and as a complicating factor in understanding the traumatogenic aspects of combat. In the studies we report, the data collection included measures of bereavement response as well as the investigation of elements of the trauma component.

In the first study, the impact of comrade loss on 53 participants who had served in combat was assessed (Mor Yosef, 2003). Of these, 14 had lost a comrade during a combat or training event at which the participants were present, and 14 had lost a comrade without being involved in that particular event. The remainder had not been bereaved of comrades. The mean time elapsed since the event was 5½ years. Posttraumatic symptoms were assessed with the Impact of Event Scale (Horowitz, Wilner, & Alvarez, 1979), and grief responses were assessed with the Texas Revised Inventory of Grief (Faschingbauer, Zisook, & Devaul, 1987). The findings showed that the degree of intrusive memories was significantly higher among the bereaved soldiers who had been present at the event in which their comrade had died when compared to those who had lost a friend but had not been present and those who had not lost a comrade. In addition, they showed that soldiers who were present at the time of loss have a more difficult and less resolved loss response compared to soldiers who were not present at the event. This was true both at the time of loss and years later. Taken together, these findings suggest that the combination of exposure to combat and bereavement at the same time both exacerbate the experience of trauma and interfere with the processing of interpersonal loss.

In seeking to understand the nature of the relationships as experienced by the participants, the relationships of some soldiers to living comrades and of others to deceased comrades were compared. When participants described themselves in relation to other comrades, the bereaved soldiers reported feelings of guilt that did not characterize the nonbereaveds' relationships with their living comrades. Living friends were seen as more central to the life course of the nonbereaved. In contrast, the bereaved viewed their deceased comrades more positively and in an idealized fashion while confining thoughts about such relationships to aspects associated with their army experience. The sense of distance from the relationship with the deceased was greater than the distances in relationships with living comrades. This was the picture that emerged overall. At the same time, preloss intimacy was an important aspect of the response to loss. The closer the preloss relationship, the stronger was the grief response. This held true for the time period immediately following the loss and years later. To summarize, comrade loss is a significant experience for the bereaved soldier. At the same time, in these as in other relationships, closeness to a particular person is a factor that affects the response to loss (Mor Yosef, 2003).

We (Mor Yosef, 2003) also explored the cumulative effects of losing multiple friends and comrades. When we compared bereaved soldiers who had lost one or two comrades with those who had lost more on perceptions of military bereavement loss, there was a significant effect. Those who had suffered more losses showed greater sensitivity to the suffering, guilt, life impact, and emotional needs of those who experience military bereavement. Similarly, the loss of more comrades was associated with a trend toward greater difficulties in processing the loss both early on and later.

Based on the findings from this pilot study, we conducted a second study that sought to pay closer attention to the interaction between bereavement and trauma. To accomplish this goal, we compared posttraumatic responses measured with the Posttraumatic Symptom Scale (Foa, Riggs, Dancu, & Rothbaum, 1993) and grief reactions measured with the Texas Revised Inventory of Grief. The participants had been in combat and were divided into four groups on the basis of their exposure to comrade loss and having been wounded. Interim findings from this study show that loss of a comrade does not significantly affect posttraumatic symptomatology but do show strong effects on measures of self-esteem and bereavement (Laron, 2009). The impact of comrade loss was found to vary as a result of the number of comrades lost in the individual combat events. In this study, those who had lost a greater number of comrades showed a clear tendency toward higher scores on the Posttraumatic Symptom Scale and measures of grief, although these did not reach statistical significance. In contrast to the number of comrades lost, however, one's closeness to an individual comrade who had died emerged as a significant and very strong predictor of the adjustment to loss. As in the earlier study reported above (Mor Yosef, 2003), the closer the relationship, the worse is the adjustment to loss.

In our new study (Mor Yosef, 2011), bereavement was shown to interact with the experience of being wounded in the same combat event. Wounded and uninjured bereaved soldiers differed on the degree to which their descriptions of the deceased were presented in a coherent manner. The wounded soldiers' descriptions of the deceased were significantly less well organized than those of the nonwounded soldiers. This finding is consistent with the impact of being wounded or injured as a contributing factor to the development of PTSDs (Koren, Arnon, & Klein, 2001). Its significance, however, lies in the bereavement components of a soldier's response to the trauma along Track II, the nature of the relationship to the deceased.

When these written descriptions of the deceased were analyzed and scored according to a number of dimensions as is standard with the Object Representations Inventory (Blatt, Wein, Chevron, & Quinlan, 1979; Sadeh, Rubin, & Berman, 1993), a number of interesting findings emerged. The strongest emotions communicated by the bereaved soldiers were negative feelings and guilt triggered by thoughts about the deceased. For all the bereaved, these scores hovered near the upper level on a 7-point Likert-type scale assessing only negative indicators. A separate index of the positive feelings associated with the deceased comrade was present, but the results here were less pronounced and hovered below the midpoint. The most severely affected index measured the degree to which the descriptions reflected coherence and narrative structure. Disorganization was present.

Overall, these results convey part of how the traumatic nature of the combat loss event served to interfere with the reorganization of thoughts and feelings associated with the deceased. The dysphoric affects associated with the comrade who had died remain strong, whereas the positive emotions are more limited. At the same time, however, the death event serves to disrupt the basic thoughts and feelings about the deceased and the meaning of the relationship to him or her. This disorganization and the generally negative aspects of thoughts involving the deceased interfere with the emotional and cognitive reorganization necessary in bereavement (Rubin, Malkinson, & Witztum, in press).

The Experience of Comrade Loss: Soldier Narratives

In this final section, we introduce qualitative material from the written descriptions and interviews conducted with soldiers bereaved of comrades. The data reported below further underscore the importance of retaining a bereavement perspective in considering the traumas of combat that require assessment and understanding.

The first quote we bring communicates a bereaved soldier's point of view of the significance of military loss. He shares his view of why the loss of a comrade is such a highly significant relational loss.

> To lose a comrade is not something you can accept. It was very hard for me to understand that he was killed in war and not by something else. I cannot accept that I will not see him again. For me, to lose a friend is harder than to die or to lose a family member. . . . I saw my buddy as a family member in another form, and therefore I cannot accept that he is not with me. (Laron, 2009, p. 40)

In this heartfelt description, connections to military buddies are described as variations on family connections. Although there are specific references to the cause of death in combat as a distressing experience, the emphasis on the interpersonal connections is predominant. This shows why the death of a comrade would be experienced as significant specifically with regard to the connection to the deceased. From the two-track bereavement perspective, combat-related losses are associated both with the traumatic nature of combat experiences overall (Track I) and with the relationship bonds to the deceased (Track II). In cases similar to this one, in which intervention is deemed necessary, moving from the sense of shock and trauma to the specifics of the relationship with the particular person who died can be helpful for the reworking of the experience.

This can be seen in the report of a soldier who lost a close friend while narrowly escaping death himself. The small physical distance that separated the two soldiers conveys how small the distance between life and death can be.

> I found out the person who picked up the other end of the stretcher was my friend G, and he was killed. Just like that, like we picked up the

stretcher, and he took a direct hit. . . . Think about it. 6 feet separated us, which is the stretcher, and one guy takes a direct missile hit, and you, nothing happens to you. (Laron, 2009, p. 46)

Here the sense of shock and wonder at how close death was, claiming his friend and sparing him, seems predominant. The capricious nature of the death event is paramount. In clinical practice, these factors can serve to highlight the threat to self communicated in the experience and may overshadow exploration of the significance of the loss of the friend and its meaning. The mention of the loss of a specific friend, however, should lead to an exploration of the significance of the deceased in accordance with the perspective afforded by Track II.

The next narrative begins with a description of the traumatic loss event, which conveys the reworking of the relationship to the deceased. This is characteristic of the way death and combat are encoded. At the same time, there is an evolution and continual reworking of the meaning of the death. The narrative shows that the death and trauma event is not fixed and that the relationship to the deceased continues to be a topic that tugs at and continues to preoccupy the surviving comrade.

The death of A was my first brush with the tragic death of a close friend, someone who I spoke to minutes before he was killed. . . . My attempt to remember A and our time together raises difficult feelings, a lot of sadness in that he did not get to see us as a tight group, as we had never been before, doing things other than army stuff, and [sad] that he did not manage to do all the things he had dreamt about, travel and study. . . . Lots of time I ask myself what kind of relationship we would end up having, it is hard to tell. (Mor Yosef, 2003, p. 46)

The reference to feelings of sadness as well as additional mixed feelings related to leaving the deceased behind are present. The comrade in arms (A) who died is someone whose evolution alongside his buddies has stopped. What A might have been like and what the relationship with him would have been like are questions and thoughts raised in this quote. They hint at the potential inherent in the exploration of the meaning of the relationship with the deceased. Bonds with the deceased are not confined to what happened in the past but also involve thoughts and emotions related to what might have been. Working with themes associated with the relationship to the deceased can evolve in different ways, but all of these themes share an appreciation for the significance of bereavement overall.

Not just participating in combat but the loss of comrades can be overwhelming. The need to function in the here and now, which often entails closing off powerful emotions, sometimes interferes with the reconnection to the experience. This, in turn, can interfere with the processing of the loss and bereavement and with the integration of the story and the meaning of the relationship with the deceased into the bereaved's life story. In reading the next quotation, it is not hard to understand why an overly trauma-focused perspective that does not allow for the exploration and integration of the deceased colleague would be of limited value (Rubin et al., 2003).

In the next account, the loss is directly addressed, and the respondent makes it clear that the relationship to his dead comrade was and remains meaningful for him. It also communicates how difficult it is to process and deal with loss early on. This type of response, which demonstrates limited capacity to respond to the loss at the time it occurs, can contribute to experiences of unresolved and disenfranchised grief, which may continue for years (Doka, 1989).

> It took less time for me than for the others to understand what happened and what that meant. The coping with loss was dictated to me and to my buddies by the army by virtue of the fact that we remained in Lebanon for two more weeks. The daily routine at the position was so busy and demanding that for young soldiers, there was really no time to listen to feelings and thoughts except at night between one shift of guard duty to the next. I don't think this was the best way for me to deal with loss, but it was probably the best way for the Army. Today, six years later, I have put together ways to be alone with Z and to enjoy his memory and to be sad about his loss, although there are things that I think that should have come out in the days after the tragedy but did not. Today, if they [the thoughts and feelings] are still there, they are deep inside and I don't know what they are. I don't blame myself for the situation and life is good for me, but at times I regret that I did not get to know Z better than I managed. (Mor Yosef, 2003, p. 56)

The above description reiterates why there are obstacles to grieving during military activity that interfere with processing of loss. For clinicians working with soldiers who have lost comrades, it is important to understand the obstacles to grieving that were present at the time of death. At the same time, here too, it is valuable to attend to who the deceased was and what the relationship to him was like.

The narratives of the soldiers presented here convey the impact of combat and loss that communicates the following: (a) the confusion during combat experiences that makes the loss event something that is difficult to narrate in a cohesive manner, (b) awareness of the elements of life threat that pervade the experience for soldiers who were in the same combat sequences in which comrades and commanding officers were killed, and (c) the need to renarrate one's own life in the wake of the combat experience and how one emerges from that. There is more to bereavement of comrades than the confusion, life threat, and reorganization of one's own life. The narratives presented also clearly convey the sense that in many cases, the comrades who died are people whose lives were intertwined with those of the survivors in more than simply functional ways—and that it is important to grieve such losses and reorganize the relationship to the deceased. The combination of affiliation and attachment is a recurring motif in these narratives.

Space does not allow for a fuller consideration of the clinical implications of using the Two-Track Model of Bereavement. The interested reader is referred to an article addressing the clinical utility of the bifocal perspective of the Two-Track Model of Bereavement in a case of combat trauma and bereavement (Rubin et al., 2003). The case study discussed illustrates how working with a focus on the relationship to the deceased was therapeutically beneficial for a soldier who developed stress reactions following a traumatic combat event.

Concluding Remarks

The material considered in this chapter supports the importance of focusing on the loss of comrades as a significant aspect of the trauma of combat. The Two-Track Model of Bereavement is a framework particularly well suited to clinical assessment and therapeutic intervention with soldiers who have experienced the loss of comrades and friends. Although intervention with aspects of stress and PTSD has demonstrated effectiveness in assisting soldiers and veterans who suffer from diagnosable disorders, it has not sufficiently targeted the bereavement component of military service for intervention (Foa et al., 2008; Rubin et al., 2003).

The affiliative and attachment bonds formed among soldiers and soldiers' identification with the military unit as a family-like source of support and attachment serve numerous adaptive functions for soldiers in peace and in war. Their significance, however, does not lie in the adaptive nature of such relationships but rather in the depth of the bonds, identifications, and meanings formed. The use of the term *band of brothers* succinctly communicates this aspect of combat soldiers' connections with one another. The loss of members of one's core unit is similar to the loss of family members in several important respects. The loss of a comrade serves as a potential trauma as it brings with it the realization of one's vulnerability. These thoughts and feelings are magnified and compounded when such death occurs in combat in which the survivor is involved. At the same time, there is an important interpersonal bereavement component in comrade loss. This varies as a function of the significance of the relationship and closeness to the particular person who died. The Two-Track Model of Bereavement focuses on those twin areas of adaptation to the stresses of combat when bereavement is involved. Track I directs us to the areas of biopsychosocial functioning, which allows for an evaluation of the degree of dysfunction present. Functioning includes stress and trauma responses as well as depression, meaning construction, and management of life tasks. Track II directs us to the nature of the relationship to the deceased. The psychological relationship of the bereaved individual to the deceased is critical to the evaluation of grief and mourning (Rubin, Malkinson, & Witztum, 2011).

In situations wherein the traumatic nature of the death obstructs or dominates the narrative of the relationship, it is important to attend to the repair and construction of a link to a fuller, nontraumatic connection with the memories of the deceased. Understanding the importance of the relationship to the deceased is the first step in assisting soldiers and veterans who have lost comrades to rework and reorient the relationship to the remembered comrade and the meaning of that relationship for them. Clearly, the bonds and relationships soldiers form with each other are highly significant.

But we in it shall be remembered—
We few, we happy few, we band of brothers;
For he to-day that sheds his blood with me
Shall be my brother.

—Shakespeare (1599/1982, IV, iii)

References

American Psychiatric Association. (1958). *Diagnostic and statistical manual of mental disorders*. Washington, DC: Author.

American Psychiatric Association. (1968). *Diagnostic and statistical manual of mental disorders* (2nd ed.). Washington, DC: Author.

American Psychiatric Association. (1980). *Diagnostic and statistical manual of mental disorders* (3rd ed.). Washington, DC: Author.

American Psychiatric Association. (1994). *Diagnostic and statistical manual of mental disorders* (4th ed.). Washington, DC: Author.

American Psychiatric Association. (2000). *Diagnostic and statistical manual of mental disorders* (4th ed., text revision). Washington, DC: Author.

Blatt, S. J., Wein, S. J., Chevron, E. S., & Quinlan, D. M. (1979). Parental representations and depression in normal young adults. *Journal of Abnormal Psychology, 88,* 388–397.

Bowlby, J. (1980). *Attachment and loss: Vol. 3. Loss.* New York: Basic Books.

Crisp, A. H., & Priest, R. G. (1972). Psychoneurotic status during the year following bereavement. *Journal of Psychosomatic Research, 16,* 351–355.

Doka, K. (Ed.). (1989). *Disenfranchised grief: Recognizing hidden sorrow.* Lexington, MA: Lexington Books.

Elder, G. H., & Clipp, E. C. (1988). War time losses and social bonding: Influences across 40 years in men's lives. *Psychiatry, 51,* 177–198.

Faschingbauer, T. R., Zisook, S., & Devaul, R. (1987). The Texas Revised Inventory of Grief. In S. Zisook (Ed.), *Biopsychosocial aspects of bereavement* (pp. 111–124). Washington, DC: American Psychiatric Press.

Figley, C. R. (1978). Symptoms of delayed combat stress among a sample of Vietnam veterans. *Military Medicine, 143,* 107–111.

Foa, E., Riggs, D., Dancu, C., & Rothbaum, B. (1993). Reliability and validity of a brief instrument for assessing post-traumatic stress disorder. *Journal of Traumatic Stress, 6,* 459–474.

Foa, E. B., Keane, T. M., Friedman, M. J., & Cohen, J. E. (Eds.). (2008). *Effective treatments for PTSD: Practice guidelines from the International Society for Traumatic Stress Studies* (2nd ed.). New York: Guilford.

Freud, S. (1957). Mourning and melancholia. In J. Strachey (Ed.), *The standard edition of the complete psychological works of Sigmund Freud* (Vol. 14, pp. 239–258). London: Hogarth. (Original work published 1917)

Garb, R., Bleich, A., & Lerer, B. (1987). Bereavement in combat. *Psychiatric Clinics of North America, 10,* 421–436.

Harvey, J. H., Stein, S. K., & Scott, P. K. (1995). Fifty years of grief: Accounts and reported psychological reactions of Normandy invasion veterans. *Journal of Narrative Life History, 5,* 315–332.

Horowitz, M. J., Wilner, N. R., & Alvarez, W. (1979). Impact of event scale: A measure of subjective stress. *Psychosomatic Medicine, 41,* 209–218.

Jones, E., & Wessely, S. (2007). A paradigm shift in the conceptualization of psychological trauma in the 20th century. *Journal of Anxiety Disorders, 21*(2), 164–175.

Kinzie, D., & Goetz, R. (1996). A century of controversy surrounding post-traumatic stress syndromes: The impact of *DSM-III* and *DSM- IV. Journal of Traumatic Stress, 9,* 159–179.

Koren, D., Arnon, I., & Klein, E. (2001). Long term course of chronic posttraumatic stress disorder in traffic accident victims: A three-year prospective follow-up study. *Behavior Research and Therapy, 39*(12), 1449–1458.

Lamprecht, F., & Sack, M. (2002). Posttraumatic stress disorder revisited. *Psychosomatic Medicine, 64*(2), 222–237.

Laron, Y. (2009). *Loss and trauma: The impact of comrade-loss during a combat operation on the psychological adaptation of soldiers who participated in the operation.* Unpublished MA thesis, University of Haifa.

Levy, A., Witztum, E., & Solomon, Z. (1996). Lessons relearned—When denial becomes impossible: Therapeutic response to combat stress reaction during the Yom Kippur War (1973), the Lebanon War (1982) and the Intifada. *Israel Journal of Psychiatry, 33,* 88–102.

Lorch, N. (2003). *The Arab-Israeli wars.* Retrieved June 21, 2010, from http://www .mfa.gov.il/MFA/History/Modern+History/Centenary+of+Zionism/The+Arab-Israeli+Wars.htm

Malkinson, R. (2007). *Cognitive grief therapy.* New York: Norton.

Malkinson, R., Rubin, S., & Witztum, E. (Eds.). (2000). *Traumatic and non traumatic loss and bereavement: Clinical theory and practice.* Madison, CT: Psychosocial Press.

Malkinson, R., Rubin, S., & Witztum, E. (2005). Terror, trauma, and bereavement: Implications for theory and therapy. In Y. Danieli, D. Brom, & J. Sills (Eds.), *The trauma of terrorism: Sharing knowledge and shared care, an international handbook* (pp. 467–477). Binghamton, NY: Haworth Maltreatment & Trauma Press.

Malkinson, R., Rubin, S., & Witztum, E. (2006). Therapeutic issues and the relationship to the deceased: Working clinically with the Two-Track Model of Bereavement. *Death Studies, 30*(9), 797–815.

Malkinson, R., & Witztum, E. (2000). Collective bereavement and commemoration: Cultural aspects of collective myth and the creation of national identity. In

R. Malkinson, S. Rubin, & E. Witztum (Eds.), *Traumatic and nontraumatic loss and bereavement: Clinical theory and practice* (pp. 295–320). Madison, CT: Psychosocial Press.

Mor Yosef, S. (2003). *War and bereavement: The impact of the loss of comrades in arms and friends upon young men.* Unpublished MA thesis, University of Haifa.

Mor Yosef, S. (2011). *The influence of combat on the emotional functioning of combat veterans: The contribution of being wounded, and comrade loss as a function of attachment and coping style.* Unpublished doctoral dissertation, University of Haifa, Israel.

Neria, Y., Gross, R., Litz, B., Maguen, S., Insel, B., Seirmarco, G., et al. (2007). Prevalence and psychological correlates of complicated grief among bereaved adults 2.5–3.5 years after September 11th attacks. *Journal of Traumatic Stress, 20*(3), 251–262.

Neria, Y., & Litz, B. (2004). Bereavement by traumatic means: The complex synergy of trauma and grief. *Journal of Loss and Trauma, 9,* 73–87.

Pivar, I. L., & Field, N. P. (2004). Unresolved grief in combat veterans with PTSD. *Anxiety Disorders, 18,* 745–755.

Pivar, I. L., & Prigerson, H. G. (2005). Traumatic loss, complicated grief, and terrorism. In Y. Danieli, D. Brom, & J. Sills (Eds.), *The trauma of terrorism: Sharing knowledge and shared care, an international handbook* (pp. 279–289). Binghamton, NY: Haworth Maltreatment & Trauma Press.

Rabinovich, A. (2004). *The Yom Kippur War: The epic encounter that transformed the Middle East.* New York: Schocken Books.

Rubin, S. (1981). A two-track model of bereavement: Theory and research. *American Journal of Orthopsychiatry, 51*(1), 101–109.

Rubin, S. (1984). Mourning distinct from melancholia: The resolution of bereavement. *British Journal of Medical Psychology, 57,* 339–345.

Rubin, S. (1992). Adult child loss and the Two-Track Model of Bereavement. *Omega, 24*(3), 183–202.

Rubin, S. (1999). The Two-Track Model of Bereavement: Overview, retrospect and prospect. *Death Studies, 23*(8), 681–714.

Rubin, S., Bar Nadav, O., Malkinson, R., Koren, D., Gofer-Shnarch, M., & Michaeli, E. (2009). The Two-Track Model of Bereavement Questionnaire (TTBQ): Development and findings of a relational measure. *Death Studies, 33,* 1–29.

Rubin, S., Malkinson, R., & Witztum, E. (2003). Trauma and bereavement: Conceptual and clinical issues revolving around relationships. *Death Studies, 27,* 667–690.

Rubin, S., Malkinson, R., & Witztum, E. (2008). Clinical aspects of a DSM complicated grief diagnosis: Challenges, dilemmas, and opportunities. In M. S. Stroebe, R. O. Hansson, H. Schut, & W. Stroebe (Eds.), *Handbook of bereavement research and practice: Advances in theory and intervention* (pp. 187–206). Washington, DC: American Psychological Association Press.

Rubin, S., Malkinson, R., & Witztum, E. (2011). The Two-Track Model of Bereavement: The double helix of research and clinical practice. In R. Neimeyer, H. Winokuer, D. Harris, & G. Thornton (Eds.), *Grief and bereavement in contemporary society: Bridging research and practice.* New York: Routledge.

Rubin, S., Malkinson, R., & Witztum, E. (in press). *A clinician's guide to working with loss and bereavement.* New York: Routledge.

Rynearson, E. (Ed.). (2006). *Violent death: Resilience and intervention beyond the crisis.* New York: Routledge.

Sadeh, A., Rubin, S., & Berman, E. (1993). Parental and relationship representations and experiences of depression in college students. *Journal of Personality Assessment, 60*(1), 192–204.

Shakespeare, W. (1982). *Henry V* (G. Taylor, Ed.). Oxford, UK: Oxford University Press. (Original work published 1599)

Stroebe, M., Gergen, M., Gergen, K., & Stroebe, W. (1992). Broken hearts or broken bonds. *American Psychologist, 47*(10), 1205–1212.

Sundin, J., Fear, N. T., Iversen, A., Rona, R. J., & Wessely, S. (2010). PTSD after deployment to Iraq: Conflicting rates, conflicting claims. *Psychological Medicine, 40,* 367–382.

Weiss, R. (2001). Grief, bonds, and relationships. In M. Stroebe, R. Hansson, W. Stroebe, & H. Schut (Eds.), *Handbook of bereavement research: Consequences, coping and care* (pp. 47–62). Washington, DC: American Psychological Association Press.

Widdison, H. A., & Salisbury, H. G. (1990). The delayed stress syndrome: A pathological delayed grief reaction? *Omega, 20*(4), 293–306.

Witztum, E., & Kotler, M. (2000). Historical and cultural construction of PTSD in Israel. In A. Shalev, R. Yehuda, & C. Mcfarlane (Eds.), *International handbook of human response to trauma* (pp. 103–114). New York: Plenum.

Witztum, E., Levy, A., & Solomon, Z. (1996). Lessons denied: A history of therapeutic response to combat stress reaction during Israel's War of Independence (1948), the Sinai Campaign (1956) and the Six Day War (1967*). Israel Journal of Psychiatry, 33,* 79–88.

Witztum, E., Malkinson, R., & Rubin, S. (2001). Death, bereavement and traumatic loss in Israel: A historical and cultural perspective. *Israel Journal of Psychiatry, 38,* 157–170.

Zisook, S., Chentsova-Dutton, Y., & Shuchter, S. R. (1998). PTSD following bereavement. *Annals of Clinical Psychiatry, 10,* 157–163.

8

The Trauma of Bullying Experiences

Faye Mishna and Jami-Leigh Sawyer

The pervasiveness of bullying among children is well documented. The effects may be far-reaching both for children who are victimized and for those who bully. Bullying is recognized as a complex phenomenon that is a relationship problem (Pepler et al., 2006), characterized by the assertion of power through aggression (Pepler & Craig, 2000). The power differential between the child who bullies and the child who is victimized becomes entrenched with repeated bullying, thereby increasing the powerlessness of the child who is bullied (Craig & Pepler, 2003). Children who are bullied repeatedly become increasingly unable to defend themselves and thus require protection from adults. The power possessed by children who bully may exist due to individual characteristics, such as size, strength, or age (Olweus, 1993), or from awareness of others' vulnerabilities (Sutton, Smith, & Swettenham, 1999). Power may also be obtained as a result of social advantage, such as higher social status among peers or strength in numbers, with more than one child bullying another (Craig, Pepler, & Blais, 2007).

An ecological theoretical framework is considered essential to understanding bullying and intervening. According to this perspective, individual characteristics, social interactions, and ecological and cultural conditions all play a role in social behavioral patterns (Atlas & Pepler, 1998; Cairns & Cairns, 1991). To understand and intervene with bullying, therefore, it is essential to extend the focus beyond the child who bullies or the child who is bullied to include the peer group, classroom, family, community, and broader society (Atlas & Pepler, 1998; Craig, Pepler, & Atlas, 2000; Hanish & Guerra, 2000; Olweus, 1994).

Bullying may be experienced as traumatic (Janson & Hazler, 2004) and can have serious short- and long-term effects on the lives of children and adolescents. Although not all children and youth experience bullying as traumatic, research is needed to explore the individual, interpersonal, and ecological factors and conditions that contribute to bullying when it is experienced as traumatic. Such knowledge would be essential in informing education and treatment programs and interventions both to prevent the traumatization of children and to effectively address the experience of being traumatized. Factors to examine include the frequency, nature, severity, and type of bullying (Janson & Hazler, 2004) as well as adults' responses to the victimized children, for example, whether adults believe and validate the children, or whether the children are held responsible for their own victimization (Mishna, 2004; Mishna, Pepler, & Wiener, 2006).

Bullying is a pervasive problem in many countries (Olweus, 1994) and is often a predictable and unspoken, albeit painful, part of childhood. Bullying can take many forms, including physical bullying (e.g., hitting, spitting), social bullying (e.g., social exclusion, gossip), verbal bullying (e.g., threats, insults), and cyberbullying (e.g., malicious messages spread through the Internet or by cell phone) (Craig et al., 2007). Bullying can be direct (e.g., face-to-face aggression) or indirect (e.g., malicious acts without confrontation, such as social exclusion). Regardless of the form bullying takes, concern is warranted for all children and youth who are chronically victimized by their peers due to the potential long-lasting detrimental effects that may persist into adulthood (Nansel et al., 2001).

Bullying frequently occurs at school, particularly in areas with low supervision (Pepler, Craig, Ziegler, & Charach, 1993). Bullying may also occur, however, in the community (Craig & Pepler, 2003) or online (Mishna, Saini, & Solomon, 2009). The Internet and other forms of communication technology, which include social networking sites, YouTube, e-mail, and webcams (Burgess & Green, 2008; Hinduja & Patchin, 2009; Lange, 2007; Lenhart & Madden, 2007; Livingstone & Bober, 2004; Mitchell, Wolak, & Finkelhor, 2008; Palfrey & Gasser, 2008; Schrock & Boyd, 2008), give young people unprecedented opportunities to communicate with others both in and out of their existing face-to-face social networks (Gross, 2004; Lenhart & Madden, 2007; Media Awareness Network, 2005; Wolak, Mitchell, & Finkelhor, 2003) and provide youth with unparalleled exposure to a vast array of ideas, knowledge, and images that would not otherwise be within their reach. The Internet does offer many benefits for youth, such as social support, identity exploration, and cross-cultural interactions (Jackson et al., 2006; Valkenburg & Peter, 2007). It also puts youth at risk, however, for online victimization, including cyberbullying, and provides an arena for misconduct, such as bullying others online. A recent study focusing on children's and youth's perceptions found that cyberbullying often occurs within children's friendship and social circles (Mishna et al., 2009), thereby highlighting the increased ease of and access to bullying peers. As a result of cyberbullying, it is plausible that many children find themselves unable to escape bullying by their peers, even within their own homes. One child termed this phenomenon "non-stop bullying" (Mishna et al., 2009).

Children respond to bullying in varied ways. Research has found that bullying tends to be prolonged when children react emotionally, either passively or aggressively (Mahady-Wilton, Craig, & Pepler, 2000). In contrast, reactions that focus on problem-solving strategies such as assertiveness have been linked to a de-escalation of bullying behaviors (Craig et al., 2007). In a study examining the ways in which children responded to bullying and their evaluations of the effectiveness of the strategies they employed, Craig and colleagues (2007) found that a significant number of youth did "nothing" to stop the bullying. When children did attempt to stop their victimization by peers, this was often motivated by a need to exert control and assertiveness. In addition, children reported that the longer the bullying had continued, the more likely it was that their strategies were ineffective. This finding highlights the need to promote effective strategies by children and youth who are being bullied and also underscores the importance of adult support to assist children who are victimized (Craig et al., 2007).

Gender differences have been well documented in bullying relationships, particularly regarding the use of aggression. Boys tend to be bullied more often than girls (Atlas & Pepler, 1998; Nansel et al., 2001; Olweus, 1994), although girls are more likely to report being bullied compared to boys (Cowie, 2000; Craig et al., 2007). Whereas boys tend to use direct aggressive behavior that includes physical aggression, declaration of dominance, and yelling (Cairns & Cairns, 1994), girls are more likely to use indirect aggression, particularly in relation to social relationships (e.g., exclusion) (Crick & Grotpeter, 1993; Underwood, 2003). Girls who are victimized by their peers are at increased risk of developing internalizing symptoms such as somatic complaints and withdrawn behaviors (Baldry, 2004).

Research has identified common characteristics of children who are victimized and those who bully. Recognizing that we must be cautious when making generalizations, children who are victimized by their peers may be characterized by loneliness, unhappiness, school avoidance (Kochenderfer & Ladd, 1996), and low self-esteem (Slee & Rigby, 1993b). These children tend to be rejected by their peers (Slee & Rigby, 1993a) and to lack friends (Olweus, 1994). Moreover, children who are victimized are often labeled as passive or submissive, withdrawn, and physically weak. Whether a child or youth is bullied depends largely on several factors, including personal characteristics and behaviors, school climate, and peer group dynamics and interactions (Hanish & Guerra, 2000). In comparison, children and youth who bully are more prone to be stronger than their peers and depicted as impulsive and aggressive (Olweus, 1993). Children who bully are more likely to be convicted of a criminal offense by the age of 24 (Olweus, 1993) and are at higher risk of antisocial (Nansel et al., 2001) and delinquent behaviors (Farrington, 1993). Furthermore, when compared to their peers, children who bully are 5 times more likely to report using alcohol and 7 times more likely to report drug use (Pepler, Craig, Connolly, & Henderson, 2001). Approximately 10% to 20% of victimized children both bully and are victimized (Olweus, 1978). This group of children is the most severely rejected by peers (Pellegrini, 1998; Perry, Kusel, & Perry, 1988), and these children experience particularly serious adjustment problems

(O'Moore & Kirkham, 2001; Perry et al., 1988) in many areas (Schwartz, Proctor, & Chien, 2001).

Characteristics of families of children involved in bullying have also been identified (Oliver, Oaks, & Hoover, 1994). For example, families of children who bully have been reported to lack warmth or to demonstrate excessive permissiveness (Olweus, 1994) and to display a high degree of conflict, which may include violence (Baldry & Farrington, 2005; Olweus, 1994). In contrast, families of children who are victimized tend to be described as overly involved or enmeshed (Oliver et al., 1994). It is unclear, however, whether this close relationship precedes or follows the child's victimization (Oliver et al., 1994).

Bullying as a Traumatic Experience

For many children and adolescents, being a victim of bullying can be experienced as traumatic. Van der Kolk, McFarlane, and Weisaeth (1996) referred to psychological trauma as any critical incident (such as repeated emotional and verbal abuse and neglect) that results in individuals' experiencing uncharacteristically strong emotional reactions that cause psychological changes and that may affect their functioning at work, at home, or in other areas of their lives. According to Stolorow and Atwood (1992), who emphasized the relational context in which trauma occurs, "pain is not pathology. It is the absence of adequate attunement and responsiveness to the child's painful emotional reactions that renders them unendurable and thus a source of traumatic states and psychology" (p. 54). The authors contended that this conceptualization pertains both to dramatic and discrete traumatic events and to more subtle forms of traumatic injuries. Research has found that the symptoms of trauma and their severity are linked to the repetition of exposure over time (McFarlane & deGirolamo, 1996). Such findings are consistent with the bullying research literature, which highlights the detrimental effects of repeated acts of physical or verbal aggression as a key factor in bullying relationships (Craig & Pepler, 2003; Olweus, 1993). It is reasonable, therefore, to examine bullying and its effects in relation to trauma.

Although not all children or youth who are bullied experience trauma associated with their victimization, it is crucial to recognize and acknowledge the potentially devastating effects of peer victimization. Indeed, bullying has been linked to many detrimental and long-lasting effects. Children who bully and those who are victimized are both at risk of developing social, emotional, academic, and psychiatric problems, which may persist into adulthood (Fekkes, Pijpers, Fredriks, Vogels, & Verloove-Vanhorick, 2006; Nansel et al., 2001; O'Connell, Pepler, & Craig, 1999; Olweus, 1993). More particularly, negative outcomes associated with being bullied include poor psychological well-being and social adjustment, psychological distress, and physical unwellness (Rigby, 2003). Children who are victimized are more likely to suffer from psychological disorders such as anxiety or depression

(Baldry, 2004), report feeling afraid at school, avoid school more frequently (Slee, 1994), and may experience academic difficulties (Clarke & Kiselica, 1997). Bullying has also been associated with suicidal ideation both for children who bully and for those who are victimized (Kaltiala-Heino, Rimpelä, Marttunen, Rimpelä, & Rantanen, 1999; Klomek et al., 2008; Klomek, Marrocco, Kleinman, Schonfeld, & Gould, 2009).

Although the negative consequences associated with bullying have been well documented, an unfortunate reality for many school-aged children is that bullying is still often accepted as a hurtful yet common aspect of childhood, an attitude that can minimize the potentially traumatic effects of bullying. Children are consequently often encouraged to solve bullying problems on their own (Craig et al., 2007), an attitude that fails to recognize the powerlessness of the victimized child (O'Connell et al., 1999). A study conducted by Hazler, Miller, Carney, and Green (2001) examines the ability of 251 professionals (counselors and teachers) to differentiate bullying from other forms of conflict. Twenty-one scenarios were presented to participants to gauge whether they judged the situations to constitute bullying. Findings reveal that professionals were more likely to rate physical conflicts as bullying, regardless of whether the actions fit the definition of bullying. Furthermore, professionals rated scenarios with physical threat or abuse as more severe than verbal or social/emotional bullying behaviors. This finding highlights the need for adults to understand the detrimental effects of all forms of bullying and to recognize that just as physical bullying requires adult intervention, so too do verbal and relational bullying. Hazler (1997) contended that the difficulty in deciding whether a situation is defined as bullying is the main reason why most adults do not intervene. Similarly, Mishna et al. (2006) found that although the respondents in their study, consisting of children who self-identified as experiencing bullying and their parents and teachers, included indirect bullying in their definitions, they often considered this form of bullying less serious. The authors concluded that this view of indirect bullying as less serious, together with the absence of repetition within the children's, parents', and educators' definitions, suggests that the respondents do not fully grasp the potentially damaging effects of many bullying behaviors.

Schools play a major role in determining the interpersonal context, such as tolerance of and ability to handle social aggression (Twemlow, Fonagy, & Sacco, 2003). In particular, a lack of connectedness among students and between students and teachers can result in a number of detrimental outcomes (Twemlow, Fonagy, & Sacco, 2002). An extreme example of the violence that may ensue is the Columbine tragedy, which occurred at what some students, teachers, and parents described as a school that tolerated bullying (Greenfield & Juonen, 1999; Kass, 2000). Although this tragic situation represents an extreme and does not occur in the majority of schools, it highlights the fact that a toxic school environment in which bullying is common inevitably results in tremendous suffering and perhaps trauma for many children who are victimized; in extreme circumstances it can result in horrific violence and trauma affecting the entire school and community (Aronson, 2004; Greenfield & Juonen, 1999; Twemlow et al., 2003).

Evidence suggests that peer victimization can have a traumatic effect on bystanders (Janson & Hazler, 2004). It has been documented that bystanders can experience traumatic reactions similar to those of the victimized children or youth (Boney-McCoy & Finkelhor, 1995). Janson and Hazler (2004) conducted a study examining psychological distress and physiological reactivity in 77 participants. Each participant was interviewed twice, first to recall an instance of when he or she was a bystander and second to recall a situation in which he or she was the victim of a prevalent form of repetitive abuse (e.g., bullying). Results indicated that bystanders and victims may be similarly affected by repetitive abuse both at the time of event occurrence and over time (Janson & Hazler, 2004).

Shame and Humiliation

Shame plays a central role in bullying dynamics, which has been demonstrated through applying shame management theory to explain bullying behaviors (Ahmed, 2006). Research in the field of restorative justice indicates that individuals have a higher risk of partaking in wrongdoing in the future when they are unable to feel shame associated with harming others (Ahmed & Braithwaite, 2006). Two types of shame management have been identified: shame acknowledgment and shame displacement. According to this perspective, individuals who acknowledge shame associated with their wrongdoing are more likely to abstain from such actions in the future due to their appreciation of the consequences associated with such actions. Conversely, those individuals who displace their feelings of shame by blaming others will more likely increase their acts of wrongdoing because of their lack of appreciation of the consequences (Ahmed & Braithwaite, 2006).

Very little research has directly examined the role of shame in bullying (Menesini & Camodeca, 2008). The majority of the extant research has been conducted in a few countries, including Spain, Italy (Menesini & Camodeca, 2008; Menesini et al., 2003), Australia (Ahmed, 2006), and Bangladesh (Ahmed & Braithwaite, 2006). Menesini and colleagues (2003) conducted parallel studies in three European cities, one in Spain and two in Italy, to examine the role of shame and guilt in relation to bullying situations. A total of 121 children between the ages of 9 and 11 were assigned to one of three status groups based on peer nominations: bully, victim, or outsider. Children were told a fictional story about bullying and were then asked to put themselves in the role of the bully and describe their feelings of responsibility (shame and guilt) and disengagement (indifference and pride). The researchers recognized cross-cultural differences within their sample as children from different parts of Europe displayed varying degrees of disengagement. Specifically, when compared to children from Spain, children from the southern part of

Italy revealed an attitude of higher disengagement toward the bully as they exhibited a lack of negative emotions in response to the bullying behavior and a sense of satisfaction with their actions (Menesini et al., 2003).

Ahmed's (2006) study in Australia finds that children manage their shame differently depending on their role in bullying experiences. Children who bully were found to displace their shame by externalizing blame and anger, with little acceptance of wrongdoing. Conversely, children who are victims of bullying tended to internalize their shame, resulting in overwhelming feelings of rejection in which they did not feel that others considered them worthy.

Ahmed and Braithwaite (2006) found an association between shame management and bullying behaviors within the cultural context of Bangladesh in their study that examined the relationships among forgiveness, reconciliation, shame, and school bullying. Parental forgiveness and reconciliation were important factors in this study as parents were regarded as children's most significant authority figures. The researchers hypothesized that forgiveness and reconciliation would be associated with shame management abilities and thus linked to bullying. Data were collected from 1,875 Bangladeshi adolescents in Grades 7 through 10 using the Life at School Survey. Results indicated that high shame acknowledgment (e.g., accepting responsibility, making amends) was associated with less bullying whereas high shame displacement (e.g., using anger or blaming others) was associated with more bullying.

Because the aforementioned findings are specific to particular countries, it is unclear what role culture may have played in relation to shame and bullying as culture may affect shame differently. Bedford and Hwang (2003) examined the emotions of guilt and shame in Chinese culture compared to American culture. They described a differential sensitivity to shame for Chinese culture, whereby Chinese individuals are sensitive to feeling shame from the actions or lack of actions of others. There is therefore a need for further research to examine the role of shame in bullying, including the cultural determinants related to shame. Because bullying occurs throughout the world, it is imperative to examine the role of culture, particularly as it relates to shame in bullying.

Humiliation, defined as "feelings of disgrace and public disparagement that may shatter a youngster's healthy sense of narcissism and sense of identity, and loss of a basic sense of one's worthwhileness" (Pfeffer, 1990, p. 81), has also been linked to bullying. Research indicates that humiliation as a result of being bullied has been associated with devastating consequences (Stillon, 1994). Indeed, Pfeffer (1990) contended that humiliation is one of the critical factors that precipitate suicidal ideation due to relationship problems. Pfeffer argued that feelings of humiliation, which can be brought about by repeated bullying, are a "powerful force to increase thoughts of self-annihilation" (p. 81).

Bullying Interventions

Interventions to address bullying, typically school based, have had mixed success. Reasons for this varying effectiveness include factors such as inconsistent institutional and societal commitment, prohibitive time and personnel demands, and teacher and school variables (Kallestad & Olweus, 2003). There is consensus, nevertheless, that interventions must encompass all levels of the system, including the school, classroom, peers, parents, and individual children or youth involved in bullying, and must be supported by broader structural initiatives (Olweus, 1993). Effective programs involve identifying and intervening with students considered at risk; providing education to all students about skills, strategies, and nonviolent problem solving; furnishing information to foster a positive social and learning environment; and developing interventions that promote a safer, more caring, and responsive climate (Twemlow & Cohen, 2003). Twemlow and Cohen (2003) contended, "At the end of the day all violence prevention programs come down to relationships: our ability to listen to ourselves, to recognize others' experience and use this information to solve problems, to learn and be creative together" (p. 121).

Albeit critical, the interpersonal is but one level among the overlapping levels and processes that must be taken into account to address bullying fully. The focus in this chapter is on responses at the interpersonal level. Within the interpersonal domain there are a number of crucial relationships that must be examined and addressed: the relationship between the child or youth who bullies and the child or youth who is victimized (individual or group), the relationship between the teacher and involved children, the relationship between the involved children and their parents, the relationship between the parents and teachers, and the interpersonal relationships and interchanges within the larger school environment, for instance, between the teacher and principal or between the parents and school administration.

Model of Clinical Intervention

The emphasis in clinical social work practice on the person in the environment, and the importance of the therapeutic relationship, is congruent with contemporary psychoanalytic theories such as self psychology (Kohut, 1977; Kohut & Wolf, 1978), intersubjectivity theory (Stolorow, 1994; Stolorow & Atwood, 1992), and relational theory (Mitchell, 1988, 2000). As bullying is considered to be a relationship problem, contemporary psychoanalytic theories that focus on the relationship are integral in illustrating the clinical process and interventions for childhood bullying. These theories provide a valuable conceptual framework through which to capture the complex interactions inherent in the counseling relationship.

Clinical Illustration

Erin is a bright and talented 10-year-old girl in Grade 5 who has recently transferred to her current school. She was born in Canada shortly after her parents emigrated from China and lives with them and her older brother in a large Canadian urban center. Erin attends a school that is categorized in the second-highest income level. Schools at this level have a moderate to low percentage of single-parent families and mixed to high education levels, with most families living in single detached housing, and a low to moderate percentage of recent immigrants (*Schools Like Us Project Description*, 2001–2002). The school Erin attends is renowned for its all-around excellence. Indeed, one teacher expressed concern that the school's reputation as "nice" reduced teachers' and parents' vigilance with respect to bullying. He believed that the degree of bullying within the school

> is just as much. It's much more covert. I think because the majority of our bullying is not physical, most parents don't perceive that we have a bullying problem. In fact many of them may have the same attitude that I heard from teachers when I first arrived, saying, "Oh, our kids are nice to each other; there is no bullying."

The teacher's portrayal of the nature of bullying within this school corresponded to Erin's perceptions. Erin described having been "bullied physically" at her previous school. Erin had come to expect, and even to accept, being victimized by her peers, which was palpable in her belief, "I was a kid to be bullied." After transferring to her current school, Erin felt "relief" because the bullying she had anticipated did not occur. Rather, she thought, "Oh wow, nothing bad is happening." Completing the survey administered as part of a research study drastically altered Erin's view, however. She explained,

> There is a group of people I know, and I thought that they were my friends. But they tell secrets in front of me. And they'll say, "Could you go away?" and I would. I didn't think it was my business. But now I remember the tone of voice that they used, and they meant it meanly. So I rethought that and I thought, "I guess they were bullying me."

Erin often dreaded going to school but for the most part forced herself to attend. Prior to her interview for the research, Erin had not discussed these experiences or feelings with anyone. Clearly struggling with issues related to her exclusion, especially now that she recognized the behavior as bullying, Erin was willing to see a school social worker to receive help coping with her feelings and this problem. The researcher made the referral (as had been preplanned) as part of the research ethics protocol, which had been approved by the university.

Erin was susceptible to feeling traumatized due to her bullying experiences as a result of several coinciding and interacting elements. It was important for the clinician to understand the whole ecological context. Even before her current experience of repeated and chronic exclusion by peers, Erin had a history of being physically bullied and indeed spoke in a manner that suggested she had resigned herself to this state of affairs. Erin's anticipation that the physical bullying she had previously endured would continue when she transferred to her new school was such that Erin not only felt relieved but did not recognize the exclusion as bullying. Rather, Erin believed that her peers, including those she considered friends, were justified in treating her as they did.

Another factor to consider is that although Erin described her relationship with her parents and particularly her mother as close and supportive, she stated that in the past, her mother had not always believed her when she divulged her bullying experiences. She offered as one example the time she reported to her mother that she had been "chased around the schoolyard by this kid waving his fists and saying, 'I'm going to hurt you.'" Moreover, Erin's mother, like many others as revealed by the research evidence, did not appreciate the seriousness of relational bullying. Thus, her mother reported that when Erin expressed the desire to participate in our research study and self-identified as being bullied, she "worried that it was something worse. I thought somebody was pushing her or hitting her or something like that." Erin's mother stated that she felt "relieved" when she found out that her daughter was being excluded by peers because "this is what kids do." It is interesting to note that this feeling of relief was similar to Erin's.

Not fitting typical expectations about how a victimized child presents and behaves, Erin fell beneath the radar of her school. Her teacher was unaware that Erin might be experiencing bullying and expressed surprise to learn that Erin reported being bullied: "It never occurred to me that Erin would be bullied because she can stand up for herself and is liked and well adjusted." The fact that neither Erin nor the significant adults in her life (her parents and teacher) recognized that she was being bullied by her peers left her at greater risk of feeling traumatized and was a contributing factor to the situation's escalating.

The social worker gently probed and listened as Erin talked about her experiences with peers and friends and as she contemplated her newfound realization that their behavior constituted bullying. Appreciating the seriousness and impact of indirect bullying, the social worker responded empathically to Erin's description of the effect of her repetitive exclusion and to her growing expressions of hurt and anger.

At her current school, Erin was repeatedly subjected to exclusion by peers, including those she considered friends. Despite not having identified herself as experiencing bullying, Erin nonetheless was clearly affected. Reading a definition of bullying that included social exclusion allowed Erin to realize that she had the right not to be treated in such a manner. Reflecting on how she felt when excluded, for example, being told to "go away," Erin began to make links between the bullying experiences and her emotional issues and low self-esteem:

It makes me really sad. I think it's my fault. And well, I don't know why but I think that may affect me. Well, now when I make a mistake for some reason, I feel like I have to punish myself so I hit myself. And I think that could be related to the bullying.

Erin added that when upset with herself she had recently begun to hit her head with a book or pinch herself so hard that she drew blood. The social worker validated her pain and helped Erin to articulate her responses to find more effective, less destructive ways of coping.

The clinician was informed by contemporary psychodynamic theories, including self psychology theory, intersubjectivity theory, and relational theory. Accordingly, she considered empathy to be central to both development and the therapeutic process (Kohut, 1984). She understood that in the treatment process, Erin's previously frustrated selfobject needs would likely be reactivated through an empathic connection developed with the therapist. Informed by these theories, the clinician recognized that listening empathically was integral to developing and sustaining a solid therapeutic relationship with Erin. The clinician therefore prioritized the relational context of the therapy and considered Erin's subjectivity within the context to be most important. According to self psychology theory, the self is the core of the personality, integrating central ambitions and goals. Although each child is born with an innate sense of self, a responsive and empathic environment is crucial to the child's achieving a coherent sense of self (Goldstein, Miehls, & Ringel, 2009; Kohut, 1984), which contributes to a child's healthy self-esteem.

The clinician's inquiry, interest, and empathic understanding provided Erin with needed mirroring and validation, which strengthened her sense of self, increased her self-esteem, and fostered her ability to increasingly recognize and identify her feelings, for example, hurt and anger at how her peers treated her. At times, Erin commented that it was "weird" that the clinician believed her.

As Erin's previous selfobject needs emerged in the context of this new relational interaction with the clinician, Erin not only reconsidered her friends' treatment of her but began to contemplate some aspects of her relationship with her mother (Goldstein et al., 2009). The focus of intersubjectivity theory is "on the interplay between the differently organized subjective worlds of the observer and the observed" (Atwood & Stolorow, 1984, p. 41), particularly on the subjective experiences of the participants (Stolorow, Atwood, & Brandchaft, 1994). Healthy and pathological patterns of development are seen as arising from, and being maintained within, the interaction of subjectivities, for example, parent-child or therapist-client (Orange, Atwood, & Stolorow, 1997). Erin and her mother both described their relationship as "close," and Erin expressed feeling supported by her mother. As the therapy progressed, she told her therapist that in the past her mother had not always "believed" her when she told her about being bullied. Erin explained that her mother "thought it was happening so often that she was thinking, 'Is Erin really telling me the truth, because this is happening so often?'" Erin exclaimed, "And of course I was!" She continued,

> To assume that it is true is much better than to assume that it's not true. When my mom doesn't believe me, it's sort of hard because then

you have no support. So when you have no support in dealing with the issue, it is not going to stop. Although kids can do something, children cannot always deal with this kind of situation. I mean we just can't on our own. It is not as if we were born with some sort of sense of what to do here, what to do there. So we need help in that situation.

Feeling "believed" by the clinician allowed Erin to reflect on her own needs, which were to have her parents believe and validate her subjective experiences. Erin is remarkably insightful for a child so young; her statements correspond to the literature with respect to the importance of feeling understood and validated for healthy development and self-esteem. Failure to validate a child's experience of victimization can lead to the child's feeling traumatized (Stolorow & Atwood, 1992), to being unsure about his or her own feelings. Indeed, Erin had not appeared to register her own feelings, manifest by not consciously identifying feeling bullied when repeatedly excluded by her peers. Erin's self-destructive behavior, which consisted of such actions as hitting or pinching herself in response to flaws, mistakes, or not being treated well, indicated that she was deeply affected. After reading the definition, Erin reconsidered and recognized her peers' treatment of her as bullying behavior. Despite this change in her view, Erin did not discuss this newfound understanding with anyone, nor had the adults in her life recognized that she was in need of help. She then disclosed her bullying experiences first when completing the questionnaire and later when interviewed as part of the research.

As noted, even after recognizing that she was bullied, Erin did not tell her parents or teacher. This corresponds with a troubling and consistent finding that many children do not tell an adult about being victimized by their peers (Hanish & Guerra, 2000). In a study that examined the perspectives of children who self-identified as bullied and of their parents and educators, it emerged that adults at times doubted the children's subjective responses or did not view incidents as bullying—even though the child expressed or displayed distress or felt bullied (Mishna, 2004; Mishna, Scarcello, Pepler, & Wiener, 2005). The adult's conclusion shapes his or her response to the child and thus influences whether a child will report the bullying (Craig, Henderson, & Murphy, 2000). Doubting a child's perspective may contribute to his or her lack of disclosure to teachers (Mishna, 2004; Mishna et al., 2006). Discussing the effect on children of educators' not responding to children's accounts of victimization, Clarke and Kiselica (1997) contended, "The victims internalize the implied message that the adults have discounted their worth as individuals, and they carry this message forward into adulthood" (p. 316).

Fundamental to Winnicott's (1960, 1965) perspective of object relations theory is the concept of the "holding environment," whereby the mother or caregiver creates a world in which the baby or child feels "held, safe, and protected from dangers without and protected as well from the danger of emotions within" (Flanagan, 2008, p. 131). The concept of the holding environment can extend beyond the mother-child relationship to include the therapeutic relationship: "Clients, too, need the therapist to construct a holding environment that creates a safe physical and psychological space wherein they feel protected so that spontaneous interactions, feelings, and experiences can occur" (Flanagan, 2008, p. 131). Erin's social worker was able to create a holding environment by listening and demonstrating an appreciation of the seriousness of indirect bullying and by responding to her in ways that other adults, such as her mother and teacher, had not. Relational aggression has only recently been recognized as a distinct form of bullying and has been used to capture the nature through which girls tend to bully (Crick & Grotpeter, 1993). There is compelling evidence of the potentially devastating effects of relational bullying (Owens, Shute, & Slee, 2000). Nevertheless, like Erin and her mother, children and adults often do not consider indirect or relational aggression a form of bullying or consider it to be less severe (Craig et al., 2000; Hanish & Guerra, 2000; Mishna, 2004; Mishna et al., 2006). This attitude can lead to overlooking the damage of this form of bullying. By appreciating the seriousness of indirect or relational bullying and its devastating effect on Erin, the therapist created an environment in which Erin felt safe and supported and in which she was able to begin to examine and identify her feelings and responses with respect to her peers' bullying behavior and her mother's lack of validation of her subjective experiences.

Central to intersubjectivity theory is the view that the context is foundational to understanding the emotional life of an individual (Orange et al., 1997; Stolorow & Atwood, 1992). In addition to providing Erin individual therapy, therefore, it was imperative that the therapist understand the larger context in which Erin lived. The clinician's assessment highlighted the gap in knowledge about bullying by Erin's mother and teacher, which impeded their ability to recognize that Erin was enduring victimization by peers. Their lack of recognition compounded the problem for Erin. As noted, this lack of validation could prove traumatic. After receiving permission from Erin, the therapist provided her parents with information about bullying, including the potentially devastating effects of bullying behaviors that are not overt or do not seem serious, such as exclusion (Craig, Henderson, & Murphy, 2000), and when the timing seemed right helped them to determine how to respond appropriately. Similarly, the clinician realized that it was necessary to work with the teacher to increase her understanding of the complexity of bullying. It appeared that the teacher's assumptions about characteristics that victimized children would display, for example, that they would not be well adjusted or well liked, might be a factor that prevented her from recognizing the possibility that Erin could be bullied and that this could have a traumatic impact on her. There is a need for the social worker to balance information about the characteristics that victimized children may exhibit with the recognition that these characteristics need not be present in all bullying situations (Mishna et al., 2005; Mishna et al., 2006).

Finally, it was important that the social worker work with both Erin's parents and her teacher to emphasize the importance of their validating her experiences. Her mother corroborated Erin's view that in the past she did not always believe Erin's accounts of being bullied, which she attributed to her daughter's tendency to be "dramatic," and the consequent "difficulty to sort of gauge is she upset, is she exaggerating . . . what is going on?"

Organizing principles are a key component of an individual's subjectivity, and they reflect "the emotional conclusions a person had drawn from lifelong experience of the emotional environment, especially the complex mutual connections with early caregivers" (Orange et al., 1997, p. 7). Erin's therapist understood that she had an important role in helping Erin's parents and teacher understand and respond to Erin's perspective and feelings. The potential damage when adults do not validate a child is such that "what the children learn from the adults' handling of bullying incidents must be more frightening to them than the individual bullying incidents" (Clarke & Kiselica, 1997, p. 316). Hence, it is critical that adults listen to and validate the child's experience of victimization because failure to do so can lead to the child's feeling traumatized (Stolorow & Atwood, 1992) and can contribute to development of organizing principles with the expectation that adults and others will not listen to or validate the individual. Erin eloquently argued that she and other children need to be believed and helped by adults with bullying situations and poignantly articulated the danger when this does not occur. Her ability to recognize the need for adult help was a protective factor yet did not negate Erin's vulnerability should adults not listen to or believe her account.

To confuse matters, Erin considered the children who bullied her to be friends. Having or desiring a friendship with the child who bullies may complicate the situation and inhibit the victimized child's ability to disclose (Mishna, 2004). The clinician therefore had to weigh her recognition that this behavior constitutes bullying with an understanding that Erin might be afraid of acknowledging to herself or disclosing this problematic behavior to others for fear of losing the friendship. Despite her newfound awareness that her friends should not exclude her as they were, Erin was faced with the dilemma of whether and how to act on this recognition as the potential loss of her friends may have felt too big a risk to take. According to a study on help-seeking behaviors among children in Grades 3 and 4, children were more likely to ask teachers for help when they did not care about maintaining friendships with the children who were the aggressors (Newman, Murray, & Lussier, 2001), suggesting that the children were aware that loss of a friendship might be the cost of telling a teacher. In another study (Mishna, 2004), one girl explained that she could not use her teacher's advice to stay away from a boy who physically bullied her "because we've been a little bit friends for a year."

Overall, friendship is depicted as positive and as a source of protection for victimized children (Grotpeter & Crick, 1996). Having friendships can ameliorate the negative effects of victimization and can decrease the likelihood that a child will continue to be bullied (Hanish & Guerra, 2000). It must be recognized, however, that "dyadic friendships can either diminish or reinforce the peer victimized child's vulnerabilities" (Crick & Nelson, 2002, p. 599). Children's friendships are foundational for the acquisition of skills and competencies (Newcomb & Bagwell, 1995) and may serve as prototypes for later relationships such as ones with romantic partners (Laursen & Bukowski, 1997). Without information to the contrary, adults might assume that leaving children to their own devices in navigating friendship fosters growth. Social workers have a key role to play in working with adults to intervene to help children deal with bullying within friendships. For instance, Erin clearly needed support to recognize the bullying and to believe that she should not accept being bullied as part of her friendships. It is not sufficient for Erin to be told, "Just don't be friends"; she requires help navigating how to address the bullying behaviors that are occurring within the friendship and needs to know that she is not alone to deal with it.

Paradoxically, because Erin appeared to do well socially and academically, so much so that her teacher was surprised she would report being victimized, the clinician had to be mindful not to minimize Erin's concerns. Erin had begun to display concerning and negative effects of being bullied along with potentially traumatic effects of the experience, such as dreading and wanting to avoid school despite being a strong student and self-blaming and physically hurting herself. Without support and interventions by trusted adults, Erin's behavior could have potentially escalated into sustained self-harming behavior and school avoidance, resulting in deterioration of her current excellent grades. Erin had many protective factors such as her ability for self-reflection and insight and her positive relationships with her parents and teacher on which it was important to build (Baldry & Farrington, 2005). The clinician tried to balance empathizing with the pain and problems with building on Erin's strengths and including significant adults in the treatment.

Conclusion

Erin entered therapy somewhat shell-shocked, having quite suddenly realized that she had been unaware that her peers, including friends, were bullying her. In the therapy, Erin explored her experiences with peers and her family, which helped her to recognize the traumatic nature of her experiences and ultimately transform the trauma.

Bullying is a pervasive and concerning phenomenon that can have long-lasting negative consequences for children involved, a phenomenon contributing to many societal problems associated with interpersonal violence (Pepler et al., 2006). A recent focus on victimization among children and adolescents largely stems from the human rights movement and recognition that individuals' rights are too commonly abused (Smith, 1997). Bullying can be experienced by children as traumatic. Regardless of the nature or per-ceived severity of the bullying, however, a child can feel traumatized if adults do not listen, respond, or intervene appropriately. Thus, if adults blame or do not believe or validate the child's experience of victimization, the child could feel further victimized (Astor, 1995). The relationship problem that is bully-ing calls for a perspective that accounts for the inherent complexities involved—the individual, the social, and the environmental context.

The perspective presented in this chapter offers a frame through which traumatic experiences of peer victimization can be understood and addressed therapeutically. A clinical example illustrates concepts and strategies includ-ing the role of the therapist, the nature of the therapeutic relationship, and the therapeutic process and interventions. As this example demonstrates, it was important for the clinician to appreciate and understand the relational context of the therapy and to also recognize and work with the ecological context system in which Erin lived, thus extending beyond work with Erin to include her mother, teachers, and the larger school system. While addressing other levels of the system, the clinician was mindful of creating a holding environment that emphasized safety and recognized the primacy of Erin's subjectivity.

References

Ahmed, E. (2006). Understanding bullying from a shame management perspective: Findings from a three-year follow-up study. *Educational & Child Psychology, 23*(2), 25–39.

Ahmed, E., & Braithwaite, V. (2006). Forgiveness, reconciliation, and shame: Three key variables in reducing school bullying. *Journal of Social Issues, 62*(2), 347–370.

Aronson, E. (2004). How the Columbine high school tragedy could have been pre-vented. *Journal of Individual Psychology, 60*(4), 355–360.

Astor, R. A. (1995). School violence: A blueprint for elementary school interven-tions. *Social Work in Education, 19*(2), 101–115.

Atlas, R. S., & Pepler, D. J. (1998). Observations of bullying in the classroom. *Journal of Educational Research, 92*(2), 86–99.

Atwood, G. E., & Stolorow, R. D. (1984). *Structures of subjectivity: Explorations in psychoanalytic phenomenology.* Hillsdale, NJ: Analytic Press.

Baldry, A. C. (2004). The impact of direct and indirect bullying on the mental and physical health of Italian youngsters. *Aggressive Behavior, 30,* 343–355.

Baldry, A. C., & Farrington, D. P. (2005). Protective factors as moderators of risk factors in adolescence bullying. *Social Psychology of Education, 8,* 263–284.

Bedford, O., & Hwang, K. K. (2003). Guilt and shame in Chinese culture: A cross-cultural framework from the perspective of morality and identity. *Journal for the Theory of Social Behavior, 33*(2), 127–144.

Boney-McCoy, S., & Finkelhor, D. (1995). Psychosocial sequelae of violent victim-ization in a national youth sample. *Journal of Consulting & Clinical Psychology, 63*(5), 726–736.

Burgess, J. E., & Green, J. B. (2008). Agency and controversy in the YouTube community. In *Proceedings. IR 9.0. Rethinking communities, rethinking place—Association of Internet research conference*. Copenhagen: IT University of Copenhagen, Denmark.

Cairns, R. B., & Cairns, B. D. (1991). Social cognition and social networks: A developmental perspective. In D. Pepler & K. Rubin (Eds.), *The development and treatment of childhood aggression* (pp. 249–278). Hillsdale, NJ: Lawrence Erlbaum.

Cairns, R. B., & Cairns, B. D. (1994). *Lifelines and risks: Pathways of youth in our time*. Cambridge, UK: Cambridge University Press.

Clarke, E. A., & Kiselica, M. S. (1997). A systemic counselling approach to the problem of bullying. *Elementary School Guidance & Counselling, 31*, 310–325.

Cowie, H. (2000). Bystanding or standing by: Gender issues in coping with bullying in English schools. *Aggressive Behaviour, 26*, 85–97.

Craig, W., Pepler, D., & Blais, J. (2007). Responding to bullying: What works? *School Psychology International, 28*(4), 465–477.

Craig, W. M., Henderson, K., & Murphy, J. G. (2000). Prospective teachers' attitudes toward bullying and victimization. *School Psychology International, 21*(1), 5–21.

Craig, W. M., & Pepler, D. J. (2003). Identifying and targeting risk for involvement in bullying and victimization. *Canadian Journal of Psychiatry, 48*(9), 577–582.

Craig, W. M., Pepler, D. J., & Atlas, R. (2000). Observations of bullying on the playground and in the classroom. *International Journal of School Psychology, 21*, 22–36.

Crick, N., & Grotpeter, J. (1993). Relational aggression, gender, and social-psychological adjustment. *Child Development, 66*, 710–722.

Crick, N. R., & Nelson, D. A. (2002). Relational and physical victimization within friendships: Nobody told me there'd be friends like these. *Journal of Abnormal Child Psychology, 30*(6), 599–607.

Farrington, D. P. (1993). Understanding and preventing bullying. *Crime and Justice, 17*, 381–458.

Fekkes, M., Pijpers, F. I. M., Fredriks, M., Vogels, T., & Verloove-Vanhorick, S. P. (2006). Do bullied children get ill, or do ill children get bullied? A prospective cohort study on the relationship between bullying and health-related symptoms. *Pediatrics, 117*(5), 1568–1574.

Flanagan, L. M. (2008). Object relations theory. In J. Berzoff, L. M. Flanagan, & P. Hertz (Eds.), *Inside out and outside in: Psychodynamic clinical theory and practice in contemporary multicultural contexts* (2nd ed., pp. 121–160). Northvale, NJ: Jason Aronson.

Goldstein, E., Miehls, D., & Ringel, S. (2009). *Advanced clinical social work practice: Relational principles and techniques*. New York: Columbia University Press.

Greenfield, P. M., & Juonen, J. (1999). A developmental look at Columbine. *APA Monitor Online, 30*(7).

Gross, E. F. (2004). Adolescent Internet use: What we expect, what teens report. *Journal of Applied Developmental Psychology, 25*(6), 633–649.

Grotpeter, J. K., & Crick, N. R. (1996). Relational aggression, overt aggression, and friendship. *Child Development, 67*, 2328–2338.

Hanish, L. D., & Guerra, N. G. (2000). Children who get victimized at school: What is known? What can be done? *Professional School Counseling, 4*(2), 113–119.

Hazler, R. J. (1997). Bystanders: An overlooked factor in peer-on-peer abuse. *Journal for the Professional Counselor, 11,* 11–21.

Hazler, R. J., Miller, D. L., Carney, J. V., & Green, S. (2001). Adult recognition of school bullying situations. *Educational Research, 43*(2), 133–146.

Hinduja, S., & Patchin, J. W. (2009). *Bullying beyond the schoolyard: Preventing and responding to cyberbullying.* Thousand Oaks, CA: Sage.

Jackson, L. A., von Eye, A., Biocca, F. A., Barbatsis, G., Zhao, Y., & Fitzgerald, H. E. (2006). Does home Internet use influence the academic performance of low-income children? *Developmental Psychology, 42*(3), 429–435.

Janson, G. R., & Hazler, R. J. (2004). Trauma reactions of bystanders and victims to repetitive abuse experiences. *Violence and Victims, 19,* 239–255.

Kallestad, J. H., & Olweus, D. (2003). Predicting teachers' and schools' implementation of the Olweus bullying prevention program: A multilevel study. *Prevention & Treatment, 6*(21), Article A. Retrieved January 15, 2006, from http://content.apa.org/journals/pre/6/1/21

Kaltiala-Heino, R., Rimpelä, M., Marttunen, M., Rimpelä, A., & Rantanen, P. (1999). Bullying, depression, and suicidal ideation in Finnish adolescents: School survey. *British Medical Journal, 319,* 348–351.

Kass, J. (2000). Witnesses tell of Columbine bullying. *Rocky Mountain News.* Retrieved March 3, 2006, from http://www.denver-rmn.com/shooting/1003col4.shtml

Klomek, A. B., Marrocco, F., Kleinman, M., Schonfeld, I. S., & Gould, M. (2009). Bullying, depression, and suicidality in adolescents. *Journal of the American Academy of Child & Adolescent Psychiatry, 46*(1), 40–49.

Klomek, A. B., Sourander, A., Kumpulainen, K., Piha, J., Tamminen, T., Moilanen, I., et al. (2008). Childhood bullying as a risk for later depression and suicidal ideation among Finnish males. *Journal of Affective Disorders, 109*(1/2), 47–55.

Kochenderfer, B. J., & Ladd, G. W. (1996). Peer victimization: Cause or consequence of school maladjustment? *Child Development, 67,* 1305–1317.

Kohut, H. (1977). *The restoration of the self.* New York: International University Press.

Kohut, H. (1984). *How does analysis cure?* Chicago: University of Chicago Press.

Kohut, H., & Wolf, E. S. (1978). The disorders of the self and their treatment: An outline. *International Journal of Psycho-Analysis, 59,* 413–425.

Lange, P. G. (2007). Publicly private and privately public: Social networking on YouTube. *Journal of Computer-Mediated Communication, 13*(1), 361–380.

Laursen, B., & Bukowski, W. M. (1997). A developmental guide to the organisation of close relationships. *International Journal of Behavioral Development, 21*(4), 747–770.

Lenhart, A., & Madden, M. (2007). *Teens, privacy & online social networks.* Washington, DC: Pew Internet & American Life Project. Retrieved June 29, 2007, from http://www.pewinternet.org/~/media//Files/Reports/2007/PIP_Teens_Privacy_SNS_ReportFinal.pdf

Livingstone, S., & Bober, M. (2004). *UK children go online: Surveying the experiences of young people and their parents.* London: LSE Research Online. Retrieved from http://eprints.lse.ac.uk/archive/0000395

Mahady-Wilton, M., Craig, W. M., & Pepler, D. J. (2000). Emotional regulation and display in classroom bullying: Characteristic expressions of affect, coping styles and relevant contextual factors. *Social Development, 2,* 226–244.

McFarlane, A. C., & deGirolamo, G. (1996). The nature of traumatic stressors and the epidemiology of posttraumatic reactions. In B. A. van der Kolk,

A. C. McFarlane, & L. Weisaeth (Eds.), *Traumatic stress: The effects of overwhelming experience on mind, body and society* (pp. 129–154). New York: Guilford.

Media Awareness Network. (2005). *Young Canadians in a wired world.* Retrieved April 11, 2009, from http://www.media-awareness.ca/english/research/ycww/phaseII/key_findings.cfm

Menesini, E., & Camodeca, M. (2008). Shame and guilt as behaviour regulators: Relationships with bullying, victimization and prosocial behaviour. *British Journal of Developmental Psychology, 26,* 183–196.

Menesini, E., Sanchez, V., Fonzi, A., Ortega, R., Costabile, A., & Lo Feudo, G. (2003). Moral emotions and bullying: A cross-national comparison of differences between bullies, victims and outsiders. *Aggressive Behavior, 29,* 515–530.

Mishna, F. (2004). A qualitative study of bullying from multiple perspectives. *Children & Schools, 26*(4), 234–247.

Mishna, F., Pepler, D., & Wiener, J. (2006). Factors associated with perceptions and responses to bullying situations by children, parents, teachers and principals. *Victims and Offenders, 1*(3), 255–288.

Mishna, F., Saini, M., & Solomon, S. (2009). Ongoing and online: Children and youth's perceptions of cyber bullying. *Children and Youth Services Review, 31*(12), 1222–1228.

Mishna, F., Scarcello, I., Pepler, D. J., & Wiener, J. (2005). Teachers' understanding of bullying. *Canadian Journal of Education, 28*(4), 667–691.

Mitchell, K. J., Wolak, J., & Finkelhor, D. (2008). Are blogs putting youth at risk for online sexual solicitation or harassment? *Child Abuse & Neglect, 32,* 277–294.

Mitchell, S. A. (1988). *Relational concepts in psychoanalysis: An integration.* Cambridge, MA: Harvard University Press.

Mitchell, S. A. (2000). *Relationality: From attachment to intersubjectivity.* Hillsdale, NJ: Analytic Press.

Nansel, T. R., Overpeck, M., Pilla, R. S., Ruan, W. J., Simons-Morton, B., & Scheidt, P. (2001). Bullying behaviours among US youth: Prevalence and association with psychosocial adjustment. *Journal of the American Medical Association, 285*(16), 2094–2100.

Newcomb, A. F., & Bagwell, C. L. (1995). Children's friendship relations: A meta-analytic review. *Psychological Bulletin, 117*(2), 306–347.

Newman, R. S., Murray, B., & Lussier, C. (2001). Confrontation with aggressive peers at school: Students' reluctance to seek help from the teacher. *Journal of Educational Psychology, 93*(2), 398–410.

O'Connell, P., Pepler, D. J., & Craig, W. M. (1999). Peer involvement in bullying: Insights and challenges for intervention. *Journal of Adolescence, 22,* 437–452.

Oliver, R., Oaks, I. N., & Hoover, J. H. (1994). Family issues and interventions in bully and victim relationships. *School Counselor, 41,* 199–202.

Olweus, D. (1978). *Aggression in the schools: Bullies and whipping boys.* Washington, DC: Hemisphere.

Olweus, D. (1993). *Bullying at school: What we know and what we can do.* Cambridge, MA: Blackwell.

Olweus, D. (1994). Bullying at school: Long-term outcomes for the victims and an effective school-based intervention program. In L. R. Huesmann (Ed.), *Aggressive behavior: Current perspectives* (pp. 97–130). New York: Plenum.

O'Moore, M., & Kirkham, C. (2001). Self esteem and its relationship to bullying behavior. *Aggressive Behavior, 27,* 269–283.

Orange, D. M., Atwood, G. E., & Stolorow, R. D. (1997). *Working intersubjectively: Contextualism in psychoanalytic practice.* Hillsdale, NJ: Analytic Press.

Owens, L., Shute, R., & Slee, P. (2000). "Guess what I just heard!": Indirect aggression among teenage girls in Australia. *Aggressive Behavior, 26,* 67–83.

Palfrey, J., & Gasser, U. (2008). *Born digital: Understanding the first generation of digital natives.* New York: Basic Books.

Pellegrini, A. D. (1998). Bullies and victims in school: A review and call for research. *Journal of Applied Developmental Psychology, 19*(2), 165–176.

Pepler, D. J., & Craig, W. (2000). *Making a difference in bullying* (LaMarsh Report 59). Toronto, Canada: York University.

Pepler, D. J., Craig, W., Connolly, J., & Henderson, K. (2001). Bullying, sexual harassment, dating violence, and substance use among adolescents. In C. Wekerle & A. M. Wall (Eds.), *The violence and addiction equation: Theoretical and clinical issues in substance abuse and relationship violence* (pp. 153–168). Philadelphia: Brunner/Mazel.

Pepler, D. J., Craig, W. M., Connolly, J. A., Yuile, A., McMaster, L., & Jiang, D. (2006). A developmental perspective on bullying. *Aggressive Behavior, 32,* 376–384.

Pepler, D. J., Craig, W. M., Ziegler, S., & Charach, A. (1993). A school-based antibullying intervention: Preliminary evaluation. In D. Tattum (Ed.), *Understanding and managing bullying* (pp. 76–91). Oxford, UK: Heinemann.

Perry, D. G., Kusel, S. J., & Perry, I. C. (1988). Victims of peer aggression. *Developmental Psychology, 24,* 807–814.

Pfeffer, C. R. (1990). Manifestation of risk factors. In G. MacLean (Ed.), *Suicide in children and adolescents* (pp. 65–88). Toronto, Canada: Hogrefe & Huber.

Rigby, K. (2003). Consequences of bullying in schools. *Canadian Journal of Psychiatry, 48,* 583– 590.

Schools like us project description. (2001–2002). Toronto, Canada: Toronto District School Board.

Schrock, A., & Boyd, D. (2008). *Online threats to youth: Solicitation, harassment, and problematic content* (Research Advisory Board Report for the Internet Safety Technical Task Force, Berkman Centre for Internet & Society at Harvard University). Retrieved July 9, 2009, from http://cyber.law.harvard.edu/pub release/isttf/

Schwartz, D., Proctor, L., & Chien, D. (2001). The aggressive victim of bullying: Emotional and behavioral dysregulation as a pathway to victimization by peers. In J. Juvonen & S. Graham (Eds.), *The plight of the vulnerable and victimized* (pp. 147–174). New York: Guilford.

Slee, P. (1994). Situational and interpersonal correlates of anxiety associated with peer victimization. *Child Psychiatry and Human Development, 25*(2), 97–107.

Slee, P. T., & Rigby, K. (1993a). Australian school children's self appraisal of interpersonal relations: The bullying experience. *Child Psychiatry and Human Development, 23,* 272–282.

Slee, P. T., & Rigby, K. (1993b). The relationship of Eysenck's personality factors and self esteem to bully-victim behaviour in Australia. *Personality & Individual Differences, 14,* 371–373.

Smith, P. K. (1997). Bullying in life-span perspective: What can studies of school bullying and workplace bullying learn from each other? *Journal of Community & Applied Social Psychology, 7,* 249–255.

Stillon, J. M. (1994). Suicide: Understanding those considering premature exits. In I. B. Corless, B. B. Germino, & M. Pittman (Eds.), *Dying, death, and bereavement: Theoretical perspectives and other ways of knowing* (pp. 273–298). Boston: Jones and Bartlett.

Stolorow, R. D. (1994). The intersubjective context of intrapsychic experience. In R. D. Stolorow, G. E. Atwood, & B. Brandchaft (Eds.), *The intersubjective perspective* (pp. 3–14). Northvale, NJ: Jason Aronson.

Stolorow, R. D., & Atwood, G. E. (1992). *Contexts of being: The intersubjective foundations of psychological life.* Hillsdale, NJ: Analytic Press.

Stolorow, R. D., Atwood, G. E., & Brandchaft, B. (1994). *The intersubjective perspective.* Northvale, NJ: Jason Aronson.

Sutton, J., Smith, P. K., & Swettenham, J. (1999). Social cognition and bullying: Social inadequacy or skilled manipulation? *British Journal of Developmental Psychology, 17,* 435–450.

Twemlow, S. W., & Cohen, J. (2003). Guest editorial: Stopping school violence. *Journal of Applied Psychoanalytic Studies, 5*(2), 117–123.

Twemlow, S. W., Fonagy, P., & Sacco, F. C. (2002). Feeling safe in school. *Smith College Studies in Social Work, 72*(2), 303–326.

Twemlow, S. W., Fonagy, P., & Sacco, F. C. (2003). Modifying school aggression. *Journal of Applied Psychoanalytic Studies, 5*(2), 211–222.

Underwood, M. (2003). *Social aggression among girls.* New York: Guilford.

Valkenburg, P., & Peter, J. (2007). Preadolescents' and adolescents' online communication and their closeness to friends. *Developmental Psychology, 43*(2), 267–277.

van der Kolk, B. A., McFarlane, A. C., & Weisaeth, L. (1996). *Traumatic stress: The effects of overwhelming experience on mind, body, and society.* New York: Guilford.

Winnicott, D. (1960). The theory of the parent-child relationship. *International Journal of Psychoanalysis, 41,* 585–595.

Winnicott, D. W. (1965). Ego distortion in terms of true and false self. In D. W. Winnicott (Ed.), *The maturational processes and the facilitating environment* (pp. 140–152). New York: International Universities Press. (Original work published 1960)

Wolak, J., Mitchell, K. J., & Finkelhor, D. (2003). Escaping or connecting? Characteristics of youth who form close online relationships. *Journal of Adolescence, 26*(1), 105–119.

9

Traumas of Development in the Gay Male

James Lampe, R. Dennis Shelby, and Boris Thomas

The challenge we have faced in writing this chapter is that of applying and expanding the organizing principles of trauma theory to include circumstances that may be experienced by developing gay (or "proto-gay") males during childhood and adolescence without promoting the idea that all gay males are traumatized. The terms *gay* and *proto-gay* appear frequently throughout this chapter and refer to males who at some point in their lives choose not to hide their same-sex attraction, who seek to live openly in communities—whether small or large—as such, and who claim same-sex attraction as a portion of their identity.[1]

There is an expanding body of literature addressing the topic of trauma and the gay male, advancing theory, providing valuable interventions, and also clarifying the antiquated and erroneous hypothesis that homosexual desire is purely the result of early sexual abuse. This literature explores a wide variety of topics, including but not limited to helping those who have sustained early sexual abuse to separate the abuse from sexual identity (King, 2000; Rivera, 2002), the interplay of cultural considerations and the language spoken during the abuse (Cassese, 2000), the effects of gay men's seeking political asylum to escape torture administered because of their sexual orientation (Pepper, 2005), and HIV and AIDS in gay men who have survived early sexual abuse (Burnham, 1994). This chapter does not address the profound and deeply intrusive types of physical, sexual, and psychological abuse and trauma explored in the literature cited above. Instead, we wish to advance the idea that there are socioculturally bound phenomena that may be traumatizing to the developing gay male, that these phenomena are situated within a greater life course developmental context, and that what we will call "traumas of development" constitute early narcissistic injuries that interfere with the development of self-structure and

---

[1]The terms *gay* and *proto-gay* do not diminish the relevance and/or importance of other terms, often culturally bound, used to describe identifications with same-sex attraction, for example, *same gender loving* or *two-spirited*.

manifest themselves in a variety of defensive behaviors occurring in later life (e.g., sexualization, compulsion, and inhibition). The traumas of development also can occur in tandem with other challenges to early development, such as loss of loved ones, physical and educational challenges, socioeconomic difficulties, and conflicts within the family system.

Increasingly, there are more parents who allow for fluidity in the developing child's sense of sexual identity and maintain openness to the child's gender role presentations. The home environment presents one hurdle in development. The world outside of the home in which the proto-gay child is reared presents another hurdle. One purpose of this chapter is education: With more knowledge about how the gay male develops, we hope for sociocultural changes that will provide optimal parenting, thus supporting the development of gay male children and minimizing traumas of development. In a clinical context, however, the more immediate need is for treatment approaches that effectively assist gay males who have sustained traumas of development. We propose, generally, a psychodynamic approach that, specifically, allows for heightened responsiveness by the clinician and allows for a reworking within the therapeutic interaction.

Organization of the Chapter and Theoretical Approach

The chapter is divided into four sections. In the first, we discuss the sources of traumas of development occurring in childhood and adolescence. This is followed by a summary of developmental tasks associated with life course development occurring after adolescence. Next, we examine one defensive process, sexualization, which may manifest itself in high-risk sexual behaviors and be accompanied by an assortment of other symptoms such as depression, difficulties in maintaining romantic and familial relationships, and substance abuse. Finally, we offer a detailed case discussion that integrates developmental issues and illustrates a treatment approach focusing primarily on the use of transference and the importance of clinician responsiveness.

The range of clinical theories employed by psychodynamic clinicians is wide. This chapter is, therefore, conceptualized broadly so that clinicians of varying schools of thought will recognize the central precepts, psychodynamics, and technical ideas. However, the primary clinical perspective will be that of classical and contemporary self psychology and intersubjectivity.

Childhood and Adolescence

The Parental Discovery or Suspicion of a Gay Child

Learning (or believing) that a child has an alternative sexual identity in many cases threatens parental self-esteem and challenges hopes that the parent had for the child—all based on the parent's narcissistic ambitions (Galatzer-Levy & Cohler, 2002). Before the child actually articulates an alternative sexual identification, parents often communicate that the child's expressions of difference are injurious to their own sense of well-being. Such negative responses likely support problematic mirroring processes that communicate disapproval, a lack of receptivity, and overall discomfort with aspects of the proto-gay child's affective and attachment behavior (Blum & Pfetzing, 1997). These early parental responses—or a lack of responsiveness—serve as a source of inner conflict and guilt for the proto-gay child and later the gay adult (Isay, 1989).

The Trauma of Development

Trauma has been part of the psychoanalytic lexicon for more than 100 years, dating back to Freud's early works. More recently, trauma has been described as consisting of a threatening experience that interrupts information processing and turns what would be an expected adaptive response into a maladaptive one (Sar & Ozturk, 2005). Ornstein (1994) looked at trauma within the context of self psychology. Maintaining a sense of continuity is reliant on the establishment of a cohesive self. Over time, a cohesive self allows for an enduring sense of identity. Traumatic memories can threaten this continuity of self. Fragmentation of memory, in which a split develops between cognitive recognition and the feelings associated with the event, is evidence of traumatic experience, recognizable by the manner in which such memory fragments come into consciousness. Ornstein noted that "traumatic memories are not simple episodic memories" (1994, p. 135). The fragments of traumatic memory can intrude as flashbacks or in dreams, disrupting the cohesiveness of the self. For Ornstein, it is disavowal that accounts for the mind's inability to recall traumatic memory. Traumatic memories by their nature are unspeakable for fear that the original terror will be reexperienced.

Ornstein (1994) defined the difference between childhood trauma and adult trauma in terms of the presence of a consolidated nuclear self. "Once the nuclear self becomes consolidated in terms of its ambitions, values, and ideals, it can be expected to remain relatively intact even under extreme physical and emotional conditions" (p. 141). Symptoms due to trauma have typically been defined in terms of posttraumatic stress. Symptoms due to chronic interpersonal trauma that begin in early childhood were defined by van der Kolk, Roth, Pelcovitz, Sunday, and Spinazzola (2005) as disorders of extreme stress not otherwise specified. These are differentiated from posttraumatic stress disorder. Seven categories were described, including dysregulation of affect and impulse, attention or consciousness, self-perception, perception of the perpetrator(s), relations with others, somatization, and general systems of meaning.

Expanding on the definition of trauma, Davies (1998) cited the sense of "feeling different" experienced by many proto-gay children, intuitively linked to despised cultural images that generate emotional overstimulation and cognitive disorganization. The situation is further complicated when the child feels valued by family members who also speak derisively about "faggots" or "queers" (Blum & Pfetzing, 1997).

In this paradigm, the child lacks an empathic Other who can help him to modulate his affect states and process and encode the conflicting data he has received with language, a task that is often suspended until his adult years (Blum & Pfetzing, 1997). A splitting of consciousness or dissociation occurs without the child's being able to react emotionally and/or thoughtfully to the "traumatic" event (Blum & Pfetzing, 1997; Freud, 1893/1955). Such traumas are unarticulated and become structured internally, thus affecting the entire maturational process in gay development (Blum & Pfetzing, 1997). The often-reported sense of feeling different creates a theoretical problem. Do we view this purely as a recognition on the part of the child that something is indeed different? In a similar vein, how do we regard the child's anxiety with the emergence of sexual interests in the late phallic stage? Might this also be viewed as a response to unarticulated anxieties in the parents' minds? Does it reflect a lack of parental response to the child's fantasies of oedipal victory, that is, destroying one parent to claim the other? The origins of this often-tortured sense of difference may be multiple. Many times it lives on in an unrelenting self-scrutiny that is so familiar that the individual comes to view it as an integral aspect of his daily mentation. The sense of difference should not be viewed as a given in the lives of gay men, possessing definite meanings, but rather as another complex dynamic to be explored and understood in depth.

For developing homosexual children who face the types of environmental challenges described above, mirroring responses typically present in healthy heterosexual development go missing (Blum, Danson, & Schneider, 1997). Healthy sexual development requires that early sexual and affectionate expressions "be received, affirmed, and encouraged, allowing for healthy integration of such feelings and attachments into the developing self" (Blum et al., 1997, p. 3). Blum et al. (1997) observed that the failure to experience the needed mirroring responses creates a developmental situation in which sexual and affectional "strivings and feeling states become the source of severe and enduring inner conflict and guilt" (cited in Stolorow, 1987, p. 93). Not only are sexual strivings not mirrored for the homosexual child; if same-sex attraction is exhibited, it can be met with ridicule and shaming. This situation creates severe threats to the maintenance of self-selfobject ties (Blum et al., 1997).

Overstimulation, the Fear of Humiliation, and Acting Out

Gay male adolescents are often placed in situations in which they must manage the ever-present fear of becoming sexually aroused by other, presumably heterosexual, same-sex peers, friends, and relatives (e.g., in the shared sibling bedroom or school locker room) (Phillips, 2001). These situations are the by-product of heterosexual norms that segregate the sexes based on the assumption that there will be no within-gender attraction. Two possible clinical manifestations of this trauma are inhibition and compulsion.

The public humiliation that results from the articulation or expression of same-sex desire or from gender-nonconforming behavior is traumatic. Even after the humiliation or punishment has passed, an abiding fear may result in "hiding" activities and can also manifest itself in sexual compulsivity (Drescher, 2001). Negative images generated by society have been deemed "covert cultural sexual abuse," thus traumatizing adolescent gay males and supporting behavior such as sexual acting out, which may be considered a reenactment of the trauma (Kort, 2004). The difficulties of child-parent relations in the early development of the gay male can result in internalized homophobia, a concept that, since its early use by Maylon (1982), has been used to encompass visible externalized experiences as well as internal unconscious dynamics (Moss, 2002). The problem of internalized homophobia is that the individual's "erotic equilibrium depends upon both a vigilant avoidance of the object and a vigilant renunciation of the aim," and as a result, "success in object finding leads to subjective impoverishment, rather than to subjective enrichment" and to "disorganization rather than to synthesis" (Moss, 2002, p. 35). The manifestations of this paradox are broad and, depending on the individual, may result in a variety of symptoms, including depression, inhibition of desire, compulsive behaviors (e.g., substance abuse and risky sexual behaviors), and suicidal ideation.

Working with traumatic phenomena in which humiliation and mortification are the dominant affects may create technical challenges for the clinician. Defenses often obscure the depth of affects, and a deep sustaining transference is often needed for the patient to bring these feelings and memories fully into the treatment. The client may be consciously or unconsciously "scanning" the therapist for indications that he or she can work with the material without re-creating the original traumatic outcome. In cases wherein the client has deliberately chosen to work with an out gay therapist, the therapist's awareness of his or her own experiences and thoughts about coming out and gay development will add a dimension to the work and contribute to the transference/countertransference experiences. When the therapist is heterosexual and this is known to the client, the therapist must be more sensitive to concerns about re-creation of the original trauma. In any case, the therapist must be thinking about the total environment, including the client's family members, friends, and greater society. After all, it is within the greater societal construct that, for the most part, the gay child is not looked on either as a boon or as a neutral entity. He is more often than not seen as a problem.

Life Course Development After Adolescence

Life course theory recognizes that psychological development continues beyond childhood and adolescence, through the adult years and into old age. Individual lives are shaped continually by personal experiences that include the cultural and historic experiences one interacts with along life's path.

Generally the early and middle adult years are characterized by a forward-looking perspective and establishing and working to attain goals and aspirations. Good physical health in tandem with feelings of invincibility are carried forward from adolescence. Early adulthood is a period of developing identity, social adaptation, defining one's roles, and finding and settling into a social community with one's developing identity tied into establishing relationships within a peer group. In the early adult years, the individual's psychological development includes a comparison of self with peers and evaluation of self for achievement of life's task. Put quite simply, the young adult is dealing with the questions, Where do I fit in this world? Who are my peers? and Who am I most like? Internalization of this social experience influences and shapes healthy self-development. The basic need for selfobjects, which Kohut (1971, 1977, 1984) recognized as consistently experienced throughout life, has a focus in developing peer relationships and a search for a life partner. In the clinical realm, a gay man in his 20s is searching for a peer group to affirm or solidify his identity and place in the world.

Development of a homosexual identity goes beyond the individual's mere recognition of same-sex erotic attraction. It requires the integration of erotic desire and social aspects of life, including but not limited to the search for a significant other or life partner. This integrative process typically occurs during the early adult years. However, it is not surprising that the development of a healthy gay identity can be influenced by socially stigmatizing circumstances that delay or otherwise inhibit growth. It must be underscored that same-sex sexual orientation—and the corresponding developmental path associated therewith—does not presume psychopathology.

Historically, sexual orientation has not always been recognized as a normal developmental task. In fact, it bears comment here as there are those who utilize clinical practice in efforts to alter sexual orientation. The National Association of Social Workers supports the position that efforts to change sexual orientation are unethical. Separately, the American Psychological Association and the American Psychiatric Association have taken the position that efforts to change sexual orientation are generally not effective and are strongly discouraged. We take the position that homosexuality is not a pathological state. Development of a positive gay identity is shaped by environmental factors including family and cultural sentiment.

Midlife is considered a period of transition in which individuals examine their lives with a developing awareness of their own mortality. Social adaptation is reexamined as the individuals begin to see their elder years around the corner. Although adjustment to midlife for the general population has been studied and digested in journal articles, exploratory studies on gay men's adjustment in midlife are almost nonexistent. The maturing gay male may approach midlife with a fragmented sense of self if he has not been successful in building his self-esteem and has lived his adult life with a sense of separateness and alienation (Friend, 1987). Kertzner (2001) reviewed the literature on adult developmental perspectives in midlife and noted that the sequelae of stigmatized sexual identity are not adequately recognized, particularly insofar as this affects the psychosocial tasks of adulthood.

Although similar social experiences are reported by many gay men, cultural differences do account for heterogeneity in other life experiences. The life course experiences of non-White gay men must take into account the existence of racism and associated identity development issues. Martinez and Sullivan (1998) cited distinctions between the experiences of African Americans and Whites in regard to the gay and lesbian coming-out processes and identity development and point to specific difficulties faced by African American[2] gays. This literature also highlights disturbing findings of phenomena that differ markedly across racial and cultural lines and that may also relate to differences in identity formation (Chicago Department of Public Health, 2009; Hart, Peterson, & Community Intervention Trial for Youth Study Team, 2004; Stall et al., 2003). As one specific example, Bartholow, Goli, and Ackers (2006) cited nonadherence to safe sex practices and considerably higher HIV infection rates among African American and Hispanic men when compared with their White counterparts.

Racism and its many effects—some overt and others far more insidious—add considerable complexity to the non-White gay male's development. The psychoanalytic literature is limited in its exploration of the developmental challenges faced by African American, Latino, and Asian gay men. However, it is significant to note that the concept of chronic interpersonal trauma starting early in childhood (van der Kolk et al., 2005) sits within a greater American context that demonstrates many disparities between dominant White cultures and minority cultures.

According to Centers for Disease Control and Prevention (CDC, 2008) data, between 2004 and 2006, African Americans had the highest age-adjusted death rates among African Americans, Whites, Native Americans, Asians, and Latinos, and African American males have the lowest life expectancies of any group in the United States. Based on data collected in 2006, among men aged 15 to 34, African Americans had mortality rates higher than White, Asian, and Latino men of the same ages (CDC, 2008). Whites lead in per capita suicide, with Native Americans close behind, followed (in descending order) by Asians, Latinos, and African Americans. However, African Americans are murdered at a rate 8 times higher than Asians, nearly 6 times higher than Whites, and almost 3 times higher than both Native Americans and Latinos (CDC, 2009a). Between 1980 and 1995, the suicide rate among African American boys and young men increased 105% (CDC, 1998). Among gay and bisexual African American men, studies have found higher rates of heavy alcohol and cocaine use in comparison to their heterosexual counterparts (Richardson, Myers, Bing, & Satz, 1997), elevated levels of depression and anxiety as compared to White gay men or heterosexual

---

[2]The term *African American* is being used globally to include all Black men. However, there are often differences in identity and identifications between men who are African American, tracing their ancestors directly to the slave trade terminating in the United States, and other men of African descent who—although living in the United States—may identify as being of Caribbean or of other geonational and/or cultural origins.

African American men, and increased incidences of HIV and AIDS (CDC, 2009a, 2009b). Higher rates of poverty, lack of education, incarceration, and unemployment are additional statistics that correspond to the experiences of some African American men. In short, these conditions collectively indicate that African American men living in the United States are at considerable risk for emotional and/or health problems.

A limited body of empirical research on attitudes among African Americans toward homosexuality suggests that many African Americans hold negative views about same-sex sexuality and that this is supported by conservative religious views (Greene, 1994, 1997; Herek & Capitanio, 1995; Michael, Gagnon, Laumann, & Kolata, 1994). Also related are the sociocultural conditions that shape Black masculine identity in the United States (see, e.g., Lemelle & Battle, 2004). Where there is tolerance of homosexuality in African American communities, there is often an implied agreement that same-sex sexuality should not be explicitly disclosed or displayed (Mays, 1989; Peterson, 1992; Savin-Williams, 1996). This scenario often leads gay African American men to maintain dual existences, a position with significant psychological consequences (Greene, 1994) including compartmentalization. Compartmentalization works against integration, the cornerstone of the developmental milestone of the "committed" stage of gay identity development generated by Troiden (1993). This stage of development is marked by an acceptance of one's gayness, the fusing of sexuality and emotionality into a cohesive and integrated whole, the belief that being gay is legitimate and not secondary to a heterosexual identity, and finally, the initiation and maintenance of same-sex love relationships and disclosing of a gay identity to the general public (Troiden, 1993).

The challenges of heterosexism in African American communities and the stressors associated with being a minority in a dominant White society affect the ability of the gay African American to assume a gay identity, or more specifically, a dual gay and African American identity, without discomfort (Crawford, Allison, Zamboni, & Soto, 2002). A better integrated, dual self-identification (i.e., both African American and gay) has been associated with higher levels of self-esteem, HIV-prevention self-efficacy, stronger social support networks, greater levels of life satisfaction, and lower levels of male gender role and psychological distress among African American gay and bisexual men (Crawford et al., 2002). Although it is our position that identity formation and its many residual effects warrant further study, we believe that addressing stressors associated with having a double-minority status in American society is critical in clinical work with gay African American men (Zamboni & Crawford, 2007). These challenges, especially as they affect the developing proto-gay African American male, are implicated in the traumas of development that this chapter addresses. Generally speaking, clinical work with gay men will be less successful if there is not sufficient attention to the complexity of psychological development beyond identity formation.

The Psychodynamic Approach: Defensive Client Strategies and Clinical Process

The trauma of development generated by failures in mirroring, lack of parental (selfobject) responsivity, and fear of humiliation hamper the proto-gay child's free expression of self and thus constitute narcissistic injuries to the developing self. The lack of readily available idealizeable gay adults or adults to meet idealizing needs often creates additional vulnerability and, in some instances, an overreliance on mirroring responses. In response to this developmental trauma, which may occur as early as adolescence, gay males may demonstrate sexual acting out behavior that initially resembles sexual addiction (Kort, 2004). Dissociation is one primitive defense used in response to overwhelming or traumatic situations that cannot be fully addressed either emotionally or cognitively (Blum & Pfetzing, 1997; Davies, 1998). In the material that follows, we will address sexualization, another unconscious defensive process that may be used by the individual who sustains the trauma of development.

Another important part of the treatment will involve addressing and providing space for the expression of rage. Ignoring the narcissistic rage associated with the sometimes traumatizing experiences of growing up gay or lesbian in a society where social prejudice against gays and lesbians is very real helps maintain the victim status of gay and lesbian individuals. As Marion Tolpin (personal communication, 1998) has pointed out, "rage is often the nexus of the deficit" (Shelby, 2000).

Sexualization and Disavowal

Sex can serve as a defensive process by which men (and women) manage anxieties associated with a wide assortment of unresolved issues. Sexualization, the defensive use of sexuality (Goldberg, 1995), is an idea central to this chapter, although we are by no means asserting that gay and bisexual men employ sexualization to a greater degree than heterosexual individuals. Goldberg elaborated on the idea that sexualization serves to fill in a self-deficit. The exact nature of the deficit is highly variable and can range from self-esteem regulation, to faulty regulatory capacities, to attempts to enact fantasies related to an idealized imago that cannot be engaged in depth within an enduring relationship. The presence of a vertical split in the personality can accentuate instability and is often related to drug and alcohol abuse. Shelby (2002) linked the combination of individual dynamics and the presence of a vertical split as factors in men who find themselves in anxious if not desperate attempts to engage other men in brief sexual encounters.

Again, personality plays a central role. One of the tasks of clinical engagement is to bring all of this material into the encounter so that it may be analyzed and worked through and so that the psychological burden on the client may be decreased. An assessment and/or referral for substance abuse treatment may be in order after a careful assessment of the client's readiness to engage in drug/alcohol treatment. For some individuals, a period of psychotherapy is necessary before they feel strong enough and/or feel genuinely motivated to engage in substance treatment.

Transference and Countertransference in the Treatment

All personality styles and self-structures are represented by gay men and men who have sex with other men. These men also represent every ethnic and socioeconomic group in the country. Given this diversity and the linkage to sexuality, the range of transference and countertransference reactions is infinite. We are using Freud's enduring definition; transference is a reedition of feelings and attitudes about important people: one's mother, father, sister, or brother. This can be applied to a wide range of clinical theories. The understanding of the nature of the feelings and attitudes that are reexperienced will, of course, depend on the clinician's personal clinical theory.

Sustaining, organizing, and modulating transferences may develop quite early if the clinician is responsive and the client is in great distress. The nuances of more neurotic transferences are highly variable, and if the client has a tendency toward sexualization as a defense, then the transference may become erotized. We take the Freudian stance that the transference is like an organism with a life of its own. While the tasks may be similar among clients, how transferences evolve and how they may be employed in service of the treatment is highly variable.

Countertransference, of course, varies with the client and the clinician. The linkage to sexuality will most likely activate neurotic structures and their unconscious memories and fantasies. The continued presence of HIV in the gay community can add to countertransference burdens on the therapist. The combination of sexuality and contagion can create an intense stirring of the repressed or barely repressed anxiety and fantasies. It is important for the clinician to be aware of such phenomena and view fantasy material as well as sexual activity as opportunities for engagement rather than as attempts to talk the patient out of particular behavior or to be educative or corrective. Erotization of the transference is often met with a countertransference reaction consisting of subtle to blatant indulgence or simply the ignoring of the material or the therapist's more negative reactions. The most common countertransference reaction is in response to the client's report of compulsive or dangerous (i.e., unprotected or otherwise unsafe) sexual practices. This may cause alarm, if not anger and contempt, in the clinician. Most likely the patient is asking for help in his sexual life. The clinician needs to understand the communication behind the report of sexual experiences. The bringing in of sexual material to the treatment often represents a deepening of the transference. The clinician's awareness of transference manifestations and engagement of the transference most likely will help the client modulate his behavior in the long run. Stern educative stances risk repelling the transference and fueling the very behavior the clinician feels impelled to modulate. Of course, where clients are asking for information, a calm, steady, reassuring stance will help them integrate safer sex information. The clinician should also listen for anxieties and fantasies that may have been interfering with data that are readily available in the public domain.

Case Illustration

The following case history illustrates the complexity of clinical encounters with gay men who are also infected with HIV and the clinician's use of himself and the transference and countertransference to help effect change. An HIV-positive client is presented here for several reasons: HIV infection often causes narcissistic issues to come to the forefront of the client's mind, issues related to sexuality and mortification are also enhanced, and transference phenomena are often expressed more readily when the therapist is responsive to the client's distress. The fact that the client selected for discussion below is HIV positive does not by any means support the idea that all gay men who sustain traumas of development become HIV positive.

> Chance is an attractive and masculine-appearing 40-year-old, African American, gay man. An artist and musician, he was born and raised in an urban environment in a financially stable, two-parent household. Chance's father died when he was 28, and his mother is a cancer survivor. He has an older brother who has been estranged from the family for many years due to a falling out with their mother. Chance is out to his family members, who ostensibly accept his gay identity. However, he has occasionally been called a "faggot" and other derogatory names.
>
> When Chance first presented for treatment at the age of 33, he was depressed and confused. He was living with and trying to negotiate a tumultuous relationship with a partner 10 years his senior who, like Chance, also was HIV positive and, unbeknownst to Chance, was suffering from several addictions.
>
> Chance described having survived several family crises including caring for his ailing grandmother until her death when he was 20, helping his family—both emotionally and financially—in the wake of his father's death, providing support to his cancer-surviving mother, and managing his own HIV diagnosis. Guilt played a significant role in Chance's life. Although Chance's life was not without financial or other struggles, he had a sense of guilt over enjoying himself and having growth experiences, such as travel outside of the country, while his

family faced difficulties. Chance also experienced guilt regarding his desire to expand his life beyond the boundaries of his predominantly working-class, African American neighborhood, which his mother and other relatives scorned, saying that he was "acting White." Finally, he felt a great deal of guilt about his brother's estrangement from the family and shared that he had wrongly sided with his mother against his brother, thus supporting his brother's departure from the family and his loss of an important male figure in his life. Chance was financially generous to his family, consistently providing them with assistance, often to his own detriment. At times Chance chose giving his mother money to take care of her household over purchasing meds to maintain his compliance with his HIV antiviral regimen. Diverting funds to his family served two purposes—it assuaged his guilt and helped him to do what felt most important to him: "keeping the family together," which he stated that neither his father nor brother could do anymore.

Chance also reported a history of regular "party and play" (combination of drug use and sex) with crystal methamphetamine (colloquially called "tina") use during his 20s and early 30s and occasionally during the course of treatment. Sexual activity played a significant role in Chance's life, helping him to escape from the frequent disappointments that his family and his romantic relationship created. It also provided an avenue for him to discharge feelings of guilt that haunted him. He stated that his early use of crystal meth was a contributing factor in his becoming HIV positive. Chance was 27 years old when he tested positive.

Chance described a traumatic childhood. His parents were explosive, unempathic, and frequently cruel, and his father was occasionally physically violent toward his mother. In raising Chance and his brother, both parents employed corporal punishment and humiliation liberally and frequently ridiculed Chance for behavior that was not sufficiently masculine. Chance's mother controlled his expression of emotion, telling him what he should or should not feel and punishing him when his emotions were not to her liking. His creativity was not understood, and his brother, who was tougher than Chance, frequently protected him, on occasion bearing the brunt of punishments unfairly intended for Chance. Chance's extended family was composed mostly of women who, like his mother, were domineering and insensitive. He felt that with the exception of one uncle, who was peripheral to the family's functioning, the men in the family were controlled and emasculated by the women. Like many individuals who have suffered ongoing early trauma, Chance was hypervigilant—always scanning the environment for potential danger and extremely conscious of how others around him were feeling and responding to situations. When Chance began treatment, he had a visible facial tic, which conveyed an underlying anxiety.

Transference and Countertransference in the Treatment

In my first interaction with Chance—a brief telephone conversation to assess his situation and make a first appointment—I experienced a spontaneous paternal countertransference. I imagined myself guiding and taking care of him. When he asked if I were African American and I responded affirmatively, he seemed relieved, and it felt as if the therapeutic alliance had already begun.

The transference quickly revealed his need for me not only to be a strong paternal figure with the capacity to stand up to his domineering mother and provide mentoring but also to serve as a soothing, nurturing, and understanding maternal presence. In his life outside of the treatment room, Chance's unconscious desire for a strong and supportive male figure was manifested in his positive friendships with and attractions to older men. The difficult romantic relationship in which he was involved at the start of treatment had its genesis in his attraction to—and idealization of—a man who at the time appeared to be knowledgeable, worldly, and confident. As the work progressed, Chance frequently switched my name for that of his brother, his best friend (an older man), and an uncle in whom Chance frequently confided. He constantly sought my approval and support.

Treatment Course

At the start of treatment, Chance manifested a defensive idealization of his mother, minimizing her frequently cruel, insensitive, and hostile treatment and rationalizing her behavior by saying it was due to the many challenges she had faced in her life. Similarly, Chance also had idealized his partner, minimizing his substantial weaknesses and ignoring and accommodating the partner's addictive behaviors. The primary—and most challenging—task of treatment was to help Chance accept the toxic reality of his abusive parents and the effect that their behaviors had on him. My initial interpretations consisted of gently bringing to the surface feelings that Chance had repressed regarding his parents' mistreating him (e.g., "That must have been humiliating for you" or "I wonder if you felt disappointed when your mother responded that way"). Later interpretations focused on his unrealistic expectations and challenged his propensity for idealization (e.g., "You can never rely on your mother to respond to you in a kind way, yet you frequently find yourself hoping that she will").

When Chance began to accept the reality of his early mistreatment, he experienced much anger and a profound sense of loss, mourning for the idealized versions of his parents, images to which Chance had clung for so many years. The violent dissolution of his relationship with his partner was a catalyst for substantial growth for Chance. He was able to express what he had sought in his partner and how, rather than accepting who his partner really was, Chance had created an idealized version. My interpretations linked Chance's disappointment in his parents and the loss of his father and brother to his seeking a partner who could fill those roles. Chance was able to take in these types of interpretations. Eventually, he was able to focus on his tendency to deny the existence of those traits he found disappointing in his partner. A secondary task of treatment was to help Chance to trust his feelings and to be less hypervigilant.

Chance began to remember and recount episodes of abuse that punctuated his childhood. As he began to metabolize these experiences, he vacillated between overwhelming rage and deep sadness. As this process continued, I noticed that he began to take better care of himself, tending to both his antidepressant and his antiviral medication regimens. His facial tic virtually disappeared, reappearing only during times of great stress.

He went through a long period of having no sex, and we spent a significant amount of time reviewing the effect that his past sexual encounters had on him. He was able to discuss how at times during sex he had felt used and objectified as a "black top," a feeling that resonated with the humiliations experienced in his childhood and adolescence. Using crystal meth allowed him to escape the feeling of being used, but at the price of fusing sex with drugs. Reflecting on his prior sexual life, he stated,

> As I remember my escapades, it's hard to separate the sex from tina. I remember, it was always so tough coming off the tina high. Often, coming down would wipe out the memory of the sex, which would make me want sex and tina even more.

Chance frequently described our work together as my giving him "tools" to help him manage situations by himself. Through the transference, he allowed me to reparent him. Following a developmental arc, he articulated the ability and need to figure things out for himself without my assistance. He expressed great pride in being able to trust his feelings more, be less hypervigilant, see others for themselves rather than idealized figures, and interact with his mother while maintaining a safe emotional distance from her.

Like many gay men who become HIV positive as a result of recreational sex, Chance was using sexual activity and drugs as a way of escaping a traumatic upbringing. The defensive use of denial to manage early trauma corresponds to the denial of risk present in recreational sex with drugs. Although he had been living with HIV for many years, Chance's ability to focus on his self-care, specifically as it relates to his antiviral regimen, was directly related to his addressing early traumas, forming healthier ways of participating in old and new relationships, and forging a positive self-identity.

Discussion and Commentary[3]

This case illustrates the complexity of clinical engagement and the many components that result in a good client-therapist match. We see a young

---

[3]Case commentary provided by the second author, R. Dennis Shelby.

African American man with a combination of disavowed trauma and disappointment clinging to idealizations of his mother and the loss of his father and brother and clearly seeking to reengage and rework aspects of a problematic relationship with his father via adult love relationships. The clinician's sensitivity to issues relating to being gay, HIV positive, and also African American clearly helped the client relax and engage in treatment. The clinician offered him an alternative to problematic identifications and to frustrated efforts to engage individuals who were not at all suitable for the complex psychological tasks he was facing.

Many individuals who move out of the social and ethnic enclaves of their families of origin experience such liberation with mixed feelings. The desire and drive to have better, more exciting lives often triggers guilt. Add to the mixture denied, repressed, or disavowed rage, and the guilt is often magnified. Guilt can inhibit the full expression of talents and skills, and it can also bind patients to the more unhappy dynamics of their childhood. The clinician recognized this as something problematic and to be worked out in treatment.

In the history, we learn that the client in his 20s discovered chemical-enhanced sexuality. One has the sense of a lost young man trying to find his footing, a feeling that permeates the case discussion. The client clearly recognized that the treatment relationship was a place to begin to feel grounded and oriented. The clinician gave free reign to the client's exploration of the motivations underlying his quest to experience something psychological in his sexual adventures and love life. More important, the client was able to acknowledge and explore aspects of his experience that did not feel good—coming down off of the high and feeling used as a fetish by White men. The therapist's effort to bring the quest and unconscious motivations into the treatment resulted in a reengagement of thwarted developmental needs. Most likely the clinician's attunement to the challenges of negotiating societal and gay venues dominated by White gay ethics and values helped this African American client work through his hopes for a new and exciting life and consequent narcissistic injuries.

It is not unusual to encounter a gay man (of any race) who is the highest functioning member of his family. However, guilt, ambivalent feelings about sexuality, and disavowed trauma often leave such individuals feeling like the "defective" ones. The careful comparisons of self-image, details of family life, and current function often bring this disparity into focus. The clinician's sensitive attention to disavowed trauma may enable the client to free himself from burdensome idealizations. Evidence suggests that in this instance, the treatment became a regulatory environment. The client freed himself from an unhappy relationship, focused on his own health maintenance, and became more self-reflective. The client articulated this when he stated that his therapist "gave him the tools." Developmentally associated self-deficits are often repaired in a good psychotherapeutic encounter.

The results of this clinical encounter are a reworking of childhood traumas and problematic parental selfobject relationships, enhanced functioning in life, and greater ability to integrate and manage challenges, including HIV infection. The clinical work with this clinician clearly gave the client the tools he needed to go on living and prospering.

Conclusion

Development of the gay male is by no means monolithic. There are many more factors than could possibly be presented here that affect the course of growth and psychic maturation of the proto-gay male child and adolescent. In this chapter, a case involving developmental trauma was presented and discussed. This case involved a gay man who sought assistance from the clinician in transcending developmental traumas sustained in an early environment unresponsive to his developmental needs. A successful clinical encounter with the therapist, who maximized responsiveness and understood the challenges to the self caused by failures in early mirroring and reflectivity as well as the lack of idealization of a parental object, has the effect of reparenting the adult male. An open and accepting stance through which the clinician provided mirroring and reflective functions and permitted himself to be used as an idealized figure through the transference strengthened the therapeutic alliance with the client and allowed for exploration of his defensive manifestations of traumas of development, including but not limited to the adult gay man's use of unconscious defenses such as compulsion and sexualization. Through the strong client-therapist alliance, the effective use of transference and countertransference, and the clinician's self-awareness, other environmental issues affecting the client, including matters of loss, identity formation, and personal achievement, to name only a few, may also be addressed in the course of treatment.

References

Bartholow, B. N., Goli, V., & Ackers, M. (2006). Demographic and behavioral contextual risk groups among men who have sex with men participating in a Phase 3 HIV vaccine efficacy trial: Implications for HIV prevention and behavioral/biomedical intervention trials. *Journal of Acquired Immune Deficiency Syndromes, 43*, 594–602.

Blum, A., Danson, M., & Schneider, S. (1997). Problems of sexual expression in adult gay men: A psychoanalytic reconsideration. *Psychoanalytic Psychology, 14*(1), 1–11. Retrieved April 9, 2010, from EBSCOhost

Blum, A., & Pfetzing, V. (1997). Assaults to the self: The trauma of growing up gay. *Gender and Psychoanalysis, 2*(4), 427–442. Retrieved January 7, 2011, from http://web.ebscohost.com/ehost/detail?hid=17&sid=cd3b67c3-f288-4cc4-a0c8-186c205bac85%40sessionmgr15&vid=6&bdata=JnNpdGU9ZWhvc3QtbGl2ZQ%3d%3d#db=pph&AN=GAP.002.0427A

Burnham, R. (1994). Trauma revisited: HIV and AIDS in gay male survivors of early sexual abuse. In R. A. Burnham, S. A. Cadwell, & M. Forstein (Eds.), *Therapists on the front line: Psychotherapy with gay men in the age of AIDS* (pp. 379–404). Washington, DC: American Psychiatric Association. Retrieved January 7, 2011, from http://web.ebscohost.com/ehost/results?hid=17&sid=cd3b67c3-f288-4cc4-a0c8-186c205bac85%40sessionmgr15&vid=7&bquery=(burnham+trauma+rev isited)&bdata=JmRiPXBwaCZkYj1wc3loJnR5cGU9MSZzaXRlPWVob3N0LW xpdmU%3d

Cassese, J. (2000). Cross cultural perspectives in treating the gay male trauma survivor. In J. Cassese (Ed.), *Gay men and childhood sexual trauma: Integrating the shattered self* (pp. 153–182). Binghampton, NY: Harrington Park Press/ Haworth Press. Retrieved January 7, 2011, from http://web.ebscohost.com/ ehost/detail?hid=17&sid=cd3b67c3-f288-4cc4-a0c8-186c205bac85%40session mgr15&vid=11&bdata=JnNpdGU9ZWhvc3QtbGl2ZQ%3d%3d#db=psyh &AN=2001-16426-009

Centers for Disease Control and Prevention. (1998). Suicide among Black youths— United States, 1980–1995. *Morbidity Mortality Weekly Report, 47,* 193–196.

Centers for Disease Control and Prevention. (2008). *Health, United States, 2008, with special feature on the health of young adults.* Hyattsville, MD: National Center for Health Statistics.

Centers for Disease Control and Prevention. (2009a). *Health, United States, 2009 with special feature on medical technology.* Retrieved January 7, 2011, from http://www.cdc.gov/nchs/data/hus/hus09.pdf

Centers for Disease Control and Prevention. (2009b). *HIV/AIDS among African Americans: CDC HIV/AIDS facts.* Retrieved January 7, 2011, from http://www .cdc.gov/hiv/topics/aa/pdf/aa.pdf

Chicago Department of Public Health. (2009). *STD/HIV Division—Surveillance, epidemiology and research.* Chicago: Author.

Crawford, I., Allison, K., Zamboni, B., & Soto, T. (2002). The influence of dual-identity development on the psychosocial functioning of African-American gay and bisexual men. *Journal of Sex Research, 39*(3), 179–189.

Davies, J. M. (1998). Repression and dissociation—Freud and Janet: Fairbairn's new model of unconscious process. In N. Skolnick & D. Scharff (Eds.), *Fairbairn, then and now* (pp. 53–69). Hillsdale, NJ: Analytic Press.

Drescher, J. (2001). Attending to sexual compulsivity in a gay man. In J. Petrucelli & C. Stuart (Eds.), *Hungers and compulsions: The psychodynamic treatment of eating disorders and addictions* (pp. 267–276). Lanham, MD: Jason Aronson.

Freud, S. (1955). On the psychical mechanism of hysterical phenomena: Preliminary communication. In J. Strachey (Ed. & Trans.), *The standard edition of the complete psychological works of Sigmund Freud* (Vol. 2, pp. 1–17). London: Hogarth Press. (Original work published 1893)

Friend, R. (1987). The individual and social psychology of aging: Clinical implications for lesbians and gay men. *Journal of Homosexuality, 14*(1/2), 307–331.

Galatzer-Levy, R. M., & Cohler, B. J. (2002). Making a gay identity: Coming out, social context, and psychodynamics. *Annual of Psychoanalysis, 30,* 255–286. Retrieved January 7, 2011, from http://web.ebscohost.com/ehost/detail?hid= 17&sid=d6994b5e-4498-459b-8f93-6cc5413266e3%40sessionmgr11&vid=11 &bdata=JnNpdGU9ZWhvc3QtbGl2ZQ%3d%3d#db=pph&AN=AOP.030 .0255A

Goldberg, A. (1995). *The problem of perversion.* New Haven, CT: Yale University Press.

Greene, B. (1994). Ethnic minority lesbians and gay men: Mental health and treatment issues. *Journal of Clinical and Consulting Psychology, 62,* 243–251.

Greene, B. (1997). Ethnic minority lesbian and gay men: Mental health and treatment issues. In B. Greene (Ed.), *Ethnic and cultural diversity among lesbians and gay men: Psychological perspectives on lesbian and gay issues* (pp. 216–239). Thousand Oaks, CA: Sage.

Hart, T., Peterson, J. L., & Community Intervention Trial for Youth Study Team. (2004). Predictors of risky sexual behavior among young African American men who have sex with men. *American Journal of Public Health, 94*(7), 1122–1124.

Herek, G. M., & Capitanio, J. (1995). Black heterosexuals' attitudes towards lesbians and gay men in the United States. *Journal of Sex Research, 32,* 95–105.

Isay, R. A. (1989). *Being homosexual: Gay men and their development.* New York: Avon Books.

Kertzner, R. M. (2001). The adult life course and homosexual identity in midlife gay men. *Annual Review of Sex Research, 12,* 75–93. Retrieved January 7, 2011, fromhttp://web.ebscohost.com/ehost/detail?hid=17&sid=d6994b5e-4498-459b-8f93-6cc5413266e3%40sessionmgr11&vid=15&bdata=JnNpdGU9ZWhvc3QtbGl2ZQ%3d%3d#db=psyh&AN=2002-18276-003

King, N. (2000). Childhood sexual trauma in gay men: Social context and the imprinted arousal pattern. In J. Cassese (Ed.), *Gay men and childhood sexual trauma: Integrating the shattered self* (pp. 19–35). Binghampton, NY: Harrington Park Press/Haworth Press. Retrieved January 7, 2011, from http://web.ebscohost.com/ehost/detail?hid=17&sid=d6994b5e-4498-459b-8f93-6cc5413266e3%40sessionmgr11&vid=17&bdata=JnNpdGU9ZWhvc3QtbGl2ZQ%3d%3d#db=psyh&AN=2001-16426-002

Kohut, H. (1971). *The analysis of the self.* New York: International Universities Press.

Kohut, H. (1977). *The restoration of the self.* New York: International Universities Press.

Kohut, H. (1984). *How does analysis cure?* (A. Goldberg & P. E. Stepansky, Eds.). Chicago: University of Chicago Press.

Kort, J. (2004). Covert cultural sexual abuse of gay male teenagers contributing to etiology of sexual addiction. *Sexual Addiction & Compulsivity, 11*(4), 287–300.

Lemelle, A., & Battle, J. (2004). Black masculinity matters in attitudes toward gay males. *Journal of Homosexuality, 47*(1), 39–51.

Martinez, D., & Sullivan, S. (1998). African American gay men and lesbians: Examining the complexity of gay identity development. *Journal of Human Behavior in the Social Environment, 1*(2/3), 243–264. Retrieved January 7, 2011, from http://web.ebscohost.com/ehost/detail?hid=17&sid=d6994b5e-4498-459b-8f93-6cc5413266e3%40sessionmgr11&vid=19&bdata=JnNpdGU9ZWhvc3QtbGl2ZQ%3d%3d#db=psyh&AN=2000-12305-013

Maylon, A. K. (1982). Psychotherapeutic implications of internalized homophobia in gay men. *Homosexuality and Psychotherapy, 7,* 59–69.

Mays, V. M. (1989). AIDS prevention in Black populations: Methods of a safer kind. In V. M. Mays, G. W. Albee, & S. F. Schneider (Eds.), *Primary prevention of AIDS: Psychological approaches* (pp. 264–279). Newbury Park, CA: Sage.

Michael, R. T., Gagnon, J. H., Laumann, E. O., & Kolata, G. (1994). *Sex in America: A definitive survey.* Boston: Little, Brown.

Moss, D. (2002). Internalized homophobia in men: Wanting in the first person singular, hating in the first person plural. *Psychoanalytic Quarterly, 71*(1), 21–50. Retrieved January 7, 2011, from http://web.ebscohost.com/ehost/detail?hid=

17&sid=d6994b5e-4498-459b-8f93-6cc5413266e3%40sessionmgr11&vid=21
&bdata=JnNpdGU9ZWhvc3QtbGl2ZQ%3d%3d#db=pph&AN=PAQ.071
.0021A

Ornstein, A. (1994). Trauma, memory, and psychic continuity. In A. Goldberg (Ed.),
A Decade of Progress: Progress in Self Psychology, 10. Hillsdale, NJ: The
Analytic Press.

Pepper, C. (2005). Gay men tortured on the basis of homosexuality: Psychodynamic
psychotherapy and political asylum advocacy. *Contemporary Psychoanalysis,
41*(1), 35–54. Retrieved January 7, 2011, from http://web.ebscohost.com/ehost/
detail?hid=17&sid=d6994b5e-4498-459b-8f93-6cc5413266e3%40sessionmgr
11&vid=23&bdata=JnNpdGU9ZWhvc3QtbGl2ZQ%3d%3d#db=pph&AN=
CPS.041.0035A

Peterson, J. L. (1992). Black men and their same sex desires and behaviors. In
G. Herdt (Ed.), *Gay culture in America: Essays from the field* (pp. 147–164).
Boston: Beacon.

Phillips, S. (2001). The overstimulation of gay and lesbian lives: Social and psychoanalytic perspectives. *Journal of the American Psychoanalytic Association, 50*(2),
674–678. Retrieved January 7, 2011, from http://web.ebscohost.com/ehost/
detail?hid=17&sid=d6994b5e-4498-459b-8f93-6cc5413266e3%40sessionmgr11
&vid=25&bdata=JnNpdGU9ZWhvc3QtbGl2ZQ%3d%3d#db=pph&AN=APA
.049.1235A

Richardson, M. A., Myers, H. F., Bing, E. G., & Satz, P. (1997). Substance use and
psychopathology in African American men at risk for HIV infection. *Journal of
Community Psychology, 24*(4), 353–370.

Rivera, M. (2002). Informed and supportive treatment for lesbian, gay, bisexual and
transgendered trauma survivors. *Journal of Trauma & Dissociation, 3*(4),
33–58.

Sar & Ozturk (2005). What is trauma and dissociation? *Journal of Trauma Practice,
4,* 7–12.

Savin-Williams, R. C. (1996). Ethnic and sexual-minority youth. In R. C. Savin-
Williams & K. M. Cohen (Eds.), *The lives of lesbians, gays and bisexuals:
Children to adults* (pp. 393–415). Fort Worth, TX: Harcourt Brace.

Shelby, R. (2000). Narcissistic injury, humiliation, rage, and the desire for revenge:
Thoughts on Drescher's psychoanalytic therapy and the gay man. *Gender and
Psychoanalysis, 5*(3), 275–289. Retrieved January 7, 2011, from http://web
.ebscohost.com/ehost/detail?hid=17&sid=d6994b5e-4498-459b-8f93-6cc5413
266e3%40sessionmgr11&vid=31&bdata=JnNpdGU9ZWhvc3QtbGl2ZQ%3d
%3d#db=pph&AN=GAP.005.0275A

Shelby, R. D. (2002). About cruising and being cruised. *Annual of Psychoanalysis,
30,* 191–208.

Stall, R., Mills, T. C., Williamson, J., Hart, T., Greenwood, G., Paul, J., et al. (2003).
Associations of co-occurring psychosocial health problems and increased
vulnerability to HIV/AIDS among urban men who have sex with men. *American
Journal of Public Health, 93,* 939–942.

Stolorow, R. (1987). *Psychoanalytic treatment: An intersubjective approach.*
Hillsdale, NJ: Analytic Press.

Troiden, R. R. (1993). The formation of homosexual identities. In L. Garnets &
D. Kimmel (Eds.), *Psychological perspectives on lesbian and gay male experiences* (pp. 191–217). New York: Columbia University Press.

van der Kolk, B., Roth, S., Pelcovitz, D., Sunday, S., & Spinazzola, J. (2005). Disorders of extreme stress: The empirical foundation of a complex adaptation to trauma. *Journal of Traumatic Stress, 18,* 389–399.

Zamboni, B. D., & Crawford, I. (2007). Minority stress and sexual problems among African-American gay and bisexual men. *Archives of Sexual Behavior, 36*(4), 569–578. Retrieved January 7, 2011, from http://web.ebscohost.com/ehost/detail?hid=17&sid=d6994b5e-4498-459b-8f93-6cc5413266e3%40sessionmgr11&vid=29&bdata=JnNpdGU9ZWhvc3QtbGl2ZQ%3d%3d#db=psyh&AN=2008-00095-007

10

Cultural and Historical Trauma Among Native Americans

Shelly A. Wiechelt and Jan Gryczynski

Even the seasons form a great circle in their changing, and always come back again to where they were. The life of a man is a circle from childhood to childhood, and so it is in everything where power moves.

—Black Elk, Oglala Sioux Holy Man
(cited in Neihardt, 1932/2008, p. 155)

Biological, psychological, and social system processes affect individuals in the way that they perceive and function in the world. Complex interactions between these systems within individuals influence how they think, feel, and behave in relation to themselves and others. Individuals' current statuses reflect their lived experience to date. Traumatic events that occur in the lives of individuals have the potential to dramatically affect those individuals' functioning in terms of physical health, mental health, and social behavior.

Similar to an individual, a culture consists of complex processes that sustain and nourish it. Internal processes such as values, beliefs, symbols, and norms uphold the culture. External forces such as interaction with other cultures and effects of nature may put pressure on a culture. To a certain extent external pressures may challenge a culture to change and grow. However, sudden and catastrophic pressures may overwhelm the cultural system's ability to cope and thus can be traumatic to the culture. Less sudden pressures such as oppression and aggressive encroachment on a culture will stress the culture as well as the individuals and systems within it with potentially traumatic effects.

Native Americans have experienced individual and cultural traumas that have profoundly affected their individual and communal lives. Some of these events occurred in the remote past in the lives of prior generations and generated effects that rippled across subsequent generations even unto this day. Others occurred more recently in the lives of individuals, families, and communities. The effects of cultural traumas from the remote past intermingle with effects of recent traumas, resulting in a cumulative and compounding spiral of traumatic effects. To understand trauma in the lives of Native Americans and ways of promoting healing, it is important to begin with a foundation in relevant concepts.

Native American

First and foremost, it is important to understand to whom the term *Native American* refers. The term *Native American* is misleading as it implies that a single group of indigenous people exists in the United States. In fact, hundreds of different tribes, each with its own unique cultural rubrics, beliefs, and practices, exist in the United States today. There are 564 federally recognized tribes as well as many other unrecognized tribes. More than 4 million individuals in the United States identify their race as American Indian or Alaska Native, making American Indian or Alaska Native one of the smallest racial minorities in the nation (Ogunwole, 2006). Although many Native Americans reside on reservations, 64% live outside of tribal areas, and many reside in urban centers (National Urban Indian Family Coalition, 2008; Ogunwole, 2006). Any reference to Native Americans in this chapter encompasses an array of diverse groups whose commonality is in their indigenousness to the continental land now known as the United States of America. Because the focus of this chapter is on the experience of indigenous people of the United States in general rather than a specific tribal group, the term *Native American* is used despite its limitations. In many population statistics, the term *American Indian/Alaska Native* is commonly used as a racial designation. In this chapter, the terms *Native American* and *American Indian/Alaska Native* are used interchangeably.

Trauma

The current conception of trauma in Western cultures is based largely on the definition encompassed in the posttraumatic stress disorder (PTSD) criteria listed in the *Diagnostic and Statistical Manual of Mental Disorders* (fourth edition, text revision; *DSM-IV-TR*) (American Psychiatric Association, 2000). Essentially, a traumatic event is one in which an individual experiences, witnesses, or learns that a close associate has experienced an event that "involves actual or threatened death or serious injury, or other threat to one's physical integrity" (American Psychiatric Association, 2000, p. 463). For such events to be considered traumatic, the individual must have responded to the event with feelings of intense fear, helplessness, or horror. The criteria for a diagnosis of PTSD include three symptom clusters: reexperiencing, avoidance/numbing, and arousal. Simply experiencing an event such as those described in the *DSM-IV-TR*—

> military combat, violent personal assault [sexual assault, physical attack, robbery, mugging], being kidnapped, being taken hostage, terrorist attack, torture, incarceration as a prisoner of war or in a concentration camp, natural or manmade disasters, severe automobile accidents, or being diagnosed with a life-threatening illness (p. 463)—

does not mean that an individual will perceive the event as being traumatic or experience traumatic effects. Research suggests that it is likely that an interaction between the pretrauma characteristics of the individual, the nature and severity of the traumatic event, the individual's perception of the event, and posttrauma experiences interact in ways that determine the nature and severity of traumatic reactions to the event or lack thereof (Briere & Scott, 2006; Carlson, 1997).

Although trauma reactions are often discussed in terms of PTSD and acute stress disorder, individuals can experience reactions that meet criteria for other disorders alone or in tandem with PTSD or acute stress disorder such as depressive disorders, brief psychotic disorder, dissociative disorders, other anxiety disorders, substance use disorders, adjustment disorders, conversion disorder, somatization disorder, and personality disorders. Furthermore, individuals may experience trauma reactions that do not meet criteria as outlined by the *DSM-IV-TR*; they may exhibit symptoms that either do not fully meet or exist entirely outside of *DSM* criteria. Two issues to consider in this regard are complex PTSD (C-PTSD) and culture-bound trauma.

Herman (1992) coined the term *complex PTSD*. She posited that individuals who experience prolonged repeated traumatic stressors (such as hostages, prisoners of war, and survivors of domestic violence, childhood physical abuse, childhood sexual abuse, and organized sexual exploitation) experience alterations in affect regulation, consciousness, self-perception, perception of the perpetrator, relations with others, and systems of meaning. Individuals who manifest this syndrome are often misdiagnosed with other disorders that may be pejorative in nature (e.g., borderline personality disorder) and receive fragmented treatment that never addresses the underlying trauma. Complex trauma syndromes have been described extensively in the clinical literature but were not included in the *DSM-IV-TR*. The inclusion of a complex trauma syndrome, "disorders of extreme stress not otherwise specified" (DESNOS), in the *DSM-IV* was discussed and is again under consideration for *DSM-V*. The inclusion of DESNOS in the *DSM* heretofore has been highly controversial. A separate DESNOS diagnostic category was not included in the *DSM-IV* because field trials showed that most of the individuals who had DESNOS also met criteria for PTSD, and thus they were thought to be covered by the existing diagnostic criteria (Roth, Newman, Pelcovitz, van der Kolk, & Mandel, 1997; van der Kolk et al., 1996). Nevertheless, it is apparent that individuals who experience prolonged and repeated traumatic stress present with a complex constellation of problems and have different treatment needs than those who experience single-incident events.

As noted above, PTSD is a Western conception of a disorder that develops in response to a traumatic event that is in part contingent on the perceptions, characteristics, and environment of the afflicted person. Certainly, the constructed meanings of events, ways of coping, and social and physical environments vary by culture. It follows then that what one perceives as being a traumatic event and how one reacts to that event, even to the extent of a pathologic response, is influenced by culture. The PTSD construct does not exactly fit all cultures, but it is useful in understanding traumatic experiences when care is taken to recognize ethnocultural differences (Friedman & Marsella, 1996). The reexperiencing and arousal symptoms appear to be more consistent across cultures than the avoidance/numbing symptoms and likely have more of a biological basis (Marsella, Friedman, Gerrity, & Scurfield, 1996; McFall & Resick, 2005). The PTSD classification does not incorporate symptoms of complex, prolonged, or cumulative trauma, which are so often experienced by indigenous people. Nor does it take into account the cultural context of the trauma experience, which includes the intrapsychic, interpersonal, and sociopolitical domains (Drozdek, 2007). Although PTSD can be applied across cultures, the symptom clusters should be considered in the context of culture, and it should be recognized that the construction of what is traumatic as well as the trauma response may fall entirely outside the parameters of the PTSD diagnosis.

Culture

Culture is a complex concept that many have endeavored to define. The definition presented by Marsella (2005) incorporates the various facets of culture:

> Culture is a shared learned behavior and meanings that are socially transferred in various life-activity settings for purposes of individual and collective adjustment and adaptation. Cultures can be (1) transitory (i.e., situational even for a few minutes), (2) enduring (e.g., ethnocultural life styles), and in all instances are (3) dynamic (i.e., constantly subject to change and modification). Cultures are represented (4) internally (i.e., values, beliefs, attitudes, axioms, orientations, epistemologies, consciousness levels, perceptions, expectations, personhood), and (5) externally (i.e., artifacts, roles, institutions, social structures).

Cultures (6) shape and construct our realities (i.e., they contribute to our world views, perceptions, orientations) and with this ideas, morals, and preferences. (p. 657)

According to Marsella (2005), the notion that cultures can be temporary or transitory is included because cultures can develop in all social settings (e.g., classrooms, youth gangs) and the cultures that emerge in such settings can be in conflict with others. The most salient point, however, is that "culture constructs our realities and shapes the way we perceive and experience reality" (Marsella, Johnson, Watson, & Gryczynski, 2008, p. 5). Culture provides a structure and a context in which members can define themselves and make meaning out of the events in their own lives as well as in the collective. Cultures often contain a paradigm as to how the world operates in relation to a divine force. Rules for behavior and associated benefits and consequences are clear. Members of the culture understand the power hierarchy and know what characteristics and behaviors will gain them value and worth (Salzman, 2001). The culture also creates a context for living in which goods and services can be produced and utilized. The structure and context of the culture creates a sense of belonging, safety, and protection. The many facets of culture come together to buffer members from the effects of external stressors. Individuals and systems within the culture rely on the culture to provide them with the structure and context for their lives; the disintegration of a culture is thus traumatic (deVries, 1996).

Cultural Trauma

It is difficult to determine when the concept of cultural trauma first appeared in the literature, but as early as 1925 the notion that a society could be damaged by dramatic social change was discussed (Sorokin, 1925/1967). Sorokin (1925/1967) argued that rampant societal damages caused by the political, economic, epistemological, and spiritual upheaval of the Soviet revolution included dramatic increases in poverty, violence, sexual assault, disease, psychological disorders, familial instability (increasing divorce and declining birth rates), death rates, and alcoholism. These changes, caused by the trauma of the revolution, contributed to an overall cultural decline and a period of "primitivization." Thus, he was one of the first to discuss damages to a culture as a result of traumatic actions on the culture itself.

Sztompka (2000) suggested that the conditions for cultural trauma exist in an atmosphere of cultural disorientation that emerges when sudden and unexpected disruptions occur. Radical changes in technological, economic, or political conditions (e.g., revolution, market collapse, forced migration or deportation, genocide, terrorism, violence, assassination of a political leader) can affect core values, beliefs, and norms, creating cultural disorientation and possibly cultural trauma. Like the personal experience of an event that could lead to PTSD, the experience of the cultural event in and of itself is not traumatic; the interpretation and meaning that is attached to the event by a given culture influences whether it becomes traumatic for the culture. It is likely that the nature of the event, the social construction of the meaning of the event, and the degree to which the culture is able to resume its functions following the event affect the extent and severity of the trauma experience or lack thereof. For example, Bracken (2002) noted that the expected rise in mental health and social problems associated with the effects of war in the homeland (e.g., bombing raids, food shortages) in England during World War II did not occur. The English people constructed the experience as a time for solidarity and strength, coming together in a culturally sustaining way rather than experiencing it as trauma leading to societal deterioration. Taken a step further, the meaning that the world made of the British stand against the Blitzkrieg was one of a courageous people standing against the Nazi evildoers. This type of narrative allows for memorialization and healing. If England had lost the war, a vastly different narrative may have been constructed. Others who have experienced violent assaults against their culture continue to struggle to have their voices heard and their experience validated in the eyes of the world: the Armenians who continue to struggle for recognition of the genocide that they experienced at the hands of the Turkish government in 1915, the women of Congo who struggle against present-day systematic rape and violence, and Native Americans who contend with a revisionist history that purports that massacres of their people by American forces were actually heroic battles won against a savage force.

In summary, cultural trauma is a complex concept whose components are discussed in a variety of ways in the literature (see Stamm, Stamm, Hudnall, & Higson-Smith, 2004). It is clear that when a culture is overwhelmed by trauma, it loses its ability to protect and support its members. Homeostatic mechanisms that normally operate within the culture do not function, and the stress-buffering properties of the culture are diminished or destroyed (deVries, 1996). Such has been the case with Native Americans as well as with other ethnocultural groups subjected to widespread disturbances as a result of colonization, slavery, forced relocation, genocide, disease, war, or any number of events that cause an entire group of people to suffer tragically (Neal, 1998).

Theoretical Perspectives on Cultural Trauma

Alexander (2004) posited that "cultural trauma occurs when members of a collectivity feel they have been subjected to a horrendous event that leaves indelible marks upon their group consciousness, marking their memories forever and changing their future identities in fundamental ways" (p. 1). Members of the collective do not need to directly experience the event to experience the dramatic loss of identity and meaning that the trauma brings about. Nor does the trauma have to be a sudden event; it can be a slow process working its way into the psyche of the collective. The trauma process as described by Alexander begins with a claim that a fundamental injury to a social group has occurred; the claim-making carrier groups within the collective struggle to make meaning out of the event(s). Once the members of the wounded group recognize their traumatization, the claim can be broadened to the wider social community. This meaning-making process includes the nature of the pain, the nature of the victim, the relation of the trauma victim to the wider audience, and attribution of responsibility. Social institutions in the domains of religion, law, science, aesthetics, mass media, and state bureaucracy affect the representational process and may constrain or expand claims based on their own interests or agendas and may themselves be agents of trauma. The distribution of power among these institutions is often uneven and affects how trauma is or is not represented in a culture. Once meaning is made from the traumatic experience, it becomes incorporated into the collective identity, and a process of reparation, reconstruction, and healing can occur. When carrier groups do not have the resources to disseminate trauma claims and/or social institutions constrain trauma claims, perpetrators of collective suffering can avoid assuming responsibility for the damage they have caused, and the healing components of the trauma process are stymied.

Salzman (2001) and Salzman and Halloran (2004) applied terror management theory (see Greenberg, Solomon, & Pyszczynski, 1997; Solomon, Greenberg, & Pyszczynski, 2004) to the concept of cultural trauma, particularly among indigenous people. In essence, terror management theory contends that human beings' self-consciousness makes them aware of the inevitability of their own death, and thus they experience an underlying terror of personal annihilation. This fear of mortality would be immobilizing if not for the anxiety-buffering effects of self-esteem and cultural worldview. Culture provides the standards for success and makes meaning of life. Individuals who conform to cultural standards and are deemed successful have both enhanced self-esteem and a meaningful world in which to live. The cultural worldview is essential for buffering anxiety. When a culture is threatened, members will coalesce to protect it from being diminished. When a culture experiences trauma and its cultural worldview is damaged, anxiety flourishes, and serious psychological and behavioral effects emerge.

Stamm et al. (2004) developed a theory of cultural trauma and loss that is based on the idea of cultural clash, whereby a hegemonic "arriving" culture challenges the "original" culture and disrupts fundamental cultural, social, and economic processes. Colonialism is the clearest example of a context for such a clash to occur. However, it is also possible for cultural clash to occur within one culture where conflict exists between subgroups. In Stamm et al.'s model, the repercussions of cultural clash—characterized by disruptions such as expanded trade, intellectual innovations, epidemics, competition for scarce resources between the arriving culture and original culture, incongruent belief systems, and war—precede an era of cultural loss in which members of the challenged group, still struggling to adjust to the new social reality, continue to experience an erosion of their shared identity and the loss of familiar social structures (cultural memory, language, self-rule, place, family system, economic resources, and healing systems). By the time this era of continued cultural disintegration emerges, the arriving culture may have established itself as a powerful and overbearing social, political, and military force, institutionalizing its dominance and structuring the distribution of resources and benefits to the detriment of the original culture (see also Walters & Simoni, 2002).

Multigenerational and Historical Trauma

The recognition that trauma experienced by one generation could be passed on to later generations emerged when children of Nazi Holocaust survivors were found to be experiencing psychiatric symptoms seemingly related to their parents' traumatic experiences (Kansteiner, 2004). The phenomenon responsible for these symptoms was termed *transposition,* meaning that the trauma experience was transposed from one generation to another; that is, the children of Holocaust survivors relived the experiences of their parents in an unconscious way (Kestenberg, 1989; Laub, 2002). This transposition is thought to pass from generation to generation as even the grandchildren of Holocaust survivors have been observed to experience traumatic effects. The notion of transposition is not without critics, who suggest that the negative effects experienced by the children are an effect of poor parenting by traumatized parents rather than a direct effect of the past trauma (i.e., the Holocaust) (Kansteiner, 2004). Rather than debating the merits of these arguments, Auerhahn and Laub (1998) pointed to their research, which suggests that "knowledge of psychic trauma weaves through the memories of several generations," also that "massive trauma has an amorphous presence . . . [and] shapes the internal representation of reality of several generations, becoming an unconscious organizing principle passed on by parents and internalized by their children" (p. 22). Research indicates that although the trauma response is heterogeneous in terms of individual and collective constructions, it is likely that the multigenerational experience of trauma across groups that experienced mass trauma is a universal phenomenon (see Danieli, 1998).

Drawing from the literature on the intergenerational transmission of trauma among the descendents of Nazi Holocaust survivors and other massively victimized populations, Maria Yellow Horse Brave Heart developed the theory of historical trauma and delineated the historical trauma response as it occurs among Native American people (Brave Heart, 2003; Brave Heart & DeBruyn, 1998). Historical trauma is defined as "the cumulative emotional and psychological wounding, over the lifespan and across generations, emanating from massive group trauma experiences" (Brave Heart, 2003, p. 7). The historical trauma response occurs in reaction to historical trauma and involves an array of problems that may include substance abuse, self-destructive behavior, suicidal thoughts and gestures, depression, anxiety, low self-esteem, anger, difficulty recognizing and expressing emotions, survivor guilt, intrusive trauma imagery, identification with ancestral pain, fixation on trauma, somatic symptoms, and elevated mortality rates (Brave Heart, 2003, 2007). Historical unresolved grief is associated with the historical trauma response. The unresolved grief is a result of a long history of personal, familial, and communal losses that could not be mourned. These include massacres; premature death due to disease, suicide, or poverty; loss of language; changes in spirituality and belief systems; and disrupted family structure due to forced repression of Native social systems and children's coerced or forced attendance at boarding schools. Grief is a normal response to loss, and various cultures have ways of mourning and expressing their grief. Native Americans were often unable to mourn in traditional ways or were compelled to detach from the pain of tremendous grief by a hegemonic culture that delegitimized their lived experience (Brave Heart & DeBruyn, 1998). This historical unresolved grief gets passed on from generation to generation.

More recently, Evans-Campbell (2008) elaborated on historical trauma theory by suggesting a multilevel framework for understanding the phenomenon that includes impacts at the individual, family, and community levels. She further suggested a dynamic interplay between direct trauma experiences and transgenerational trauma: that high rates of current violence, victimization, and trauma among Native American populations are best understood against the backdrop of temporally distal patterns of collective harm.

Native American Trauma Experience: History and Present Day

Native Americans contend with present-day events that have the potential to be traumatic at the individual and cultural level at much higher rates than other racial groups. They also contend with the cumulative effects of cultural and intergenerational traumas from the past, which are conceptualized as historical trauma. To help the reader understand the magnitude of the trauma that is part of the Native American experience, we provide an overview of the traumatic events that have occurred and continue to occur in the lives of Native Americans in this section.

The era of European discovery and subsequent colonization of the Americas marked the beginning of great suffering for the indigenous people of the American continents. The Native American population decreased from greater than 5 million in 1492 to 250,000 in the decade between 1890 and 1900 (Thornton, 1987). This massive depopulation is attributed to a number of factors including disease, genocidal acts, war, and subsistence-disrupting policies. Europeans brought with them an array of diseases, such as small pox, that the Native American people had never encountered. With the population's lacking the biological immunities that come with disease exposure, the introduction of European illnesses devastated many Native American tribes with recycling epidemics. The devastation of illness would be compounded by the destructions of war and displacement as Europeans spread throughout the continent.

As the European presence grew, peaceful relations with Native American tribes gave way to conflicts over land and resources. These conflicts escalated as the republic of the United States of America formed and expanded. The competition for land in the East and the Americans' belief in their own manifest destiny led to the passage of the Indian Removal Act of 1830, which forced southeastern tribes (even those that were "civilized," that is, had adopted White ways such as the owning and farming of land, entrepreneurialism, Christianity, and European-style governmental systems) to relocate to reservations in the West (Wilson, 1998). Thousands of Native Americans died on these brutal forced marches to the West, the most notorious of which is the Cherokee Trail of Tears. When tribes were forced to relocate from their homelands, a vital cultural connection to place was severed. As the young nation pushed further westward, it engaged in a series of conflicts that came to be known collectively as the Indian Wars. Although the manifest social policy of the U.S. government toward the Native Americans was one of relocation, in actual practice the result was too often annihilation. Tribal groups that did not relocate from their lands to reservations were attacked and in many instances massacred. Those that did move onto reservations were compelled to abandon traditional spiritual practices and adopt Christianity along with other White ways of being.

Early U.S. government policies regarding Native Americans often functioned under the implicit assumption that the White culture was superior to indigenous cultures. Practices aimed at "civilizing the savages" proliferated. Sometimes, such policies and practices were driven by benevolent motives, but nevertheless the message conveyed was one of Native Americans' cultural inferiority. A systematic pattern of policies evolved with the explicit goal of hastening Native American assimilation into the hegemonic culture, which was often pursued through force or coercion and involved attempts to destroy or suppress elements of Native American tribal cultural and traditional practices (Brave Heart & DeBruyn, 1998; Johnson et al., 2008). One of the most damaging assimilation practices was forcing Native American children to attend boarding schools. The Carlisle Industrial Indian School was founded in 1879 and served as a model for other Indian schools. The motto of Richard Pratt, who was the founder of the Carlisle Indian School, was, "Kill the Indian, and save the man." This motto is emblematic of the notion that replacing Indian cultural practices among the children with skills and practices from the White culture would allow them to assimilate and somehow save them. To that end, Native American children were forced to discard their familiar traditional ways and adopt the ways of the Whites. They were compelled to adopt Christian names, cut their hair, wear uniforms, eat unfamiliar foods from the White culture, and speak only English. Children were severely beaten if they engaged in traditional behaviors or spoke their own language. Thousands of children died from disease and sheer loneliness (Luther Standing Bear, cited in Wilson, 1998). Boarding schools lasted well into the 20th century, and many report experiencing violence and victimization there in the form of physical and sexual abuse.

After the Wounded Knee Massacre in 1890 in which 300 men, women, and children along with Chief Big Foot were mowed down by the bullets of the U.S. Army and left lying on the frozen ground, the Indian Wars were over. However, the traumatization of the Native American people was not. Along with Native American children's being sent to boarding schools, transracial adoptions were frequent until the passage of the Indian Child Welfare Act in 1978. Religious and cultural practices were squelched until the passage of the Indian Religious Freedom Act in 1978. The repression of Native American cultural practices has led to a number of cultural losses such as the loss of Native languages. Microaggressions such as offensive team mascots and slogans depicting or referring to Native Americans and the use of the term *squaw* to refer to Native American women continue to occur today (Walters, Evans-Campbell, Stately, & Old Person, 2006). In addition, many Native Americans continue to contend with poverty, prejudice, discrimination, and various other forms of oppression.

During the 20th century, many Native Americans left reservation lands to migrate to urban settings in search of economic opportunities, and the U.S. government policies encouraged such urban relocation (Brave Heart & DeBruyn, 1998; Johnson et al., 2008; Snipp, 1992). The majority of Native Americans now live outside of reservations (Ogunwole, 2006), where they may have more limited access to the tribal culture and its attendant social support systems. Although many urban Native Americans have been successful in retaining ties to culture practices and cultural identity through various mechanisms (see Cheshire, 2001; Snipp, 1992), some urban Native American communities have experienced a loss of community and cultural cohesion that may have adverse impacts on health and well-being (Johnson, Gryczynski, & Wiechelt, 2007).

Currently, Native Americans experience very high rates of lifetime traumatic events. They experience death rates 1.2 times higher than all other races in the United States in general and have much higher death rates from certain diseases (8.5 times for tuberculosis, 4.2 times for chronic liver disease and cirrhosis, and 2.9 times for diabetes), substance abuse (6 times for alcohol-related deaths and 1.5 times for drug-related deaths), and unintentional injuries (2.5 times) (Indian Health Service, 2009). Native Americans experience violent crimes in general and rape/sexual assault in particular at more than twice the rate of the general population; they are more likely to report the offender as being from a different race than Black and White victims, with Whites making up the highest number of offenders for such crimes against Native Americans (Perry, 2004). The homicide rate for Native Americans is twice the rate for all other races in the United States (Indian Health Service, 2009). Native American women are at least twice as likely to experience intimate partner violence as any other racial group (Bureau of Justice Statistics, 2010). American Indian/Alaska Native children experience elevated rates of maltreatment (physical abuse, sexual abuse, neglect; 14.2 per 1,000 American Indian or Alaska Native children vs. 9.1 per 1,000 White children), with the second-highest rates of child victimization after African American children (U.S. Department of Health and Human Services, 2009).

Reactions to Trauma

Given their high incidence of trauma exposure, it is not surprising that Native Americans experience elevated rates of PTSD as compared to the general population (Beals et al., 2005; U.S. Department of Health and Human Services, 2001). Nor is it surprising that they experience higher rates of substance use disorders than other racial groups (10.7% vs. 7.6% for past year alcohol use disorders and 5.0% vs. 2.9% for past year drug use disorders) given that substance use disorders are known to be associated with trauma and PTSD (Ouimette & Brown, 2003; Substance Abuse and Mental Health Services Administration, 2007). Existing research indicates that Native Americans have high rates of psychological distress and mental health problems when compared to other races as well as the highest rates of unmet needs for such problems (Harris, Edlund, & Larson, 2005). With regard to psychological distress, a recent report on American Indian/Alaska Native health indicates that Native Americans report experiencing feeling sad, restless, hopeless, and worthless at a higher rate than any other racial/ethnic group (Barnes, Adams, & Powell-Griner, 2010). In addition, studies suggest that depression and anxiety are commonly experienced by Native Americans, particularly as comorbid disorders with substance use disorders or PTSD, and that depression may be expressed in atypical ways (Beals et al., 2005; B. Duran et al., 2004; Robin, Chester, & Goldman, 1996; U.S. Department of Health and Human Services, 2001). The interpersonal, prolonged, and cumulative nature of the traumatic events that are experienced by Native Americans may produce a trauma reaction that is more consistent with C-PTSD/DESNOS rather than PTSD as it is more inclusive of the broad range of psychological distress that Native Americans experience. In any case, the fact that Native Americans are 1.7 times more likely to commit suicide than the general population indicates that careful assessment of their mental health status is warranted (Indian Health Service, 2009).

The heterogeneity of Native Americans in the United States is an important consideration in any effort to understand their life experience in general and their experience of mental health and substance abuse problems in particular. The mental health system and its associated epistemology in the United States are constructed in such a way that they reflect the dominant Western culture. Mental health and substance abuse problems as experienced by Native Americans may not fit neatly into mainstream constructions. For example, it is well known that standard measures of depression fail to detect depression in Native American individuals in many instances (Beals et al., 2005; U.S. Department of Health and Human Services, 2001). Despair that is experienced in association with the loss of sacred places or intrusions on identity does not easily fit into hegemonic nosological systems, nor is it resolved by mainstream intervention strategies (Gone, 2006; Robin et al., 1996). For Native Americans, the experiences of trauma and trauma responses are likely much broader than those that are included in existing classification systems. Also, constructions of trauma and trauma effects are likely to have some variation by tribal group, gender, sexual orientation, reservation versus urban status, and degree of assimilation (Balsam, Huang, Simoni, & Walters, 2004; Beals et al., 2005; Cole, 2006; B. Duran et al., 2004; Evans-Campbell, Lindhorst, Huang, & Walters, 2006). Finally, current-life traumatic experiences and trauma reactions among Native Americans occur against a backdrop of cumulative cultural traumas whose effects were passed on across generations, albeit in different ways depending on the experiences of the various tribes.

Cultural Trauma and Its Effects on Native Americans

The arrival of Europeans to North American soil launched an epoch of cultural trauma for the indigenous people. The Europeans viewed themselves as being on the right side of God and entitled to the newly found beautiful lands. Further, they believed that they had the right to civilize the "savage" inhabitants of the land and to eradicate those inhabitants who did not comply. The presence and attitudes of the colonizing force inevitably produced cultural clashes resulting in disease, war, forced relocation, and challenges to traditional belief systems as outlined in brief above. Such clashes would be reproduced over the course of several hundred years throughout the expanding country. Napoleon (1996, as cited in Salzman & Halloran, 2004, p. 234) described the effects of exposure to European disease (influenza) and the sudden death of 60% of the Yup'ik people to illustrate the process and effect of cultural trauma on indigenous people:

> The suffering, the despair, the heartbreak, the desperation, and confusion these survivors lived through is unimaginable. People watched helplessly as their mothers, fathers, brothers, and sisters grew ill, the efforts of the *angalkuq* [medicine men] failing. . . . Whether the survivors knew or understood, they had witnessed the fatal wounding of *Yuuraraq* [way of being a human being] and the old Yup'ik culture. . . .

The Yup'ik world was turned upside down, literally overnight. Out of the suffering in confusion, desperation, heartbreak, and trauma was born a new generation of Yup'ik people. They were born into shock. They woke to a world in shambles, many of their people and their beliefs strewn around them, dead. Their medicines and their medicine men and women had proven useless. Everything they had believed in had failed. Their ancient world had collapsed. . . . The world the survivors woke to was without anchor. They woke up in shock, listless, confused, bewildered, heartbroken, and afraid. (pp. 10–11)

Today we know that efforts to restore a culture should be undertaken as soon as possible following a culturally traumatic event to promote healthy coping and minimize the effects of traumatic stress and potential damage to the culture. To that end, deVries (1996) suggested that the following should be done following an event that is potentially traumatic to a culture:

- employ remaining cultural structures to help victims manage horror,
- facilitate rituals and customs that order emotions,
- create self-help opportunities,
- legitimize suffering,
- bring order and continuity into the posttraumatic period,
- incorporate rituals and places to carry them out into the rehabilitative processes,
- reestablish symbolic places (churches, school yards, and other important gathering places), and
- work to reinstitute traditional social relationships.

The Native American people received no such restoration. The focus of the dominant U.S. culture was to do away with the indigenous cultures whether by annihilation or assimilation. Thus, the Native people were left to struggle with each successive traumatic event. There were, of course, opportunities to relocate and to accept White ways of being, but these came at the great costs of loss of connection with the land, loss of connection with the spirit world, loss of identity, and loss of family structures and other familiar ways of being that were all in and of themselves traumatic. The disintegration of culture results in a diminished sense of trust, aggression, anxiety, and other negative affective states among individuals from within that culture. According to Salzman (2001), the decimation of a culture leaves its members with a shattered worldview and no prescribed way of living; thus, they are left with no means for maintaining anxiety-buffering self-esteem and resort to other, often self-destructive, means of managing their anxiety. The effects of cultural trauma continue to reverberate through the lives of Native Americans and their communities. Understanding cultural trauma and its impact on Native Americans is an essential building block toward comprehending the multiplicative complex effect of ongoing cumulative individual and cultural traumas that is known as historical trauma.

Historical Trauma: The Native American Experience

The theoretical literature on the phenomenon of historical trauma among Native Americans has had a multipronged, transtemporal emphasis spanning the micro and macro levels. At the micro or individual level, the cumulative effects of intergenerational trauma manifest as an individual-level psychological response that can mimic the symptoms of PTSD and disrupt the individual's psychological functioning and coping systems. Brave Heart (2003) termed the range of maladaptive psychological and behavioral reactions to historical trauma the "historical trauma response," arguing that the established diagnostic criteria for PTSD do not sufficiently reflect the culturally and historically grounded traumas experienced by Native Americans. Early applications of intergenerational trauma to the Native American experience also suggested a link between temporally distal experiences of cultural loss and subjugation in the group's shared history and the collection of health and social problems that continue to affect Native Americans as a group in the modern era (Brave Heart, 2003; Brave Heart & DeBruyn, 1998). This explicit dual conceptualization of intergenerational trauma as affecting not only individuals' psychological processes but also population-level disparities in health and access to resources was a significant theoretical advance. More recently, scholars have continued to elaborate on these kinds of multilevel conceptualizations of historical trauma (see, e.g., Evans-Campbell, 2008; Sotero, 2006).

Brave Heart and others have contended that the contemporary plights faced by the Native American population—as indicated by racial disparities in such domains as violent victimization, substance use disorders, domestic violence, and health outcomes—could be seen as a direct consequence of historical trauma through its role in shaping the social and cultural contexts in which individuals operate (Brave Heart & DeBruyn, 1998; Evans-Campbell, 2008; Sotero, 2006; Whitbeck, Adams, Hoyt, & Chen, 2004). Health disparities continue to be evident in Native American communities, particularly in the realm of behavioral health, both in rural and in urban areas (Castor et al., 2006; Steele, Cardinez, Richardson, Tom-Orme, & Shaw, 2008; Urban Indian Health Institute, 2008). Empirical research suggests that the theorized link between trauma and health disparities is a plausible one given the relationship between PTSD and illness. For example, research has found that PTSD is associated with a range of health problems (Sareen et al., 2007; Sledjeski, Speisman, & Dierker, 2008). Moreover, the association between PTSD and chronic health conditions is explained by the number of traumatic events experienced during the life course (Sledjeski et al., 2008). Hence, there is evidence indicating that repeated exposure to traumatic events has a cumulative impact on the development of a range of chronic illnesses. If individuals internalize the cultural traumas experienced by their ancestors, it is possible that both historical and contemporary traumas might exert a cumulative adverse impact on human health.

The concept of historical trauma, its vital components, and the theorized pathways by which it perpetuates health and resource disparities in the affected population resonates well with a parallel body of scholarship in the field of social epidemiology that has sought to develop more nuanced understandings of risk-shaping processes at multiple levels of social organization (see, e.g., Berkman, Glass, Brissette, & Seeman, 2000; Glass & McAtee, 2006; Link & Phelan, 1995). Historical trauma can be seen through the prism of what Link and Phelan (1995) described as fundamental causes of disease. The fundamental cause conceptualization shifts emphasis away from proximal risk factors and encourages researchers to "contextualize" risk factors by appreciating the role of social conditions in structuring resource disparities that give rise to such risks. Although Link and Phelan's conceptualization is by and large temporally static and fixed in the present, historical trauma theory complements their approach to understanding what puts people "at risk of risks" by postulating a process and mechanism that generates risk for the health-demoting fundamental causes themselves. Although it is admittedly an imperfect metaphor, the phenomenon of historical trauma and its intergenerational transmission can be seen as giving rise to the contemporary social conditions that structure risk for disease and social problems.

Working from a perspective of public health and social epidemiology, Sotero (2006) has outlined a comprehensive conceptual model of historical trauma that details the physiological, psychological, and social consequences resulting from primary exposure to a mass trauma experience. Sotero argues that intergenerational transmission of the trauma response can occur through multiple vectors, including genetic, environmental, psychosocial, and social-economic-political systems as well as discrimination. A key feature of enduring historical trauma is that some part of the mass trauma was perpetrated against the culture in a deliberate, purposeful way. Although Native Americans experienced their share of unintentional disasters (e.g., a large number of deaths from illness due to lack of immunity to European diseases), much of the shared mass trauma in the group's history emanates from human decisions and contact with other cultures (e.g., war, policies of forced or coerced assimilation, attempts to suppress cultural and religious practices of the Native American people by a powerful White majority). Native Americans faced a systematic and drawn-out series of injustices that were perpetrated on them by the colonizing forces and the U.S. government (Thornton, 1987; Wilson, 1998).

Historical status inequalities and group subjugation are often intergenerational phenomena that leave societal, cultural, and institutional legacies that are difficult to dismantle. Nevertheless, it is important to remember that an individual from a specific cultural group that has a shared history of mass trauma will not automatically exhibit a pattern of symptoms attributable to a historical trauma response. The degree to which an individual experiences problems in psychosocial functioning that can be linked to a historical trauma response may vary depending on an array of considerations, including but not limited to cultural identification, cultural knowledge, existing support systems, and available outlets for cultural expression.

A graphical depiction of historical trauma and the pathways by which some of its effects may become manifest, drawing from several sources (Brave Heart & DeBruyn, 1998; Evans-Campbell, 2008; Sotero, 2006; Stamm et al., 2004) as well as our own understanding of the phenomenon, is shown in Figure 10.1. Mass cultural traumas experienced by one generation result in disruption of cultural roles and protective processes. These disruptions stifle culturally grounded opportunities for healing from the effects of acute PTSD. The trauma experience does not emanate from a singular event but rather is characterized by a sequential collection of cultural traumas that generate momentum for processes of cultural loss and disintegration (which continue to endure through subsequent generations). Policies and systems of subjugation—some intentionally designed to destroy or fundamentally transform the culture—are put in place by the new hegemonic order. Children who never experienced the first set of traumas are adversely affected throughout the developmental process by the acute psychosocial problems experienced by their parents and elders. The children are also directly affected by subsequent trauma events that are a feature of the new sociopolitical environment. The cumulative intergenerational experiences of trauma and cultural loss act to perpetuate legacies of social systems, policies, and institutions that disrupt the natural protective and adaptive features of a culture. Over time, critical cultural protective factors are displaced by the shared experience of the cumulative trauma. In this way, historical trauma becomes a self-perpetuating phenomenon, woven into the tattered tapestry of cultural identity.

A Bridge From the Past to the Present: Historical and Contemporary Traumas

An interesting and still emergent area of research is the interaction between historical trauma response and modern-day experiences of trauma, injustice, mistreatment, or discrimination (see Evans-Campbell, 2008). It is useful to distinguish between the adverse psychosocial effects stemming from such contemporary experiences and the enduring effects of historical trauma on an individual whose cultural group was exposed to massive trauma events at some point in the group's distant history. Contemporary exposure to trauma, injustice, or mistreatment does not in and of itself indicate the presence of a

Figure 10.1   A model of the generational flow and consequences of historical trauma

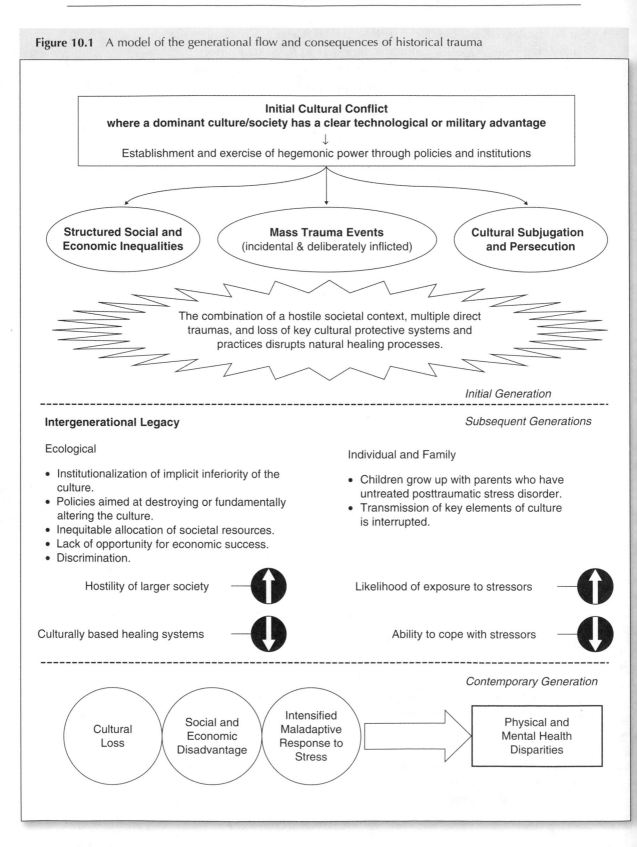

historical trauma response in the individual (although some theorists would argue that the risk of such contemporary harm is inflated as a result of historical trauma). However, the historical trauma response may be reified and intensified in the face of modern-day adverse experiences to the extent that the individual views such experiences as fitting within a broader pattern of historical abuses. In one of the few advanced quantitative studies examining the effects of historical trauma on health behavior, Whitbeck, Chen, Hoyt, and Adams (2004) demonstrated that historical loss mediated the effects of experienced discrimination on alcohol abuse among Native American women. Furthermore, enculturation had an independent protective effect against alcohol abuse. These findings highlight the complex interrelationships between historical trauma (as experienced by the individual) and contemporary stress-producing experiences such as discrimination as well as the potential for gender differences in the link between historical loss and practice of health-demoting behaviors (see also Brave Heart, 1999; Walters & Simoni, 2002).

Native Americans as a group are at elevated risk for experiencing trauma, violence, and stress-inducing events (see reviews in Brave Heart & DeBruyn, 1998; Evans-Campbell, 2008; Johnson et al., 2008). Understanding the way that historical trauma or cultural loss shape these experiences and continue to prevent healing could have important implications for culturally focused intervention development and clinical work. If historical trauma plays a role in intensifying subjective experiences of stress and promulgating maladaptive behavioral responses, providing opportunities for the expression of healthy grieving processes and coping skills could presumably buffer against poor outcomes. Because historical trauma affects individuals, families, communities, and the broader Native American population, efforts to hasten healing through fostering empowerment, resiliency, and reclamation of cultural identity should target all of these areas (Evans-Campbell, 2008; Sotero, 2006).

Challenges for Conducting Research on Historical Trauma and Future Directions

Conducting empirical research that directly tests the theorized underpinnings of historical trauma and its repercussions is challenging due to the numerous dimensions that characterize the concept and complicate accurate measurement. The issues that pose particular difficulties for empirical inquiry include teasing apart the deleterious impacts of historical trauma at the individual (psychopathological and maladaptive behavioral response) versus ecological (health disparities and economic inequalities) levels, clarifying and testing the precise mechanisms by which intergenerational transmission is thought to occur, and examining the real-world repercussions of historical trauma in how it shapes temporally proximate cultural stress-inducing events experienced during the life course.

The majority of the scholarly literature on historical trauma among Native Americans has been theoretical and practice oriented. The result has been the development and continued refinement of a rich and elegant body of theory that is ripe for empirical investigation. Research on historical trauma is poised to take off in the coming years and decades. An important development has been advances in quantitative measurement of constructs central to historical trauma. Whitbeck, Adams, et al. (2004) developed and psychometrically validated two measures of critical importance in this regard. These brief structured scales measure the degree to which individuals think about losses that are unique to the Native American experience and the degree to which they attribute negative emotional responses (e.g., shame and rage) to these losses. It is imperative that future researchers continue to refine measurement of such central concepts. This will pave the way for more advanced studies that can empirically test the various theoretical underpinnings of historical trauma. Although not without its pitfalls, intervention research should be an indispensible ingredient for historical trauma scholarship in the next decade. Indeed, given the challenges associated with observational research of an inherently transtemporal and multilevel phenomenon, randomized trials of interventions may provide the best evidence of the merits of historical trauma theory. It would be a compelling validation of the theory if it turns out that addressing historical trauma within structured programs or therapeutic interventions leads to improved outcomes relative to interventions that do not address such issues. Investigating and interrupting the adverse effects of historical trauma on individuals, families, and communities will almost certainly require an interdisciplinary approach as myriad issues that are derived from historical trauma theory lie at the heart of social work, psychology, sociology, and public health.

Healing

The complex and heterogeneous nature of trauma and trauma reactions among Native Americans as well as the heterogeneity that exists among Native Americans themselves mean that there is not now, nor is there ever likely to be, an easy, prescribed, or uniform approach to resolving the effects of trauma among them. It is clear that multiple considerations regarding the individual are needed in the assessment and treatment planning process:

- experience of traumatic event(s);
- experience of PTSD and C-PTSD symptoms;
- experience of other psychiatric symptoms, for example, depression and anxiety;
- substance use behaviors;
- experience of psychological or spiritual distress that is not captured by *DSM* classifications;

- experience of health-related problems;
- degree to which the individual identifies with the Native culture;
- extent to which the individual engages in traditional practices and behaviors;
- awareness of and identification with cultural and historical trauma;
- economic, political, geographic, and cultural contexts in which the individual lives;
- individual strengths and capacity for resilience;
- connection with family and Native American community; and
- the capacity of the family or the community to support the healing process.

The treatment needs of an individual are going to be radically different depending on the individual's experiences relative to the above factors. For example, a Native American man who experiences PTSD symptoms related to his experiences in war and resides on the Navajo reservation in Arizona where he embraces traditional practices and feels a close connection to his family and community is likely to have very different needs and strengths than does a woman of Cherokee descent residing in Baltimore, Maryland, who experiences C-PTSD symptoms related to a past history of ongoing childhood physical abuse and is only vaguely aware of her Native American ancestry. In the first case, the integration of traditional healing practices along with familial and community support would likely be extremely important early in the treatment process (see Manson, 1997). In the second case, efforts to integrate traditional healing practices early in the treatment process would likely be perceived as weird and perhaps even emblematic of prejudice or at least cultural insensitivity on the part of the clinician (if the clinician were not a Native American). However, in both cases historical trauma is likely to be playing a role by possibly creating the circumstances in which trauma occurs in the case of childhood physical abuse (historic disruptions in family system functioning and parenting practices) as well as increasing the individual's vulnerability to developing PTSD and potentially amplifying the trauma experience in either case (see Evans-Campbell, 2008). Attention to historical trauma will be an important component in the healing process in both cases; the only questions are how and when.

A careful assessment of the individual's sense of Native American identity and cultural connection will be useful to the clinician in determining an appropriate course of action. Aragon (2006) suggested that the use of a genogram and a timeline diagram can provide useful insight into family connections and patterns as well as lifetime milestones and setbacks that will help to clarify the individual's status regarding culture and identity. In the case of the Cherokee woman above, the assessment may reveal that she has assimilated into the dominant culture, and current mainstream strategies for addressing C-PTSD are indicated (see Foa, Keane, Friedman, & Cohen, 2009; Herman, 1992). Nevertheless, historic trauma may still be playing a role in her life, and the clinician should at least be cognizant of that possibility. As treatment progresses, deeper healing of the disengaged historical trauma may be possible by reconnecting her with her ancestral past in a slow and careful way (E. Duran, 2006).

According to E. Duran (2006), the soul wound, now known as historical trauma, has long been acknowledged by Native American elders as the result of the ancestral wounding of the people and of the earth. He asserts that healing for the problems faced by Native Americans today (e.g., depression, anxiety, substance abuse, violence) occurs via a decolonizing process aimed at healing the soul wound. Clinicians who work with Native Americans must use care not to perpetuate the trauma of colonialism. Epistemological hybridism whereby clinicians can understand and value the worldview of Native Americans in addition to their own is needed to practice in decolonizing ways. The helping process should "address the immediate problem and simultaneously set in motion the act of decolonizing" (p. 14). An important component of the process is to answer the question, Who are you (i.e., Who is your tribe? Who is its God? and What is its tribal creation story?)? The clinician must also answer these questions for him- or herself as being disconnected from one's own ancestral path makes it impossible to help others connect with theirs. The healing work in this model is aimed at making the connections between current life problems and historic trauma. E. Duran's model is instructive for all clinicians who work with Native Americans in that cultural competency, respect for different ways of knowing and being, and connection with one's own self are necessary regardless of the specific therapeutic approach being used.

Clinicians who work with Native Americans may work with a particular tribal group on or near a reservation or with an array of tribal groups in urban Indian centers. In addition, because most Native Americans now live away from tribal lands, clinicians in any geographic area or type of practice setting may come into contact with Native Americans in their practices. Therefore, it is incumbent on all clinicians to have at least a basic understanding of the experience of Native Americans in the United States and the effects of historical trauma on behavioral and physical health (see Johnson, Baldwin, Gryczynski, Wiechelt, & Haring, 2010; Johnson et al., 2007). Clinicians who work with a particular tribal group should be very familiar with the history and practices of that tribe. To be culturally competent practitioners with Native Americans, clinicians should go beyond simply acquiring knowledge, reflect on their own biases and the biases of the helping professions toward Native Americans, and redress those biases in their work with and on behalf of Native Americans (Weaver, 1998).

Community-level healing is vital to ameliorating the effects of historical trauma in the long term. Salzman (2001) described cultural recovery movements in which Native American people are identifying and making use of their traditional values and practices in association with political struggles to regain power. Such struggles restore the cultural worldview and the people's faith in their ways of being, thus restoring the anxiety-buffering properties of the culture. The Yup'ik people, whose dramatic cultural loss was briefly described above, are working to heal from historical trauma and have incorporated their traditions into behavioral health treatment (Mills, 2003). Brave Heart (1998) developed the historical trauma and unresolved grief intervention, which addresses generational and lifespan trauma using empowerment principles in the context of the Lakota culture. The intervention has been extended to a number of other tribal groups and is now identified as a tribal best practice by the First Nations Behavioral Health Association. Brave Heart (1999) implemented a parenting curriculum among Lakota parents to redress the effects of the boarding school–era traumatization on families. In 1986, the Lakota people initiated the Big Foot Memorial Ride, which allowed them to finally grieve the tragic massacre of Chief Big Foot and 300 people at Wounded Knee in 1890. It was also an opportunity to celebrate their strength in that the Lakota as a people continue to survive (Weaver, 1998). The Wellbriety movement emerged in 1999 to help Native Americans with alcohol and other drug problems recover (White Bison, 2002). There are many other examples of how the Native American people as a whole and as tribal groups have entered an era of revitalization (Stamm et al., 2004). In the face of overwhelming odds, Native Americans have survived and are reclaiming their various cultures to empower themselves and promote ongoing healing and revitalization for generations to come. They are indeed a resilient people.

Case Vignette: Joe

Joe is a 62-year-old Native American man who is a member of the Lumbee tribe. He currently resides with his wife of 40 years who is also Lumbee. The couple has five adult children and seven grandchildren. Joe primarily grew up in Robeson County, North Carolina, where the Lumbee tribe is mainly located. His family of origin relocated to Baltimore, Maryland, when he was 12 years old in an effort to find a better source of income. (Some members of the Lumbee tribe began migrating to Baltimore in the late 1930s to seek work; the flow of migration peaked during the 1940s and 1950s. A large group of Lumbee and their offspring currently reside there.) He reports that when he was a boy in North Carolina, segregation between Whites, Blacks, and "Indians" (Joe uses the term *Indian* to describe himself) was commonplace. Thus, he affiliated with only other Lumbee people when he lived there; the school, church, and other community activities all comprised Lumbee. He found the relocation to Baltimore to be difficult as he now had to attend school and interact in an urban community with many fewer Indians and more Black and White people. Joe reports that even though people in North Carolina often treated the Lumbee people with disdain and discriminatory practices, they knew that they were Native Americans. In Baltimore, people were unsure what race the Lumbee were and often cast them as being mixed-race people (i.e., Black and White). Joe reports that he grew up in impoverished conditions, both of his parents were alcoholics, and his father was physically violent toward his mother and him as well as his siblings. When the family lived in North Carolina, the whole family picked cotton and tobacco to subsist economically. The family was economically better off once they settled in Baltimore as Joe's father was able to obtain work as a roofer. The Lumbee community in Baltimore lived in a certain area of the city's east side (i.e., Butcher's Hill) until recent years, when the area underwent economic development and gentrification. Joe recalls frequent community picnics and other activities that he enjoyed.

Joe began using alcohol at age 14 and drank heavily until he began to use heroin at age 24. He developed an addiction to heroin and used it daily. He continued to drink alcohol during that time, although less often as he was more interested in using heroin. Joe's alcohol and drug use caused him to be arrested and incarcerated on multiple occasions for crimes such as possession, public intoxication, and theft. He also got into numerous fights in the community and was shot once and was stabbed on several occasions during such fights. Joe primarily socializes at the corner bar, which is frequented by members of the Lumbee community. Joe is currently unemployed but has worked under the table as a roofer for most of his adult life.

At first glance, Joe's experience of trauma and substance abuse is not atypical for individuals with substance abuse problems in Baltimore City. However, when Joe's issues are considered in the context of what we now know about historical and cultural trauma and the Lumbee experience, we get a better sense of what Joe needs to support his recovery efforts and help him to heal.

Dial and Eliades (1996) provided a history of the Lumbee Indians. A few of their key points are described here to help the reader get a sense of what might constitute historical trauma for the Lumbee people. The Lumbee strongly identify as Native Americans but adopted European ways so long ago that they are disconnected from their language and other cultural traditions. It is believed that the ancestors of the Lumbee tribe helped the members of the "Lost Colony" of Roanoke by allowing them to merge into the tribe. This merger likely resulted in the White and Native peoples' exchanging cultural practices, which is a possible explanation for the Native group's early use of the English language in addition to other European ways of being. The Lumbee's geographic isolation and degree of acculturation protected them from colonial aggression against Indians. As anti-Indian sentiment and fear of non-Whites in general grew in the southern United States during the 1800s, the Lumbee increasingly experienced race-based discrimination and oppression. Prior to 1952 the Lumbee were known as Croatan or the Indians of Robeson County.

The Croatan name had become a source of derision and abuse; consequently, the tribe adopted the name *Lumbee* and petitioned the government to be recognized under its chosen name. The Lumbee are recognized as a Native American tribe by the state of North Carolina and the U.S. government. However, the federal recognition was not granted until 1956, and the language of the bill recognizing them contained the caveat that they would not receive federal Indian services as offered to other tribes. The Lumbee tribe continues to struggle for full recognition and eligibility for federal services. The Lumbee also struggle for full recognition as a Native American tribe with other Native Americans who sometimes discount the Lumbee because of their assimilated history and lack of a distinct Native culture (e.g., language, dance, foods).

A review of Lumbee history makes it apparent that disconnection, diffusion, oppression, and mixed messages are core features of the tribal experience. The Lumbee were assimilated and isolated enough not to be subjected to forced relocation to reservations in the 19th century but Indian enough to be deprived of their basic rights and be recipients of derision and discrimination. Nevertheless, the Lumbee people are strongly connected to one another, their homeland, and their spirituality and function as a unified force to retain and advance their community. This strong connectivity in the community has maintained the group's Native American identity. The Lumbee of Baltimore retain strong ties with the main tribal group in North Carolina. To this day, many Lumbee Indians living in Baltimore continue to refer to Robeson County as home and frequently visit the area.

Joe experienced trauma in the form of family violence and race-based oppression as a child. He felt safe in Robeson County in the company of his tribal group. Moving to Baltimore and being disconnected from his identity and his cultural group was extremely disruptive to his life. He also experienced a different kind of prejudice in Baltimore in that Whites treated him poorly because he was Black in their eyes and Blacks treated him poorly because they saw him as being White. He did not belong with either group, and his formerly prominent identity as an Indian had become invisible to those around him. The invisibility issue remained a problem throughout Joe's life in Baltimore as medical, social service, and justice system personnel typically misidentified him and did not know how to interact with him. Joe's struggle to be seen and valued as a Native American person is consistent with the struggle of the Lumbee people to be seen and valued as a Native American tribe.

Joe's family history of alcoholism, exposure to childhood abuse and domestic violence, poverty, and social disruption all placed him at high risk for developing substance abuse problems. Violence and victimization are associated with substance abuse, and thus, Joe's alcohol and heroin use placed him at high risk for the shooting and stabbings that he experienced. All of this occurred against the backdrop of the historical trauma experienced by the Lumbee people, which sets up the context for violence, poverty, and a diffuse sense of self.

Joe sought help from a local community agency whose mission is to work with the Native American community. Joe's physical health and substance abuse behavior were initially the primary concerns. Joe distrusted the mainstream medical system and was reluctant to accept a referral. He was angry that he had been racially misclassified in the past and felt medical personnel did not respect him or listen to his needs. Joe was referred to a clinic in the community that provides physical health as well as mental health and substance abuse treatment services. One of the case managers there is Native American and worked with Joe to help him negotiate the system and accept services. Joe received medical treatment and enrolled in a methadone maintenance program through the clinic. Simultaneously, Joe began to attend programming and received ongoing case management services from the local community agency serving Native Americans. The agency worked with Joe to obtain economic resources and dental care. Joe joined a therapist-led weekly recovery support group. He also attended educational groups on HIV/AIDS and hepatitis prevention and tobacco cessation. The groups at the agency are all designed for Native Americans and are particularly sensitive to the needs of the Lumbee community. The group format is used to facilitate community connections and draw on the strong affiliations that the Lumbee feel for one another. The recovery support group incorporates sober living skills with an exploration of Lumbee identity and the establishment of non-drug-using community connections. The educational groups are delivered from a cultural-strengths perspective and incorporate Native American concepts, symbols, and worldviews into disease prevention and health maintenance. Joe benefits from these types of services because they allow him to feel respected as a Native American, help him feel connected to the community (prior disconnections were extremely upsetting to him), help him to explore his identity as a Native American as well as his connection to his tribe, and provide him with skills to address his substance abuse and trauma-related issues. The agency provides community activities that allow Joe to socialize with other Lumbee in a substance-free environment, thus reducing his need to affiliate at the corner bar.

This case illustrates the complex links between historic cultural trauma, family trauma, and individual trauma in the life of Joe. It also highlights the importance of reconnecting Joe with the strength of his community and his own cultural identity. Given Joe's particular circumstances, services that are designed to foster that reconnection may help to keep him engaged in therapeutic interventions from which he stands to benefit. The case of Joe reflects a typical case in a particular agency that serves Native Americans in Baltimore, Maryland. Both of this chapter's authors are affiliated with this agency. The agency is staffed with both Native and non-Native personnel and provides culturally sensitive services. It is important to note that Joe hesitated to seek help because he felt disrespected and misunderstood by other social service and health care agencies from which he sought help in the past. All helping professionals should be sensitive to the cultural identification of the individuals whom they serve and provide services in response to their needs.

_____ **Conclusion**

Native American tribal groups have experienced cultural and historical traumas that play a role in the health and social problems that many Native Americans contend with today. It is incumbent on helping professionals to have an understanding of cultural and historical trauma and its interaction with current individual and communal life challenges to provide sensitive and effective services to Native Americans in both urban and rural settings. This chapter is designed to help readers to develop a beginning understanding of how current life traumas and struggles among Native Americans may be related to cultural and historical trauma and to recognize that pathways to healing come through a reconnection to the strength and resilience of the community. Native Americans are diverse in terms of their experience of current and historical trauma as well as their reactions to such experiences. Therefore, care must be taken to understand the story of each person and each tribal group to provide meaningful healing pathways, services, and interventions that respect and honor the "who" of the person sitting before the clinician.

_____ **References**

Alexander, J. C. (2004). Toward a theory of cultural trauma. In J. C. Alexander, R. Eyerman, B. Giesen, N. J. Smelser, & P. Sztompka (Eds.), *Cultural trauma and collective identity* (pp. 1–30). Berkeley: University of California Press.

American Psychiatric Association. (2000). *Diagnostic and statistical manual of mental disorders* (4th ed., text revision). Washington, DC: Author.

Aragon, A. M. (2006). A clinical understanding of urban American Indians. In T. M. Witko (Ed.), *Mental health care for urban Indians: Clinical insights from Native practitioners* (pp. 19–31). Washington, DC: American Psychological Association.

Auerhahn, N. C., & Laub, D. (1998). Intergenerational memory of the Holocaust. In Y. Danieli (Ed.), *International handbook of multigenerational legacies of trauma* (pp. 21–41). New York: Plenum.

Balsam, K. F., Huang, B., Simoni, J. M., & Walters, K. L. (2004). Culture, trauma, and wellness: A comparison of heterosexual and lesbian, gay, bisexual, and two-spirit Native Americans. *Cultural Diversity and Ethnic Minority Psychology, 10*, 287–301.

Barnes, P. M., Adams, P. F., & Powell-Griner, E. (2010). *Health characteristics of the American Indian or Alaska Native population: United States 2004–2008* (National Health Statistics Report No. 20). Washington, DC: U.S. Department of Health and Human Services, Centers for Disease Control and Prevention, National Center for Health Statistics. Retrieved March 15, 2010, from http://www.cdc.gov/nchs/data/nhsr/nhsr020.pdf

Beals, J., Manson, S. M., Whitesell, N. R., Spicer, P., Novins, D. K., & Mitchell, C. M. (2005). Prevalence of *DSM-IV* disorders and attendant help-seeking in 2 American Indian reservation populations. *Archives of General Psychiatry, 62*, 99–108.

Berkman, L. F., Glass, T., Brissette, I., & Seeman, T. E. (2000). From social integration to health: Durkheim in the new millennium. *Social Science & Medicine, 51,* 843–857.

Bracken, P. (2002). *Trauma: Culture, meaning, and philosophy.* London: Whurr.

Brave Heart, M. Y. H. (1998). The return to the sacred path: Healing the historical trauma and historical unresolved grief response among the Lakota through a psychoeducational group intervention. *Smith College Studies in Social Work, 68,* 287–305.

Brave Heart, M. Y. H. (1999). Oyate Ptayela: Rebuilding the Lakota Nation through addressing historical trauma among Lakota parents. *Human Behavior in the Social Environment, 2,* 109–126.

Brave Heart, M. Y. H. (2003). The historical trauma response among Natives and its relationship with substance abuse: A Lakota illustration. *Journal of Psychoactive Drugs, 35,* 7–13.

Brave Heart, M. Y. H. (2007). The impact of historical trauma: The example of the Native community. In M. Bussey & J. B. Wise (Eds.), *Trauma transformed: An empowerment response* (pp. 176–193). New York: Columbia University Press.

Brave Heart, M. Y. H., & DeBruyn, L. M. (1998). The American holocaust: Healing historical unresolved grief. *American Indian and Alaska Native Mental Health Research, 8*(2), 60–82.

Briere, J., & Scott, C. (2006). *Principles of trauma therapy: A guide to symptoms, evaluation, and treatment.* Thousand Oaks, CA: Sage.

Bureau of Justice Statistics. (2010). *Intimate partner violence in the U.S.: Victim characterisics.* Retrieved March 10, 2010, from http://bjs.ojp.usdoj.gov/content/intimate/victims.cfm

Carlson, E. B. (1997). *Trauma assessments: A clinician's guide.* New York: Guilford.

Castor, M. L., Smyser, M. S., Taualii, M. M., Park, A. N., Lawson, S. A., & Forquera, R. A. (2006). A nationwide population-based study identifying health disparities between American Indians/Alaska Natives and the general populations living in select urban counties. *American Journal of Public Health, 96,* 1478–1484.

Cheshire, T. C. (2001). Cultural transmission in urban American Indian families. *American Behavioral Scientist, 44,* 1528–1535.

Cole, N. (2006). Trauma and the American Indian. In T. M. Witko (Ed.), *Mental health care for urban Indians* (pp. 115–130). Washington, DC: American Psychological Association.

Danieli, Y. (Ed.). (1998). *International handbook of multigenerational legacies of trauma.* New York: Plenum.

deVries, M. W. (1996). Trauma in cultural perspective. In B. A. van der Kolk, A. C. McFarlane, & L. Weisaeth (Eds.), *Traumatic stress: The effects of overwhelming experience on mind, body, and society* (pp. 398–413). New York: Guilford.

Dial, A. L., & Eliades, D. K. (1996). *The only land I know: A history of the Lumbee Indians.* Syracuse, NY: Syracuse University Press.

Drozdek, B. (2007). The rebirth of contextual thinking in psychotraumatology. In B. Drozdek & J. P. Wilson (Eds.), *Voices of trauma: Treating survivors across cultures* (pp. 1–25). New York: Springer Science + Business Media.

Duran, B., Sanders, M., Skipper, B., Waitzkin, H., Malcoe, L. H., Paine, S., et al. (2004). Prevalence and correlates of mental disorders among Native American women in primary care. *American Journal of Public Health, 94,* 71–77.

Duran, E. (2006). *Healing the soul wound: Counseling with American Indians and other Native peoples.* New York: Teachers College Press.

Evans-Campbell, T. (2008). Historical trauma in American Indian/Native Alaska communities. *Journal of Interpersonal Violence, 23,* 316–338.

Evans-Campbell, T., Lindhorst, T., Huang, B., & Walters, K. L. (2006). Interpersonal violence in the lives of urban American Indian and Alaska Native women: Implications for health, mental health, and help-seeking. *American Journal of Public Health, 96,* 1416.

Foa, E. B., Keane, T. M., Friedman, M. J., & Cohen, J. A. (Eds.). (2009). *Effective treatments for PTSD: Practice guidelines from the International Society for Traumatic Stress Studies.* New York: Guilford.

Friedman, M. J., & Marsella, A. J. (1996). Posttraumatic stress disorder: An overview of the concept. In A. J. Marcella, M. J. Friedman, E. T. Gerrity, & R. M. Scurfield (Eds.), *Ethnocultural aspects of posttraumatic stress disorder: Issues, research, and clinical applications* (pp. 11–32). Washington, DC: American Psychological Association.

Glass, T. A., & McAtee, M. J. (2006). Behavioral science at the crossroads in public health: Extending horizons, envisioning the future. *Social Science and Medicine, 62,* 1650–1671.

Gone, J. P. (2006). Mental health, wellness, and the quest for authentic American Indian identity. In T. M. Witko (Ed.), *Mental health care for urban Indians: Clinical insights from Native practitioners* (pp. 55–80). Washington, DC: American Psychological Association.

Greenberg, J., Solomon, S., & Pyszczynski, T. (1997). Terror management theory of self-esteem and cultural worldviews: Empirical assessments and conceptual refinements. In M. P. Zanna (Ed.), *Advances in experimental social psychology* (Vol. 29, pp. 61–139). San Diego, CA: Academic Press.

Harris, K. M., Edlund, M. J., & Larson, S. (2005). Racial and ethnic differences in mental health problems and use of mental health care. *Medical Care, 43,* 775–784.

Herman, J. L. (1992). *Trauma and recovery.* New York: Basic Books.

Indian Health Service. (2009). *Trends in Indian health, 2002–2003 edition.* Washington, DC: Government Printing Office.

Johnson, J. L., Baldwin, J., Gryczynski, J., Wiechelt, S. A., & Haring, R. C. (2010). The Native American experience: From displacement and cultural trauma to resilience. In H. McCubbin (Ed.), *Multiethnicity & multiethnic families: Development, identity, and resilience.* Honolulu, HI: Le'a.

Johnson, J. L., Baldwin, J., Haring, R. C., Wiechelt, S. A., Roth, S., Gryczynski, J., et al. (2008). Essential information for disaster management and trauma specialists working with American Indians. In A. J. Marsella, J. L. Johnson, P. Watson, & J. Gryczynski (Eds.), *Ethnocultural perspectives on disaster and trauma* (pp. 73–113). New York: Springer Science + Business Media.

Johnson, J. L., Gryczynski, J., & Wiechelt, S. A. (2007). HIV/AIDS, substance abuse, and hepatitis prevention needs of Native Americans: In their own words. *AIDS Education & Prevention, 19,* 531–544.

Kansteiner, W. (2004). Testing the limits of trauma: The long-term psychological effects of the Holocaust on individuals and collectives. *History of the Human Sciences, 17*(2/3), 97–123.

Kestenberg, J. (1989). Transposition revisited: Clinical, therapeutic, and developmental considerations. In P. Marcus & A. Rosenberg (Eds.), *Healing their wounds: Psychotherapy with Holocaust survivors and their families* (pp. 67–82). New York: Praeger.

Laub, D. (2002). Testimonies in the treatment of genocidal trauma. *Journal of Applied Psychoanalytic Studies, 4,* 63–87.

Link, B. G., & Phelan, J. (1995). Social conditions as fundamental causes of disease. *Journal of Health and Social Behavior, 35*(extra issue), 80–94.

Manson, S. M. (1997). Cross-cultural and multiethnic assessment of trauma. In J. P. Wilson & T. M. Keane (Eds.), *Assessing psychological trauma and PTSD* (pp. 239–266). New York: Guilford.

Marsella, A. J. (2005). Culture and conflict: Understanding, negotiating, and reconciling conflicting constructions of reality. *International Journal of Intercultural Relations, 29,* 651–673.

Marsella, A. J., Friedman, M. J., Gerrity, E. T., & Scurfield, R. M. (1996). Ethnocultural aspects of PTSD: Some closing thoughts. In A. J. Marsella, M. J. Friedman, E. T. Gerrity, & R. M. Scurfield (Eds.), *Ethnocultural aspects of posttraumatic stress disorder: Issues, research, and clinical applications* (pp. 529–538). Washington, DC: American Psychological Association.

Marsella, A. J., Johnson, J. L., Watson, P., & Gryczynski, J. (2008). Essential concepts and foundations. In A. J. Marcella, J. L. Johnson, P. Watson, & J. Gryczynski (Eds.), *Ethnocultural perspectives on disaster and trauma: Foundations, issues, and applications* (pp. 3–13). New York: Springer Science + Business Media.

McFall, G. J., & Resick, P. A. (2005). A pilot study of PTSD symptoms among Kalahari Bushmen. *Journal of Traumatic Stress, 16,* 445–450.

Mills, P. (2003). Incorporating Yup'ik and Cup'ik Eskimo traditions into behavioral health treatment. *Journal of Psychoactive Drugs, 35,* 85–88.

Napoleon, H. (1996). *Yuuyaraq: The way of the human being.* Fairbanks: University of Alaska Fairbanks, Native American Knowledge Network.

National Urban Indian Family Coalition. (2008). *Urban Indian America: The status of American Indian and Alaska Native children and families today.* Retrieved February 24, 2010, from http://www.aecf.org/KnowledgeCenter/Publications.aspx?pubguid={CCB6DEB2-007E-416A-A0B2-D15954B48600}

Neal, A. G. (1998). *National trauma and collective memory.* Armonk, NY: M.E. Sharpe.

Neihardt, J. G. (2008). *Black Elk speaks: Beginning the life story of a holy man of the Oglala Sioux* (premiere ed.). Albany: State University of New York Press. (Original work published 1932)

Ogunwole, S. U. (2006). *We the people: American Indians and Alaska Natives in the United States, census 2000 special report (CENSR-28).* Washington, DC: U.S. Census Bureau. Retrieved January 10, 2010, from http://www.census.gov/prod/2006pubs/censr-28.pdf

Ouimette, P. C., & Brown, P. J. (Eds.). (2003). *Trauma and substance abuse: Causes, consequences, and treatment of comorbid disorders.* Washington, DC: American Psychological Association.

Perry, S. W. (2004). *American Indians and crime: A BJS statistical profile, 1992–2002.* Washington, DC: U.S. Department of Justice, Bureau of Justice Statistics. Retrieved February 15, 2010, from http://bjs.ojp.usdoj.gov/content/pub/pdf/aic02.pdf

Robin, R. W., Chester, B., & Goldman, D. (1996). Cumulative trauma and PTSD in American Indian communities. In A. J. Marsella, M. J. Friedman, E. T. Gerrity, & R. M. Scurfield (Eds.), *Ethnocultural aspects of posttraumatic stress disorder: Issues, research, and clinical applications* (pp. 239–253). Washington, DC: American Psychological Association.

Roth, S., Newman, E., Pelcovitz, D., van der Kolk, B. A., & Mandel, F. S. (1997). Complex PTSD in victims exposed to sexual and physical abuse: Results from the *DSM-IV* field trial for posttraumatic stress disorder. *Journal of Traumatic Stress, 10,* 539–555.

Salzman, M. B. (2001). Cultural trauma and recovery: Perspectives from terror management theory. *Trauma, Violence, & Abuse, 2,* 172–191.

Salzman, M. B., & Halloran, M. J. (2004). Cultural trauma and recovery: Cultural meaning, self-esteem, and the reconstruction of the cultural anxiety buffer. In J. Greenberg, S. L. Koole, & T. Pyszczynski (Eds.), *Handbook of existential pscyhology* (pp. 231–246). New York: Guilford.

Sareen, J., Cox, B. J., Stein, M. B., Afifi, T. O., Fleet, C., & Asmundson, G. J. (2007). Physical and mental comorbidity, disability, and suicidal behavior associated with posttraumatic stress disorder in a large community sample. *Psychosomatic Medicine, 69,* 242–248.

Sledjeski, E. M., Speisman, B. A., & Dierker, L. C. (2008). Does number of lifetime traumas explain the relationship between PTSD and chronic medical conditions? Answers from the National Comorbidity Survey–Replication (NCS-R). *Journal of Behavioral Medicine, 31,* 341–349.

Snipp, C. M. (1992). Sociological perspectives on American Indians. *Annual Review of Sociology, 18,* 351–371.

Solomon, S., Greenberg, J., & Pyszczynski, T. (2004). The cultural animal: Twenty years of terror management theory and research. In J. Greenberg, S. L. Koole, & T. Pyszczynski (Eds.), *Handbook of experimental psychology* (pp. 13–34). New York: Guilford.

Sorokin, P. (1967). *The sociology of revolution.* New York: Howard Fertig. (Original work published 1925)

Sotero, M. A. (2006). A conceptual model of historical trauma: Implications for public health practice and research. *Journal of Health Disparities Research and Practice, 1*(1), 93–108.

Stamm, B. H., Stamm, H. E., Hudnall, A. C., & Higson-Smith, C. (2004). Considering a theory of cultural trauma and loss. *Journal of Loss and Trauma, 9,* 89–111.

Steele, C. B., Cardinez, C. J., Richardson, L. C., Tom-Orme, L., & Shaw, K. M. (2008). Surveillance for health behaviors of American Indians and Alaska Natives—Findings from the behavioral risk factor surveillance system, 2000–2006. *Cancer, 113,* 1131–1141.

Substance Abuse and Mental Health Services Administration. (2007). *The National Survey on Drug Use and Health report: Substance use and substance use disorders among American Indians and Alaska Natives.* Retrieved January 5, 2010, from http:www.oas.samhsa.gov/2k7/AmIndians/AmIndians.htm

Sztompka, P. (2000). The other face of social change. *European Journal of Social Theory, 3,* 449–466.

Thornton, R. (1987). *American Indian holocaust and survival: A population history since 1492.* Norman: University of Oklahoma Press.

Urban Indian Health Institute. (2008). *Reported health and health-influencing behaviors among urban American Indians and Alaska Natives.* Retrieved February 21, 2010, from http://www.uihi.org/publications/reports

U.S. Department of Health and Human Services. (2001). *Mental health: Culture, race, and ethnicity—A supplement to mental health: A report of the surgeon general.* Rockville, MD: U.S. Department of Health and Human Services,

Substance Abuse and Mental Health Services Administration, Center for Mental Health Services. Retrieved February 15, 2010, from http://mentalhealth.samhsa.gov/cre/default.asp

U.S. Department of Health and Human Services, Administration on Children, Youth, and Families. (2009). *Child maltreatment 2007*. Washington, DC: Government Printing Office.

van der Kolk, B. A., Pelcovitz, D., Roth, S., Mandel, F. S., McFarlane, A., & Herman, J. L. (1996). Dissociation, somatization, and affect dysregulation: The complexity of adaptation to trauma. *American Journal of Psychiatry, 153*(Festschrift Suppl. 7), 83–93.

Walters, K., & Simoni, J. (2002). Reconceptualizing Native women's health: An indiginest stress-coping model. *American Journal of Public Health, 93,* 520–524.

Walters, K. L., Evans-Campbell, T., Stately, A., & Old Person, R. (2006, May 5). *Historical trauma, microaggressions, and colonial trauma response: A decolonization framework for HIV prevention efforts among indigenous communities.* Paper presented at the Embracing Our Traditions, Values, and Teachings: Native Peoples of North America HIV/AIDS conference, Anchorage, AK.

Weaver, H. N. (1998). Indigenous people in a multicultural society: Unique issues for human services. *Social Work, 43,* 203–211.

Whitbeck, L. B., Adams, G. W., Hoyt, D. R., & Chen, X. (2004). Conceptualizing and measuring historical trauma among American Indian people. *American Journal of Community Psychology, 33*(3/4), 119–130.

Whitbeck, L. B., Chen, X., Hoyt, D. R., & Adams, G. W. (2004). Discrimination, historical loss and enculturation: Culturally specific risk and resiliency factors for alcohol abuse among American Indians. *Journal of Studies on Alcohol, 65,* 409–418.

White Bison, Inc. (2002). *The red road to wellbriety: In the Native American way.* Colorado Springs, CO: Author.

Wilson, J. (1998). *The earth shall weep: A history of Native America.* New York: Grove Press.

11

The Effects of Trauma Treatment on the Therapist

Brian Rasmussen

For the clinician, therapy with individuals who have experienced trauma firsthand frequently provides rewarding therapeutic experiences. Facilitating individuals' healing and growth offers a glimpse into the strength and resiliency of the human spirit and people's capacity for overcoming some of life's most cruel and tragic events. Inspiring stories abound regarding people's courage to face unimaginable assaults and personal indignities. Indeed, there is some evidence to suggest that therapeutic work with people who have been traumatized may have growth-producing effects for the therapist (Linley & Joseph, 2007).

Nonetheless, therapists who bear witness to the traumatic suffering of others may, like the people they treat, suffer negative effects. Repeated stories of physical assaults, rape, torture, hate crimes, war, incest, shootings, and emotional cruelty, to mention just a few possible traumatic events, do, in layman's terms, begin to get to you. But how does this work get to you? What impact does it have on the clinician? Does it change the therapist? Are any of these possible changes lasting? How are these effects similar to and/or different from older and more familiar terms—*burnout* or *countertransference?* Do all therapists who treat trauma victims experience negative effects? What are the mechanisms or processes that facilitate these potential negative effects? What empirical evidence exists to support the constructs that have been developed to understand these effects? What impact do these negative effects have on the clinical process? What can be done to mitigate the possible negative effects? A growing body of literature is helping us to answer these questions—but the answers at this time are far from certain or straightforward. Although it is widely accepted that psychotherapy can be a rewarding and meaningful, if not personally enriching, career, it nonetheless holds the potential for exacting a toll on therapists (Kadambi & Ennis, 2004), particularly those helping the traumatized.

In this chapter I will examine the concepts of vicarious trauma (VT) and, more broadly, the effect that therapeutic work with people who have been traumatized has on the therapist. I will also examine some related concepts, including the ideas of compassion fatigue (CF), burnout, and countertransference. Each of these concepts is distinct yet similar and indeed interrelated. Distinguishing among them is important for both research and clinical practice because there has been increasing conceptual confusion with the proliferation of terms (Canfield, 2005). I will also review some of the empirical support for VT, a body of literature that has become ever more complex over the years. The implications of VT will be addressed, particularly as they influence the therapeutic relationship and the treatment process. Finally, the chapter examines the need for self-care and effective organizational responses that hold potential for mitigating the deleterious effects of trauma treatment. Case examples will be selectively employed to highlight the concepts and processes involved. I begin by exploring the concept of VT.

VT

McCann and Pearlman (1990) first coined the term *vicarious trauma* 20 years ago. Since that time there has been a great deal of attention drawn to ill effects on therapists who work with trauma survivors. In their groundbreaking article they wrote,

> While an extensive knowledge base exists on the psychological consequences of traumatic experiences for victims, less attention has focussed on the enduring psychological consequences for therapists of exposure to the traumatic experiences of victim clients. Persons who work with victims may experience profound psychological effects, effects that can be disruptive and painful for the helper and can persist for months or years after work with traumatized persons. We term this process "vicarious traumatization." (p. 133)

McCann and Pearlman (1990) distinguished their thinking from existing concepts of countertransference and burnout, issues I will examine later, and situated the concept of VT within a constructivist self-development theory. This theory examines the relationship among traumatic events, cognitions, and our adaptation to the external world. A constructivist foundation to the theory posits that people develop cognitive structures through the process of interpreting their life events. For instance, people are said to develop cognitive structures or schemas that anchor some of their basic beliefs about the world—for instance, who can be trusted, what causes what, and one's place in the world. But what if someone's external world is fraught with danger, abuse, and violence? Trauma, these authors argue, disrupts these schemas depending on the saliency of the events for that particular person. For the therapist, exposure to clients' traumatic stories is theorized to disrupt the same schemas related to basic needs of safety, dependency, trust, power, esteem, and intimacy.

Symptomatically, therapists may begin to develop some of the same post-traumatic stress disorder (PTSD) symptoms as their clients. Such disturbances may include intrusive thoughts or images, painful emotional reactions, emotional withdrawal, anxiety, and alterations of their sense of personal safety and trust of others. Pearlman and Saakvitne (1995) outlined five significant areas of impact on the therapist: (a) frame of reference—including alterations in how one sees oneself, values, and spirituality; (b) self-capacities—changes in affect regulation, self-soothing capacities, and enjoyment of daily life; (c) ego resources—referring to "the inner facilities the individual uses to navigate the interpersonal world and to meet his psychological needs"; (d) psychological needs—including safety, trust, esteem, intimacy, and control; and (e) sensory system—disturbances to memory, imagery, and bodily sensations (p. 66). Important to note, VT is defined as a transformation of the inner experience of the therapist with respect to these areas.

How does VT come about? Pearlman and Saakvitne (1995) argued that it is therapists' empathic engagement with clients that creates a vulnerable state for them. The very quality that helps to heal also puts therapists at risk. They described four types of empathic engagement with survivor clients. *Cognitive empathy* refers to a cognitive understanding of the traumatic events, their meaning, and their effects. Affective empathy suggests that therapists feel some of the client's pain, rage, despair, and other dysphoric affects connected to clients' experiences. In addition, there are temporal dimensions of past and present. Consequently, *"there are four realms into which we can enter empathically with our clients: the past cognitive experience, the present cognitive experience, the past affective experience, and the present affective experience"* (p. 297). Pearlman and Saakvitne suggest that the realm of past affective empathic attunement is one that makes therapists most vulnerable to vicarious traumatization. That is to say, their empathic connection to the client as a child, experiencing the overwhelming nature of powerful affects as they were once felt, moves them deeply. It may indeed force them to challenge their cherished beliefs about the world and the goodness of others.

Case Example 1: Christine

Christine is a 30-year-old, White, single clinician who provides therapeutic services to victims of violence and sexual abuse. She has been doing this job since graduating with her MSW. She finds the work challenging and rewarding but lately has been questioning her own abilities and motivation for work with this clientele. On a daily basis she hears stories of physical and sexual abuse from both recent and past experiences. Early on she struggled to "leave work at work," and for a while she thought she was doing better compartmentalizing her therapeutic work. Lately she finds herself thinking more about some clients in the evening. Often thoughts of clients just "pop into her mind" in an intrusive manner, and she can't stop thinking about the clients. Not infrequently, these thoughts about clients are accompanied by disturbing imagery—a kind of replay of the therapeutic sessions. She wonders whether she is being helpful to these clients, often replaying in her mind moments in the sessions when she wished she had something more soothing or effective to say or do.

Christine grew up the eldest of three in a middle-class family. Both parents were university educated; her father was a high school teacher and her mother a nurse. Her liberal-minded parents instilled in the children the values of social justice and giving to others. Although the family was not actively religious, family vacations were frequently combined with missionary-style work in impoverished countries such as Haiti and Mexico. There she was exposed to severe levels of poverty but always came away inspired by the resilient spirit of the people she tried to help. Nothing, however, had prepared her for the horrors of sexual and physical abuse she was to hear in practice. Most disturbing was discovering that some of the men in her community whom she had known in various capacities were the reported perpetrators of such violence. One alleged perpetrator of sexual abuse was her high school teacher, a person whom she had previously admired and from whom she received an academic reference. It made her wonder whom she could trust. Christine began to sleep poorly, often awakened by disturbing dream content. Gradually she began to withdraw from others, preferring to stay in on the weekends. She had had a few long-term relationships and was interested in a committed relationship but during the past year had stopped dating. Christine pondered changing professions, making occasional inquires into various MBA programs.

In this case, negative effects of providing trauma treatment were becoming evident in Christine's perception of herself and others and in her behavior. Pearlman and Saakvitne's (1995) model would suggest that Christine is experiencing internal shifts in her cognitive schemas related to basic needs of safety, dependency, trust, power, esteem, and intimacy. Further, she is beginning to experience some symptoms of PTSD, in particular the intrusive thoughts and the nightmares.

CF

Another way of understanding the effects of working with people who have been traumatized is the concept of secondary traumatic stress (STS)—or what later came to be known as CF (Figley, 1995, 2002). Simply put, people who work in caring professions and whose daily tasks involve providing emotional support for clients can frequently suffer psychological distress as a result of these interactions (Bride, 2007). CF is defined as "the formal caregiver's reduced capacity or interest in being empathic or 'bearing the suffering of clients'" and comprises the "natural consequent behaviors and emotions resulting from knowing about a traumatizing event experienced or suffered by a person" (Adams, Boscarino, & Figley, 2006, p. 103). Similar to the concept and process of VT, CF is thought to be a consequence of empathic engagement with trauma clients. The observable negative consequences are similar to those of VT and include intrusive thoughts, avoidant behaviors, emotional depletion, and feelings of helplessness (Figley, 1995). How is this conceptualization different from VT? Kadambi and Ennis (2004) offer the following analysis:

> In contrast to vicarious trauma, which is proposed to be an inevitable, irreversible consequence of working with trauma survivors, the experience of compassion fatigue is conceptualized as an expected, yet, treatable and preventable by-product of working with people who are suffering (Figley, 1995). The experience of compassion fatigue results from empathizing with those who are experiencing emotional pain and suffering. It is therefore not inextricably bound to the notion that the exposure to descriptions of traumatic events and human cruelty is a necessary condition for the experience of stress symptoms in therapists. Consequently, compassion fatigue is quite applicable to trauma therapists, but is easily generalized to mental health professionals working with a variety of client populations. (p. 6)

The idea of CF has a certain "user friendly appeal" as it is intuitively grasped (Bride, Radey, & Figley, 2007). Even if we have never worked with trauma survivors, we can imagine the emotional exhaustion of giving of ourselves day after day. If we associate the problem of trauma work with some specific settings such as emergency rooms or victim assistance services, it's easy to minimize the number of trauma histories there are in other populations. In a paper that deserves bonus marks for a most creative title, "The Unbearable Fatigue of Compassion: Notes From a Substance Abuse Counsellor Who Dreams of Working at Starbuck's," Fahy (2007) described the personal impact of the unique conditions of this work. In the words of one of the therapists,

> How many of my clients have trauma? How about try all of 'em. I've heard it's 80% but I think that it's higher. It's definitely higher in women. I did a women's group once with nine women and all of them had had at least one rape that they remembered. Compassion Fatigue—I don't know what that is but I know I got it. These clients are so needy. Services are being cut and residential beds are evaporating. Sometimes I come home from my job and I just sit and stare. I tell my kids "Mommy can't talk for a while." (p. 202)

Smith (2007) reflected on the problem of CF as experienced by himself and graduate students who provided psychotherapy services to people living with HIV/AIDS, a practice area that has received very little attention in this regard. Like the clinical population of substance misusers, this service population also presented with a significant history of abuse in childhood and adulthood. Indeed, Smith cited evidence that a history of "childhood sexual abuse is a predictor of adult engagement in behaviours that increase risk of HIV transmission" (p. 194). Although his data with respect to CF are descriptive and anecdotal, he provided a compelling argument for the need to research this important area of clinical practice.

Given the definition of CF it would seem obvious that people who have direct combat-related trauma would be prime examples of those at risk for experiencing the negative effects of secondary trauma. Clearly, the mental health effects of deployment to Iraq and Afghanistan are significant and include a high incidence of PTSD (Hoge, Auchterlonie, & Milliken, 2006). Further, the notion of shared trauma has been evoked to capture those instances in which the clinician and client experience the same traumatic event—for instance, helpers embedded in war zones or directly affected by the terrorist attacks of 9/11/01.

Burnout

It is important to consider the potential negative effects of trauma work within the context of the external conditions of the clinician's work environment. As is frequently the case in many agencies, clinicians are faced with increased demands, larger caseloads, higher levels of acuity, less support by way of supervision, greater accountability, and fewer sessions in which to do their work. Not surprisingly, some workers experience what has traditionally been referred to as burnout. The term predates the concept of VT, and like CF, it has wider applicability inasmuch as exposure to trauma clients is not a prerequisite for this "syndrome." The term *burnout* refers to a state of overwhelming exhaustion; feeling depleted, detached, and cynical; and a sense that one's work is lacking in accomplishment (Maslach, 1982; Maslach, Jackson, & Leiter, 1996). Accordingly, burnout is thought to be intimately related to the stress of the modern-day realities of a clinician's work life. Therefore, all workers are potentially at risk for experiencing burnout. Fortunately, the effects of burnout, unlike those of VT, are not considered to be long lasting.

Case Example 2: Jeff

Jeff is a 38-year-old supervisor in a large family service agency. With multiple funders, this agency provides clinical services to a wide range of clients, including victims of violence against women, sexual assault, and incest. He has been working for the agency for 7 years and during the past 3 has moved into a supervisory role with limited direct clinical responsibilities. In recent years he has witnessed significant funding cuts and a corresponding increase in the demand for services. At the same time, the current funders require increased accountability via complex and detailed reporting systems. He feels frustrated that so much of his time is spent doing paperwork, grant proposals that seem to go nowhere, and bureaucratic "make work projects" that he has little time to support his frontline staff. His long hours at the office do not seem to translate into a sense of productiveness. He constantly feels drained and increasingly bitter over his lack of control of his work life. He dreads falling asleep on Sunday evenings as he knows what is in store for him once he awakens.

Jeff is showing signs and symptoms of burnout. Although he rarely questions his choice in career, he is convinced that work conditions have changed significantly during his career. When the agency executive director encouraged Jeff to take a lengthy vacation he didn't hesitate to comply with this advice. Two weeks into a month-long holiday, Jeff began to "feel himself again." His energy and outlook improved, and he actually looked forward to returning to work. After he had been back at work for 2 weeks, his holiday seemed like a distant memory.

Countertransference

Countertransference is an inescapable dimension of all clinical practice and indeed a critical element in the therapeutic process with people who have been traumatized. Freud introduced the term *countertransference* in 1910 as a way to capture the impact of the patient's unconscious on the analyst (Orr, 1954/1988). Freud's thinking at the time was that the analyst needed to recognize these feelings and overcome them for otherwise the analyst would be unable to properly treat the patient. This view of countertransference suggests a phenomenon that is detrimental to treatment. Reich (1951, 1960), a leading proponent of the classical view of countertransference, warned that emotional intensity on the part of the therapist can suggest unresolved conflicts for this clinician. Although this perspective is undeniably valuable, Freud's stance of 100 years ago stands in contrast with much of the current literature suggesting that countertransference can be more broadly defined to include a full range of subjective experiences a therapist has toward a particular client. For example, Racker (1957/1988) showed how countertransference can be used as a tool for understanding the mental processes of a patient. He identified two forms of countertransference, concordant and complementary identifications. Concordant identifications are empathic resonating experiences in response to the patient's thoughts and feelings. However, with complementary identifications the therapist begins to feel like some disowned (projected) aspect of the patient's self. For instance, the therapist may begin to feel, uncharacteristically, punitive or harsh toward the patient. Likewise, Sandler (1976) introduced the concept of "role responsiveness" to capture the dynamic interaction between the patient's transference and the therapist's countertransference, such that pressure is exerted on the therapist to play out a certain role in this interrelationship. From an intersubjective view, the therapeutic process, and indeed countertransference, flows from the interplay of two differently organized subjectivities (Stolorow, Brandchaft, & Atwood, 1987).

Although the literature on countertransference is vast and beyond the scope of this chapter to review, it is important to emphasize that these various theoretical positions on countertransference do have significant implications for treatment. That is, holding a classical stance—that the countertransference arises from the therapist's own history—or a totalist stance—that the countertransference emerges from a full range of internal and external factors and dynamics—does influence understanding and intervention. The limits of both perspectives were pointed out by Tansey and Burke (1989), who stated,

> Whereas the classicist may be too quick to attribute an intense personal response to the therapist's exclusively private concerns, the totalist runs the risk of too readily concluding that the countertransference response to the patient constitutes a royal road to the patient's unconscious rather than a detour into his own. (p. 28)

More recently, Davies and Frawley (1994), in their work with adult survivors of sexual abuse, articulated eight "relational positions" that are alternatively enacted within four "relational matrices." From a relational perspective, these positions include "the uninvolved nonabusing parent and the neglected child; the sadistic abuser and the helpless, impotently enraged victim; the idealized, omnipotent rescuer and the entitled child who demands to be rescued; and the seducer and the seduced" (p. 167). Davies and Frawley argued that because these positions reflect self and object representations that are often split off from consciousness, they are more accessible through careful attention to one's countertransference.

Pearlman and Saakvitne (1995) recognized the importance of countertransference in their seminal book *Trauma and the Therapist* and devoted considerable attention to its role and relationship to VT. They wrote, "While vicarious traumatization and countertransference are distinct constructs and experiences, they affect one another" (p. 33). Further, these authors distinguished between these concepts in temporal terms. Although VT is said to be accumulative across many therapies, countertransference is particular to any given therapy. Further, the effects of countertransference are limited in time, whereas the impact of VT is argued to be "permanently transformative." Nonetheless, countertransference and VT are highly interactive.

Indeed, the relationship between the two concepts is such that one can intensify or even set the stage for the other. This is particularly the case when the therapist is unable to hold or contain strong affects that need to be kept outside of awareness and consequently outside of the treatment process. Pearlman and Saakvitne (1995) offered the following case example:

> A therapist was working with a survivor client who had recently suf-fered a number of significant losses. He was himself anticipating the death of a loved one. Over time, he found himself feeling increasingly unable to maintain hope and a belief in his client's ability to heal from grief. As the client ruminated endlessly on the potential losses and was unable to engage in life, the therapist found himself experiencing the client as physically different: pallid, grey, unappealing, unenlivened. As this perception emerged into the therapist's awareness and he sought consultation, he realized he was engaged in a multidetermined reenact-ment. He recognized in his perception the repetition of the client's life-threatening illness early in childhood, and the parallel in his response to the client's mother's disconnection and helpless despair. The therapist realized that there was a further parallel in his own his-tory, in his experience of his own mother as helpless in the face of his own childhood medical trauma. As the therapist began to question the effectiveness of this particular therapy process, he became more reac-tive, less emotionally available, and more withdrawn with all his cli-ents, and specifically less able to tolerate death themes and despair in all therapies. This generalization reflects the impact of the counter-transference despair on the hope that maintains therapies, thus creat-ing a vicarious traumatization response. (p. 319)

Conversely, VT can set the stage for countertransference responses (Pearlman & Saakvitne, 1995). Because VT affects the self of the therapist, it would logically hold that changes in one's emotional responsiveness would alter and shape one's countertransference responses. For example, one's reactions to a new traumatic story by a client might be altered if the therapist were feeling depleted, withdrawn, and cynical. In turn, I (Rasmussen, 2005) have suggested that this process, as understood from an intersubjective perspective, would alter the clinical process, shaping and altering the transference/countertransference process. Given the mutual, reciprocal, and interactional nature of the therapeutic process, changes in the subjectivity of one participant inevitably affects the other. The follow-ing vignette offers an illustration:

Case Example 3: Leslie and Anne

Leslie has recently begun therapy with Anne, a White, 29-year-old, single woman. This is Anne's first experience with therapy. She was sexually abused by her father between the ages of 6 and 12. Until this time, Anne has talked to no one about this abuse. Anne has sketched out for her therapist the "basics" of what happened but now is returning to these memories and beginning to share more details of the sexual abuse, aspects of which are more horrifying than her earlier reports suggested.

On this particular day, the session takes place late in the afternoon. Leslie is tired and depleted, having provided several hours of intensive treatment by this point in the day. Anne, however, has arrived at the session determined to reveal more about her abuse history—in particular, one story that occasionally replays in her mind as a nightmare. At the same time, she is terrified to verbalize this memory. With some encouragement from Leslie, Anne begins to share the story. As she does, Anne feels an intense wave of fear wash over her. Anne pauses. She fleetingly makes eye contact with Leslie and notices that Leslie averts her gaze and shuffles in her seat. Leslie says, "Please, go on," in a flat tone. After a lengthy pause, Anne continues to share the story, only much later in the evening to realize that she left out the most horrific part. (Rasmussen, 2005, p. 27)

With this example I shift my analysis of the problem of vicarious traumatization from an intrapsychic problem to a relational problem. Changes in the subjective state of the therapist affected the treatment relationship. It is reasonable to assume that clients are perceptive about the subjective states of therapists and adjust their content accordingly (Aron, 1991). This perspective suggests that there is no place to hide for therapists and that, for better or worse, "we are in this together."

Applications to Various Populations

The clinical populations and practice domains relevant to the problem of VT are vast and diverse. What they hold in common is the respective psychological adversity faced by both the survivor and the helper. Here, I will briefly explore some of the practice areas mentioned above in which the clinician is called on to provide assistance and the ways in which these traumas pose psychological challenges to the helper.

Pearlman and Saakvitne (1995) focus their writing primarily on psychotherapy with adult survivors of childhood sexual abuse. Their interest in this area is understandable given its prevalence in general populations and its extraordinarily high rate in people with mental health and psychiatric disorders. Further, they argue that this population experiences high levels of symptomatology, requiring a trusting therapeutic relationship with someone willing to hold intense affect, because such clients often evoke complicated and intense countertransference responses and may overwhelm survivor therapists who may have experienced similar traumatic events. Similarly, Herman (1992) has noted how therapists working with this population might be drawn toward a rescuing role and identify with the survivors' feelings of rage and grief. Moreover, therapists working with people who have been sexually traumatized can be overwhelmed with the staggering cruelty inflicted on children. Repeated stories of sexual molestation do make one question basic assumptions about humanity.

Although many therapists work with victims of sexual assault, others have chosen to work with sexual offenders. The impact on these therapists, who are required to read and hear about sexual offences in graphic detail, may present different dynamics for therapists who are also expected to maintain an empathic stance with their clients. Although less has been written about these therapists from a VT perspective, Moulden and Firestone (2007) suggested that there are several factors related to VT in sexual offender therapists. These factors include client characteristics, therapist characteristics, and therapy characteristics. Some of these therapists are said to report symptoms in the moderate to clinical range. The length of time working with this population is thought to be an important factor—with those early on in their careers and those with lengthy service being the most negatively affected. Moulden and Firestone called for "more systematic analyses of the relationship between the contributors and consequences of VT as well as mediators and moderators of this relationship" (p. 78). The call for additional research will be addressed later in the chapter.

Hospital social workers who are indirectly exposed to trauma run the risk of experiencing STS or VT (Badger, Royse, & Craig, 2008). Work in these settings is often fast paced and allows for little down time to reflect on feelings or to debrief. Similarly, social work practice in mental health centers (Ting, Jacobson, Sanders, Bride, & Harrington, 2005), substance abuse centers (Fahy, 2007), and child welfare agencies (Horwitz, 2006) is also fast paced, with workers exposed to an accumulation of traumatic events. In the latter, child welfare workers are frequently exposed to stories of cruelty and abuse suffered by children of all ages, including infants (Horwitz, 2006; Perron & Hiltz, 2006). When interventions go badly, child welfare workers are often held accountable, if not blamed outright, for attempting to resolve extraordinarily difficult situations. The following report of a recurring dream comes from a young dedicated child welfare worker:

> I had this recurring dream for months. . . . In the dream I was always drowning. My head would bob underwater. But in the hand of my one outstretched arm, above the water, was a baby. And I would be screaming "would someone please take this baby!" But no one did and I would wake in a panic. (personal communication)

Given our basic assumptions about VT, it is not surprising that treating torture survivors holds potential for ill effects on therapists. Interesting to note, Deighton, Gurris, and Traue (2007) reported that it is not so much the exposure to clients' descriptions that is related to VT symptoms but rather what the therapist does when faced with such exposure. Likewise, mental health professionals working with combat-related trauma are considered to be at high risk for developing CF (Tyson, 2007).

Another area of traumatic exposure includes therapeutic response to large-scale disasters, both natural and human caused. On the natural side, such disasters may include earthquakes, floods, tornados, wildfires, and severe storms (Byrne, Lerias, & Sullivan, 2006; Leitch, Vanslyke, & Allen, 2009). The sheer enormity of the disaster can have an overwhelming effect on a helper responding to the situation. For example, the emotional contagion evident when large groups of displaced people congregate can be infectious to everyone touched by it. Accordingly, the sense of helplessness, uncertainty, and loss of control is very difficult to soothe. Examples of large-scale disasters of the man-made type include terrorist attacks, school and workplace shootings, and industrial accidents (Naturale, 2007).

Empirical Research

In this section I will explore some of the research that has sought to determine the effects of working with trauma survivors. This growing body of literature has become increasing complex, with the findings leading to more nuanced understandings. What seems increasingly clear is that some clinicians treating traumatized individuals will experience symptoms of VT and CF. But the questions, Who? How? When? and Why? have yet to be definitively answered. As Chouliara, Hutchison, and Karatzias (2009) asserted, "while the concept of vicarious traumatisation appears to have been enthusiastically embraced by practitioners, the empirical research remains fragmented and inconsistent and does not yet represent a coherent body of work" (p. 48). In a critical examination of this body of research we must be mindful of the following empirical challenges: (a) differentiating the various conceptualizations of negative impacts of trauma treatment, (b) defining terms as well as operationalizing and validating measures, (c) methodological limitations of recent studies, (d) problems of self-reports, and (e) theoretical limitations of etiological processes. Although mindful of the related concepts of countertransference and burnout, my focus here is primarily on the research literature on VT and STS. As Kadambi and Ennis (2004) remind us, the field has not "reached a consensus on the identification of a single descriptor that accurately reflects the uniqueness and range of responses to providing trauma therapy" (p. 4).

VT

First I will examine some of the research that explores the construct of VT, beginning with an early investigation by Pearlman and MacIan (1995) that studied a sample of 188 trauma therapists. Participants were asked to complete questionnaires about their work with trauma survivors and their own psychological well-being. Included in this study was the Traumatic Stress Institute Belief Scale. Results suggested that newer therapists experience more psychological difficulty, as do therapists who have a history of personal traumas. These findings pointed toward the needs for emotional support for trauma therapists, more training, and more supervision. At the same time, Schauben and Frazier (1995) found that a counselor's history of victimization was not related to his or her own level of symptomatology. They did, however, find that counselors who had greater exposure on their caseloads to trauma experienced higher levels of VT.

Dane and Chachkes (2001) explored the factors that might lead to VT in hospital social workers. The methodology used focus groups with 12 participants who worked in various medical specialties throughout a large urban hospital. The four major themes that emerged from the qualitative analysis of this data included (a) organizational stress, (b) guilt, (c) problems with the emotional impact of cases, and (d) social supports. In contradiction to one of the major hypothesis of Pearlman and Saakvitne's (1995) work, these authors concluded that

> based on the results of the findings there is no evidence to support the hypothesis that hospital social workers in this study experienced an actual transformation of their inner world resulting from empathic engagement with the patients, which is the hallmark of VT. (p. 45)

However, the methodological limitations of this investigation suggest that further study on this question may be useful.

Comparing clinicians who treat survivors of sexual abuse with clinicians who treat sexual offenders, Way, VanDeusen, Martin, Applegate, and Jandle (2004) sought to determine the level of VT in both groups as well as the clinicians' means of coping and its relationship to the work with differing populations. A total of 347 clinical members (252 working with offenders and 95 treating survivors) responded to a survey that included the Impact of Events Scale and the Childhood Trauma Questionnaire. In particular, the researchers were interested in two factors believed to interfere with trauma treatment: intrusion and avoidance. Interestingly, the findings showed that the two clinical groups did not differ with respect to the levels of VT measured, although the majority of the sample fell within the clinical range for VT. Further, the clinicians treating the survivors were found to use more positive personal and organizations strategies for coping with this work. Consistent with the findings of Schauben and Frazier (1995), they did not find that a personal history of trauma was significantly associated with VT.

In a review of the research literature on VT in practitioners working with adult survivors of child sexual abuse, Chouliara et al. (2009) found that all studies report some degree of negative effects of this specific work on a range of professionals. Some of the studies report high levels of PTSD symptomatology, including disruptions in belief systems, avoidance and intrusive thoughts, and disruptions in trust, intimacy, and safety. However, a clear picture does not emerge when studies attempt to compare groups of professionals for measures of VT. Accordingly, it is important to establish that VT is intimately related to the effects of trauma work as distinguished from other forms of counseling and therapy. In their review of these studies a worker's personal history of sexual abuse did not show a strong association with higher symptomatology. I'll return a bit later to the methodological limitations of these and other related studies.

In another recent study of VT, STS, and burnout by Devilly, Wright, and Varker (2009), the researchers cast similar doubts about what we have assumed about the direct effects of exposure to traumatic experiences of others. The authors agreed that it makes intuitive sense that exposing oneself to the traumatic stories of others in an empathic context should affect the therapist at an emotional level—whether consciously or unconsciously. But they were also concerned about the confusion around the terminology and the difficulty in teasing out significant differences between the constructs. In their study of 152 mental health professionals, all participants completed questionnaires that contained measures of STS, VT, and burnout. In addition, the design included a control group of nontrauma therapists, as it is commonly argued that it is the trauma work in particular that leads to VT and CF, not other variables common to the therapeutic encounter. This research found that "STS, VT and burnout are highly convergent constructs, but the measures for STS and VT do not display construct validity whereas burnout does" (p. 381). Further, the findings led the researchers to conclude that all three constructs appear to measure the same phenomenon. However, an important finding indicates that there were no significant differences in VT or STS for clinicians who were exposed to either high levels of client trauma or low levels of exposure to trauma patients. Interestingly, they did suggest that the findings point to work-related stressors as the strongest predictors of practitioner stress. This finding is in keeping with the commonly heard refrain from clinicians that "it's not the clients that get to you—it's the craziness of working here!"

CF

Although there are obvious similarities between CF and VT, for the purposes of research the definitions reveal an important difference (Baird & Kracen, 2006). Figley (1995) defines STS as "the natural and consequent behaviors and emotions resulting from knowing about a traumatizing event experienced by a significant other—the stress resulting from helping or wanting to help a traumatized or suffering person" (p. 7). Although the effects are indirect, the impact of CF bears very close resemblance to symptoms of PTSD.

These symptoms include hyperarousal, intrusive imagery, distressing emotions, cognitive changes, avoidance, and functional impairment (Figley 1995, 2002). In measuring CF, several standardized instruments have been developed including the Compassion Fatigue Test, the Compassion Satisfaction and Fatigue Test, and the Compassion Fatigue Scale (Adams, Figley, & Boscarino, 2008). Also included in their discussion of measurements are the Professional Quality of Life Scale, the Secondary Traumatic Stress Scale, the Impact of Event Scale, the Trauma and Attachment Scale, and the World Assumptions Scale. For a full description and discussion of the uses of these tests, see Bride et al. (2007). In a study that sought to determine the psychometric properties of a Compassion Fatigues Scale and its predictive validity, Adams et al. (2006) analyzed data taken from a survey of social workers living in New York City following the terrorist attacks of 9/11/01. Although their conclusions are admittedly tentative, they did find that the Burnout and Secondary Trauma scales "seemed to be quite appropriate assessment tools, either separately or combined into the CF–Short Scale, for identifying caregiving professionals at risk for CF and psychological problems" (p. 107).

But what happens when you survey master's-level social workers who were randomly selected from a large body of licensed professionals? Bride (2007) analyzed data from 294 surveys of social workers who were administered a demographic questionnaire and the Secondary Traumatic Stress Scale. This group of participants was primarily female, had on average 16 years of experience, and was engaged in a wide range of service fields, including mental health, health care, child welfare, school social work, and community organizing. Participants were asked to rate the extent to which their client population was traumatized. Some of the interesting findings from this study included the report that 40% of the respondents found that they had thoughts about their clients without intending to—in other words, intrusive thoughts. Almost 20% experienced psychological distress or physiological reactions when recalling their work with traumatized clients. Further, 27% reported irritability and problems with concentration. The authors concluded that social workers engaged in work with traumatized populations are likely to experience at least some of the symptoms of STS, and important to note, a significant minority (15.2%) meet the diagnostic criteria for PTSD.

Critique of Research

Since the early 1990s, clinicians have been drawn to the idea that therapeutic work with traumatized people can have a negative effect on themselves as people and therapists. And indeed, some of the early research seems to support these disturbing contentions. However, the more recent research and critique around conceptual models have stirred debate around practically every aspect of this phenomenon and have challenged many to reflect on what has been taken for granted. This is not surprising and clearly not an unfortunate development. Research and interest in this complex area was bound to lead to conflicting results and, in some cases, diverging opinions. Next, I will examine some of the conceptual concerns and research limitations that currently exist in the literature.

First, we can consider the problem and validity of self-reports. Both qualitative and quantitative approaches to understanding this problem area are reliant on therapists' self-reports of subjective states; the history of their own traumatic pasts; previously held beliefs, values, and convictions; and the nature of their own work. Here is an important dilemma, although one rarely mentioned in the literature: given that the process by which VT is thought to come into being is the empathic connection a therapist has with his or her client—and that this is the main avenue by which VT occurs—what therapist would be willing to claim that he or she is unaffected by this work? The obvious implication would have to be that such a therapist is a singularly unempathic clinician—and who among us would want to be subjected to that suspicion? It may be possible that some therapists have been more inclined to express the negative effects to conform to an internalized and externalized ideal version of the empathic healer. Setting aside for the moment the possibility that there are some unempathic clinicians out there, it seems more likely that some other variables (in addition to empathy) play a role in the transmission process.

Much of the current research literature is time limited and cross-sectional in nature. Consequently, there is an important need for longitudinal study of this phenomenon. Because VT is thought to alter beliefs, worldviews, and other enduring dimensions of one's subjectivity, it would make sense for these to be explored over a lengthy period of time, such that the hypothesized shifts in the inner world of the therapist could be measured with baselines in mind.

In addition, much of the literature supporting the idea of VT has been generated from studies that have not had control groups or even comparison groups to help eliminate contributing variables (Chouliara et al., 2009). This makes it challenging to uphold the claim that it is specifically the work with trauma that affects the therapist. Further study is required with therapists working with trauma survivors as compared to therapists working with non–trauma survivors. In addition, we need to control for the variable of the therapist's own trauma history. Here, the findings have been inconsistent as to predicting VT. Some studies of VT with therapists who possess personal trauma histories have found higher levels of traumatic stress (Cunningham, 1999; Pearlman & MacIan, 1995), whereas Schauben and Frazier (1995) were unable to support this finding. Although intuitively we might surmise that a personal history of abuse would leave one vulnerable to VT, more research is needed in this area to clarify this important concern.

There are, as Kadambi and Ennis (2004) and others (Devilly et al., 2009) argued, some conceptual limitations to the study of VT. For instance, there has been some debate as to whether VT is a chronic versus acute state among therapists working with trauma survivors. Consequently, Kadambi and Ennis suggested that "this possibility may provide some insight as to why research investigating vicarious trauma has been characterized by such inconsistency" (p. 15). Further, they concluded, "An often overlooked aspect of much of the research in the area of vicarious trauma is the fact that the majority of professionals providing trauma therapy appear to be coping well with the demands of their work," and consequently, "vicarious trauma as it is currently conceptualized is limited in its ability to account for aspects of providing trauma therapy that are positive and enriching for professionals" (p. 15). Being able to account in conceptual and theoretical ways for both negative and positive is important as we further our understanding of trauma treatment.

Self-Care

Despite the fact that research has not shown ill effects on all therapists who engage in trauma treatment, it does seem prudent to reflect on one's self-care and ongoing emotional health and vitality (Venart, Vassos, & Pitcher-Heft, 2007). Decades of psychotherapy research have consistently demonstrated the relationship of a caring and compassionate therapist to positive therapeutic outcomes. The absence of a healthy, emotionally resilient, and attentive therapist is bound to affect both the client and the therapeutic process (Rasmussen, 2005). Here I will explore some of the ways in which therapists can maintain optimal self-care strategies. Many of the ideas and recommendations below may seem patently obvious, yet it is surprising how many clinicians struggle to take care of themselves as their first order of business. Perhaps as therapists, we are more inclined to attend to the needs of others before our own. We could speculate as to why this is—but that would be another chapter.

First and foremost, self-care, as it relates to being an effective therapist, means healing oneself. Very often people who become therapists have experienced many of the same traumas and emotional injuries that their clients have suffered. Indeed, the motivation for becoming a therapist may have important unconscious dimensions related to earlier experiences of loss and deprivation (Barnett, 2007). The idea of being "triggered" is not so abstract when the stories of the client resonate loudly within the self, such that the therapist becomes preoccupied by his or her own memories and reflections. This experience can happen in or out of therapy sessions. Although the question of the relationship between the therapist's trauma history and the development of VT requires further study, it seems reasonable to propose that a therapist with a trauma history seek therapy him- or herself. "Heal thyself" ought to be the first order of business. Beyond the specific recommendation of seeking one's own therapy, it is important for the therapist to reflect on a holistic approach to self-care. Such considerations include attention to diet, exercise, sleep, play, and social connections outside of work.

Organizational Responses

Without question, agencies and organizations that provide services to traumatized people have an obligation to ensure that their settings provide the optimal conditions for therapists to conduct their work (Kosny & Eakin, 2008). Given the extensive research literature on VT and CF, it would be reasonable to conclude that providing therapy to traumatized individuals poses a potential occupational hazard. Accordingly, organizations need to be familiar with the latest research and work to create positive working conditions for their clinicians (Geller, Madsen, & Ohrenstein, 2004). Some of the measures that an organization can take to help mitigate the negative effects of trauma treatment include (a) providing the best possible training and educational opportunities for clinicians, (b) providing clinical supervision and case consultation, (c) providing opportunities for peer support, (d) creating a flexible work environment, (e) balancing the caseload and workload of clinicians, and (f) where possible, supporting a collegial decision-making environment.

Case Example 4: Jen

Early on in her MSW program Jen knew that she wanted to be a clinician who worked in the field of mental health. Throughout her program she streamlined her course selection as well as possible to take courses in clinical practice, group and family therapy, substance misuse, family violence, and psychopathology. For her two practica, she was placed in nationally recognized treatment facilities where she received very good clinical supervision and some excellent training. When Jen graduated she quickly found a clinical position in a mid-sized agency in a small-size city, far away from the high powered university-based settings to which she had become accustomed. With some background in the area of treating children who had been sexually abused, Jen quickly established a reputation for herself as "the person to refer to" in her community when it came to these cases. She worked independently and with considerable autonomy. Early on, Jen relished this opportunity to experiment with various approaches with what was to become a very large and almost exclusive caseload of sexually abused children. As time went on, however, she began to feel more and more isolated.

Organizationally, she reported to a supervisor who had long since given up psychotherapy and now mostly engaged in administrative duties. Supervision, when it occurred, largely consisted of questions and issues related to bureaucratic details of stats and discussion of agency politics. After instances when Jen tried to focus concerns on questions of treatment, transference, and countertransference, she quickly realized that her supervisor was largely ineffectual in helping her reflect on her practice and think through treatment options for some of the more difficult cases. In one memorable supervisory session, risking perceptions of incompetence, Jen disclosed that in a recent session with a highly traumatized child, she froze and had no idea what to say or do in the moment. Her supervisor was surprised by her admission and seemed, in Jen's perception, to be disappointed in her.

Moreover, when in supervision, the supervisor and Jen seemed to be talking different languages, each bringing divergent concerns to the table. Jen was concerned that the pressure to focus on immediate symptom relief for the children and bring down her overall number of sessions was interfering with her larger therapeutic goals. Jen's supervisor continued to express concern about the lengthening waiting list and the pressure from funders to see more children. Occasionally, Jen would press to attend a conference or workshop related to her growing area of expertise. Her requests were quickly deflected by her supervisor, who would retort by saying, "We hired you because you were well trained, not thinking that you needed more training."

In this situation, Jen began to feel trapped and unsupported. Two additional administrative issues added to Jen's frustration. First, her requests for taking vacation time on relatively short notice were often refused for bureaucratic reasons, that is, that she needed to notify the agency months in advance for taking time off. And second, her desire to balance her practice week by doing some couple's counseling, another area of strength, were repeatedly rebuffed as she was told that given the lengthy waitlists, her work with these children was the top priority. Jen's input into any administrative decision making was minimal. She left the agency after 2 years.

This case example highlights the ways in which organizational processes, structure, and decision making can interact with and negatively affect the well-being of the therapist. Feelings of disempowerment and lack of support for clinical practice will take its toll over time and, in combination with the already noted challenging aspects of trauma treatment, will undermine the work of the therapist. Clearly, all therapists need continuing education and advanced training for their specialized work (Phipps & Byrne, 2003; Sommer, 2008). Further, all clinicians conducting trauma treatment are highly advised to seek out some form of clinical supervision (Tehrani, 2007; VanDeusen & Way, 2006; Wheeler, 2007).

This clinical supervision may take various forms, from one-on-one supervision to peer supervision. Important in any of these forms of supervision is the development of a trusting, supportive relationship. The supervisee has to be able to risk admissions of not knowing, vulnerability, confusion, negative countertransference reactions, and personal weaknesses. And, as Pearlman and Saakvitne (1995) pointed out, "a trauma therapy supervision or consultation is always a consultation on a therapy relationship, not on the client" (p. 359).

In the same spirit, I have argued (Rasmussen, 2005) that there is a need for clinical supervision that attends to what happens between the therapist and client in a dynamic way. The clinical supervisor is in a position to note the shifts and changes in the supervisee over time. Doing so, in the context of a safe, supportive supervisory relationship, provides the path to personal and professional growth. Concealing one's limitations and vulnerabilities—or as some might say, "Fake it until you make it"—may sound like an adaptive strategy in the short run, but it is a foolish plan in the long run.

Conclusion

The developing literature on the negative effects of trauma treatment has brought our attention to effects that exposure to other people's trauma might have on clinicians. This body of literature, both conceptual and empirical, has become increasingly complex and nuanced. Indeed, the contradictory results of many of the studies to date strongly point to the value of further study. Many of the questions posed at the beginning of the chapter cannot be answered conclusively. It does seem fair to say that some clinicians working with people who have been traumatized will be negatively affected by this work. But questions, Which ones? In which ways? and For which reasons? cannot be answered with certainty. As Devilly et al. (2009) have asserted, "many simply assume that such traumatization inevitably exists, but there has been some difficulty in building a body of quality empirical support" (p. 373). In addition to understanding the ill effects of trauma treatment, we also need to understand how and why so many professionals are coping well with the demands of their work. Kadambi and Ennis (2004) have concluded that "shifting empirical focus from mental health professionals' vulnerability to traumatic stress responses, onto their resiliency against it, could serve to identify significant protective or mitigating factors that have yet to be identified" (p. 17). It may take another decade of research to provide adequate answers to these questions.

It seems timely that in addition to providing empirical support for the negative impact on the therapist/purveyor of trauma treatment, clinicians and researchers should reconsider the conceptual and theoretical underpinnings of these constructs. In particular, although the idea that empathic immersion in the subjective experience of the traumatized client is central to the etiology of VT, this theorizing needs to be refined further. What other factors, in what combination, can more predicatively produce these effects? Could the etiological variables of empathy, a personal history of abuse, and a lack of adequate training combine to provide a stronger explanation? As we take this example further, imagine being a therapist who is overwhelmed by the affect of a client's trauma, triggered by one's own traumatic history, and at a loss to know what to say or do to help the client? Imagine this experience's occurring over and over again. Of course this is only one possible configuration of dynamic interacting variables. Other possibilities could take into consideration issues of gender, culture, and life experiences, to name but a few. The important point here is that the complexity of the dynamic interaction of variables has to be accounted for both in the conceptual model and in the research that purports to comprehend it.

However, we do have enough information and understanding about the effects of providing care to people who have been traumatized to make some broad recommendations. It seems reasonable to suggest that clinicians seek the best available training, supervision, and supportive organizational practices. Many may find it helpful to maintain a balance in the clinical services they offer and, indeed, a balance in their personal lives. Finally it is recommended that therapists who have a personal history of trauma seek therapy for themselves. Although there are no easy answers to maintaining emotional health in the face of the significant challenges posed by trauma treatment, I suggest that our first order of business ought always to be ensuring our own optimal care. Only then can we optimally care for others.

References

Adams, R., Boscarino, J., & Figley, C. (2006). Compassion fatigue and psychological distress among social workers: A validation study. *American Journal of Orthopsychiatry, 76*(1), 103–108.

Adams, R., Figley, C., & Boscarino, J. (2008). The compassion fatigue scale: Its use with social workers following urban disaster. *Research on Social Work Practice, 18*(3), 238–250.

Aron, L. (1991). The patient's experience of the analyst's subjectivity. *Psychoanalytic Dialogues, 1*(1), 29–51.

Badger, K., Royse, D., & Craig, C. (2008). Hospital social workers indirect trauma exposure: An exploratory study of contributing factors. *Health and Social Work, 33*(1), 63–71.

Baird, K., & Kracen, A. (2006). Vicarious traumatisation and secondary traumatic stress: A research synthesis. *Counselling Psychology Quarterly, 19*(2), 181–188.

Barnett, M. (2007). What brings you here? An exploration of the unconscious motivations of those who choose to train and work as psychotherapists and counsellors. *Psychodynamic Practice, 13*(3), 257–274.

Bride, B. (2007). Prevalence of secondary traumatic stress among social workers. *Social Work, 52*(1), 63–70.

Bride, B., Radey, M., & Figley, C. (2007). Measuring compassion fatigue. *Clinical Social Work Journal, 35,* 155–163.

Byrne, M., Lerias, D., & Sullivan, N. (2006). Predicting vicarious traumatization in those indirectly exposed to bushfires. *Stress and Health, 22,* 167–177.

Canfield, J. (2005). Secondary traumatization, burnout, and vicarious traumatization: A review of the literature as it relates to therapists who treat trauma. *Smith College Studies in Social Work, 75*(2), 81–101.

Chouliara, Z., Hutchison, C., & Karatzias, T. (2009). Vicarious traumatisation in practitioners who work with adult survivors of sexual violence and child sexual abuse: Literature review and directions for future research. *Counselling and Psychotherapy Research, 9*(1), 47–56.

Cunningham, M. (1999). The impact of sexual abuse treatment on the social work clinician. *Child & Adolescent Social Work Journal, 16*(4), 227–290.

Dane, B., & Chachkes, E. (2001). The cost of caring for patients with an illness: Contagion to the social worker. *Social Work in Health Care, 33*(2), 31–51.

Davies, J., & Frawley, M. (1994). *Treating the adult survivor of childhood sexual abuse: A psychoanalytic perspective.* New York: Basic Books.

Deighton, R., Gurris, N., & Traue, H. (2007). Factors affecting burnout and compassion fatigue in psychotherapists treating torture survivors: Is the therapist's attitude to working through trauma relevant? *Journal of Traumatic Stress, 20*(1), 63–75.

Devilly, G., Wright, R., & Varker, T. (2009). Vicarious trauma, secondary stress or simply burnout? Effect of trauma therapy on mental health professionals. *Australian and New Zealand Journal of Psychiatry, 43*, 373–385.

Fahy, A. (2007). The unbearable fatigue of compassion: Notes from a substance abuse counsellor who dreams of working at Starbuck's. *Clinical Social Work Journal, 35*, 199–205.

Figley, C. R. (1995). *Compassion fatigue: Coping with secondary traumatic stress disorder.* New York: Brunner/Mazel.

Figley, C. R. (Ed.). (2002). *Treating compassion fatigue.* New York: Brunner/Routledge.

Geller, J., Madsen, L., & Ohrenstein, L. (2004). Secondary trauma: A team approach. *Clinical Social Work Journal, 32*(4), 415–430.

Herman, J. L. (1992). *Trauma and recovery: The aftermath of violence from domestic abuse to political terror.* New York: Basic Books.

Hoge, C. W., Auchterlonie, J. L., & Milliken, C. S. (2006). Mental health problems, use of mental health services, and attrition from military service after returning from deployment to Iraq or Afghanistan. *Journal of the American Medical Association, 295*(9), 1023–1032.

Horwitz, M. (2006). Work related trauma effects in child protection social workers. *Journal of Social Service Research, 32*(3), 1–18.

Kadambi, M., & Ennis, L. (2004). Reconsidering vicarious trauma: A review of the literature and its limitations. *Journal of Trauma Practice, 3*(2), 1–21.

Kosny, A., & Eakin, J. (2008). The hazards of helping: Work, mission and risk in non-profit social service organizations. *Health, Risk & Society, 10*(2), 149–166.

Leitch, M. L., Vanslyke, J., & Allen, M. (2009). Somatic experiencing treatment with social service workers following Hurricanes Katrina and Rita. *Social Work, 54*(1), 9–18.

Linley, A., & Joseph, S. (2007). Therapy work and therapist's positive and negative well-being. *Journal of Social and Clinical Psychology, 3*, 385–403.

Maslach, C. (1982). *Burnout—The cost of caring.* Englewood Cliffs, NJ: Prentice Hall.

Maslach, C., Jackson, S. E., & Leiter, M. P. (1996). *Maslach Burnout Inventory manual.* Palo Alto, CA: Consulting Psychologists Press.

McCann, L., & Pearlman, L. A. (1990). Vicarious traumatisation: A framework for understanding the psychological effects of working with victims. *Journal of Traumatic Stress, 3*(1), 131–147.

Moulden, H., & Firestone, P. (2007). Vicarious traumatization: The impact on therapists who work with sexual offenders. *Trauma, Violence, & Abuse, 8*(1), 67–83.

Naturale, A. (2007). Secondary traumatic stress in social workers responding to disasters: Reports from the field. *Clinical Social Work Journal, 35,* 173–181.

Orr, D. (1988). Transference and countertransference: A historical survey. In B. Wolstein (Ed.), *Essential papers on countertransference* (pp. 91–110). New York: New York University. (Original work published 1954)

Pearlman, L. A., & MacIan, P. S. (1995). Vicarious traumatization: An empirical study of the effects of trauma work on trauma therapists. *Professional Psychology, Research and Practice, 26,* 558–565.

Pearlman, L. A., & Saakvitne, K. (1995). *Trauma and the therapist: Countertransference and vicarious traumatization in psychotherapy with incest survivors.* New York: Norton.

Perron, B. E., & Hiltz, B. (2006). Burnout and secondary trauma among forensic interviewers of abuse children. *Child and Adolescent Social Work Journal, 23*(2), 216–234.

Phipps, A., & Byrne, M. (2003). Brief interventions for secondary trauma: Review and recommendations. *Stress and Health, 19,* 13–147.

Racker, H. (1988). The meanings and uses of countertransference. In B. Wolstein (Ed.), *Essential papers on countertransference* (pp. 158–201). New York: New York University Press. (Original work published 1957)

Rasmussen, B. (2005). An intersubjective perspective on vicarious trauma and its impact on the clinical process. *Journal of Social Work Practice, 19*(1), 19–30.

Reich, A. (1951). On countertransference. *International Journal of Psycho-Analysis, 32,* 25–31.

Reich, A. (1960). Further remarks on countertransference. *International Journal of Psycho-Analysis, 41,* 389–395.

Sandler, J. (1976). Countertransference and role-responsiveness. *International Review of Psycho-Analysis, 3,* 43–47.

Schauben, L. J., & Frazier, P. A. (1995). Vicarious trauma: The effects on female counselors of working with sexual violence survivors. *Psychology of Women Quarterly, 19,* 49–64.

Smith, B. (2007). Sifting through trauma: Compassion fatigue and HIV/AIDS. *Clinical Social Work Journal, 35,* 193–198.

Sommer, C. (2008). Vicarious traumatisation, trauma-sensitive supervision, and counsellor preparation. *Counselor Education & Supervision, 48,* 61–71.

Stolorow, R., Brandchaft, B., & Atwood, G. (1987). *Psychoanalytic treatment: An intersubjective approach.* Hillside, NJ: Analytic Press.

Tansey, M., & Burke, W. (1989). *Understanding countertransference: From projective identification to empathy.* Hillside, NJ: Analytic Press.

Tehrani, N. (2007). The cost of caring—The impact of secondary trauma on assumptions, values and beliefs. *Counselling Psychology Quarterly, 20*(4), 325–339.

Ting, L., Jacobson, J., Sanders, S., Bride, B., & Harrington, D. (2005). The Secondary Traumatic Stress Scale (STSS): Confirmatory factor analyses with a national sample of mental health social workers. *Journal of Human Behavior in the Social Environment, 11*(3), 177–194.

Tyson, J. (2007). Compassion fatigue in the treatment of combat-related trauma during wartime. *Clinical Social Work Journal, 35,* 183–192.

VanDeusen, K., & Way, I. (2006). Vicarious trauma: An exploratory study of the impact of providing sexual abuse treatment on clinicians' trust and intimacy. *Journal of Child Sexual Abuse, 15*(1), 69–85.

Venart, E., Vassos, S., & Pitcher-Heft, H. (2007). What individual counsellors can do to sustain wellness. *Journal of Humanistic Counseling, Education and Development, 46,* 50–65.

Way, I., VanDeusen, K. M., Martin, G., Applegate, B., & Jandle, D. (2004). Vicarious trauma: A comparison of clinicians who treat survivors of sexual abuse and sexual offenders. *Journal of Interpersonal Violence, 19,* 49–71.

Wheeler, S. (2007). What shall we do with the wounded healer? The supervisor's dilemma. *Psychodynamic Practice, 13*(3), 245–256.

Index

About the Editors_____

Shoshana Ringel, PhD, is an associate professor at the University of Maryland–Baltimore School of Social Work. She is the coauthor of two previous books, *Attachment and Dynamic Practice* (with J. Brandell) and *Advanced Clinical Practice: Relational Principles and Techniques* (with E. Goldstein and D. Miehls). She has published numerous articles and was certified on the Adult Attachment Interview by Mary Main and Eric Hesse. Dr. Ringel maintains a private practice in Baltimore.

Jerrold R. Brandell, PhD, is a Distinguished Professor at Wayne State University School of Social Work in Detroit, Michigan. He has published numerous articles and book chapters as well as nine other books, including *Attachment and Dynamic Practice* (with S. Ringel), *Psychodynamic Social Work,* and *Theory & Practice in Clinical Social Work* (2010, Sage). He is the founding editor-in-chief of the journal *Psychoanalytic Social Work,* which is now in its 18th year of publication, and he maintains a part-time private practice in psychoanalysis and psychotherapy in Ann Arbor, Michigan.

About the
Contributors

A. Antonio González-Prendes, PhD, Assistant Professor, Wayne State University School of Social Work, Detroit, Michigan

Jan Gryczynski, MA, Research Associate, Friends Research Institute, Baltimore, Maryland

Dan Koren, PhD, Professor, Department of Psychology, University of Haifa, Israel

James Lampe, PhD, Private Practice, Chicago, Illinois

Laura V. Loumeau-May, MPS, ATR-BC, LPC, Journeys Program, Valley Home Care. Inc., Paramus, New Jersey; Caldwell College, New Jersey

Ruth Malkinson, PhD, School of Social Work, Tel Aviv University, Israel

Faye Mishna, PhD, Margaret and Wallace McCain Family Chair, Professor, and Dean, Factor-Inwentash Faculty of Social Work, University of Toronto, Ontario, Canada

Brian Rasmussen, PhD, Associate Professor, Okanagan University College School of Social Work, Kelowna, British Columbia, Canada

Stella M. Resko, PhD, Assistant Professor, School of Social Work and Merrill-Palmer Skillman Institute, Wayne State University, Detroit, Michigan

Simon Shimshon Rubin, PhD, Director, International Center for the Study of Loss, Bereavement and Human Resilience; Chairman, Postgraduate Psychotherapy Program, and Professor, Department of Psychology, University of Haifa, Israel

Jami-Leigh Sawyer, Hamilton Health Sciences–McMaster Children's Hospital, Hamilton, Ontario, Canada

R. Dennis Shelby, MSW, PhD, Director of Doctoral Studies, Institute for Clinical Social Work, Chicago, Illinois

Boris Thomas, JD, PhD, Private Practice, Chicago, Illinois

Shelly A. Wiechelt, PhD, LCSW-C, Assistant Professor, University of Maryland, Baltimore County School of Social Work, Maryland

Eliezer Witztum, MD, Professor, Mental Health Center, Faculty of Health Sciences, Ben Gurion University, Beer Sheba, Israel

Shahar Mor Yosef, MA, Department of Psychology, University of Haifa, Israel

SAGE Research Methods Online
The essential tool for researchers

**Sign up now at
www.sagepub.com/srmo
for more information.**

An expert research tool

- An **expertly designed taxonomy** with more than 1,400 unique terms for social and behavioral science research methods
- **Visual and hierarchical search tools** to help you discover material and link to related methods

- Easy-to-use navigation tools
- Content organized by complexity
- Tools for citing, printing, and downloading content with ease
- Regularly updated content and features

A wealth of essential content

- The most comprehensive picture of quantitative, qualitative, and mixed methods available today
- More than **100,000 pages of SAGE book and reference material** on research methods as well as editorially selected material from SAGE journals
- More than **600 books** available in their entirety online

Launching 2011!

⑤SAGE research methods online